WORLD CONGRESS ON INTELLECTUAL CAPITAL READINGS

About KMCI Press
Powerful Knowledge for Knowledge Professionals

KMCI Press is an exciting publishing partnership that unites the Knowledge Management Consortium International (KMCI), the leading organization for knowledge management professionals, and Butterworth-Heinemann's Business group and Digital Press imprints, one of the premier publishers of knowledge management books.

KMCI Press publishes authoritative and innovative books that educate all knowledge management communities, from students and beginning professionals to chief knowledge officers. KMCI Press books present definitive and leading-edge ideas of the KMCI itself, and bring clarity and authoritative information to a dynamic and emerging profession.

KMCI Press books explore the opportunities, demands, and benefits knowledge management brings to organizations and defines important and emerging knowledge management disciplines and topics, including:

- *Professional roles and functions*
- *Vertical industry best practices and applications*
- *Technologies, including knowledge portals and data and document management*
- *Strategies, methodologies, and decision-making frameworks*

The Knowledge Management Consortium International (KMCI) is the only major not for profit member organization specifically for knowledge management professionals, with thousands of worldwide members including individuals in the professional and academic fields as well as leading companies, institutions, and other organizations concerned with knowledge management, organizational change, and intellectual capital.

Other titles published by KMCI Press include:
The Springboard, How Storytelling Ignites Action in Knowledge-Era Organizations by Stephen Denning
Knowledge Management Foundations by Steve Fuller
Knowledge Management and Enterprise Portals by Joseph Firestone
World Congress on Intellectual Capital Readings edited by Nick Bontis

For details about these books please visit www.bh.com/knowledgemanagement

WORLD CONGRESS ON INTELLECTUAL CAPITAL READINGS

EDITED BY NICK BONTIS, PH.D.
MINT RESEARCH CENTRE,
MCMASTER UNIVERSITY

KNOWLEDGE
MANAGEMENT
CONSORTIUM
INTERNATIONAL

Boston   Oxford   Auckland   Johannesburg   Melbourne   New Delhi

CONTENTS

1
THOUGHT LEADERSHIP ON INTELLECTUAL CAPITAL   1

2

MANAGING ORGANIZATIONAL KNOWLEDGE BY DIAGNOSING INTELLECTUAL CAPITAL: FRAMING AND ADVANCING THE STATE OF THE FIELD

3

DIGITAL KNOWLEDGE: COPYRIGHT INTELLECTUAL PROPERTY AND THE INTERNET

4

The Power of Knowledge-Pattern Recognition   72

5

Competitive Capital: A Fourth Pillar of Intellectual Capital?   94

6

STRATEGIC KNOWLEDGE SOURCING, INTEGRATION, AND ASSIMILATION: A CAPABILITIES-PORTFOLIO PERSPECTIVE   104

7

INTEGRATING ORGANIZATIONAL LEARNING AND KNOWLEDGE MANAGEMENT: A CASE STUDY   119

8

INTELLECTUAL CAPITAL DISCLOSURES IN SWEDISH ANNUAL REPORTS   135

9

RELEVANT EXPERIENCES IN MEASURING AND REPORTING INTELLECTUAL CAPITAL IN EUROPEAN PIONEERING FIRMS   157

10

UNDERSTANDING INTELLECTUAL CAPITAL STATEMENTS: DESIGNING AND COMMUNICATING KNOWLEDGE MANAGEMENT STRATEGIES   179

11

THE LEARNING CAPACITY INDEX A MEASUREMENT SYSTEM FOR LINKING CAPACITY TO LEARN AND FINANCIAL PERFORMANCE   203

12

DEVELOPING A MEASURE OF KNOWLEDGE MANAGEMENT   226

13

INNOVATION CAPABILITY–BENCHMARKING SYSTEM (ICBS) 243

14

DEVELOPMENT AND IMPLEMENTATION OF AN INTELLECTUAL CAPITAL REPORT FOR A RESEARCH TECHNOLOGY ORGANIZATION 266

15

FOR BETTER OR WORSE? ASSESSING THE COSTS AND BENEFITS OF CONTINGENT KNOWLEDGE-WORK AS AN INVESTMENT IN INTELLECTUAL CAPITAL   287

16

MANAGING HUMAN CAPITAL WITH COMPETENCY-BASED HUMAN RESOURCES MANAGEMENT   306

17

A DIALECTICAL MODEL FOR BEST–PRACTICES DEVELOPMENT   320

18

DE-BIASING SCIENCE AND TECHNOLOGY INVESTMENT DECISIONS 338

19

AN EXAMINATION OF THE TRANSFER OF INTELLECTUAL CAPITAL ACROSS CULTURES 356

20

KNOWLEDGE-SHARING
IN NETWORKED ORGANIZATIONS 374

ABOUT THE AUTHORS

EDITOR

Nick Bontis

DeGroote Business School, McMaster University, Hamilton, Canada
nbontis@mcmaster.ca

Dr. Nick Bontis (Ph.D. University of Western Ontario) is an award-winning professor of strategic management at McMaster University and Program Director of the World Congress on Intellectual Capital. He is Associate Editor of the *Journal of Intellectual Capital* (the leading research publication in the field) and Director of the Institute for Intellectual Capital Research (a global research think-tank and KM consulting firm). He is Chief Knowledge Officer of Knexa.com Enterprises, which is the world's first knowledge exchange and auction, and sits on a variety of advisory boards for several knowledge-based companies. He is widely recognized as a leading researcher in the fields of intellectual capital, knowledge management, and organizational learning and is an internationally sought-after keynote speaker and respected management consultant. His latest publications appear in a variety of journals, including *Journal of Management Studies, European Management Journal, Management Decision, Knowledge and Process Management, International Journal of Technology Management, Journal of Internet Research*, and *International Journal of Management Reviews*, among others. See www.Bontis.com for more information.

CONTRIBUTING AUTHORS

Philip R. Beaulieu

Faculty of Management, University of Calgary, Calgary, Canada
pbeaulie@ucalgary.ca

Phil Beaulieu (Ph.D. University of Washington) is an associate professor teaching management accounting and internal auditing at the University of Calgary, who has also authored a course in advanced management accounting for the Certified General Accountants Association of Canada. He is interested in the communication of intellectual capital measurements between firms and their investors and creditors. A related research interest is the provision of innovative assurance services, such as assurance regarding the reliability of systems, by public accountants. Dr. Beaulieu has published articles in *Contemporary Accounting Research*, *Accounting, Organizations and Society*, and *Auditing: A Journal of Practice and Theory*.

Laurie Bassi

Human Capital Dynamics, Chevy Chase, Maryland, U.S.A.
lbassi@hcdynamics.com

Dr. Laurie Bassi, an internationally recognized expert in using systems for measuring and valuing learning as a tool for continuous improvement, is the president of Human Capital Dynamics and a research fellow at the Accenture Institute for Strategic Change. In recent years, Dr. Bassi has served as the director of research at Saba and the vice president and general manager for research and enterprise solutions at ASTD. While at ASTD, she worked with a consortium of employers to develop standardized, benchmarkable metrics for measuring both employers' investments in education and training, as well as the learning outcomes that those investments create. These measurement systems, which were designed as a tool for continuous improvement, are now used in thousands of organizations around the world. Earlier in her career, Dr. Bassi was a tenured professor of economics and public policy at Georgetown University. She has also served as the director of several U.S. government commissions.

David W. Birchall

Henley Management College, Greenlands, Henley-on-Thames, Oxfordshire, U.K.
Davidbi@henleymc.ac.uk

David Birchall is Director of Educational Technologies and Information Systems at Henley Management College and Director of the Centre for Business in the Digital Economy. He has worked on many innovations within Henley, including the development of e-learning systems and an e-library. He is a founding member of both the Future Work Forum and the Knowledge Management Forum at Henley. He has research interests in the areas of innovative practices in organizations and organizational implications of IT, knowledge management, and IT and management learning. He has published widely including *Creating Tomorrow's Organization* and *The New*

Flexi Manager. David joined Henley in 1974 and has been a professor since 1983. He has held a number of senior posts at Henley, including Director of Research, Director of Corporate Programmes and Director of Graduate Business Studies.

Manfred Bornemann
Department of International Management, Karl Franzens University, Graz, Austria
manfred.bornemann@kfunigraz.ac.at

Manfred Bornemann wrote his doctoral thesis, *Measuring Instruments for Knowledge Management,* at the Karl Franzens University, Graz, Austria. He is an independent consultant in the field of knowledge management and intellectual capital evaluation. Additionally, he is part time assistant professor at the Department of International Management at the Karl Franzens University, Graz, and gives lectures in general management, organizational theory, and knowledge management. He is an active guest lecturer in various other national institutions and has published several articles in the field of intellectual capital. Dr. Bornemann has presented papers at numerous academic conferences in the U.S.A., Canada, Singapore, and Europe.

David H. Brett
Knexa.com Enterprises, Vancouver, British Columbia, Canada
david.brett@knexa.com

David Brett is considered to be one of the pioneers of Web-based knowledge exchange. David created Knexa in 1999 as a way to financially reward people for sharing their knowledge. Considered by some KM experts to be a breakthrough in knowledge capture and sharing, Knexa has developed a worldwide reputation as a leader in its field, with partners in Europe and Australia. Mr. Brett's business background includes sixteen years experience running public companies on NASDAQ, the Toronto Stock Exchange, and the Canadian Venture Exchange. He holds a bachelor's degree in Religious Studies from the University of British Columbia and is near completion in the executive M.B.A. program at Simon Fraser University.

Per Nikolaj Bukh
Aarhus School of Business, Denmark
pndb@asb.dk

Per Bukh is BDO Professor in Entrepreneurship and Growth at the Aarhus School of Business, Aarhus, Denmark. He has been a researcher for a project on intellectual capital–reporting organized by the Danish Ministry of Industry. Among his other research interests are balanced scorecard, activity-based costing, and relationship marketing. Per Bukh has published a large number of articles in scientific journals, is a frequent speaker at business conferences, executive seminars, and in companies, and has been consulting on the design of performance measurement, intellectual capital–reporting, and cost management systems with leading Nordic companies and organizations.

Michael Charney
ServiceWare, Parsippany, New Jersey, U.S.A.
mcharney@serviceware.com

Michael Charney is Director of Product Marketing and Research for ServiceWare, a developer of KM software and solutions for the eService industry. He has worked in the KM field for six years and has been responsible for KM consulting services, internal KM programs, and ongoing KM product innovations. As the original designer of ServiceWare's KM methodology, he has developed both statistical and nonstatistical models for knowledge domain analysis and has consulted on, or managed, the implementation of dozens of KM systems. He speaks and writes on KM frequently, in both the national and international arenas. Mr. Charney has a bachelor's degree from the University of California at Berkeley and a master's degree from William Paterson University in New Jersey.

Denis M. Coffey
Requirements Engineering, KM and IC, Anteon Corporation, Rhode Island, U.S.A.
dcoffey@anteon.com

Denis Coffey received his B.S., M.S., and Ph.D. in Electrical Engineering from Northeastern University in 1962, 1964, and 1969; he further received an M.A. in Public Administration from University of Northern Colorado in 1981 and an M.Ed. from Lesley College in 1991. Dr. Coffey is a Corporate Program Manager at Anteon Corporation, applying the techniques of Quality Function Deployment to corporate and customer projects. He has also applied concept engineering to the problem of large-scale information and control-systems requirements definition. He holds memberships in the Institute of Electrical and Electronic Engineers and International Society of Technology in Education. He is an adjunct professor at Lesley College and Bristol Community College.

Jenny Darroch

Department of Marketing, University of Otago, Dunedin, New Zealand
jdarroch@commerce.otago.ac.nz

Jenny Darroch is currently completing her doctorate in the area of knowledge management and innovation. Her interest in these areas stems from earlier work she did as an economist on national innovation systems that resulted in much public debate on what can be done to enhance the international competitiveness of New Zealand firms. Prior to joining the academic world, Jenny gained extensive experience in marketing research and marketing management.

C. Anne Davies

School of Management and Economics, Queen's University, Belfast, Northern Ireland
a.davies@qub.ac.uk

Anne Davies currently holds the position of Head of the School of Management and Economics at Queen's University of Belfast. Her research interests are in the contribution of information systems (in the widest sense) to organizations; examining the links between information systems, knowledge management, and the learning organization, and developing an organizational information strategy. Previous publications have been in the area of information systems failure, especially in the public sector.

Bryan Davis

The Kaieteur Institute for Knowledge Management, Toronto, Canada
bdavis@kikm.org

Bryan is an independent researcher, educator, consultant, and analyst. He is currently engaged in advanced research into e-knowledge markets, knowledge-enabling software, knowledge business models, and knowledge pattern recognition. He has been transforming information, document, and knowledge management theory into practice for over twenty years. He is a philosophy graduate from York University and is currently on the Advisory Board of Knexa.com Enterprises. He has served as vice president of KM Strategies and Research with the Delphi Group Canada. He has previously been an IT consultant with the Municipality of Metropolitan Toronto, Manager of the Corporate Records Centre for Metro Toronto, Regional Superintendent of Records, Management Transport Canada, and Assistant Chief of the Toronto Federal Records Centre, National Archives Canada. He currently teaches a new seminar on e-knowledge–based innovation and is also an instructor in the University of Toronto School of Continuing Studies.

G. Scott Erickson

Division of Economics and Business, SUNY College at Oneonta, New York, U.S.A.
erickss@oneonta.edu

Scott Erickson is assistant professor of marketing in the Division of Economics and Business at SUNY College at Oneonta, Oneonta, New York, U.S.A. He consults in areas such as entrepreneurial high technology and marketing strategy. He holds a Ph.D. from Lehigh University, an M.I.M. from AGSIM (Thunderbird) and an M.B.A. from Southern Methodist University. Research interests include intellectual property and intellectual capital protection.

Deborah Hurst

Centre for Innovative Management, Athabasca University, Alberta, Canada
deborahh@athabascau.ca

Dr. Deborah Hurst is an associate professor with the Centre for Innovative Management, Athabasca University in Alberta, Canada. Her area of specialization is located within the study of cultural organization change with an interest in knowledge work and development of intellectual capital through ongoing competency development and virtual learning. Her work is a balance of applied and academic research that draws from a diverse background in her pursuit of this specialization. Her current research program is concerned with the experiences of contingent knowledge workers, the development, retention and valuation of intellectual capital, the use of virtual learning environments to enhance intellectual capital, transmission and alignment of cultural values, and the de-institutionalization of the psychological employment contract. For more information regarding Deborah's work or background, check the Athabasca University, Centre for Innovative Management Website.

Eila Järvenpää

Department of Industrial Engineering and Management, Helsinki University of Technology, Finland
Eila.Jarvenpaa@hut.fi

Dr. Eila Järvenpää is professor in organizational behavior and knowledge management at the Department of Industrial Engineering and Management, Helsinki University of Technology (HUT). Her research interests include knowledge management, communication in organizations, cross-cultural management, competence development and media industry, and ICT and quality of working life. She is a research director at the TAI Research Centre in HUT, responsible for the research area Organizational Development. She is responsible for the InPhD program, a doctoral program for experts and managers in industry.

Joseph J. Kranz
Requirements Engineering, KM and IC, Anteon Corporation, Rhode Island, U.S.A.
jkranz@anteon.com

Joseph Kranz provides decision-making, knowledge management, intellectual capital, and requirements engineering consulting to government and industry and is a corporate program manager at Anteon Corporation. In addition to collaborative and team process developments, and knowledge management organizational implementations, he participates in the application of genetic algorithms to science and technology investment decision-making. He has also directed major U.S. Navy command and control information system programs and received the Superior Civilian Service Award from the Secretary of the Navy. He received his B.S. in Mathematics at Loyola University in 1966 and expects to receive his Ph.D. in Business, Technology Policy, and Management in 2002 from Berne University International Graduate School. He is a member of the Society for Judgement and Decision-Making.

Laurent M. Lapierre
Human Resource Systems Group Ltd., Ottawa, Canada
llapierre@hrmcanada.com

Dr. Lapierre is currently a consultant with Human Resource Systems Group Ltd., a management consulting firm specializing in the development of competency-based human resource management systems. He currently assists government and high technology organizations in developing customized competency profiles for their employee groups. He also provides guidance in the development of competency-based human resource management processes for employee selection, performance management, and learning and development. Dr. Lapierre received his Ph.D. in human resources and management from McMaster University and his M.A.Sc. in industrial/organizational psychology from the University of Waterloo. His doctoral dissertation, entitled "Understanding the links between work commitment constructs," explored how employee work commitment affects employees' intentions to quit both their organization and their occupation. His research is currently in press in the *Journal of Vocational Behavior.*

Heine Thorsgaard Larsen
Copenhagen Business School, Denmark
htl.om@cbs.dk
Heine Thorsgaard Larsen is assistant professor of Intellectual Capital Management at Copenhagen Business School, Copenhagen, Denmark, researching mainly in the areas of strategic management, intellectual capital, knowledge management, management of intangibles, management control, and performance management. Heine Thorsgaard Larsen has been researcher on the Danish Ministry of Industry project on intellectual capital. He holds an M.Sc. in Management Accounting and Organization from Copenhagen Business School, and an M.Sc. in International Development Studies and Business Studies from Roskilde University and completed his doctoral education at Copenhagen Business School in August 2001. Heine Thorsgaard Larsen has co-authored several articles and a book on intellectual capital. Heine Thorsgaard Larsen also acts as a consultant for industry.

Karl-Heinz Leitner
Department for Technology Policy, Austrian Research Centers, Seibersdorf, Austria
karl-heinz.leitner@arcs.ac.at
Since graduating from the University of Vienna in the field of business administration and computer science, Karl-Heinz Leitner has been a scientist in the Department for Technology Policy at Austrian Research Centers, Seibersdorf. His research examines the innovative behaviors of organizations, the role of information technology in organizational change, and strategic management. Mr. Leitner also researches the micro- and macro-level perspectives of the innovation process. He has carried out theoretical and empirical studies on Austrian firms and conducted consulting projects for both public agencies and private firms.

Shelley MacDougall
Manning School of Business Administration, Acadia University, Nova Scotia, Canada
shelley.macdougall@acadiau.ca
Dr. Shelley MacDougall is assistant professor of Finance at Acadia University, Wolfville, Nova Scotia, Canada. Her area of specialization

is capital budgeting, with particular emphasis on strategic investments in new technology. Her research principally involves the identification and valuation of the intangible benefits and costs of information technology, intellectual capital, and advanced manufacturing technology. Her other research deals with the capital budgeting implications of implementing complex investments. Dr. MacDougall is also co-owner of Engineered and Environmental Products, Inc. (EEP). Further information on her work history and research can be viewed at http://ace.acadiau.ca/fps/business/smacdoug/Shelley.htm.

Joseph Magowan
School of Management and Economics, Queen's University, Belfast, Northern Ireland
mcgowans@lineone.net

Joseph Magowan graduated in English and Modern History and went on to a successful career in financial services. He has had extensive experience in a number of European banks. He is currently completing a Masters of Business Administration from Queen's University of Belfast.

Eerikki Mäki
Department of Industrial Engineering and Management, Helsinki University of Technology, Finland
Eerikki.Maki@hut.fi

Eerikki Mäki is a postgraduate student at the Department of Industrial Engineering and Management, Helsinki University of Technology (HUT). His research interests include knowledge management, interpersonal trust in knowledge intensive work, and organizational communication. He teaches knowledge management to undergraduate students.

Karen McGraw
Cognitive Technologies, Marietta, Georgia, U.S.A.
kmcgraw@mindspring.com

Dr. Karen McGraw is the Director of Learning and Performance Management for Cognitive Technologies and a research fellow at the Accenture Institute for Strategic Change. Dr. McGraw provides consultation and guidance to clients to help them gain maximum value from their human capital assets through the use of learning and performance technologies. Previously, Dr. McGraw was the director of Strategic Services for Saba, guiding clients as they implemented e-learning, learning management, and competency management. Prior to entering the consulting field, Dr. McGraw managed research and development projects in intelligent computer managed instruction, knowledge engineering, and performance support for BDM, Loral, and Texas Instruments. Her current research interests include organizational and individual learning to enable better business performance. Dr. McGraw has written several textbooks and numerous articles and is a frequent speaker for industry events. She received her doctorate in educational psychology and instructional technology from Texas Tech University.

Lorraine McKay
Human Resource Systems Group Ltd., Ottawa, Canada
lmckay@hrmcanada.com

Ms. McKay is currently a partner with Human Resource Systems Group Ltd., a management consulting firm specializing in the development of competency-based human resource management systems. She has twelve years of experience as a human resources practitioner in a wide variety of programs within the public and private sector. She has managed a variety of human resource projects and activities including: job analysis and competency profiling projects, the development and implementation of systems for selection, performance management and career planning, the deployment of large-scale employee surveys, and the development and implementation of assessment center programs and career development programs.

Daniel P. McMurrer
Human Capital Dynamics, Chevy Chase, Maryland, U.S.A.
dmcmurrer@hcdynamics.com

Daniel McMurrer is director of research at Human Capital Dynamics, based in Chevy Chase, Maryland, and a research fellow at the Accenture Institute for Strategic Change. Previously, he has been research manager at Saba Software in Redwood Shores, California, and senior research associate at the American Society for Training and Development in Alexandria, Virginia. His research has included efforts to create and extend the use of standard measures for valuing training investments and outcomes and to apply those measures in a market environment. He worked previously at the Urban Institute in Washington, D.C., where his book, *Getting Ahead: Economic and Social Mobility in America* (co-authored with Isabel Sawhill), was published in 1998. He holds degrees from Princeton University and

Georgetown University and currently works from his home in Amherst, Massachusetts.

Rod McNaughton
Eyton Chair in Entrepreneurship, University of Waterloo, Waterloo, Canada
rmcnaugh@engmail.uwaterloo.ca

Professor McNaughton's specialty is international marketing strategy, focusing on the rapid entry into overseas markets by knowledge-intensive new ventures. The results of his research into export channel selection, industrial clusters and networks, export policy, the venture capital industry, strategic alliances, and foreign direct investment are published in numerous refereed journals and books. Prior to joining the University of Waterloo, Dr. McNaughton held a chair in Marketing at the University of Otago School of Business.

José Manuel Montes Peón
Faculty of Economics, University of Oviedo, Spain
jmmontes@econo.uniovi.es

José Manuel Montes has taught in technical schools and in the Faculty of Economics since 1992. His doctoral thesis is related to the study of the resource-based view of the firm. He was awarded the Special Degree prize, Flores de Lemus (1992), and his doctorate (1997). He is currently vice-dean of the Faculty of Economics at Oviedo University.

Jan Mouritsen
Copenhagen Business School, Denmark
jm.om@cbs.dk

Jan Mouritsen is professor of management control at Copenhagen Business School and has interests in intellectual capital and knowledge management, technology management, performance management, organizational design, and operations management. He has been research coordinator on the Danish Ministry of Industry's projects aimed at developing intellectual capital statements in Denmark. Jan Mouritsen has published widely in international journals, he is on the editorial board of several international journals, and he is on the board of European Institute of Advanced Studies in Management. Jan Mouritsen also consults for industry and the public sector.

Danny Nikitopoulos

DeGroote Business School, McMaster University, Hamilton, Canada
danny_nikitopoulos@hotmail.com
Danny Nikitopoulos is a research associate at the DeGroote Business School, McMaster University. He is a recent graduate of McMaster's undergraduate commerce program. His research interests lie in understanding how intellectual capital and knowledge management practitioners operationalize theory into action.

Patricia Ordóñez de Pablos

Faculty of Economics, University of Oviedo, Spain
patricia@econo.uniovi.es
Patricia Ordóñez de Pablos is a lecturer for Oviedo University (Spain) in the Department of Business Administration. As a Ph.D. candidate, her fields of interest are knowledge management, intellectual capital, and organizational learning. Her doctoral thesis is entitled *Knowledge Management and Intellectual Capital Measuring in the International Firm*. She has presented and published various papers, including *Intellectual Capital Report as a Reflection of the Invisible Balance Sheet, Strategic Tools for Intellectual Capital Measurement*, and *Knowledge Management and Intellectual Capital Reports*.

Susana Pérez López

Faculty of Economics, University of Oviedo, Spain
sperez@econo.uniovi.es
Susana Pérez López completed her bachelor's degree in Economics and Management. She has taught in technical schools and on the Faculty of Economics and Management since 1998. Her research activity has been based on the study of intellectual capital, knowledge management, learning organization, and firm strategy. She is currently pursuing her doctorate in knowledge management at the University of Oviedo.

Helen N. Rothberg

School of Management, Marist College, Poughkeepsie, U.S.A.
hnrothberg@aol.com
Helen Rothberg is assistant professor of Management in the School of Management of Marist College, Poughkeepsie, New York, U.S.A. She is also the principal of HNR Associates, a consulting firm specializing in competitive intelligence and the development of shadow teams. She holds a Ph.D. from City University Graduate Center (New York), an M.Phil., also from City University, and an M.B.A. from Baruch College. Research interests

include competitive intelligence and the use of shadow teams as an information-gathering tool.

Ursula Schneider

Department of International Management, Karl Franzens University, Graz, Austria
ursula.schneider@kfunigraz.ac.at

Ursula Schneider heads the Department of International Management at Karl Franzens University, Graz, and directs the program of European Studies in Human Resource Development at the College of Europe in Brugge. Her research is focused on the process of globalization, on new business models in a knowledge-based economy, on knowledge and learning (epistemology), on knowledge management, and on the monitoring and measuring of intangible assets.

George Tovstiga

ABB Business Services Ltd., Business Consulting, Baden, Switzerland
George.tovstiga@ch.abb.com

George Tovstiga currently leads the knowledge management consultancy practice at ABB Business Services Ltd. (Baden, Switzerland). Additionally, he is associate professor of Technology and Innovation Management at the University of Twente (Netherlands) and associate faculty member at Henley Management College (U.K.). His current work focuses on developing practical concepts, tools, and approaches for managing organizational knowledge and innovation in knowledge-intensive firms. Previously, Dr. Tovstiga has held engineering and management positions in industry with multinationals including Xerox Research (Canada) and Bayer AG (Germany). He has held a number of visiting professorships at international business schools in Europe and the U.S.A. and has numerous publications in international management journals and books. George Tovstiga graduated with degrees in chemical engineering from the University of Ottawa (Canada), University of Massachusetts (U.S.A.), a doctorate in engineering from the Swiss Federal Institute of Technology (Zürich, Switzerland), and an M.B.A. from the University of Twente (Netherlands).

Camilo José Vázquez Ordás

Faculty of Economics, University of Oviedo, Spain
cvazquez@econo.uniovi.es

Camilo José Vázquez has been teaching since 1987 in technical schools and on the Faculty of Economics. His research activity has been based on the study of firm management, especially the formulation of strategy and production and growth policies. He was awarded the Special Degree prize, Flores de Lemus (1987), and his doctorate (1992). He has been sub-director of the University Institute of the Firm and director of Teaching Staff and Postgraduate Courses at Oviedo University.

José María Viedma Marti
Polytechnic University of Catalonia and ESADE, Barcelona, Spain
icms.viedma@terra.es

José María Viedma Marti is a Doctor of Industrial Engineering, a graduate in Economics, and professor of Business Administration at the U.P.C., Polytechnic University of Catalonia, and ESADE in Barcelona, Spain. He has held top executive positions in computer services and management consultancy firms. He is the president and founding partner of Intellectual Capital Management Systems and M&A Fusiones y Adquisiciones. His current field of research and interest is focused on knowledge management and intellectual capital management, and he has consulted and developed management frameworks and systems on those matters worldwide.

S. Mitchell Williams
Faculty of Management, University of Calgary, Calgary, Canada
mwilliams@mgmt.ucalgary.ca

Mitchell Williams (Ph.D. Murdoch University in Perth, Western Australia) is an associate professor at the University of Calgary. Previously, he occupied university faculty positions in Australia and Hong Kong. Initially, Dr. Williams' research interests were international and corporate social disclosure practices, and papers based on this research were published in *International Journal of Accounting* and *The European Accounting Review*. His interest in intellectual capital initially focused on the disclosure of related accounting information and has expanded to encompass factors affecting intellectual capital performance at organizational, national, and international levels. In 2001, a paper by Mitchell Williams on intellectual capital was awarded the Best Academic Paper at the 4th World Congress on Intellectual Capital in Hamilton, Ontario, Canada.

Michael E. Wright

Faculty of Management, University of Calgary, Calgary, Canada
wright@mgmt.ucalgary.ca

Michael Wright (Ph.D. Queen's University) has been a member of the University of Calgary since 1989 and is currently an associate professor. Dr. Wright teaches financial accounting and accounting theory in the B.Comm. program, financial statement analysis in the M.B.A. programs, and philosophy of science in the Ph.D. program. His research interests include intellectual capital, oil and gas accounting, international accounting, environmental disclosures, and the use of financial information by creditors and analysts in decision-making. He has received research grants from such funding organizations as the Certified General Accountants Research Foundation, the Canadian Academic Accounting Association, and the Society of Management Accountants. He has published in *Accounting, Organizations and Society* and *Auditing: A Journal of Practice and Theory.*

FOREWORD

As the world's first intellectual capital director (ten years ago at Skandia) and now the first IC professor at the University of Lund in Sweden, I am often considered the *grandfather of intellectual capital*. In spite of this, I am committed to learning, and I do this by marking down the dates of the World Congress on IC on my calendar because it is without a doubt the most stimulating experience in which I participate. McMaster University has, for the fourth time, organized a successful, world-class event and continues to show how they play a pioneering role in intellectual capital knowledge-sharing. Dr. Vishwanath Baba (Dean of the DeGroote Business School) and Dr. Chris Bart (Program Chair) deserve to be commended for their vision and commitment to the community of researchers and practitioners they help cultivate. In addition, the fact that this event is primarily run by students is a testament to the fantastic knowledge workers that McMaster generates. The most recent event in January, 2001, highlighted the tremendous growth of the subject area, with several hundred insightful presenters, researchers, practitioners, consultants, senior executives, and government officials in attendance. McMaster University is clearly at the forefront of intellectual capital and knowledge management research, and this is very much driven by the innovation, commitment, and endless energy of Dr. Nick Bontis.

A lot has happened during the first ten years of IC evolution. IC, sometimes also referred to as *intangible assets*, has become an increasingly visible item on the new economic agenda for corporations as well as nations. An IC taxonomy has evolved and with it we have established a common conceptualization for human capital, structural capital, and relationship capital (with subcomponents). Assessment, rating, and accounting processes for IC and other knowledge assets continue to be adopted. Knowledge management initiatives and the hiring of CKOs have become common practice. Technological tools, which enable knowledge effectiveness, continue to develop. Innovation research centers for IC are being prototyped throughout the world. Intellectual property rights and processes for how to extract more value out of intangible assets are now on every CEO's agenda. Guidelines and recommendations for how to disclose intellectual assets on financial statements continue to be proposed. More recently, Denmark has accepted a law on the reporting of IC, and both the Securities and Exchange Commission as well as the International Accounting Standards Board continue to support strong recommendations for IC recognition and valuation.

What was once a small group of early pioneers has quickly become a global community with thousands of practitioners and academics trying to refine the agenda for the new intangible economy. McMaster has become a natural focal point for this global effort as it continues to position itself as *the event* for IC growth. The chapters in this book represent the latest research and best practices in the field and should be a mandatory read for anyone interested in learning about intellectual capital.

Finally, I would like to offer some insight as to how I see the field shaping up in the future. First, there is a tremendous need for academic research to collaborate with business and government. Some of the key frontiers to be addressed include (1) a continual refinement of the measurement, assessment, and accounting of intangible assets towards standardization, (2) the capitalizing, valuation, and commercialization of knowledge assets by knowledge exchanges, and (3) the examination of human brain behavior, talent migration, and how to tap the world's intellectual potential for general wealth creation. Ultimately, we would benefit from a research program that tries to explain *knowledge ergonomics,* so that we can build a more caring knowledge worker context.

Leif Edvinsson
CEO, Universal Networking Intellectual Capital
Associate Professor of Intellectual Capital, University of Lund
Vice President of Intellectual Capital, Knexa.com Enterprises
E-mail: leif.edvinsson@unic.net

INTRODUCTION

The 4th World Congress on Intellectual Capital took place at McMaster University in Hamilton, Ontario, Canada, from January 17–19, 2001. The chapters in this special collection highlight some of the most cutting-edge research in the field from that event. The conference itself was the largest academic gathering for intellectual capitalists and knowledge management theorists in the world, attracting 536 delegates from thirty-two countries. This compilation represents the latest research from forty-one of the world's experts in the fields of intellectual capital and knowledge management. The underlying theme in this book is to explain how an organization can identify, measure, manage, leverage, and act upon its collective intelligence toward the pursuit of sustainable innovation. The book is divided into three main parts that first establish a foundation of literature, then examine various measurement approaches, and finally conclude with a variety of applications.

The first chapter, by Nick Bontis and Danny Nikitopoulos, provides an overview of the keynote presentations at the World Congress. The chapter highlights the key messages of such luminaries as Shahla Aly, VP Communication Sector at IBM, Canada; Stephen Denning, KM Director of the World Bank; Don Tapscott, Chairman of Digital 4Sight; Ante Pulic and Ursula Schneider, Directors at the Austrian Intellectual Capital Research Center; Tom Jenkins, CEO of OpenText; Leif Edvinsson, VP of Knexa.com Enterprises; Verna Allee, President of Integral Performance Group; and Don Morrison, COO of Research in Motion.

Chapter 2 represents a literature review by Nick Bontis originally presented at the 2nd World Congress on Intellectual Capital. It highlights the field of intellectual capital from a variety of perspectives focusing on its main conceptualizations and measurement challenges and sets forth a research agenda for the future.

David Brett introduces his concept of knowledge transactions in chapter 3. When tacit knowledge is codified, it becomes copyrighted intellectual property. Unfortunately, today's digital networks disrupt the traditional market exchanges that could have been used to trade these knowledge assets.

In the rapidly emerging knowledge-based economy, knowledge is a fundamental factor input. The problem is, with all the information bombardment we suffer from, how does one make sense of the dissonance? Bryan Davis explains the importance of knowledge pattern recognition in chapter 4.

Chapter 5, by Helen Rothberg and Scott Erickson, considers the similarities between intellectual capital management systems and competitive intelligence systems. They argue for the conceptualization of a fourth intellectual capital construct that encompasses the knowledge embedded in competitors.

George Tovstiga and David Birchall present a new methodology in chapter 6 that can be used to identify key knowledge capabilities for firms. It examines (1) knowledge-sourcing, (2) the internalization of new knowledge streams, and, ultimately, (3) the reconfiguration of existing knowledge in the firm for maximum impact.

In chapter 7, Susana Pérez López, J. M. Montes Peón, and C. J. Vázquez Ordás integrate the fields of organizational learning with knowledge management. Using seven Spanish firms as case studies, they offer hints for improving their operational knowledge management strategies.

Chapter 8 represents the first of several intellectual capital disclosure studies. Philip Beaulieu, S. Mitchell Williams, and Michael Wright were interested in determining the extent of intellectual capital disclosure practices in Swedish corporate annual reports. Their research results indicate that organizational size is significantly associated with intellectual capital disclosure.

Patricia Ordóñez de Pablos follows a similar research trajectory in chapter 9 with an examination of intellectual capital disclosure practices in Danish and Spanish firms. Her findings suggest a three-stage path in which firms begin by (1) implementing a model, (2) developing nonfinancial measures, and finally (3) initiating disclosure practices.

In chapter 10, J. Mouritsen, H. T. Larsen, and P. N. D. Bukh try to understand whether or not intellectual capital statements communicate knowledge management strategies. They examine the reporting approaches of two Danish organizations and link their statements to their overall strategies.

Karen McGraw, Daniel McMurrer, and Laurie Bassi report on the Saba Learning Capacity Index in chapter 11. The index is a self-assessment survey instrument that consists of a total of thirty-nine questions. It was designed and implemented to improve the state of measurement with regard to organizational learning.

Chapter 12 represents the conceptual development of an instrument developed to measure knowledge management. Jenny Darroch and Rod McNaughton develop the items based on the Kohli-Jaworski market-orientation instrument, which was created to measure a firm's ability to acquire, disseminate, and use market information.

José María Viedma Marti describes the Innovation Capability–Benchmarking System in chapter 13. This system benchmarks core innovation capabilities by considering the following factors: emerging needs, project objectives, new products and services, new processes, new core capabilities, new professional core capabilities, company innovation, and infrastructure financial results.

In chapter 14, Karl-Heinz Leitner, Manfred Bornemann, and Ursula Schneider describe the development of the first ever intellectual capital report at the Austrian Research Centers, Seibersdorf, which is the largest research technology organization in Austria. The authors explain the background context, model development, and implementation of the report.

Shelley MacDougall and Deborah Hurst introduce the contingent worker dilemma in chapter 15. On the one hand, contingent workers bring in stimulating new ideas and importing public domain knowledge to an organization. On the other hand, these workers are also exposed to private organizational knowledge, thereby jeopardizing the firm's strategic position.

Chapter 16 outlines the practice of competency-based human resource management as a method for effectively managing an organization's human capital. Laurent LaPierre and Lorraine McKay rationalize that processes developed in accordance with such a framework are designed to hire applicants holding the most promise in terms of the human capital they bring to a firm.

Michael Charney introduces a seven-stage framework in chapter 17. It is based on dialectical theory and recognizes that knowledge management projects are themselves constantly evolving creations, dependent on both the specific business and cultural factors being addressed as well as the individual capabilities and talents of those performing the work.

In chapter 18, Joseph Kranz and Denis Coffey document a meta-process that enables the development of a methodology that mitigates organizational and naturalistic decision-making biases in science and technology investment decision-making.

Assessing the transferability of intellectual capital across geographic and cultural boundaries is the focus of chapter 19. By presenting a case study of the experience of a West European bank in acquiring a Polish bank, Anne Davies and Joseph McGowan warn that cultural sensitivity and sufficient time and effort are required for a successful result.

In chapter 20, Eila Järvenpää and Eerikki Mäki deal with knowledge-sharing in two different networked organizations. They argue that prerequisites for knowledge-sharing include trust, personal relationships, joint professional interests, and common goals. However, the importance of each of these is contingent on network type.

Finally, there are several individuals I would like to thank who were instrumental in the compilation of this book. I would like to recognize President Peter George, Dean Vishwanath Baba, Dr. Chris Bart, and Dr. Milena Head, whose unwavering support of the conference is a testament to their continued commitment and positioning of intellectual capital and knowledge management research as a critical strategic thrust for the DeGroote Business School at McMaster University. I would also like to recognize the twenty students who volunteered several thousand hours and numerous endless nights in organizing and running the conference. Much of the success behind the record-breaking results can be attributed to the three student cochairs Meaghan Stovel, Don Newton, and Constantinos Coursaris. I would also like to highlight two other students in particular who personally assisted me in recruiting speakers and organizing the conference: Brent McKnight and Anna Poliszot. The conference has secured some high-profile sponsorship by corporate partners whose support is much needed and much appreciated. They include OpenText, Research In Motion, the Austrian IC Research Center, MCB University Press, Knexa.com Enterprises, Canadian Business Magazine, Dofasco, Bell Canada, General Motors, IBM, AMS, AT Kearney, Gennum, BitNet, the Canadian Institute of Chartered Accountants, and the Management of Innovation and New Technology Research Centre at McMaster University. Last, but not least, I would like to thank Jennifer Pursley of Butterworth-Heinemann and Steve Cavaleri of KMCI for making this project as smooth as possible.

I invite you to participate in future conferences and join in the growth of our intellectual capital community. Please be sure to visit our website at http://worldcongress.mcmaster.ca for further information.

Dr. Nick Bontis
Program Director, World Congress on Intellectual Capital
Assistant Professor of Strategic Management, McMaster University
Associate Editor, Journal of Intellectual Capital
Chief Knowledge Officer, Knexa.com Enterprises
Director, Institute for Intellectual Capital Research
E-mail: nbontis@mcmaster.ca
http://www.Bontis.com

1

THOUGHT LEADERSHIP ON INTELLECTUAL CAPITAL[1]

Nick Bontis
DeGroote Business School, McMaster University, Hamilton, Canada
nbontis@mcmaster.ca

and

Danny Nikitopoulos
DeGroote Business School, McMaster University, Hamilton, Canada
danny_nikitopoulos@hotmail.com

ABSTRACT

A synopsis of key topics, issues, and findings, as presented at the 4th World Congress on Intellectual Capital, hosted by McMaster University in Hamilton, Ontario, Canada. There were 536 delegates from thirty-two countries who discussed the growing importance of intellectual capital. This paper highlights the key messages from the keynote speakers of the conference. We include a summary of the presentations of such luminaries as Shahla Aly (VP Communication

[1]This chapter was reprinted with permission from MCB University Press © 2001. Bontis, Nick and Danny Nikitopoulos. 2001. "Thought leadership on intellectual capital," *Journal of Intellectual Capital* 2: 3, 183-191.

Sector at IBM Canada), Stephen Denning (KM Director of the World Bank), Don Tapscott (Chairman of Digital 4Sight), Ante Pulic and Ursula Schneider (Directors of the Austrian Intellectual Capital Research Centre), Tom Jenkins (CEO of OpenText), Leif Edvinsson (VP of Knexa.com Enterprises), Verna Allee (President of Integral Performance Group), and Don Morrison (COO of Research in Motion).

INTRODUCTION

The World Congress on Intellectual Capital, hosted by McMaster University in Hamilton, Ontario, Canada, took place from 17–19 January, 2001. In attendance were 536 delegates from thirty-two countries who discussed and presented papers on the growing importance of intellectual capital. This event is recognized as the premier conference for academic researchers in the field of intellectual capital. The conference program included several guest practitioner speakers as well as exhibitors and an interactive knowledge café.

The World Congress attracts the leading thought leaders in the IC field, and the 2001 roster of keynote speakers represented luminaries from a variety of industries. The following highlights the key messages from the keynote speakers. We include a summary of the presentations of such luminaries as Shahla Aly (VP Communication Sector at IBM Canada), Stephen Denning (KM Director of the World Bank), Don Tapscott (Chairman of Digital 4Sight), Ante Pulic and Ursula Schneider (Directors of the Austrian Intellectual Capital Research Centre), Tom Jenkins (CEO of OpenText), Leif Edvinsson (VP of Knexa.com Enterprises), Verna Allee (President of Integral Performance Group), and Don Morrison (COO of Research in Motion).

SHAHLA ALY–VP COMMUNICATION SECTOR, IBM CANADA

Shahla Aly commenced the proceedings of the World Congress by commenting on the developments of knowledge-intensive e-business and giving those in attendance a keen insight into what can be expected from the sector and IBM in the future.

At the heart of her discussion, Aly described the three major technological forces that will evolve the Internet and the way people and companies share knowledge and do business: (1) increase in bandwidth; (2) pervasive computing, and (3) deep computing.

As bandwidth increases and broadband networks continue to be deployed, the quality and experience of the Internet will increase dramatically. Aly equated the impact of bandwidth on humanity to that of the impact of electricity on the same, and said it would allow us to share a more natural interactive experience on the Web.

What we can expect from this advanced interactivity is what she described as *pervasive computing*. Pervasive computing will allow people to share a more personal and interactive experience that is more responsive to the user's patterns, trends, and personal characteristics and preferences. To much bemoaning in the audience, Aly provided the example that one day our alarm clocks will sound 15 minutes earlier, as they will be able to input and process information of a traffic jam on the sleeper's route to work.

Deep computing is the third major technological force she discussed. Most people are familiar with Gary Kasparov's infamous chess matches against IBM's Deep Blue computer. The ability to do mass calculations of algorithms and permutations by machines in the future will provide users with a variety of extremely complex applications at their fingertips.

With respect to commerce, Aly assured the conference delegates that, in the next generation of e-business, the companies who emerge as global players will be those who successfully bind these new technological forces with robust business models. Aly explained that the "dot-com" crash of 2000 was a result of a lack of relevant business models among many nascent e-businesses who did not consider business first, and technology second.

Overall, in the next generation of e-business we can expect a world of change and growth. Aly gauged that on a scale of 1 to 10, the Internet at the time of the conference sat at about a 1.5 or, alternately, at the stage of the automobile around the year 1910. Commenting on the proceedings of the congress, Aly emphasized the importance of exploring every aspect of intellectual capital: "There is no aspect too little to be explored."

Stephen Denning—Knowledge Management Director, World Bank

As Knowledge Management Director at the World Bank, Stephen Denning has spearheaded the bank's knowledge program since 1996. At the World Congress, Denning discussed how storytelling can serve as a powerful tool for organizational change and knowledge management to further develop an organization's intellectual capital.

Through countless transactions over time, the bank had accumulated a tremendous amount of know-how. What seized the attention of Denning was that none of this intellectual capital was organized by the World Bank to help the people of the world solve their problems more efficiently. Most people were making the same mistakes over and over again.

As with any major organizational change, especially in the field of intellectual capital, Denning discussed the obstacles involved in his ambition to transform the World Bank from a historically entrenched lending institution to a new "knowledge bank." It was the idea of storytelling that became the catalyst for the transformation of the World Bank. Denning shared with the audience many anecdotal reports of storytelling that served as an effective medium to communicate the importance of intellectual capital development within the bank.

Storytelling implies using the story as an means to convey a message or idea, whether it be regarding intellectual capital, knowledge management, total quality management, or any other organizational issue. This form of communication not only imparts information to the recipient but also allows them to get inside, to live and feel the idea.

Denning explained that storytelling can have extraordinary power in transforming individuals, organizations, and ourselves. Telling a story can enable and accelerate change by providing direct access to the living part of the organization, and so lead to change in the organization. Storytelling helps to get inside the minds of individuals and affect how they think, worry, wonder, agonize, and dream about themselves, and, in the process, create and recreate their organization and their lives. Storytelling enables the individuals in an organization to see themselves and the organization in a different light, and, through storytelling, take decisions and change their behavior in accordance with these new perceptions, insights, and identities.

DON TAPSCOTT–CHAIRMAN, DIGITAL 4SIGHT

Don Tapscott was once identified by former U.S. Vice President Al Gore as "the world's Internet guru." Tapscott argued that strong business models must be in place first before a firm can generate any wealth in the new economy. The new economy has given birth to his idea of "business webs," which are a new partnership of customers, suppliers, affinity groups, and competitors who cooperate to provide a joint, value-added service for the customer. In his keynote presentation to conference delegates, Tapscott highlighted five types of business webs:

- Agora business webs—which turn the marketplace of the Internet into a boundless meeting place where customers and firms meet to discover the price of a good or product
- Aggregation business webs—which organize and choreograph the distribution of goods, services, and information
- Value-chain business webs—which replace make/sell push models with demand-driven value chains
- Alliance business webs—which produce open free markets where selfish agents combine to maximize utility
- Distributive business webs—which facilitate the exchange of goods and services over the Web

Tapscott explained that business webs allow customers to become part of a seamless value-chain process, thus creating a transparent world. Intellectual capital flows through every facet of a business transaction, and it can be applied to all areas of knowledge assets that can be co-owned by various partners in the web. He described the following key intellectual capital assets:

- Human capital—knowledge assets contained in employees
- Structural knowledge—KM systems, databases
- Marketplace capital—brand, customers

According to Tapscott, all three facets of intellectual capital can be combined into the "business web" model. Successful companies will combine a robust business model with intellectual capital management to form a new advantage known as "digital capital." He concluded his presentation by describing a massive explosion of the "Hypernet," which connects everyone and everything using multiple smart devices that are mobile.

ANTE PULIC AND URSULA SCHNEIDER— DIRECTORS, AUSTRIAN INTELLECTUAL CAPITAL RESEARCH CENTRE

Ante Pulic and Ursula Schneider operate the Austrian Intellectual Capital Research Centre (AICRC). The AICRC is an organization that strives to enhance knowledge exchange and international cooperation in the areas of intellectual capital and knowledge management. The AICRC's primary initiatives are to raise awareness of the importance of intellectual capital in German-speaking countries and in Eastern Europe. The institute is committed to the development of intellectual capital measurement methodologies. The AICRC was founded by a cross-functional and multicultural group. The intellectual diversity has become the institute's fundamental strength in achieving its goals. The "Best Paper Award" at the World Congress is an extension of the ground-breaking research that the AICRC has conducted.

Schneider started her keynote address by reminiscing about a field that was once occupied by dreamers who sought to make intellectual capital a priority for senior managers. She argued that today's concern is not about dreaming anymore, but about measuring. In the language of Stephen Denning, she insisted, "nobody has told me the right stories to help us learn about measuring intellectual capital."

For IC initiatives to be successfully adopted, Schneider advised that they need to be embedded in everyday life: in the core operations and procedures of the organization. From the AICRC's experiences, there is leadership by European enterprises in the field of intellectual capital and knowledge management because of the diversity inherent in the continent. She described diversity as an important knowledge-building asset that is to be expected from a continent exceptionally rich in history, diverse in culture and language, and unique in structure from country to country.

Pulic's work is guided by the notion that nothing can be successfully managed if it is not adequately measured, and thus his major area of interest is the measurement of IC. Pulic and his team hope to determine the relationships between intangible and tangible assets. He argued that by measuring intellectual capital using their value added efficiency index (VAIC), companies can develop better control over the visible and invisible parts of the company. VAIC is a software-aided tool that is applicable at both the micro- and macro-level of business analysis. To date, three companies have utilized it, and Pulic shared success stories of the creation of value in their businesses.

Some of the AICRC projects intended for the future include a knowledge forum, where people can meet virtually online, and a distributed MBA program on intellectual capital in connection with three German universities, as well as knowledge-intensive companies such as Siemens and Daimler Chrysler.

Tom Jenkins—CEO, OpenText Corporation

Tom Jenkins is the Chief Executive Officer of OpenText Corporation, which is one of the largest document management companies in the world. Jenkins provided valuable insight into the field of intellectual capital from the perspective of a vendor of KM software.

The application of software tools to manage a firm's intellectual assets has driven his Waterloo, Ontario, company to achieve over $300 million in revenues. Jenkins recounted the origins of OpenText as a vendor in the knowledge management arena. What began originally as an *Oxford English Dictionary* project, moved toward developing search technology with the likes of Yahoo! and About.com. Taking into consideration the desire for long-term wealth creation, OpenText altered its strategy by moving out of the consumer markets to focus on the more lucrative business-to-business sector, where it still deals today.

In 1995 the company undertook what Jenkins referred to as a "crazy idea" and developed its first KM suite that was fully integrated into an HTML browser. In that year the company made $2 million in revenues. The growth in awareness of intellectual capital has been remarkable, as OpenText currently does over $300 million in business worldwide. Jenkins noted that the growth of intellectual capital and knowledge management can be witnessed by the change in tone, where once the words were intimidating, they have now become widely recognized as an ongoing concern for organizations.

At the heart of OpenText is the flagship product, Livelink. Livelink has developed into an innovative intranet, extranet and e-business application. The tool allows dynamic collaboration on projects and work by connecting employees, business partners, and customers across global enterprises and online trading communities. Currently, thousands of leading organizations worldwide use OpenText to address their business challenges and leverage the company's intellectual capital. In describing where markets for software tools are moving, Jenkins examined the evolution of buzzwords such as "document management," then "collaborative knowledge management," to what he now calls "collaborative commerce."

Technological platforms of the past were built in the design of document management and workflow. Document management implied that people searched for information, whereas a workflow structure assumed people talked to one another to get information as they worked on projects. Jenkins described Livelink as encompassing each of these important business aspects. He also described collaborative commerce as managing the information associated with transactions and performing this interaction with speed and efficiency (e.g., the ordering process of a CD through the entire value chain from musician, to producer, to distributor, to retailer, to consumer).

With first-hand experience in the deployment of his software across many organizations, Jenkins shared many lessons learned in the adoption of KM initiatives by his clients. He explained that most companies should first establish a project-document repository and corporate-teaming that are not geographically centered. Then they should strive to implement knowledge-sharing initiatives aided by Livelink at the department level. Enterprise-wide deployments of knowledge management are not homogeneous activities, but rather amorphous, and must be catered to each organization's characteristics. Generally, OpenText implements a department-by-department deployment of its product Livelink.

Jenkins described the experiences of several organizations, including Clarica Life Insurance, Nortel Networks, Scotland Yard, the U.S. Air Force, and Ford Motor Co. Despite this fantastic growth, Jenkins insisted that the growth days for document management are yet to come. Despite being a Canadian-based company, OpenText has an entirely global perspective, with the majority of its sales outside Canada, but primarily in G7 countries. In assessing the future of OpenText, Jenkins emphasized that technology and the Internet are here to stay, regardless of the shakedown in the financial markets in 2000 and 2001. Jenkins estimated a massive untapped revenue base during the next few years with 25 percent of that earmarked for research and development to keep OpenText's own intellectual capital fresh.

LEIF EDVINSSON—VP INTELLECTUAL CAPITAL, KNEXA.COM ENTERPRISES

It was a privilege shared by all in attendance at the World Congress to listen to a keynote presentation by Leif Edvinsson, whom some entitle the *godfather of IC*. Edvinsson gave a thought-inspiring presentation that challenged those in attendance to grasp many fascinating insights related to the study of intellectual capital.

In his earlier days at Skandia, Edvinsson began to probe the surface of IC by challenging the traditional notion of a company, asking questions such as, "what happens to companies with zero employees?" He suggested that the remains would consist mainly of intellectual property. He insisted that the awareness of IC today is greater than ever but that the formation of an arena for the exchange of intellectual capital is the true nirvana. He insisted that we must decrease the volatility of the world's stock exchanges—which he referred to as *dirty exchanges*—because the wild fluctuations show that "we have no clue how much companies are really worth." Edvinsson's main proposition was that an intellectual capital exchange can help offset some of that volatility. He believes this is possible, if there is collaboration between the SEC (Securities Exchange Commission) and the IASC (International Accounting Standards Committee), so they can map the unseen wealth of the corporate world that currently no one seems to value accurately.

He also challenged the conference delegates to examine their traditional roles and titles within organizations. He questioned how closely our business cards could describe our talents. At Skandia, he worked on the idea of "visualizing your talent" in which the roots of the term *intellectual capital* came forward. The visualization of talent is an important element to the idea of a "global knowledge nomad" or the future knowledge-worker. To the Dean of the Michael G. DeGroote School of Business, he suggested the title of *wealth creator* as opposed to *Dean*. Edvinsson suggested that our business cards should be a talking stick and that personal websites are an imperative part of visualizing one's talent.

Edvinsson also discussed the future of knowledge economics and the wealth dimensions of knowledge investments. He suggested that Europe was operating at about 45 percent of its IC potential. He also discussed the problem of knowledge automation and compared the production of telephones versus the time to achieve a college degree. He questioned why the time required to obtain a university degree was still around four years, when, since the invention of the telephone, the time to make a phone call had decreased from a few weeks to seconds. Comparatively, if the process efficiency of universities were at par with the telecommunications industry, it would require only ten weeks to earn a degree.

Edvinsson considered the idea of the *knowledge nomad* as a fundamental change in the labor market over the next ten years. A knowledge nomad is likened to an independent or contractual worker on special assignment. The more knowledgeable the worker, the more likely she is employable. Edvinsson contrasted the part-time worker versus the full-time worker today and asked, "who makes more money?" to emphasize his point. A part-time worker has the ability to link and connect to an endless number of buyers and does not lock up his or her human capital to one buyer. Unfortunately, the current labor market will not support such a framework with the existence of traditional unions, which are still prevalent in many countries. Edvinsson remarked that ventures such as Knexa.com—which is the world's first knowledge exchange—draw a bridge between human capital and structural capital to solve this problem. He predicted that, in fifty to seventy years, the current industrial society would be as dead as the feudal counties of old Europe. In considering the knowledge worker, he looked at the performance curve. The peak-performance time for a knowledge worker is about two hours, versus the current eight-hour labor contracts people are required to work. Shockingly, he added that, at six hours, there is a negative return and intellectual capital is, in fact, destroyed.

Knowledge architecture is the final challenge or frontier, and he suggested we consider what kind of architecture is needed to nourish knowledge exchange and delivery. He strongly denounced the cubicle office as an optimal framework and recommended the knowledge-café model (which also took place at the conference) to remedy this. In conclusion, he argued for strong intellectual capital leadership and a longitudinal examination of research pursuits.

Verna Allee–President, Integral Performance Group

Verna Allee provided an intuitive presentation concerning business and the field of intellectual capital. Allee explained that we have the ultimate potential to reconcile our business and economic models with the fabric of global society and the web of life. This perspective dovetailed nicely with the organic metaphors of organizations shared by Leif Edvinsson and with the concept of *business webs* proposed by Don Tapscott in their earlier presentations. Allee was convinced that people had already grasped the importance of intellectual capital, but in many important respects had missed the real point.

First, she argued that people were asking the wrong questions, especially concerning intangibles. She believed that the questions we were asking were based on old management views that shared a type of mechanistic, versus organic, thinking. Allee mentioned two important shifts that would be part of this new view:

- expand value to include all categories relevant to business success
- use methodologies that link tangibles and intangibles to continually evolving real activities

To expand our thinking on intangibles, Allee suggested we think of intangible assets in real-currency terms that can be traded for other intangibles or tangible assets. Allee presented a model of a typical asset view that encompasses three basic categories: business relationships, internal structures, and human competence, and the flow of knowledge among them. Two emerging value domains that have already begun to expand the categories of this model are social citizenship and environmental health. She provided an example of its adoption in Shell Oil's most recent annual report statements. Shell's "triple bottom line" reports have come to include people, planet, and profits, including metrics for health, safety, and environment as well as social responsibilities, such as emission targets and the diversity of their workforce.

Allee proposed that we shift toward thinking and challenging our notions about sustainability and social responsibility metrics and finding ways to incorporate these into our IC models. She presented a value-network model showing a web of relationships that generates economic value through complex dynamic exchanges of both tangible and intangible goods, services, and benefits. The idea of value networks showed the interdynamics of a business and was similar to the ideas presented by Don Tapscott in his discussion of business webs.

According to Allee's description, a value network is a new view that encompasses both business and social structures, and three new "currencies" of value exchange: the traditional transactions involving goods, services, and revenue of the old value chain; the exchange of knowledge in all forms, such as strategic and planning information, collaborative design, policy, and process knowledge; and finally, the idea of benefits that accrue to a community.

DON MORRISON–COO, RESEARCH IN MOTION

In capping off the proceedings of the 4th World Congress on Intellectual Capital, Don Morrison, Chief Operating Officer of Research in Motion (RIM), provided some final thoughts that he hoped would reverberate with listeners and allow them to make value of the ideas they gained over the last few days. RIM is famous for its revolutionary

Blackberry pagers that allow users to share corporate e-mail messages with fellow colleagues in an always-on, mobile environment.

Throughout his career with various corporations, such as AT&T and now RIM, one of the most important fundamentals Morrison has learned is to "stop thinking and start doing." He presented three critical areas that he hoped organizations would start doing more of: product innovation, service excellence, and brand recognition.

Essentially, product innovation is purely about value creation. Morrison said that, if an organization innovated the right way, they could have a transformative effect on the marketplace with a product or service that resonated with customers. Morrison stressed that RIM's process of continual innovation is an iterative, experience-based approach that pays attention to details, customers, and the market, where listening is the key.

Morrison warned that the iterative process does not constitute market research and data, but rather getting out and talking to customers who continually demand more valuable services and experiences. He stressed that a lot of organizations could further enhance the delivery of their service to gain customer loyalty. In discussing brand recognition, Morrison made reference to brand skeptics, who highlight the difference between brands, as opposed to products. He strongly supports building a brand around an idea with substance that focuses on customer experience and employs a spirit of continuous improvement, rather than a superficial two-dimensional concept or logo.

Overall, Morrison felt that, if a company truly wants to strive to be innovative, they need to learn to become a listening organization by constantly interacting with the marketplace and by trusting their collective intuitions.

2

MANAGING ORGANIZATIONAL KNOWLEDGE BY DIAGNOSING INTELLECTUAL CAPITAL:

FRAMING AND ADVANCING THE STATE OF THE FIELD[1]

Nick Bontis
DeGroote Business School, McMaster University, Hamilton, Canada
nbontis@mcmaster.ca

ABSTRACT

Since organizational knowledge is at the crux of sustainable competitive advantage, the burgeoning field of intellectual capital is an exciting area for both researchers and practitioners. Intellectual capital is conceptualized from numerous disciplines, making the field a mosaic of perspectives. Accountants are interested in how to

[1]This chapter was reprinted with permission from Inderscience Enterprises Ltd. © 1999. Bontis, Nick. 1999. "Managing Organizational Knowledge by Diagnosing Intellectual Capital: Framing and advancing the state of the field." *International Journal of Technology Management* 18, 5/6/7/8: 433–62.

measure it on the balance sheet, information technologists want to codify it on systems, sociologists want to balance power with it, psychologists want to develop minds because of it, human resource managers want to calculate an ROI on it, and training and development officers want to make sure that they can build it. The following article represents a comprehensive literature review from a variety of managerial disciplines. In addition to highlighting the research to date, avenues for future pursuit are also offered.

INTRODUCTION

> He that hath knowledge spareth words; and a man of understanding is of an excellent spirit.
>
> —*Bible, Proverbs 17:27*

Management academics strive to conduct rigorous research from which knowledge can be transferred to future generations of managers. Thus, their role is twofold: one of theorist as well as educator. This logic has some inherent implications. First, rigorous research is required to clear the publication hurdle. This generally leads to newer academics pursuing the path of least resistance. Typically, these paths are described as having voluminous amounts of researchers, and even more voluminous amounts of past research, on which to draw. The second implication lies in the notion that something out there exists to be examined. The debate of whether academics lead or lag the real world has been argued for centuries. The answer, of course, rests with which group you associate. Finally, academics must teach relevant conceptualizations in the classroom. With rising tuition costs and increasing alternatives, students are in a position to carefully scrutinize where their hard-earned money will go. Within the context of the aforementioned implications, this paper's objective is to frame and advance the field of intellectual capital. In attempting to conceptualize the phenomenon from a variety of perspectives and for different audiences, the intellectual capital field can take stock of where it has been and where it is going. This is necessary in order for it to continue its trajectory.

With the advent of the third millennium, how has the burgeoning field of intellectual capital developed? A variety of perspectives will be used to answer this question. First, the field of intellectual capital initially started appearing in the popular press in the early 1990s (Stewart 1991, 1994). Intellectual capital was described by Stewart as a "brand new tennis ball—fuzzy, but with a lot of bounce." However, this statement acts as a detriment for the survival of this field in academia. Most "bouncy" topics that are researched extensively (e.g., reengineering, quality circles, management by objectives) are frowned upon in academic circles because they are considered nothing more than popular fads. Due to their temporal shortcomings, they are deemed unworthy of serious study. On the other hand, the "fuzzy" aspect of intellectual capital captures the curious interest of practitioners who are always on the prowl for finding solutions to difficult challenges. Hence, the popularity of this topic during its genesis has been sponsored by business practitioners. It is for this audience that the conceptualization of intellectual capital resonates most.

Academics wishing to study this phenomenon face tremendous challenges. A so-called "hot topic" is just that. It has no legacy, no world-renowned researchers, and no publication trajectory to follow. This becomes a very risky proposition for developing a publication portfolio. The academic state of this field is in its embryonic stage. It is being pursued by those academics who have a very strong managerial focus and a strong appetite for a field devoid of shape or direction.

The study of the field of intellectual capital is akin to the pursuit of the "elusive intangible." Academics and practitioners alike recognize and appreciate the tacit nature of organizational knowledge. Furthermore, intellectual capital is typically conceptualized as a set of sub-phenomena. The real problem with intellectual capital lies in its measurement. Unfortunately, an invisible conceptualization—regardless of its underlying simplicity—becomes an abyss for the academic researcher. To make matters worse, intellectual capital is conceptualized from numerous disciplines, making the field a mosaic of perspectives. Accountants are interested in how to measure it on the balance sheet, information technologists want to codify it on systems, sociologists want to balance power with it, psychologists want to develop minds because of it, human resource managers want to calculate an ROI on it, and training and development officers want to make sure that they can build it. This field may be growing at a fantastic rate, but does anyone know where it is heading? Academics may want to ask their customers.

Students have spent decades learning how to manage scarce resources. The traditional economic model rests on the tenets of the scarcity assumption, which states that supply and demand determine market price. As all introductory economic students have learned, if supply goes down, then price goes up (assuming demand is constant). However, knowledge as a resource does not comply with the scarcity assumption. The more knowledge is supplied (or shared), the more highly it is valued. Furthermore, when was the last time the demand for knowledge went down? In fact, scientific folklore in the early 1900s stated that all the information in the world doubled every thirty years. As the 1970s approached, that number was reduced to seven years. Prognosticators have pushed this notion further and state that by the year 2010 all the information in the world will double every eleven hours. Do we need a better reason to appreciate the importance of educating our management students within the intellectual capital framework?

Most, if not all, premier business schools around the world continue, or are planning, to redesign their programs. A quick scan through most course outlines yields a standard offering of functional courses with integrative modules using a variety of pedagogical techniques. One of the key issues that is being addressed is how to reflect in the classroom the onslaught of new initiatives such as intellectual capital, organizational learning, knowledge management, and other "knowledge era" initiatives. Professors continue to publish new texts to help fill the void in this new burgeoning market of course redesign. In the United States, "discussions with colleagues around the country led [professors] to conclude that [they] were not the only ones struggling to find an appropriate text for teaching the business strategy course" (Besanko, Dranove, and Shanley 1996, p. iv). Similarly, in Canada "the primary stimulus for [revising] the book was [the program's] ongoing need for new material" (Beamish and Woodcock 1996, p. vii). Business schools that can tap into the need for managerial training that is reflective of the knowledge era will be well positioned to ride the current wave of interest in intellectual capital as well.

Intellectual Capital Is an Organizational Resource

It seems that every month a new management technique emerges that CEOs, hungry for new ways to improve the performance of their business, readily devour. Companies are rightsizing, downsizing, and reengineering. They are promoting a culture of leaders and followers. They are striving to be "learning organizations" and promoting team building and self-empowerment. The options are overwhelming. But all these techniques have one thing in common; they are seeking to discover better ways of utilizing organizational resources.

In our present economy, more and more businesses are evolving, whose value is not based on their tangible resources but on their intangible resources (Itami 1987). Tangible resources are those typically found on the balance sheet of a company, such as cash, buildings, and machinery. The other category comprises intangible resources: people and their expertise, business processes and market assets, such as customer loyalty, repeat business, reputation, and so forth. The annual reports of companies such as Skandia (1994, 1995a, 1995b, 1996a, 1996b, 1997) are working toward a new balance sheet that makes more sense in today's marketplace. This new balance sheet highlights the difference between visible (explicit) accounting and invisible (implicit) accounting. Traditional annual reports have concentrated on reporting what can be explicitly calculated, such as receivables, fixed assets, and so forth. Skandia has made an effort to report on their invisible assets, such as intellectual capital, which provides the company with much of its market-value-added. Examples of other organizations that are following Skandia's lead can be found in the service sector and any enterprise where businesses, such as software development start-ups, management consultants, high-technology ventures, life sciences and health care, media and entertainment and law firms, rely primarily on people (Bontis 1996a).

Although intangible assets may represent competitive advantage, organizations do not understand their nature and value (Collis 1996). Managers do not know the value of their own intellectual capital. They do not know if they have the people, resources, or business processes in place to make a success of a new strategy. They do not understand what know-how, management potential, or creativity they have access to with their employees. Because they are devoid of such information, they are rightsizing, downsizing, and reengineering in a vacuum.

That organizations are operating in a vacuum is not surprising, as they do not have any methods or tools to use that would enable them to analyze their intellectual capital stocks and organizational learning flows. To that end, a methodology and valuation system is required that will enable managers to identify, document, and value their knowledge management. This will enable them to make information-rich decisions when they are planning to invest in the protection of their various intellectual properties.

In this paper, the management of organizational knowledge encompasses two distinct, but related, phenomena: organizational-learning flows and intellectual capital stocks. Knowledge stocks and flows are interrelated because organizations that have a higher capacity to absorb knowledge will also have a higher propensity to utilize and circulate it (Cohen and Levinthal 1990). The question of whether or not organizations are efficient purveyors of knowledge (Pavitt 1971) ignores the complex cognitive and behavioral changes that must occur before learning can take place. It is important to study how knowledge travels and changes in organizations (Hedlund and Nonaka 1993).

As mentioned earlier, intellectual capital research has primarily evolved from the desires of practitioners (Bassi and Van Buren 1998; Bontis 1996a; Darling 1996; Edvinsson and Sullivan 1996; Saint-Onge 1996). Consequently, recent developments have come largely in the form of popular press articles in business magazines and national newspapers. The challenge for academics is to frame the phenomenon using extant theories in order to develop a more rigorous conceptualization. This paper coalesces many perspectives from numerous fields of study in an attempt to raise the understanding and importance of this phenomenon. The objective here is to conceptualize and frame the existing literature on intellectual capital as a foundation for further study.

Knowledge creation by business organizations has been virtually neglected in management studies even though Nonaka and Takeuchi (1995) are convinced that this process has been the most important source of international competitiveness for some time. Even management guru Peter Drucker (1993) heralds the arrival of a new economy, referred to as the *knowledge society*. He claims that in this society, knowledge is not just another resource alongside the traditional factors of production—labor, capital, and land—but the only meaningful resource today.

Until recently, there has been little attempt to identify, and give structure to, the nature and role of intangible resources in the strategic management of a business. This is partly due to the fact that it is often very difficult for accountants and economists to allocate an orthodox valuation to intangibles as they rarely have an exchange value. In consequence, they usually lie outside the province of the commodity-based models of economics and accountancy (Hall 1992). Johnson and Kaplan state that

A company's economic value is not merely the sum of the values of its tangible assets, whether measurable at historic cost, replacement cost, or current market value prices. It also includes the value of intangible assets: the stock of innovative products, the knowledge of flexible and high-quality production processes, employee talent, and morals, customer loyalty and product awareness, reliable suppliers, efficient distribution networks and the like. Reported earnings cannot show the company's decline in value when it depletes its stock of intangible resources. Recent overemphasis on achieving superior long-term earnings performance is occurring just at the time when such performance has become a far less valid indicator of changes in the company's long-term competitive position (1987: 202).

Charles Handy (1989) suggests that the intellectual assets of a corporation are usually three or four times the tangible book value. He warns that no executive would leave his cash or factory space idle, yet, if CEOs are asked how much of the knowledge in their companies is used, they typically say only about 20 percent. The importance of this topic is also reflected in the growth of the professional services industry and the many new knowledge-based firms that have fuelled our economy. Top MBA recruits no longer find as many positions in manufacturing companies as they did in the 1950s and 1960s. Nowadays, the Career Services offices of many business schools report that most new graduates secure positions with management consultants, accounting firms, investment banks, law firms, software developers, and information brokers. The common element found in each of these organizations is the abundance of intellectual capital.

To grasp the importance of why it is necessary to measure intellectual capital, we must understand the concept of "Tobin's q" from the accounting and finance literature. This ratio measures the relationship between a company's market value and its replacement value (i.e., the cost of replacing its assets). The ratio was developed by the Nobel Prize–winning economist James Tobin (White et al. 1994). In the long run, this ratio will tend toward 1.00, but evidence shows that it can differ significantly from 1.00 for very long periods of time (Bodie et al. 1993). For example, companies in the software industry, where intellectual capital is abundant, tend to have a Tobin's q ratio of 7.00, whereas firms in the steel industry, noted for their large capital assets, have a Tobin's q ratio of nearly 1.00.

Having discussed the importance of the intellectual capital field from multiple perspectives, we now turn to a review of the literature in order to understand the genesis of its conceptualization.

Review of the Literature

Although the importance of knowledge can be traced back to the ancient Greeks, the first evidence of codification of knowledge may have its roots in scientific management. Frederick Taylor (1911) attempted to formalize workers' experiences and tacit skills into objective rules and formulae. Barnard (1938) extended scientific management by also considering "behavioural knowledge" in management processes. As the two perspectives merged, a new synthesis of knowledge management was born that laid the foundation of organization theory. It was Simon (1945) who was influenced by the development of the computer and cognitive science, which recognized the nature of decision making while performing administrative functions. Simon further recognized the limitations of human cognitive capacity and coined the term *bounded rationality*. Whereas traditional inputs of capital are limited by physical space or monetary constraints, intellectual capital generation may be limited by the collective "bounded rationality" of the organization.

Schumpeter (1934) was primarily concerned with the process of change in the economy as a whole. He attributed the emergence of new products and processes to new *recombinations* of knowledge. Taking this view further, it was not until Penrose (1959) that the organization was considered as a *knowledge repository*. She pointed out the importance of experience and knowledge accumulated within the firm. Evolutionary theorists (Nelson and Winter 1982) also viewed the firm as a repository of knowledge. According to Nelson and Winter, knowledge is stored as regular and predictable behavioral patterns or *routines*.

Today, the nature and performance consequences of the strategies used by organizations to develop, maintain, and exploit knowledge for innovation, constitutes an important topic in the field of business strategy but one that has received inadequate treatment in the extant literature (McGrath, Tsai, Venkatraman, and MacMillan 1996). Orthodox economics side-steps the topic completely by assuming that all firms may choose from a set of universally accessible *production functions* that completely determine production cost structures and therefore do not lead to any knowledge-based performance differences (Nelson 1991; Teece 1982). The industrial organization literature on learning by doing is a partial exception (see Fudenberg and Tirole 1986).

Partly in response to this shortcoming, a number of theories have developed during the past several decades in the field of strategy. Organizational economics and organization theory hold that firm-level differences in knowledge do exist and, moreover, that these differences play a large role in determining economic performance. These approaches include mainstream strategy (Ansoff 1965; Andrews 1971), the resource-based view of the firm (Penrose 1959; Rubin 1973; Teece 1982; Wernerfelt 1984; Barney 1986a, 1991; Dierickx and Cool 1989; Hall 1992), evolutionary theory (Nelson and Winter 1982; Winter 1987), and core competencies (Prahalad and Hamel 1990).

Economic analysis of competitive advantage focuses on how industry structure determines the profitability of firms in an industry. However, firm differences, not industry differences, are thought by many to be at the heart of strategic analysis (Nelson 1991; Rumelt 1991). Furthermore, while most formal economic tools are used to determine optimal product-market activities, the traditional concept of strategy is phrased in terms of the resource position of the firm (Learned, Christensen, Andrews, and Guth 1969; Wernerfelt 1984). Generally speaking, the indifferent treatment of knowledge in the neoclassical economics tradition endures. Firms are assumed to have the same fixed knowledge as they are jockeyed around by the invisible hand of the market. This theoretical lens is deficient in describing the phenomenon of knowledge because of two important assumptions. Neoclassical economics assumes that all parties have perfect and complete information and that resources are completely mobile. These two assumptions are in conflict with the notion that individuals have limits to their cognitive abilities (Simon 1991) and that some forms of tacit knowledge are impossible to articulate (Polanyi 1967). This form of tacit knowledge that is embedded in the organization can be better explained by the evolutionary theory of the firm.

Polanyi's (1967) tacit-explicit distinction was introduced into the literature by Nelson and Winter (1982) in their evolutionary theory of the firm. At the crux of Nelson and Winter's evolutionary theory are *organizational routines* that allow firms the special context in which tacit and explicit knowledge interact:

> Organizational routines are the organization's genetic material, some explicit in bureaucratic rules, some implicit in the organization's culture. The interaction between the explicit and the tacit is evolutionary in that the choices made by individuals are selected in or out according to their utility in a specific historical and economic reality, and eventually embedded in organizational routines which then shape and constrain further individual choices (1982: 134).

Although the evolutionary theory of the firm improves on the deficiencies of the neoclassical economic tradition, it still lacks the contextual implications of a changing business environment. It may be true that organizational knowledge is embedded in routines, but evolutionary theory does not describe persistence or change of routines over time. For example, if explicit rules have been codified at one point in time, one can argue that these routines may not be appropriate at some later point in time when environmental conditions have forced an alternative strategic orientation. Pushing this notion forward, it is argued that organizational routines represent a collection of embedded rules from different times representing different environmental contexts. This internal focus on the firm's rules and resources is the basis for the resource-based view of the firm.

The resource-based view of the firm has been developed in work by Wernerfelt (1984), Barney (1986a, b), Teece (1988) and his colleagues (Teece, Pisano, and Shuen 1994), and Prahalad and Hamel (1990), among others, largely as a reaction against the dominant competitive forces analysis of firm strategy. Other important anticipations of, and contributions to, this theory include Penrose (1959) and Chandler (1977, 1990). The resource-based view of the firm suggests that a business enterprise is best viewed as a collection of sticky and difficult-to-imitate resources and capabilities (Penrose 1959; Barney 1986a, b; Wernerfelt 1984). Firm-specific resources can be physical, such as production techniques protected by patents or trade secrets, or intangible, such as brand equity or operating routines.

A confusing issue with the resource-based view begins with definitions (Nanda 1996). There is an embarrassing profusion of riches in phrases such as *distinctive competence* (Selznick 1957), *strategic firm resources* (Barney 1986b), *invisible assets* (Itami 1987), *strategic firm-specific assets* (Dierickx and Cool 1989), *core competencies* (Prahalad and Hamel 1990), *corporate capabilities* (Nohria and

Eccles 1991), *dynamic capabilities* (Teece, Pisano, and Shuen 1994), *combinative capabilities* (Kogut and Zander 1992), and others just waiting to be published. Although some researchers claim differences in meanings, a few have simply found an opportunity to add their own two cents worth to a growing market of definitions. An alternate route to the nomenclature regurgitation would be to start with a general definition of resources as inputs and then to analyze the circumstances under which they are useful (Nanda 1996).

The resource-based view has other limitations. Given the emphasis on firm resources, it is argued that the only feasible unit of analysis for the resource-based view paradigm is the organization. However, past research has shown that this is somewhat limiting. Empirically, Schmalense (1985) discovered that profit differences are attributable mostly to industry effects, and firm effects are insignificant. Hansen and Wernerfelt (1989) found that both industry and firm effects were significant and independent. Later, Kessides (1990) discovered significant firm effects but these were dominated by industry effects. In sum, the resource-based view may have too much of an internal focus on the firm. Other researchers have taken the resource-based view further by emphasizing knowledge and learning as the critical resource. Thus, the knowledge-based view of the firm was created as an extension of the resource-based view.

Knowledge management theorists argue that knowledge is the preeminent resource of the firm (Grant 1996a, b; Spender 1994, 1996; Baden-Fuller and Pitt 1996; Davenport and Prusak 1997). The knowledge-based view of the firm identifies the primary rationale for the firm as the creation and application of knowledge (Demsetz 1991; Kogut and Zander 1992; Nonaka 1994; Spender 1994; Nonaka and Takeuchi 1995; Foss 1996; Grant 1996a, b; Bierly and Chakrabarti 1996; Connor and Prahalad 1996, Choi and Lee 1997). The knowledge-based view of the firm "can yield insights beyond the production-function and resource-based theories of the firm by creating a new view of the firm as a dynamic, evolving, quasi-autonomous system of knowledge production and application" (Spender 1996: 59). Viewing the firm as a knowledge system focuses the attention not on the allegedly given resources that the firm must use but, to use Penrose's (1959: 25) language, on the *services* rendered by a firm's resources.

Much of the literature on intellectual capital stems from an accounting and financial perspective. Many of these researchers are interested in answering the following two questions: (1) what is causing firms to be worth so much more than their book value? and (2) what specifically is in this intangible asset? Stewart (1997) defines intellectual capital as the intellectual material that has been formalized, captured, and leveraged to create wealth by producing a higher-valued asset. Following the work of Bontis (1996a; 1988), Roos, Roos, Dragonetti, and Edvinsson (1998), Stewart (1991; 1994; 1997), Sveiby (1997), Edvinsson and Malone (1997), Saint-Onge (1996), Sullivan and Edvinsson (1996) as well as Edvinsson and Sullivan (1996), among others, intellectual capital is defined as encompassing: (1) human capital, (2) structural capital, and (3) relational capital. These subphenomena encompass the intelligence found in human beings, organizational routines, and network relationships, respectively. This field typically looks at organizational knowledge as a static asset in an organization—a so-called "stock." This concerns many theorists who are also interested in the flow of knowledge. Furthermore, intellectual capital research does not cater to changes in cognition or behavior of individuals that are necessary for learning and improvement. The field of organizational learning has an extensive history in dealing with these limitations.

Change is the only constant variable in business today (Senge 1990). Kanter (1989) notes that organizations attempt to develop structures and systems that are more responsive to change. The field of organizational learning has thrived in this context because managers believe that the more they learn about the process of change and learning itself, the better they will be in handling it and the better their firms will perform. However, Miller (1996) describes the organizational learning literature as maddeningly abstract and vague. Managers have little experience with organizational learning concepts (EUI and IBM 1996). Veilleux (1995) surveyed 186 human resource executives and found that, although 98 percent of the respondents believed in the concept of organizational learning, only 52 percent responded that their organization had an average ability to learn. Since the seminal article by Cangelosi and Dill (1965), organizational learning has been described at three different levels: individual, group, and organization. Although many organizational learning theorists have argued for the existence of learning at these levels, some researchers, especially academics in the field of international management, have extended the framework to include learning at the transorganizational level.

Individual learning is a prerequisite for organizational learning (Kim 1993). Individual-level learning occurs simply by virtue of being human (McGee and Prusak 1993). As Senge puts it, "Organizations learn only through individuals who learn. Individual learning does not guarantee organizational learning but without it no organizational learning occurs" (1990:139). The notion here is that organizational knowledge resides in the minds of employees. Nonaka and Takeuchi also point out that individual-level learning is the foundation:

> Knowledge is created only by individuals. An organization cannot create knowledge on its own without individuals. Organizational knowledge creation should be understood as a process that organizationally amplifies the knowledge created by individuals and crystallizes it at the group level through dialogue, discussion, experience sharing, or observation (1995: 239).

For the most part, researchers generally agree that individual learning is a necessary precursor to learning at a higher level (Greeno 1980). Some theorists support group level learning as an alternative to the limitations of individual learning. Group knowledge is not a mere gathering of individual knowledge. The knowledge of individual members needs to be shared and legitimized through integrating interactions and information technology before it becomes group knowledge (Tsuchiya 1994). Once organizational teams integrate their own respective learning, learning at the organizational level starts. This level of the IGO (individual-group-organizational) framework highlights the importance of the learning that resides in the organization's systems, structures, procedures, routines, and so forth (Fiol and Lyles 1985). This level of organizational learning requires the conversion of individual and group learning into a systematic base of organizational intellectual capital (Shrivastava 1986). Several other theorists concur that learning at the organizational level is an accepted component of learning in organizations (Duncan and Weiss 1979; Hedberg 1981; Shrivastava 1983; Levitt and March 1988; Stata 1989; Huber 1991; Crossan et al. 1995; Inkpen and Crossan 1995).

Businesses are typically well versed in assessing and valuing tangible assets, such as buildings, machinery, cash, and so forth, but such measures do not include the value of the workforce, their knowledge, the way they use computer systems, and so on. In an information society, such intangible assets may represent significant competitive advantage. Itami (1987) has argued that successful organizations recognize that most activities offer the potential to either enhance, or degrade, their key invisible assets, which they define as including reputation, know-how etc. These businesses expect to accumulate invisible assets, as well as conventional assets, as they complete each turn of the business cycle.

The traditional financial performance measures worked well for the industrial era, but they are out of step with the skills and competencies companies are trying to master today (Kaplan and Norton 1992). Over the last fifteen years management accounting has been redefining itself to accommodate the vast changes that have taken place in the world economy. Management accounting researchers and practitioners alike have acknowledged that many of the ways in which organizations structure and implement their management planning and control systems lack relevance for the new economy. Quinn (1992) argues that the new economy is a service-based economy, where even manufacturers need to identify their core competencies as those "services" that they offer that are valued-added and of a "best-in-the-world" caliber.

Many organizations are still philosophically wedded to outmoded, inward-looking management planning and control systems, which use wealth measures based on physical assets and evaluation of performance linked to these measures. Rather than an organization's physical assets, the new economy will require a valuation of an organization's total assets that includes its intellectual assets. Hence, to be relevant, organizations need to develop planning, control, and performance measurement systems that account for (i.e., predict, measure, and evaluate) these intellectual assets.

Kaplan and Norton (1992) proposed using what they called a *balanced scorecard* approach to performance measurement. One element of the balanced scorecard is an innovation and learning perspective that tries to assess the way in which the organization can continue to improve and create value. Vitale et al. (1994) and Vitale and Mavrinac (1995) have also developed a model and a means of evaluating a performance evaluation system on the basis of the organization's strategy which they term a *strategic performance evaluation* system. The strategic performance evaluation system is very much an outgrowth of Kaplan and Norton's balanced scorecard concept, but it moves beyond it by providing a more direct implementations focus. Although all of these authors acknowledge the importance of learning, none of them provides specific guidance on ways in which to measure and evaluate an organization's intellectual capital stocks or organizational learning flows. Thus, although their recommendations should help organizations to bring their management planning and control systems more in line with the reality of the new economy, they still overlook the significance of knowledge management as a critical success factor of the new economic entity and its key to long-run survival.

To understand the intellectual expertise embedded in an organization requires organizational members to assess their core competencies: those areas where they can achieve or have achieved "best-in-the-world" status (Prahalad and Hamel 1990; Quinn 1992). The intellectual capital of an organization represents the wealth of ideas and ability to innovate that will determine the future of the organization. Why have management accountants and financial analysts avoided this area until recently? The most obvious answer is that intellectual capital is not only difficult to measure but also difficult to evaluate. In the past, accountants have assumed a position that either ignores the problems or writes them off as impossible to solve (Luscombe 1993). It is important to realize that intellectual capital is real and provides value. One need only look at the hackneyed example of Microsoft, whose accounting book value is significantly less than its market value based on share price, to see that there must be some explanation of this "excess" market valuation. Arguably this "excess" is the market valuation of the intellectual capital stocks and organizational learning flows of the company.

Another measurement tool that is finding increased usage among large corporations is Economic Value Added (EVA) (Bontis 1996b). In defining and refining EVA, Stewart (1991; 1994) identified over 120 shortcomings in conventional GAAP accounting to measure real economic income. However, McConville (1994) and Ochsner (1995) warn that although EVA makes useful adjustments for decision-making purposes, its exotic allure often leaves top executives with no clear instructions on its implementation. Accounting for such assets was also the aim of human resource accounting (HRA) back in the 1960s.

As defined earlier, human capital represents the human factor in the organization: the combined intelligence, skills, and expertise that give the organization its distinctive character. The human elements of the organization are those that are capable of learning, changing, innovating, and providing the creative thrust that, if properly motivated, can ensure the long-run survival of the organization. As per Lynn's (1998) overview of HRA, since Hermanson's classic study in 1964, the topic of how to and whether to value human assets has been debated by accountants and human resource theorists. Indeed, the arguments for and against human resource accounting are especially pertinent to the valuation of intellectual assets in the new economy, since they involve essentially the same issues.

According to Sackmann, Flamholtz, and Bullen (1989:235) the objective of HRA is to "quantify the economic value of people to the organization" to provide input to management and financial decisions. Three types of HRA measurement models have been proposed by researchers:

1. COST MODELS, that is, historical or acquisition cost (Brummet, Flamholtz, and Pyle 1968), replacement cost (Flamholtz 1973), and opportunity cost (Hekimian and Jones 1967)
2. HUMAN RESOURCE VALUE MODELS, that is, a nonmonetary behavioral emphasis model (Likert 1967) and combined nonmonetary behavioral and monetary economic value models (Likert and Bowers 1973; Gambling 1974)
3. MONETARY EMPHASIS, that is, a discounted earnings or wages approach (Morse 1973; Friedman and Lev 1974)

Sackmann, Flamholtz, and Bullen (1989) discuss these models extensively and also summarize the numerous attempts to apply the models in various types of organizations. Although none of the experiments in HRA have been long-run successes, it is interesting to note that the majority of systems developed were in service organizations (i.e., CPA firms, banks, insurance, and financial services firms) where human capital constitutes a significant proportion of organizational value.

HRA has always had its critics. All of the models suffer from subjectivity and uncertainty and lack reliability in that they cannot be audited with any assurance. Both of these are measurement problems. Other criticisms of HRA include whether it is morally acceptable to treat people as assets and whether such measures are too easily manipulated. Although these arguments are salient comments on HRA, they beg the question of whether human assets in organizations do have value. As was said earlier, if intellectual capital does not exist in organizations, then why does stock price react to changes in management? Obviously, investors and financial markets attach value to the skills and expertise of CEOs and other top management. Investors value the people, their skills, and their potential in such organizations. In fact, the criticisms of HRA arise largely from the fact that such valuations of intellectual capital are "soft" measures rather than objective auditable numbers. The question thus arises, are auditable valuations of intellectual capital necessary in the conventional sense? The answer is being debated by such bodies as the FASB, CICA, SEC, and IASC right now. We shall soon see where the accountants will lead us. In the meantime, we can continue with further development of intellectual capital's conceptualization.

Proposed Conceptualization

Adopting Kogut and Zander's (1992) perspective on higher-order organizing principles, a proposed conceptualization of intellectual capital is put forth (see Figure 1-1). Intellectual capital is a second-order multidimensional construct. Its three subdomains include: (1) HUMAN CAPITAL—the tacit knowledge embedded in the minds of the employees, (2) STRUCTURAL CAPITAL—the organizational routines of the business, and (3) RELATIONAL CAPITAL—the knowledge embedded in the relationships established with the outside environment (Bontis 1996a; Edvinsson and Sullivan 1996).

Organizational learning, as described by Chris Argyris at Harvard (1992), among others, has been thought of as the flow of knowledge in a firm; it follows, then, that intellectual capital is the stock of knowledge in the firm. To marry the two concepts, it may be useful to consider intellectual capital as the stock unit of organizational learning. However, intellectual capital cannot necessarily be taught through education and training. The most precious knowledge in an organization often cannot be passed on (Levitt 1991).

Prior to continuing the conceptualization of intellectual capital stocks, it may be helpful to define *what it is not*. Intellectual capital does not include intellectual property. Intellectual properties are assets that include copyrights, patents, semiconductor topography rights, and various design rights. They also include trade and service marks. Undertaking an intellectual property audit is not a new idea. However, many organizations find that the results of an intellectual property audit are not particularly useful. After all, knowing that you own a patent is not a lot of use if that fact is not accompanied with information concerning its potential. This is evaluated from the various aspects that the patent can be viewed from, including return on investment, commercial potential, competitive advantage, and so on. It is important to note that intellectual property assets are usually considered from their legal perspective, which should mirror that "raison d'être." A patent for its own sake has no point or value. Therefore, intellectual property and intellectual capital are considered mutually exclusive, but the former can be considered an output of the latter.

The conceptualization of intellectual capital shall continue with an examination of the "organizational knowledge" literature. Although theories differ in their terminology and the degree to which they explicitly discuss the attributes of organizational knowledge, they all concur that superior performance, including the procurement of economic profits, results at least in part from the exploitation of distinctive process knowledge that is not articulable and that can be acquired only through experience—in short, knowledge that is "tacit" in nature (Polanyi 1967; Winter 1987). Yet, in emphasizing the positive effects of tacit knowledge on economic performance, these theories suffer from a serious shortcoming as well. Although they concede that tacit knowledge limits the ability of the organization to compete in a new industrial environment in which a substantially different knowledge base is required for competitive success, they fail to recognize that tacit knowledge also limits the ability of the organization to adapt to the changing competitive requirements of the existing industry within which it already operates.

The phenomenon of intellectual capital can be dissected into three subdomains. Each will be described in the context of its essence, scope, parameter, and codification difficulty (see Figure 2-1). Subsequent to that description, two drivers—"trust" and "culture"—will be evaluated for their impact on intellectual capital development.

Human Capital

First, the organization's members possess individual tacit knowledge (i.e., inarticulable skills necessary to perform their functions) (Nelson and Winter 1982). In order to illustrate the degree to which tacit knowledge characterizes the human capital of an organization, it is useful to conceive of the organization as a productive process that receives tangible and informational inputs from the environment, produces tangible and informational outputs that enter the

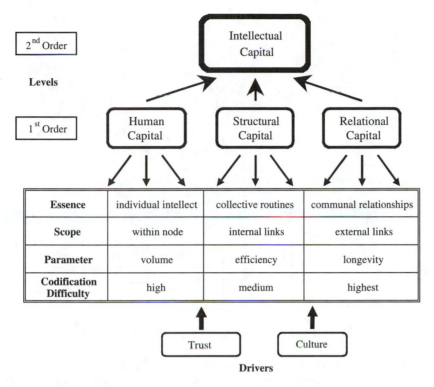

Figure 2-1 *Conceptualization of Intellectual Capital*

environment, and is characterized internally by a series of flows among a network of nodes and ties or links (see Figure 2-2).

A node represents the work performed—either pure decision-making, innovative creativity, improvisation (Crossan et al. 1996) or some combination of the three—by a single member of the organization or by parallel, functionally equivalent members who do not interact with one another as part of the productive process (see Figure 2-2). Thus, individual tacit knowledge, when present, exists at the nodes themselves. A tie or link is directional in nature and represents a flow of intermediate product or information from a given node. Every node has at least one tie or link originating from it, whereas multiple ties originating from a single node imply that the task performed at the node includes a decision about where to direct the subsequent flow. Structural tacit knowledge, when present, implies that no member of the organization has an explicit overview of these ties and consequently of the corresponding arrangement of nodes (see subsequent discussion on structural capital). Accordingly,

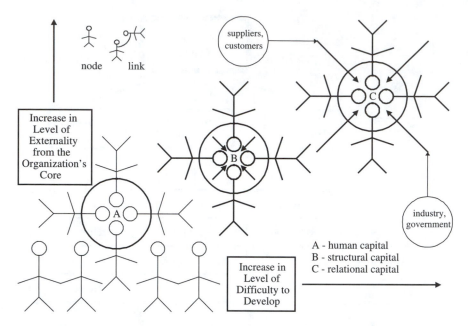

Figure 2-2 *Discriminating Intellectual Capital Sub-domains*

a productive process characterized by a substantial degree of tacit knowledge is arranged as a hodgepodge of nodes lacking any discernible organizational logic.

Point A in Figure 2-2 represents the core of human capital. Multiple nodes (human-capital units) attempt to align themselves in some form of recognizable pattern, so that intellectual capital becomes more readily interpretable. This point represents the lowest level of difficulty for development as well as the lowest level of externality from the core of the organization.

Human capital has also been defined on an individual level as the combination of these four factors: (1) genetic inheritance, (2) education, (3) experience, and (4) attitudes about life and business (Hudson, 1993). Human capital is important because it is a source of innovation and strategic renewal, whether it is from brainstorming in a research lab, daydreaming at the office, throwing out old files, reengineering new processes, improving personal skills, or developing new leads in a sales rep's little black book. The essence of human capital is the sheer intelligence of the organizational member. The scope of human capital is limited to the knowledge node (i.e., internal to the mind of the employee). It can be measured (although it is difficult) as a function of volume (i.e., a third-degree measure encompassing size, location, and time). It is also the hardest of the three subdomains of intellectual capital to codify.

Wright et al. (1994), working from a resource-based perspective, argue that in certain circumstances sustained competitive advantage can accrue from "a pool of human capital" that is larger than those groups, such as senior managers and other elites, who are traditionally identified as determining organizational success or failure. This is achieved through the human capital adding value, being unique or rare, imperfectly imitable, and not substitutable with another resource by competing firms. Storey supports this focus:

> This type of resource [human capital] can embody intangible assets such as unique configurations of complementary skills, and tacit knowledge, painstakingly accumulated, of customer wants and internal processes (1995: 4).

Structural Capital

The organization itself embodies structural tacit knowledge, which exists in "the myriad of relationships that enable the organization to function in a coordinated way [but] are reasonably understood by [at most] the participants in the relationship and a few others. . . ." This means that "the organization is . . . accomplishing its aims by following rules that are not known as such to most of the participants in the organization" (Winter 1987:171).

This construct deals with the mechanisms and structures of the organization that can help support employees in their quest for optimum intellectual performance and therefore overall business performance. An individual can have a high level of intellect, but if the organization has poor systems and procedures by which to track his or her actions, the overall intellectual capital will not reach its fullest potential.

An organization with strong structural capital will have a supportive culture that allows individuals to try things, to fail, to learn, and to try again. If the culture unduly penalizes failure, its success will be minimal. Structuring intellectual assets with information systems can turn individual know-how into group property (Nicolini 1993). It is the concept of structural capital that allows intellectual capital to be measured and developed in an organization. In effect, without structural capital, intellectual capital would just be human capital. This construct therefore contains elements of efficiency, transaction times, procedural innovativeness, and access to information for codification into knowledge. It also supports elements of cost minimization and profit maximization per employee. Structural capital is the critical link that allows intellectual capital to be measured at an organizational level.

Point B in Figure 2-2 illustrates the structural ties or links of human capital nodes that are required to transform human capital into structural capital. The arrows within structural capital represent the focus of intellectual capital development from the nodes into the organization's core. The essence of structural capital is the knowledge embedded within the routines of an organization. Its scope lies internal to the firm but external to the human capital nodes. It can be measured (although it is difficult) as a function of efficiency (i.e., an output function per some temporal unit). Organizational processes (such as those found in structural capital) can eventually be codified.

Infrastructure assets are those technologies, methodologies, and processes that enable the organization to function. Examples include methodologies for assessing risk, methods of managing a sales force, databases of information on the market or customers, communication systems such as e-mail and teleconferencing systems—basically, the elements that make up the way the organization works. Such elements are peculiar to each business, and their value to the organization can only be ascertained by survey within the target organization. Sadly, the acquisition of infrastructure assets is frequently as a result of some crisis, positioning them as a necessary evil rather than the structure that makes the organization strong. Marketing the value of infrastructure assets to the individuals within the organization is also important, in order to share with them the aspects in which infrastructure protects, enhances, and coordinates organizational resources.

Structural capital can be further differentiated between its technological component and its architectural competencies. The *technological component* can be defined as the local abilities and knowledge (e.g., tacit knowledge, proprietary design rules, unique modes of working together) that are important to day-to-day technological problem solving. The *architectural competencies* can be defined as the ability of the firm to integrate the firm's component competencies together in new and flexible ways and to develop new competencies as they are required (e.g., communication channels, information filters, and problem-solving strategies that develop between groups, control systems, cultural values, and idiosyncratic search routines). Research focusing on the architectural or integrative capabilities of firms can offer "insights into the source of enduring differences in firm performance" (Henderson and Cockburn 1994:64) and highlight the importance of exploring the sources of structural capital.

Relational Capital

Knowledge of market channels, customer and supplier relationships, as well as a sound understanding of governmental or industry association impacts, are the main themes of relational capital. Frustrated managers often do not recognize that they can tap into a wealth of knowledge from their own clients and suppliers. After all, understanding what customers want in a product or a service better than anyone else is what makes someone a business leader as opposed to a follower.

Relational capital represents the potential an organization has due to ex-firm intangibles. These intangibles include the knowledge embedded in customers, suppliers, the government, or related industry associations. Point C in Figure 2-2 illustrates that relational capital is the most difficult of the three subdomains to develop since it is the most external to the organization's core. The arrows represent the knowledge that must flow from outside the organization (i.e., its environment) into the organization's core by way of linked nodes. The essence of relational capital is knowledge embedded in relationships external to the firm. Its scope lies external to the firm and external to the human capital nodes. It can be measured (although it is difficult) as a function of longevity (i.e., relational capital becomes more valuable as time goes on). Due to its external nature, knowledge embedded in relational capital is the most difficult to codify.

One manifestation of relational capital that can be leveraged from customers is often referred to as *market orientation*. There is no consensus on a definition of market orientation, but two recent definitions have become widely accepted. The first is from Kohli and Jaworski (1990), who define market orientation as the organization-wide generation of market intelligence pertaining to current and future needs of customers, dissemination of intelligence horizontally and vertically within the organization, and organization-wide action or responsiveness to market intelligence. Similar definitions are found in Deng and Dart (1994) and Lichtenthal and Wilson (1992).

The second is from Narver and Slater (1990), who define market orientation as a one-dimensional construct consisting of three behavioral components and two decision criteria—customer orientation, competitor orientation, interfunctional coordination, a long-term focus, and a profit objective. With close parallels to Kohli and Jaworski (1990), Narver and Slater (1990) include the generation and dissemination of market intelligence as well as managerial action. Hulland (1995) posits that there exist two dimensions of organizational learning in the marketing context: market orientation (as discussed above) and market learning systems (which, in the context of this particular conceptualization of intellectual capital, will be considered as a function of structural capital).

Kogut and Zander (1992) argue that what firms do better than markets is the sharing and transfer of knowledge embedded in the organizing principles of an organization. They have suggested that a firm's innovative capabilities "rest in the organizing principles by which relationships among individuals, within and between groups, and among organizations are structured" (Kogut and Zander 1992: 384).

Teece (1988) discussed the importance of interorganizational and intraorganizational relationships and linkages to the development and profitable commercialization of new technology. He argued that as firms have moved from a serial product-delivery process (i.e., a sequential, lock-step process through the value chain) to a parallel product-delivery process (i.e., simultaneous development throughout the various functions), the need for cooperative and coordinating capabilities has increased. Pennings and Harianto (1992) also presented a theory of innovation that presumes that new technologies emerge from a firm's accumulated stock of skills (i.e., internal innovative capabilities) and its history of technological networking (i.e., external innovative capabilities). Relational capital builds on the intraorganizational relationships (Teece 1988) and technological networking (Pennings and Harianto 1992) that are available in the environment.

The organizing principles established in an innovative firm include rules by which work is coordinated and by which information is gathered and communicated. This social knowledge is not easily disseminated because it is embedded in the idiosyncratic firm-specific history and routines of the organization's entire system (Zander and Kogut 1995; Barney 1992). Companies need intelligence-gathering capabilities to keep up with technology development both inside and outside the industry. This includes not only formal processes and information systems but informal systems based on tacit understanding by employees and senior managers that they have a responsibility to the company to gather and disseminate technological information (Hamel 1991; Kodama 1992). Effective communication between partners is essential in technology collaboration and can prove difficult to build (Dodgson 1992). However, once established, this communication channel serves as an important source of information about the other interdependent organization.

Trust and Culture as Intellectual Capital Drivers

As depicted in Figure 2-1, the conceptualization of intellectual capital includes two supporting drivers for subdomain development. Trust is a very important element of both inter- and intra-organizational cooperation (Barney and Hansen 1994). Although the importance of trust has always been evident and is widely articulated in the nonacademic literature, it has only recently become a topic of major academic concern. Organizational group members need to have mutual confidence that tasks can be delegated (i.e., that others know what to do, are motivated to do it, and are competent to do it) and that monitoring can be fairly casual. The literature on external cooperative relationships suggests that choosing an external partner with complementary technologies and strategies and building a cooperative relationship based on trust and mutual respect can be problematic (Dodgson 1992). Trust, mutual respect, and compatible modes of behavior cannot be decreed or even adequately specified as an abstract entity. That is why many firms typically begin a relationship by cooperating in less strategically central areas and build up a body of experience in working with a partner over a period of years (Gulati 1995). Generally, all participants are seen to have an effect on the trust in a relationship (Mayer et al. 1995).

As organizations become more flat, more geographically dispersed, and more prone to reorganization, traditional notions of control are being updated to reflect an increased need to trust individuals and groups to carry out critical organizational tasks without close and frequent supervision (Moingeon and Edmondson 1996). Trust is a belief (Lazaric and Lorenz 1995) related to likely outcomes, a belief that reflects an actor's cognitive representations of situational contingencies. Since researchers have tended to have difficulty separating antecedents and outcomes of trust (Mayer, Davis, and Schoorman 1995), this dual role may also be salient in the context of intellectual capital.

Organizations that have a culture that supports and encourages cooperative innovation should attempt to understand what it is about their culture that gives them a competitive advantage and develop and nurture those cultural attributes (Barney 1986a). Culture constitutes the beliefs, values, and attitudes pervasive in the organization and results in a language, symbols, and habits of behaviour and thought. Increasingly, it is recognized as the conscious or unconscious product of the senior management's belief (Hall 1992). Barney discussed the potential for organizational culture to serve as a source of sustained competitive advantage. He concluded that "firms that do not have the required cultures cannot engage in activities that will modify their cultures and generate sustained superior performance because their modified cultures typically will be neither rare nor imperfectly imitable" (1986a:656).

The core of culture is formed by values (Hofstede 1991). In most organizations that have pursued formalized intellectual capital management initiatives, the common component that drives the program is value alignment. Hall (1995: viii) agrees and claims that values are the key to any successful organizational transformation because "values are basically a quality information system that when understood tell about what drives human beings and organizations and causes them to be exceptional." Another important element of culture within the context of intellectual capital is the important distinction between "knowledge hoarding" versus "knowledge sharing." Unfortunately, this conflict is all too common in today's organizations, with the former outdoing the latter.

Belasco and Sayer (1994:31) propose an "intellectual capitalism paradigm" that charts a changing distribution of the power of the "tools of production" from owners to managers and then to the "talents of the people." They assert that the possessors of the intellectual tools of production—organizational employees (or nodes of human-capital units)—will come to exercise effective power. Hedlund (1994) proposes that a new organizational form called the *N-form corporation* builds on the interplay of tacit-knowledge transfer between different levels. This is done through a variety of ways including: temporary constellations of people, lateral communication, a catalytic role for top management, and hierarchical structures.

Agency theorists (Jensen and Meckling 1976; Eisenhardt 1988) have made large inroads in the study of principal-agent relationships. For example, in the context of compensation, agency theory posits that as the proportion of outcome-based compensation (i.e., commission versus salary) increases for the agent, so does the effective management of that relationship, in that their goals are now more aligned. In other words, the principle can effectively limit the divergent behavior of the agent if the latter's compensation more closely matches that of the former. In the knowledge era, real power may lie in the human capital of an organization. If the nodes (employees of an organization) are the genesis of the intellectual capital in a firm, how will principals leverage off its effective utilization? This may, perhaps, become an exciting new research program for agency theorists in the future.

Recognizing that "power" is an important—some might say the most important—dynamic in organizations, it is also concerned with reviewing how knowledge management and power relate and the extent to which maximizing the potential of intellectual capital requires a radical transformation in the generation and distribution of power in organizations.

An increasingly strong case is being made that, as organizations respond to environmental turbulence, particularly increased worldwide competitive pressures, and swift technological and social change, they need to pay particular attention to the development and deployment of knowledge and hence to the learning needs of their employees at all levels (McGill et al. 1992; Brown et al. 1993; Parker et al. 1994; Pfeffer 1994; West 1994).

For example, Kornbluh et al. (1987) suggest that the pressure of international competition and the failure of the "technological solution" in many enterprises has focused attention on the importance of learning in order to deal with both turbulent environments and the desire of many workers for more challenging jobs. Meyer-Dohm (1992) points to the inherent errors and risks in even the most automated technology-based work systems, requiring human intervention and the design of workplaces that permit the individual a higher degree of independence.

Argyris (1994:77) appears to be clear on this issue that knowledgeable employees will reign supreme:

> Twenty-first century corporations will find it hard to survive, let alone flourish, unless they get better work from their employees . . . employees who've learned to take active responsibility for their own behavior, develop and share first-rate information about their jobs and make good use of genuine empowerment to shape lasting solutions to fundamental problems.

If these more empowering and involving managerial practices are indeed an imperative for organizational survival and growth, their implementation may lead to the employees concerned feeling more in control of their own work and lives. Being able to play a greater part in organizational decision making and development and being able to cope with increased delegation from people above them in the hierarchy may, in fact, be a consequence of the increased value of their intellectual capital to the organization. However, it is also possible to hypothesize the existence of counterforces, especially the response of the dominant managerial coalition, which may resist this power redistribution and, consequently, block the utilization of the full potential of the organization's intellectual capital for innovation. Before investigating these counterforces in more detail, it is important to establish the potential links between intellectual capital and innovation.

The links between learning, innovation, and organizational survival have been developed by a number of writers (see, for example, Bouwen and Fry 1991; Argyris 1992; Senge 1990). Sadler (1994) has highlighted the growth of knowledge- or talent-intensive industries and the importance of the "knowledge worker." The potential of learning and knowledge as the basis of power has been recognized by, among others, French and Raven (1959), Zimmerman (1990), Thomas and Velthouse (1990), and Townley (1993). Hence it seems possible to posit a link between intellectual capital, innovation, and power.

In his meta-analysis of the determinants of innovation at the organizational level, Damanpour (1991) reported a positive correlation between innovation and a number of variables that could be said to reflect intellectual capital and its usage, including specialization (i.e., providing a greater knowledge base), professionalization (i.e., increased boundary-spanning activity), technical knowledge resources, and external and internal communications. Centralization of decision-making authority was found to be negatively correlated, as Damanpour predicted (based on the work of Thompson 1965), which suggests that a dispersion of power may be necessary for innovation. Damanpour's analysis also recognized the importance of managerial support for innovation, especially in terms of leadership and coordination. Furthermore, leadership in the form of a change agent has been reviewed as being an important antecedent to organizational learning (Bontis 1995).

Also of particular interest is the hypothesis by McGill et al. (1992) that, in order to innovate, organizations need to employ "generative" rather than "adaptive" learning practices that involve, among other things, a move from hierarchical position to knowledge as the dominant power base. There is an obvious need for further research to see if organizational success is related to truly empowering people and preparing and enabling them to become "highly involved" in Eccles' terms (1991).

Research to Date

Intellectual capital research thus far has been primarily of the anecdotal variety. Most researchers have conducted case-based reviews of organizations that have established intellectual capital initiatives. Other researchers have documented the metrics that have been developed by Skandia and others. What the field needs at this point is a more concentrated focus on rigorous metric development and quantitative evaluation.

Using survey data, Bontis (1998) has already shown a very strong and positive relationships between Likert-type measures of intellectual capital and business performance in a pilot study. The explanatory power of the final specified model was highly significant and substantive (R^2 = 56.0 percent, p-value < 0.001).

Several other researchers have also supplied evidence of a positive relationship between an organization's financial, as well as organizational performance, and its level of one of the subdomains of intellectual capital: relational capital. As discussed previously, contained within the conceptualization of relational capital is market orientation. Narver and Slater find that market orientation and business performance (ROA) are strongly related (Narver and Slater 1990). Jaworski and Kohli (1993) report on a study of 222 U.S. business units, suggesting that market orientation is an important determinant of performance, regardless of market turbulence, competitive intensity, and technological turbulence. Also, Ruekert (1992) reports a positive relationship between degree of market orientation and long-run financial performance. In the United Kingdom, Greenley (1995) observed that a group of companies with higher market orientation performed better (ROI) than a group with lower market orientation. Back in 1987, Lusch and Laczniak investigated how a company's increased emphasis on an extended marketing concept, similar to market orientation, is positively associated with financial performance. Not directly related to business performance, but yet in line with intellectual capital, Atuahene-Gima (1995) infers from an Australian sample that market orientation is an important contributor to new product success. Biemans and Harmsen (1995) have also concluded on the basis of several other studies that having a market orientation in product development has proven to be a highly critical factor for new product success.

Recent trends in organizational structure have seen a move toward "de-layering," "lean production," making decisions "closer to the customer," establishing "semiautonomous work groups" and an emphasis on employee involvement and empowerment (see Wellins et al. 1991; Docherty 1993; Papahristodoulou 1994; Yeatts et al. 1994). Again it seems reasonable to hypothesize that, other things being equal, the increased intellectual capital development, and thus "nodal" power generated by environmental turbulence, should be more evenly distributed throughout the organization in these "leaner," "flatter" structures.

Empirical research has shown that top executives in large U.S. and Canadian businesses agree that new intellectual capital measures are required to help manage knowledge assets. Stivers et al. (1998) surveyed 253 companies among the U.S. Fortune 500 and Canadian Post 300 in their study of nonfinancial measure usage. Results showed that even though 63 percent of the sample felt that measuring innovation was important, only 14 percent were actually measuring it, and only 10 percent were actually using the measures for strategy development. Stivers and her colleagues argue that these results show a significant measurement-use gap. This may be more significant for measures of intellectual capital. To assist managers with this gap, Bontis et al. (1999) have developed a knowledge toolbox that helps practitioners differentiate between a variety of knowledge-based tools, including intellectual capital, human resource accounting, economic value added, and the balanced scorecard.

Another empirical research study conducted in this field was a Ph.D. dissertation by Bontis (1999). He used a psychometrically developed survey instrument to measure knowledge stocks and flows in 32 mutual fund companies. By surveying 15 respondents across three levels of management in each organization, Bontis found that knowledge stocks and flows were closely related to business performance. He concluded that although knowledge stocks had a positive association with business performance, the misalignment of knowledge stocks with knowledge flows acted as a detriment to the overall efficiency of the organization's learning system. This research shows the importance of integrating intellectual capital with research in the knowledge management and organizational learning domains.

CONCLUSION

Some critics have argued that intellectual capital is just another organizational fad that will last for three to five more years, and then managers will move on to the next attempt at finding the philosophical silver bullet. In a recent ASAP feature article, Rutledge (1997) blasts the intellectual capital field and emphatically claims that "you are a fool if you buy into this." He warns managers that, if by chance they meet people with the word "knowledge" or "intellectual capital" on their business cards, they should walk quickly and quietly away. His argument centers around the fact that the driving force behind this field are stakeholders and not shareholders of companies, and therefore social agendas, not performance, will drive business decisions. Although he is correct in touting the importance of the "softer stuff" related to intellectual capital, he cannot argue against its mass appeal. Dozens upon dozens of conferences, workshops, and seminars are being offered all over the world on how to measure and value intellectual capital each year. Practitioners are voting with their feet.

Although its popularity is not disputed, it is important to be skeptical when anyone claims that they have found the magical formula or calculation for intellectual capital. It will never be measured in the traditional dollar terms we know. At best, we will see a slow proliferation of customized metrics that will be disclosed in traditional financial statements as addenda. Metrics such as those used by Skandia and others in the financial services industry (Bontis 1997) will continue to be developed and analyzed longitudinally. Bassi and Van Buren (1998) note that, even though the stock market is already providing handsome rewards to companies that successfully leverage their intellectual capital, few firms have formalized a measurement process. The significance and lack of progress on the issue are also clear from a recent survey of 431 organizations in the United States and Europe who ranked "measuring the value and performance of knowledge assets" highest in importance more than any other issue except "changing people's behavior": 43 versus 54 percent, respectively (Skyrme and Amidon 1997).

If it is a fad, when will it end? The immense proliferation of the Internet as an information-sharing vehicle supports the argument that knowledge management and the development of intellectual capital are most sustainable as an organizational goal (Prusak 1996). As long as the economic forces embrace new knowledge-intensive industries, the field of intellectual capital will have an important place in the minds of academics and practitioners.

As with the human body's muscles, intellectual capital management may suffer from, "if you don't use it, you lose it." There is an increasing emphasis on survival of the fittest in international competitiveness. In order to stay alive, organizations must win the race (Hampden-Turner 1992). Future research in this area may want to tap into comparisons of intellectual capital characteristics by personality type, with the use of the Myers-Briggs Type Indicator (Wiele 1993). Also, researchers could correlate intellectual capital metrics with cultural diversity and values (Hofstede 1978;1991).

Finally, all business leaders should be appreciative of the power intellectual capital can have on business performance. The study of intellectual capital stocks and their exponential growth due to organizational learning flows produces a tremendous amount of energy, energy that can take companies far beyond their current vision (Ward 1996). It requires people to rethink their attitudes on this elusive intangible asset and to start recognizing that measuring and strategically managing intellectual capital may in fact become the most important managerial activity as we enter the third millennium.

REFERENCES

Andrews, Kenneth R. 1971. *The Concept of Corporate Strategy.* Homewood, Ill.: Dow Jones-Irwin.

Ansoff, H. I. 1965. *Corporate Strategy: An Analytical Approach to Business Policy for Growth and Expansion.* New York: McGraw-Hill Book Company.

Argyris, Chris. 1992. *On Organizational Learning.* Cambridge, Mass.: Blackwell.

Argyris, Chris. 1994. "Good Communication That Blocks Learning." *Harvard Business Review* (July-August) 77–85.

Atuahene-Gima, K. 1995. "An exploratory analysis of the impact of market orientation on new product performance. A contingency approach." *Journal of Product Innovation Management* 12. 275–93.

Baden-Fuller, C. and M. Pitt. 1996. "The nature of innovating strategic management." In *Strategic Innovation*, eds. Baden-Fuller and M. Pitt. London: Routledge.

Barnard, C. 1938. *The Functions of the Executive*. Cambridge: Harvard University Press.

Barney, Jay B. 1986a. "Organizational culture: Can it be a source of sustained competitive advantage?" *Academy of Management Review* 11, 3: 656–65.

Barney, Jay B. 1986b. "Strategic factor markets: Expectations, luck, and business strategy." *Management Science* 32, 10: 1231–41.

Barney, Jay B. 1991. "Firm Resources and Sustained Competitive Advantage." *Journal of Management* 17: 99–120.

Barney, Jay B. 1992. "Integrating organizational behavior and strategy formulation research: A resource based analysis." In *Advances in Strategic Management*, eds. P. Shrivastava, A. Huff, and J. Dutton 8: 39–62. Greenwich, Conn.: JAI Press.

Barney, Jay B. and M. H. Hansen. 1994. "Trustworthiness as a source of competitive advantage." *Strategic Management Journal* 15: 175–90.

Bassi, L. J. and Mark E. Van Buren. 1998. "Investments in intellectual capital: Creating methods for measuring impact and value." *ASTD working paper*, American Society of Training and Development.

Beamish, P. W. and C. P. Woodcock. 1996. *Strategic Management: Text, Readings and Cases*. Fourth edition. Toronto: Irwin.

Belasco, J. A., and R. C. Sayer. 1995. "Why Empowerment Doesn't Empower: The Bankruptcy of Current Paradigms." *Business Horizons* (March-April): 29–41.

Besanko, D., D. Dranove, and M. Shanley. 1996. *The Economics of Strategy*. New York: John Wiley and Sons.

Biemans, W. G. and H. Harmsen. 1995. "Overcoming the barriers to market-oriented product development." *Journal of Marketing Practice: Applied Marketing Science* 1, 2: 7–25.

Bierly, P. and A. Chakrabarti. 1996. "Generic Knowledge Strategies in the U.S. Pharmaceutical Industry." *Strategic Management Journal* 17 (Winter Special Issue).

Bodie Z., A. Kane, and Alan J. Marcus. 1993. *Investments* New York: Irwin.

Bontis, Nick. 1995. "Organizational Learning and Leadership: A Literature Review of Two Fields." *Published Proceedings of ASAC '95*, Windsor, Canada.

Bontis, Nick. 1996a. "There's a price on your head: Managing intellectual capital strategically." *Business Quarterly* (Summer).

Bontis, Nick. 1996b. "Economic Value Added." In *Society of Management Accountants of Canada Professional Program*, eds. R. Michalski and M. Sealey. Toronto: Society of CMAs, Module 5, Part 4.3.

Bontis, Nick. 1997. "Royal Bank Invests in Knowledge-Based Industries." *Knowledge Inc.* 2, 8: 1–4.

Bontis, Nick. 1998. "Intellectual Capital: An Exploratory Study That Develops Measures and Models" *Management Decision* 36, 2: 63–76.

Bontis, Nick. 1999. "Managing an organizational learning system by aligning stocks and flows of knowledge." *Ph.D. Dissertation*, University of Western Ontario.

Bontis, Nick, N. Dragonetti, K. Jacobsen, and G. Roos. 1999. "The knowledge toolbox: A review of the tools available to measure and manage intangible resources." *European Management Journal* 17, 4: 391–402.

Bouwen, R. and R. Fry. 1991. "Organizational Innovation and Learning: Four Patterns of Dialogue between the Dominant Logic and the New Logic." *International Studies of Management and Organization* 21, 4: 37–51.

Brown, C., M. Reich, and D. Stern. 1993. "Becoming a high-performance work organization: The role of security, employee involvement, and training." *The International Journal of Human Resource Management* 4, 2: 247–75.

Brummet, R. L., E. G. Flamholtz, and W. C. Pyle. 1968. "Human Resource Measurement: A Challenge for Accountants." *The Accounting Review* (April): 217–24.

Cangelosi, V. and W. Dill. 1965. "Organizational learning: Observations toward a theory." *Administrative Sciences Quarterly.*

Chandler, Alfred D. 1977. *The Visible Hand: The Managerial Revolution in American Business*. Cambridge: Belknap/Harvard University Press.

Chandler, Alfred D. 1990. *Scale and Scope: The Dynamics of Industrial Capitalism*. Cambridge: Belknap/Harvard University Press.

Choi, C. J. and S. H. Lee. 1997. "A knowledge-based view of cooperative interorganizational relationships." In *Cooperative Strategies: European Perspectives*, eds. P. Beamish and J. Killing. San Francisco: New Lexington Press.

Cohen, W. M. and D. A. Levinthal. 1990. "Absorptive capacity: A new perspective on learning and innovation." *Administrative Science Quarterly* 35: 128–52.

Collis, D. J. 1996. "Organizational Capability as a Source of Profit." In *Organizational Learning and Competitive Advantage*, eds. B. Moingeon and A. Edmondson. London: Sage.

Conner, K. and C. Prahalad. 1996. "A resource-based theory of the firm: Knowledge versus opportunism." *Organization Science* 7: 5.

Crossan, M., H. Lane, R. White, and L. Djurfeldt. 1995. "Organizational Learning: Dimensions for a Theory." *International Journal of Organizational Analysis* 3: 4.

Crossan, M., R. E. White, H. W. Lane, and Leo Klus. 1996. "The Improvising Organization: Where Planning Meets Opportunity." *Organization Dynamics* 24, 4: 20–34.

Damanpour, F. 1991. "Organizational Innovation: A Meta-Analysis of Effects of Determinants and Moderators." *Academy of Management Journal* 34, 3: 555–90.

Darling, M. 1996. "Building the Knowledge Organization." *Business Quarterly* (Winter).

Davenport, T. and L. Prusak. 1997. *Information Ecology: Mastering the information and knowledge environment*. New York: Oxford University Press.

Demsetz, H. 1991. "The theory of the firm revisited." In *The Nature of the Firm*, eds. O. Williamson and S. Winter. New York: Oxford University Press.

Deng, S. and J. Dart. 1994. "Measuring market orientation: A multi-factor, multi-item approach." *Journal of Marketing Management* 10: 725–42.

Dierickx, Ingemar and Karel Cool. 1989. "Asset Stock Accumulation and the Sustainability of Competitive Advantage." *Management Science* 35: 1504–1513.

Docherty, A. 1993. "Getting the Best out of Knowledge-Workers." *Involvement and Participation* 619: 6–11.

Dodgson, M. 1992. "The future for technological collaboration." *Futures* (June).

Drucker, Peter F. 1993. *Post-Capitalist Society*. Oxford: Butterworth Heinemann.

Duncan, R. and A. Weiss. 1979. "Organizational Learning: Implications for organizational design." In *Research Organizational Behavior*, ed. B. Straw. Greenwich: JAI Press.

Eccles, R. 1991. "The Performance Measurement Manifesto." *Harvard Business Review* (Jan-Feb.): 131–37.

Edvinsson, L. and M. Malone. 1997. *Intellectual Capital*. New York: Harper Business.

Edvinsson, L. and P. Sullivan. 1996. "Developing a Model for Managing Intellectual Capital." *European Management Journal* 14: 4.

Eisenhardt, K. 1988. "Agency- and Institutional-Theory Explanations: The Case of Retail Sales Compensation." *Academy of Management Journal* 31, 3: 488–511.

EIU and IBM. 1996. *The Learning Organization: Managing Knowledge for Business Success*, Research Report of the Economist Intelligence Unit in Cooperation with the IBM Consulting Group.

Fiol C. and M. Lyles. 1985. "Organizational Learning." *Academy of Management Review* 10: 4.

Flamholtz, E. 1973. "Human Resource Accounting: Measuring Positional Replacement Cost." *Human Resource Measurement* (Spring) 8–16.

Foss, N. 1996. "Knowledge-based approaches to the theory of the firm: Some critical comments." *Organization Science* 7: 5.

French, J. and B. Raven. 1959. "The basis of social power." In *Studies in Social Power*, ed. D. Cartwright. Ann Arbor, Mich.: Institute for Social Research.

Friedman, A. and B. Lev. 1974. "A Surrogate Measure for the Firm's Investment in Human Resources." *Journal of Accounting Research* (Autumn): 235–50.

Fudenberg, Drew and Jean Tirole. 1986. *Dynamic Models of Oligopoly.* London: Harwood.

Gambling, T. E. 1974. "A System Dynamics Approach to HRA." *The Accounting Review* (July): 538–46.

Grant, R. M. 1996a. "Prospering in dynamically-competitive environments: Organizational capability as knowledge integration." *Organization Science* 7: 4.

Grant, R. M. 1996b. "Toward a knowledge-based theory of the firm." *Strategic Management Journal* 17 (Winter Special Issue).

Greenly, G. E. 1995. "Forms of market orientation in UK companies." *Journal of Management Studies* 32, 1: 47–66.

Greeno, J. 1980. "Psychology in Learning." *American Psychologist* 35: 8.

Gulati, R. 1995. "Does familiarity breed trust? The implications of repeated ties for contractual choice in alliances." *Academy of Management Journal* 38, 1: 85–112.

Hall, Brian. 1995. *Values Shift: A Guide to Personal and Organizational Transformation.* Rockport, Mass.: Twin Lights.

Hall, Richard. 1992. "The Strategic Analysis of Intangible Resources." *Strategic Management Journal* 13: 135–44.

Hamel, G. 1991. "Competition for competence and inter-partner learning within international strategic alliances." *Strategic Management Journal* 12: 83–103.

Hampden-Turner, C. 1992. *Creating Corporate Culture: From Discord to Harmony.* Reading, Mass: Addison-Wesley.

Handy, Charles B. 1989. *The Age of Unreason.* London: Arrow Books Ltd.

Hansen, G. and B. Wernerfelt. 1989. "Determinants of firm performance: The relative importance of economic and organizational factors." *Strategic Management Journal* 10.

Hedberg, B. 1981. "How organizations learn and unlearn." In *Handbook of Organizational Design,* eds. P. Nystrom and W. Starbuck. London: Oxford University Press.

Hedlund, G. 1994. "A model of knowledge management and the N-form corporation." *Strategic Management Journal* 15. [AU: No page numbers?]

Hedlund G. and I. Nonaka. 1993. "Models of knowledge management in the West and Japan." In *Implementing Strategic Processes: Change, Learning, and Cooperation,* eds. P. Lorange, B. Chakravarthy, J. Roos, and A. Van de Ven. Oxford: Basil Blackwell.

Hekimian, J. S. and C. Jones. 1967. "Put People on Your Balance Sheet." *Harvard Business Review* (January-February): 105–113.

Henderson, R. and I. Cockburn. 1994. "Measuring competence? Exploring firm effects in pharmaceutical research." *Strategic Management Journal* 15: 63–84.

Hermanson, R. H. 1964. "Accounting for Human Assets." *Occasional Paper No. 14.* East Lansing, Mich.: Bureau of Business and Economic Research, Michigan State University, East Lansing. Republished 1986 by Georgia State University.

Hofstede, G. 1978. "Value Systems in Forty Countries." *Proceedings of the 4th International Congress of the Association for Cross-Cultural Psychology.*

Hofstede, G. 1991. *Cultures and Organizations: Intercultural Cooperation and Its Importance to Survival.* Glasgow: HarperCollins.

Huber, G. 1991. "Organizational Learning: The contributing processes and the literatures." *Organization Science,* 2.[AU: No page numbers?]

Hudson, W. 1993. *Intellectual Capital: How to Build It, Enhance It, Use It.* New York: John Wiley and Sons.

Hulland, J. 1995. "Market Orientation and Market Learning Systems: An Environment-Strategy-Performance Perspective." Working Paper, University of Western Ontario.

Inkpen, A. and M. Crossan. 1995. "Believing is seeing: Joint ventures and organizational learning." *Journal of Management Studies* 32.[AU: No page numbers?]

Itami, H. 1987. *Mobilizing Invisible Assets*. Boston: Harvard University Press.

Jaworski, B. J. and A. K. Kohli. 1993. "Market orientation: Antecedents and consequences." *Journal of Marketing 57* (July): 53–70.

Jensen, M. and W. Meckling. 1976. "Theory of the Firm: Managerial Behavior, Agency Costs and Ownership Structure." *Journal of Financial Economics* 3: 305–360.

Johnson, H. T. and R. S. Kaplan. 1987. *Relevance Lost*. Boston: Harvard Business School Press.

Kanter, R. 1989. *When Giants Learn to Dance*. London: Simon and Schuster.

Kaplan, R. S. and D. P. Norton. 1992. "The Balanced Scorecard Measures that Drive Performance." *Harvard Business Review* (January-February): 71–79.

Kessides, I. 1990. "Internal vs. external market conditions and firm profitability: An exploratory model." *Economic Journal*, 100.

Kim, D. 1993. "The link between individual and organizational learning." *Sloan Management Review* (Fall).

Kodama, F. 1992. "Technology fusion and the new R&D." *Harvard Business Review* 70 : 4.

Kogut, Bruce and Udo Zander. 1992. "Knowledge of the Firm, Combinative Capabilities, and the Replication of Technology." *Organization Science* 3: 383–97.

Kohli, A. K. and Jaworski, B. J. (1990). "Market orientation: The construct, research propositions, and managerial implications." *Journal of Marketing 54* (April): 1–18.

Kornbluh, H., R. Pipan, and S. J. Schurman. 1987. "Empowerment, Learning and Control in Workplaces: A Curricular View." *Zeitschrift für Sozialisationforschung und Erziehungssoziologie* 7, 4: 253–68

Lazaric, N. and E. Lorenz. 1995. "Trust and organizational learning during inter-firm cooperation." *Proceedings of Seminar on confiance, apprentissage et anticipation économique*. Compiègne, France.

Learned, E., C. Christensen, K. Andrews, and W. Guth. 1969. *Business Policy: Text and Cases*. Homewood, Ill.: Irwin.

Levitt, T. 1991. *Marketing Imagination*. New York: The Free Press.

Levitt, B. and J. March. 1988. "Organizational Learning." *Annual Review of Sociology.*

Lichtenthal, J. D. and D. T. Wilson. 1992. "Becoming market oriented." *Journal of Business Research* 24: 191–207.

Likert, R. M. 1967. *New Patterns of Management.* New York: McGraw-Hill Book Co.

Likert, R. M. and D. G. Bowers. 1973. "Improving the Accuracy of P/L Reports by Estimating the Changes in Dollar Value of the Human Organization." *Michigan Business Review* (March): 15–24.

Lusch, R. F. and G. R. Laczniak. 1987. "The evolving marketing concept, competitive intensity and organizational performance." *Journal of the Academy of Marketing Science* 15: 3.

Luscombe, N. 1993. "A Learning Experience." *CA Magazine* (February 3).

Lynn, B. 1998. "Performance evaluation in the new economy." *International Journal of Technology Management* 16, 1/2/3: 162–76.

Mayer, R., J. Davis, and F. Schoorman. 1995. "An integrative model of organizational trust." *Academy of Management Review* 20: 3.

McConville, D. 1994. "All about EVA." *Industry Week* (April 18).

McGee, J. and L. Prusak. 1993. *Managing Information Strategically.* New York: John Wiley and Sons.

McGill, M. E., J. W. Slocum, and D. Lei. 1992. "Managerial Practices in Learning Organizations." *Organizational Dynamics* 21, 1: 5–17.

McGrath, R., M. Tsai, S. Venkatraman, and I. MacMillan. 1996. "Innovation, competitive advantage and rent: A model and test." *Management Science* 42: 3.

Meyer-Dohm, P. 1992. "Human resources 2020: Structures of the 'learning company'." *Conference Proceedings of Human Resources in Europe at the Dawn of the 21st Century.* Luxembourg: Office for Official Publications of the European Communities.

Miller, D. 1996. "A Preliminary Typology of Organizational Learning: Synthesizing the Literature." *Journal of Management* 22: 3.

Moingeon, B. and A. Edmondson. 1996. "Trust and organizational learning." *Proceedings of Organizational Learning and Learning Organization Symposium '96.* Lancaster, U.K.

Morse, W. J. 1973. "A Note on the Relationship Between Human Assets and Human Capital." *The Accounting Review* (July): 589–93.

Nanda, A. 1996. "Resources, Capabilities and Competencies." In *Organizational Learning and Competitive Advantage*, eds. B. Moingeon and A. Edmondson. London: Sage.

Narver, J. C. and S. F. Slater. 1990. "The effect of a market orientation on business profitability." *Journal of Marketing* (October): 20–35.

Nelson, Richard R. (1991). "Why Do Firms Differ, and How Does It Matter?" *Strategic Management Journal* 12: 61–74.

Nelson, Richard R. and Sidney G. Winter. 1982. *An Evolutionary Theory of Economic Change*. Cambridge, Mass.: Belknap Press.

Nicolini, D. 1993. "Apprendimento Organizzativo e Pubblica Amministrazione Locale." *Autonomie Locali e Servizi Sociali* 16: 2.

Nohria, N. and R. Eccles. 1991. "Corporate Capability." Working Paper No. 92–038, Harvard Business School.

Nonaka, I. 1994. "A dynamic theory of organizational knowledge." *Organization Science*, 5.

Nonaka, I. and H. Takeuchi. 1995. *The Knowledge-Creating Company*. New York: Oxford University Press.

Ochsner, R. (1995. "Welcome to the new world of Economic Value Added." *Compensation & Benefits Review* (March-April).

Papahristodoulou, C. 1994. "Is Lean Production the Solution?" *Economic and Industrial Democracy* 15: 457–76.

Parker, S. K., S. Mullarkey, and P. R. Jackson. 1994. "Dimensions of Performance Effectiveness in High-Involvement Work Organizations." *Human Resource Management Journal* 4, 3: 1–21.

Pavitt, K. 1971. "The multinational enterprise and the transfer of technology." In *The Multinational Enterprise*, ed. John Dunning. London: George Allen and Unwin.

Pennings, J. M. and F. Harianto. 1992. "Technological networking and innovation implementation," *Organization Science* 3, 3: 356–83.

Penrose, Edith Tilton. 1959. *The Theory of the Growth of the Firm*. Oxford: Basil Blackwell.

Pfeffer, J. 1994. "Competitive Advantage Through People." *California Management Review* (Winter): 9–28.

Polanyi, Michael. 1967. *The Tacit Dimension*. New York: Anchor Day Books.

Prahalad, C. K. and Gary Hamel. 1990. "The Core Competence of the Corporation." *Harvard Business Review* (May-June): 79–91.

Prusak, L. 1996. "The Knowledge Advantage." *Strategy & Leadership* (March/April).

Quinn, J. B. 1992. *Intelligent Enterprise*. New York: Free Press.

Roos, J., G. Roos, N. Dragonetti, and L. Edvinsson. 1998. *Intellectual Capital: Navigating in the New Business Landscape*. New York: New York University Press.

Rubin, P. H. 1973. "The Expansion of Firms." *Journal of Political Economy* 81: 936–49.

Ruekert, R. W. 1992. "Developing a market orientation: An organizational strategy perspective." *International Journal of Research in Marketing* 9: 225–45.

Rumelt, R. P. 1991. "How much does industry matter?" *Strategic Management Journal* 12: 167–85.

Rutledge, J. 1997. "You're a fool if you buy into this." *ASAP* (7 April 1997).

Sackmann, S. A., E. G. Flamholtz, and M. L. Bullen. 1989. "Human Resource Accounting: A State of the Art Review." *Journal of Accounting Literature* 8: 235–64.

Sadler, P. 1994. "The management of talent." *Human Resource Management International Digest* (January-February): 37–39.

Saint-Onge, H. 1996. "Tacit Knowledge: The key to the strategic alignment of intellectual capital." *Strategy & Leadership* (April).

Schmalense, R. 1985. "Do markets differ much?" *American Economic Review*, 75.

Schumpeter, Joseph A. 1934. *The Theory of Economic Development*. Cambridge, Mass.: Harvard University Press.

Selznick, P. 1957. *Leadership in Administration*. New York: Harper and Row.

Senge, P. M. 1990. *The Fifth Discipline: The Art and Practice of the Learning Organization*. New York: Doubleday Currency.

Shrivastava, P. 1983. "A typology of organizational learning systems." *Journal of Management Studies* 20: 1.

Shrivastava, P. 1986. "Learning Structures for Top Management." *Human Systems Management*, 6.

Simon, Herbert A. 1945. *Administrative Behavior*. New York: Macmillan.

Simon, Herbert A. 1991. "Bounded rationality and organizational learning." *Organization Science* 2: 1.

Skandia. 1994. "Visualizing Intellectual Capital in Skandia." *A supplement to Skandia's 1994 Annual Report*. Sweden.

Skandia. 1995a. "Renewal and Development: Intellectual Capital." *A supplement to Skandia's 1995 Interim Annual Report*. Sweden.

Skandia. 1995b. "Value-Creating Processes: Intellectual Capital." *A supplement to Skandia's 1995 Annual Report*. Sweden.

Skandia. 1996a. "Power of Innovation: Intellectual Capital." *A supplement to Skandia's 1996 Interim Annual Report*. Sweden.

Skandia. 1996b. "Customer Value." *A supplement to Skandia's 1996 Annual Report*. Sweden.

Skandia. 1997. "Intelligent Enterprising." *A Supplement to Skandia's 6–Month Interim Report.* Sweden.

Skyrme, D. J. and D. M. Amidon. 1997. *Creating the knowledge-based business.* London: Business Intelligence.

Slater, S. F. and J. C. Narver. 1994. "Market Orientation, Customer Value, and Superior Performance." *Business Horizons* (March-April): 22–29.

Spender, J.-C. 1994. "Organizational knowledge, collective practice and Penrose rents." *International Business Review* 3: 4.

Spender, J.-C. 1996. "Making knowledge the basis of a dynamic theory of the firm." *Strategic Management Journal* 17 (Winter Special Issue).

Stata, R. 1989. "Organizational Learning—The Key to Management Innovation." *Sloan Management Review* (Spring).

Stewart, Thomas A. 1991. "Brainpower: How Intellectual Capital is Becoming America's Most Valuable Asset." *FORTUNE* (3 June 1991): 44–60.

Stewart, Thomas A. 1994. "Your Company's Most Valuable Asset: Intellectual Capital." *FORTUNE* (3 October 1994): 68–74.

Stewart, Thomas A. 1997. *Intellectual Capital: The New Wealth of Organizations.* Doubleday/Currency: New York.

Stivers, B., J. Covin, N. Green Hall, and S. Smalt. 1998. "How nonfinancial performance measures are used." *Management Accounting* (February).

Storey, J. 1995. "HRM: Still marching on, or marching out?" In *Human Resource Management: A Critical Text,* J. Storey. London: Routledge.

Sullivan, P. and L. Edvinsson. 1996. "A model for managing intellectual capital." In *Technology Licensing,* ed. R. Parr and P. Sullivan. New York: John Wiley and Sons.

Sveiby, K. E. 1997. *The New Organizational Wealth: Managing and Measuring Knowledge-Based Assets.* Berrett-Koehler: New York.

Stewart III, G. 1991. *The Quest for Value.* Harper-Collins.

Stewart III, G. 1994. "EVA™: Fact and Fantasy." *Journal of Applied Corporate Finance* (Summer).

Taylor, F. 1911. *The Principles of Scientific Management.* New York: Harper and Brothers.

Teece, David J. 1982. "Toward an Economic Theory of the Multiproduct Firm." *Journal of Economic Behavior and Organization* 3: 39–63.

Teece, David J. 1988. "Technological Change and the Nature of the Firm." In *Technical Change and Economic Theory,* eds. G. Dosi, C. Freeman, R. Nelson, G. Silverberg, and L. Soete. London: Frances Pinter.

Teece, David J., G. Pisano, and A. Shuen. 1994. "Dynamic Capabilities and Strategic Management." Working Paper, Center for Research in Management, University of California at Berkeley.

Thomas, K. W., and B. E. Velthouse. 1990. "Cognitive Elements of Empowerment: An Interpretative Model of Intrinsic Task Motivation." *Academy of Management Review* 15, 4: 666–82.

Thompson, V. A. 1965. "Bureaucracy and innovation." *Administrative Science Quarterly* 10: 1–20.

Townley, B. 1993. "Foucault, Power/Knowledge, and Its Relevance for Human Resource Management." *Academy of Management Review* 18, 3: 518–45.

Tsuchiya, S. 1994. "A study of organizational knowledge." *Proceedings of Management of Industrial and Corporate Knowledge ISMICK '94.* Compiègne, France.

Veilleux, R. 1995. *A nationwide descriptive study about the status of organizational learning in United States businesses.* Ph.D. dissertation. Washington D.C.: George Washington University.

Vitale, M. R. and S. C. Mavrinac. 1995. "How Effective is Your Performance Measurement System?" *Management Accounting* (August): 43–47.

Vitale, M. R., S. C. Mavrinac, and M. Hauser. 1994. "New Process/Financial Scorecard: A Strategic Performance Measurement System." *Planning Review* (July-August): 12–17.

Ward, A. 1996. "Lessons learned on the knowledge highways and byways." *Strategy & Leadership*(March/April).

Wellins, R. S., W. C. Byham, and J. M. Wilson. 1991. *Empowered Teams: Creating Self-Directed Groups That Improve Quality, Productivity and Participation.* San Francisco: Jossey-Bass.

Wernerfelt, Birger. 1984. "A Resource-Based View of the Firm." *Strategic Management Journal* 5: 171–80.

West, P. 1994. "The concept of the learning organization." *Journal of European Industrial Training* 18: 1.

White G. I., A. C. Sondhi, and Dov Fried. 1994. *The Analysis and Use of Financial Statements.* New York: John Wiley and Sons.

Wiele, B. 1993. "Competing from the neck up." *Performance & Instruction* (March).

Winter, Sidney G. 1987. "Knowledge and Competence as Strategic Assets." *The Competitive Challenge: Strategies of Industrial Innovation and Renewal,* ed. David J. Teece. Cambridge, Mass.: Ballinger Publishing Company. 159–84.

Wright, P. M., G. C. McMahan, and A. McWilliams. 1994. "Human Resources and sustained competitive advantage: A resource-based perspective." *International Journal of Human Resource Management* 5, 2: 301–326.

Yeatts, D. E., M. Hipskind, and D. Barnes. 1994. "Lessons Learned from Self-Managed Work Teams." *Business Horizons* (July-August): 11–18.

Zander, U. and B. Kogut. 1995. "Knowledge and the speed of the transfer and imitation of organizational capabilities: An empirical test." *Organization Science* 6, 1: 76–92.

Zimmerman, M. A. 1990. "Toward a Theory of Learned Hopefulness: A Structural Model Analysis of Participation and Empowerment." *Journal of Research in Personality*, 24.

3

DIGITAL KNOWLEDGE:

COPYRIGHT INTELLECTUAL PROPERTY AND THE INTERNET

David H. Brett
Knexa.com Enterprises, Vancouver, British Columbia, Canada
david.brett@knexa.com

ABSTRACT

When tacit knowledge is codified, it becomes copyright intellectual property. International conventions and laws pertaining to copyright are intended to promote the creation of new knowledge by ensuring rewards flow to the creators in order to sustain continued production of these goods. The advent of digital networks disrupts normal economic markets for digital goods by removing excludability, rivalry, transparency, reproduction costs, and delivery costs. However, online business models that leverage the Internet's digital distribution system will form the bulk of all future electronic commerce. The advent of "peer-to-peer" file-sharing systems such as Napster have created a clash of views on how copyright laws and digital goods markets should be maintained. The integrity of all intellectual capital is threatened if time-honored values that respect creations of the mind are compromised.

INTRODUCTION

At the dawn of the twenty-first century, it has become commonplace for pundits to cite the amazing rise of digital networks as a manifestation of the burgeoning knowledge economy. The Internet has

57

created a world where vast amounts of information and knowledge can flow instantaneously at extremely low cost. But does this digital transformation have an effect on the value of knowledge itself? How will we value knowledge in an age of zero costs and free delivery? Is the information explosion leading to knowledge "implosion?" The answers lie in the "economy" side of the "knowledge economy."

Within and between organizations, knowledge flows in markets. Whether through informal peer networks, formal knowledge-transfer arrangements, or ad hoc online forums, we exchange tacit and explicit knowledge in ways that we believe will maximize our own utility. As the theory and practice of knowledge management and intellectual capital valuation (Bontis 2001) lives and breathes in the context of the commercial enterprise, we cannot view the exchange of knowledge as being based on altruism. In an economy increasingly based on intangible assets, firms and individuals vie for the economic benefits that result from the possession and use of knowledge. Payment for knowledge can take many forms. For tacit knowledge, salaries, wages, fees, and other time-measured renumerations are the established norm. For explicit knowledge, however, extracting rents can be more complex. When it comes to getting paid for one's explicit knowledge, written or otherwise, codified work falls broadly into the increasingly digital and shifting world of publishing.

KNOWLEDGE PUBLISHING

According to the *Merriam-Webster Collegiate Dictionary*, the word *publish* means, "**1 a** : to make generally known **b** : to make public announcement of **2 a** : to disseminate to the public **b** : to produce or release for distribution; *specifically* : PRINT 2c **c** : to issue the work of (an author)." Generally, organizations expect employees to disseminate the knowledge that is created or gathered in the course of doing their work. To effect wide distribution, knowledge must be codified in an intelligible manner. In a mining company, for example, a geologist examining rock uses her tacit knowledge, a combination of her varied experiences and learned information, to identify the sample's minerals and to judge the significance of the information. She then writes her observations in her notes that will likely be used later for compiling a written report. The report will become an important asset to the mining company, embodying as much of the geologist's tacit knowledge as possible.

Published knowledge, whether for external sale or personal or internal organizational use, is copyright intellectual property, protected from unauthorized use by the laws of various countries worldwide. Whereas one's tacit knowledge is not susceptible to unauthorized duplication, illicit copies of explicit knowledge can bestow unpaid-for benefits to competitors or other foes. Authors therefore enjoy special rights to their creations, as outlined, for example, by the U.S. Constitution, Art. I, sec. 8, whose purpose is: "To promote the progress of science and useful arts, by securing for limited times to authors and inventors the exclusive right to their respective writings and discoveries."

Through employment, knowledge authors are generally viewed as assigning their rights to the organization. The firm "buys" these publications from the author through a paycheck. The "cost" of creation is mainly the time taken by employees, plus printing, binding, and so on. These "knowledge assets," unless sold, are not recorded on a company's financial statements. For this reason, firms would realize visible financial gains by selling knowledge assets to third parties. The prospect of using the Internet as a means to sell knowledge assets is one reason why market dynamics in digital goods have significant implications for knowledge management.

THE INTERNET ENIGMA

The rise of the Internet and the World Wide Web has created both an opportunity and a problem for copyright intellectual property markets, including digital knowledge. Creators and consumers of the written word, computer programs, music, films, voice recordings, and graphical images can now use common and inexpensive technologies to access, replicate, and globally distribute these works instantaneously at near zero cost. The reduction in costs of distribution should be a windfall for producers and the ease and speed of access should greatly increase enjoyment of the goods to consumers. However, the near elimination of duplication and distribution costs creates a disruption of normal economic forces that threatens the viability of sustained commerce in digitized copyright intellectual property (hereafter "digital goods"). The absence of cost-based pricing alternatives, the inability to exclude enjoyment of such goods, the resulting lack of rivalry, and the need to experience these goods in advance of payment all tend to obviate consumer motivation to pay significant prices. As economic realities drive prices down toward zero, producers lose motivation to create new digital goods, as they may be unable to recover the frequently high-sunk costs of creation. In spite of these economic realities, many sellers of digital goods have found ways to extract rents through various strategies. Traditional media and publishing concerns, as well as numerous start-up companies, are exploring new technologies and online business models in a race to solve the legal, ethical, and economic puzzles presented for digital goods by the new Internet communications medium.

All forms of digital goods, including all digitized explicit-knowledge assets and electronic-learning content, share the basic characteristics of being susceptible to costless, unlimited and near perfect replication and distribution. However, important distinctions are present from one type of digital good to another that affect the behavior of market participants seeking to enjoy the use of these creations. For example, consumers of recorded music typically expect recurrent enjoyment of a recording, whereas recurrent reading of the written word is less common, except for reference works and religious literature. The sustained enjoyment from repeat plays of recorded music also evokes buyer desire for choice of time and location for such enjoyment. Vinyl records, CDs, and tapes provide the listener with increased "option value" (Shapiro and Varian 1999) when compared to live performance or radio listening. For this reason, perfect copies of recorded music may display significantly different demand characteristics than Internet-delivered literature. Also, historical offline consumer behavior toward the various digital goods segments may have a significant impact on how they behave toward Internet digital goods. Recorded music is frequently consumed via radio broadcast at no direct cost to the consumer, providing a free sample of the creations in order to stimulate demand for the repeat enjoyment through purchased copies. Written works, on the other hand (except for news copy, advertising copy, and dramatic works), are not highly amenable to radio broadcast, and physical distribution of printed written works will not likely generate demand for repeat consumption. Film and video creations also display distinct use patterns and historical consumer behavior. Film "trailers" can provide limited sampling, but full screenings would cut demand for paid consumption dramatically. Certain visual goods display rapidly diminishing marginal utility of use, such as news reports, whereas animated films for children can display high utility on repeated use (Shapiro and Varian 1999).

All creations of the mind are ostensibly intangible. However, enjoyment of these intangibles is dependent in variable degrees on their manifestation in the physical world. Recorded sounds may be duplicated perfectly, but sound wave reproduction is not uniform, resulting in variable listener utility. Visual images are dependent on display mechanisms of variable quality to deliver enjoyment. Similarly, the utility of literature is a function of the medium to some degree. A barely legible hand-written novel manuscript will not yield the same utility as well as a nicely produced book. Although all digital goods can be converted into indistinguishable digital data packages, the character of market behavior is differentiated according to the process required to project these goods into the physical world. Accordingly, business practice, technology adoption, and government policy will not have uniform affects on all forms of digital goods. The author suggests a segregation of online distribution and marketing methodologies based on the character of the goods, as outlined in Figure 1.

The purpose of this chapter is to review some of the economic discourse relevant to digital goods and the Internet and review current online business models seeking to extract rents for Internet-distributed digital goods. Some commentators have suggested that technologies used to distribute recorded music such as Napster will force a fundamental alteration of the entire publishing industry across all spectrums (Shirky 2001). Others are challenging the very right of digital-goods creators to extract rents from their products (Barlow 1993). At the same time, publishing giants and start-up firms are launching online businesses seeking to capitalize on the Internet's ability to globally and instantaneously deliver digital goods at minimal cost. Policy-makers and market participants are also examining the capability of current laws to address the new economic characteristics of digital goods markets.

INTELLECTUAL PROPERTY CHARACTERISTICS

According to the World Intellectual Property Organization ("WIPO"), "intellectual property refers to creations of the mind: inventions, literary and artistic works, and symbols, names, images, and designs used in commerce." WIPO divides IP into two categories: "Industrial property, which includes inventions (patents), trademarks, industrial designs, and geographic indications of source; and Copyright, which includes literary and artistic works such as novels, poems and plays, films, musical works, artistic works such as drawings, paintings, photographs and sculptures, and architectural designs.

Rights related to copyright include those of performing artists in their performances, producers of phonograms in their recordings, and those of broadcasters in their radio and television programs" (WIPO 2001). The impact of the Internet and digital technologies on industrial property is less significant than the broad implications for copyright. The right to exploit industrial property must be conveyed by specific contracts between specific parties, whereas copyright imputes a general contract on market participants. The duplication and distribution capabilities of the Internet have little bearing on specific contractual obligations of identified parties. For these reasons, copyright intellectual property is highly affected by the Internet.

For the purpose of this chapter, digital goods will be divided into four categories: recorded sound creations, written works, visual creations, and computer programs. The later category will not be covered, as the particular and complex characteristics present are sufficient to warrant a much larger treatment. For example, network effects and lock-in possibilities peculiar to software create potential monopoly conditions that are not present with the former three categories.

THE ECONOMICS OF DIGITAL GOODS

John Perry Barlow, a widely read commentator on electronic publishing issues and former Grateful Dead lyricist, expressed the economic issues facing digitized copyright intellectual property as follows:

> "Throughout the time I've been groping around Cyberspace, there has remained unsolved an immense conundrum which seems to be at the root of nearly every legal, ethical, governmental, and social vexation to be found in the Virtual World. I refer to the problem of digitized property. The riddle is this: if our property can be infinitely reproduced and instantaneously distributed all over the planet without cost, without our knowledge, without its even leaving our possession, how can we protect it? How are we going to get paid for the work we do with our minds? And, if we can't get paid, what will assure the continued creation and distribution of such work?" (Barlow 1993).

Various economists have echoed Barlow's concerns and have written extensively on how traditional economic theory struggles with markets for digital goods, particularly with respect to cost-based pricing models: ". . . digital products fall into a gray area where such economic reasoning fails to give an insightful answer to business professionals looking to know how to price their products" (Choi, Stahl, Whinston 1997). However, various writers recommend a variety of strategies as a means of turning an apparent morass into an advantage.

DIGITAL PRODUCTS AND MARKET THEORY

According to the doctrines fundamental to most modern economic discourse, goods and services in a society are most efficiently distributed when unimpeded market forces are allowed to drive the prices and rates of production for such good and services. Revered seventeenth-century economist Adam Smith's laissez-faire philosophy held that, if all individuals in a society were allowed to freely compete for scarce resources, an "invisible hand" would operate to ensure that society's welfare as a whole would be maximized. Centuries later, it is hard to dispute that the world's wealthiest nations are those that promote free market policies. As Smith wrote in his classic treatise *The Wealth of Nations*:

> ". . . every individual . . . endeavors as much as he can . . . to direct . . . industry so that its produce may be of the greatest value . . . neither intending to promote the public interest, nor knowing how much he is promoting it . . . He intends only his own gain, and he is in this, as in many other cases, led by an *invisible hand* to promote an end that was no part of his intention . . . By pursuing his own interest, he frequently promotes that of society more effectually than when he really intends to promote it . . . ."

In order for the invisible hand to work, however, markets must display certain fundamental characteristics (De Long and Froomkin 1997). First of all, goods in the market must be *excludable*, in that market participants may exclude others from the use and enjoyment of a good. The value of air to a person's life is perhaps greater than all other resources, but to date, no one has found a way to exclude others from enjoying it, and hence it is not a source of rents in an economy. Pure oxygen, on the other hand, can be extracted from air, bottled, and sold as a good, as two cannot equally enjoy a single breath of oxygen. Secondly, market theory assumes that the scarcity of excludable goods invokes *rivalry* between buyers of the good. The price of oxygen may rise if a production plant fails as buyers compete for a smaller supply. Finally, for market forces to operate efficiently, goods must have as much as possible the quality of *transparency*, in that buyers can ascertain the nature and quality of a good before it is consumed. Most shoppers know what they are getting when they buy an apple, and a fair judgment of its quality can be made in advance. On the other hand, although the benefits of oxygen for human consumption are obvious to most people, the purity of any oxygen supply cannot be easily determined by casual observance. Oxygen buyers ultimately may never be able to easily determine the purity of the good. In this case, information asymmetry leads to a *market failure*, necessitating governments to regulate the production of oxygen.

Unlike most products and services in the economy, digital goods display only minimal levels of excludability, rivalry, and transparency. Thousands can enjoy a book displayed on a web page equally and simultaneously. Once released into a digital network, information and knowledge could become like air, floating freely with no ability to exclude anyone's use of it. Such conditions tend to dampen consumer rivalry, as the element of scarcity is removed. Information is also very opaque, where it is almost impossible to determine the quality of the good until after the information is consumed. These factors all mitigate consumer willingness to pay for digital goods. The response of most Internet publishers to date is to simply provide digital goods for free, hoping, usually in vain, to recoup their heavy production costs.

Making matters worse for digital goods is the problem of price. Traditional pricing schemes take into consideration the cost of production. Under Smith's market theory, social welfare is maximized when the price of a good is equal to the cost of producing one more unit (a good's "marginal cost"), as any price higher than this would mean that willing consumers would experience an unnecessary loss of utility due to not having the desired good. For this reason, freely competitive markets auger in favor of the consumer, as any producer selling above marginal cost will find other producers willingly meeting the unmet demand at a point where price = marginal cost. With digital goods delivered through the Internet, however, the cost of producing and delivering one more copy is essentially zero. If the principle of price = marginal cost is applied to digital goods, all digital goods should be priced at zero.

In their book *Information Rules: A Strategic Guide to the Networked Economy*, authors Hal Varian and Carl Shapiro point out how information goods typically have high costs of production and very low costs of reproduction. Given the tendency of markets to favor zero costs for digital goods, it follows that, because producers cannot cover their costs, production will cease. As economists Bradford de Long and A. Michael Froomkin observe in their article, "The Next Economy?", "charging price equal to marginal cost almost surely leaves the producer bankrupt, with little incentive to maintain the product except the hope of maintenance fees, and no incentive whatsoever to make another one except for that warm fuzzy feeling one gets from impoverishing oneself for the general good." Under these economic conditions, we can see that the production of digitally distributable knowledge is only possible on a sustained basis if the cost of production of the knowledge is covered through subsidization by governments or complementary income streams. As expected, much of the knowledge content available on the Internet for free has been indirectly funded through educational budgets or is written off as a marketing expense by knowledge-providers seeking to entice new buyers of their services. A good example of this is the legal profession.

BUSINESS STRATEGIES THAT EMBRACE THE DIGITAL DREAM

The inability to exclude the use of digital goods is not particular to the digital age. Classic examples of the promise and peril of communications technology are radio and television. Broadcast media such as radio and television transmissions can be picked up by anyone with a "receiver." Rather than struggle to find ways to scramble and de-scramble signals, early broadcasters gave birth to the advertising-supported content-delivery model. Unlike most newspapers, which had to be purchased, a "purchase" of radio waves was not possible. However, the rapt attention of listeners and viewers proved to be an extremely valuable commodity.

Given the success of the advertising model with broadcast media, it was only natural for Internet publishing concerns to adopt the free-content approach. However, the Internet lacks many key features required to make the advertising model successful. First of all, barriers to entry for new publishers are much lower on the Internet. With television, for example, significant minimum expenditures, various regulatory approvals, and critical business relationships are required before a firm can be in a position to charge advertisers for the right to send messages to an audience. The result is that the Web provides millions of "channel" selections, instead of dozens, which leads to a large dilution of viewers. Competition for viewers in the Internet landscape has driven many to continue delivering their products in spite of mounting losses, leading to eventual closure.

Cheap and faithful reproduction technologies are also not new to business. The photocopier and the videocassette recording device were originally viewed as potentially ruinous to the publishing, film, and television industries. But in a happy paradox, it appears that, far from harming the producers of written and visual goods, low-cost duplication and distribution has produced an opposite effect. As Shapiro and Varian observe with respect to printed works, "Printing presses, xerography, and the Internet have made text reproduction progressively cheaper, and express mail and fax machines have reduced distribution costs immensely. With each reduction in cost, the *amount* of information being distributed has increased dramatically. There is more being published today, and more money being made in publishing, than ever before" (Shapiro and Varian 1999: 94). The same unexpected outcome has occurred with the feature film industry. Far from losing revenue to theft of their copyright intellectual property, more money is often made from sales of videotapes than theatrical releases.

In spite of the economic challenges inherent in digital goods, many commentators predict that Internet-delivered products represent the true business promise of the new medium. According to University of Texas scholars Soon-Yong Choi, Dale Stahl, and Andrew Whinston, "the future of electronic commerce will be guided by innovative digital products and services that will emerge in the electronic marketplace." In their 1997 book *The Economics of Electronic Commerce*, the authors argue that "digital product"–pricing will be determined by payments required by copyright holders. "Although some argue that the variable reproduction cost will be zero, the author believes that it will be a substantial, albeit constant, amount due to the per-copy copyright payment" (Choi, Stahl, and Whinston 1997: 350). Furthermore, the authors suggest that the most efficient way to deliver digital goods may be through a strategy of "mixed bundling," incorporating "micropayments" for individual articles, instead of traditional bundled pricing methods typical of newspapers, magazines, journals, and music CDs. Under bundled strategies, consumers must pay for content they do not want in order to get the content they want, which may improve margins for the content. However, there is evidence that unbundled pricing may be profit-maximizing for sellers and utility-maximizing for buyers.

PEAK: PRICING ELECTRONIC ACCESS TO KNOWLEDGE

Recently, the University of Michigan spearheaded a three-and-one-half-year experiment designed to help discover optimal pricing strategies for electronically delivered academic journals (MacKie-Mason, Riveros, and Gazzale 1999). The Pricing Electronic Access to Knowledge (PEAK) project, conducted in cooperation with Elsevier Science, provided electronic access to twelve hundred scientific journals to a number of academic institutions under three pricing schemes. "Traditional subscription" pricing provided "unlimited access" to a given journal. "Generalized subscriptions" provided unlimited access to any 120 articles of the twelve hundred available. "Per article" pricing provided unlimited access to specific article by one individual. Among many interesting findings, the PEAK experiment indicated that as the users became familiar with the system, per article revenues increased dramatically. "Revenues for per article purchasing are more than fifteen times higher in 1999 than in 1998 . . ." (MacKie-Mason, Riveros, and Gazzale 1999: 9). The writers observe, "we see evidence that as they gained experience with PEAK, librarians favored the more flexible access options . . . that allow users to select the articles they want to read" (MacKie-Mason, Riveros, and Gazzale 1999: 9). These findings would suggest that for academic writings, buyer utility, and seller revenues are maximized through unbundled selection and delivery.

NAPSTER: "ALL-YOU-CAN-EAT" OR BE EATEN?

In a recent article entitled "Where Napster is Taking the Publishing World" published in the February, 2001, edition of *Harvard Business Review,* author Clay Shirky argues that the explosive growth of the Napster music "file sharing" community has dramatic implications for the entire publishing business, not just the music industry. In contrast to most digital goods delivery from large, centralized "server" computers, Napster users access music files from millions of other smaller computers owned by individual users. Known as *peer-to-peer file-sharing,* users both serve and accept files enabled by Napster's software and database service. According to Shirky, Napster has ensured that unbundled, pay-per-unit pricing schemes will not work. Describing the bias of the music industry, Shirky writes, "'one unit, one price' would be the norm, they believed, while 'all-you-can-eat' based on subscriptions and advertising would be oddities. Napster's success means that the 'all-you-can-eat' model has won." Shirky further argues that consumers who copy digital files, will not accept digital rights management, the application of technology to prevent illicit copying and distribution of electronic files.

Napster was recently successfully sued for copyright violation by a consortium of companies that hold copyrights to much of the music transferred through the Napster network. Faced with massive pecuniary damage claims, Napster has begun complying with an order to remove certain "songs" from its database as specified by the plaintiffs. Shirky's article, which was published prior to the February, 2001, court ruling against Napster, suggested that the very nature of copyright law would need to be altered to conform to the consumers appetite for free access to digital content. "The big question isn't whether Napster will win or lose on appeal. It's whether the current legal structure regarding copyright will hold. As anyone who has used Napster is aware, the answer is no. The music industry is not losing the right to enforce copyright but the ability to do so" (Shirky 2001: 6). Is Shirky right?

The author believes that, although the peer-to-peer system of file-sharing will force music copyright holders to adopt a subscription-based revenue model, the peer-to-peer model will not be prevalent with other forms of digitized copyright intellectual property. The reason for this is that the very character of music makes it amenable to multi-server file-sharing, whereas other digital goods do not. Accordingly, differentiated pricing and delivery methods are required to address the variable character and use parameters.

The following diagram (Figure 3-1) illustrates a differentiation scheme for non-software, digital intellectual property with suitable corresponding Internet-distribution models. Digital goods can be segmented according to the contrast between experiences that are purely cognitive and those that are purely sensory. Upon cognition, the brain can permanently store the concepts, ideas, and evocations of writings, reducing the need to re-read. Music, by contrast, cannot be fully reproduced by the brain, as sound waves are required. Peer-to-peer platforms such as Napster are dependent on high utility of reuse, as users must maintain files on their computers for sharing in the network. If utility per use reduced rapidly, users would tend to delete more used files, reducing the attractiveness of the network. In the case of written works, motivation to store the data is reduced, as

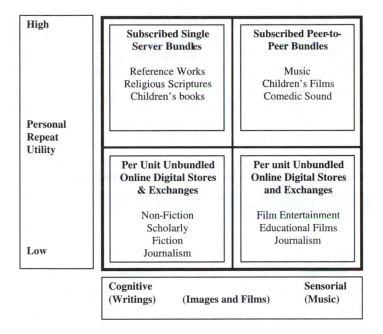

Figure 3-1 *Economic matrix for differentiated digital copyright intellectual property*

reuse renders little utility. Users would have low motivation to make their servers and files available to a network in a peer-to-peer matrix. The likelihood of a "Napster for Writings" is therefore low, forcing market participants to buy and sell written works through online stores and exchanges. As utility per use increases, so does the relative efficiency of bundled-pricing schemes. Reference works, for example, yield long-term repeat utility, as users refer back to them again and again. Since writings are not suitable for peer-to-peer networks, single-server subscription bundles are appropriate.

PEER-TO-PEER KNOWLEDGE MANAGEMENT?

Some commentators have argued that peer-to-peer networks will provide the basis for the next generation of knowledge management (KM) technologies. In their article, "KM Revolution from an Unlikely Direction" (published at Lotus.com), authors Jeff Angus and Stowe Boyd suggest that peer-to-peer systems will play an important role in KM. "Technologies such as Groove Networks, ikimbo, Engenia, and the dozens of other upstarts exploding in the P2P space are on the right track, we think—at least in principle."

The author believes that peer-to-peer technologies will not have significant applications in KM, as written materials have low repeat utility and as such motivation is absent for users to maintain sufficient searchable libraries to provide to the network.

The long-term viability of peer-to-peer use, even for music-sharing, is not a given, as the system tends to force inefficient bundling schemes. Under Napster's current system, users have access to hundreds of thousands of songs. How could any bundle cover the full costs of copyright payments for all the material? Presumably, a fair price to the copyright holders would be prohibitive to buyers. For this reason, the success of peer-to-peer systems will depend on highly creative pricing schemes.

CONCLUSIONS

The fields of knowledge management, information technology, and electronic commerce are inextricably interwoven. As the future of electronic commerce lies with markets for digital goods, the nature and status of copyright intellectual property is of fundamental importance to IT and KM. IT advances will ensure that tacit knowledge will be codified and digitized with increasing ease. Knowledge itself, therefore, will pass more fluidly from the mind, through digital networks, and into the minds of our fellow human beings. As we flow our knowledge in this manner, we need more than ever to invoke and respect the time-tested societal rules whereby we respect each other's mental creations. Recent foment over copyright laws should not be viewed as greedy stakeholders trying to extend unfair monopoly rights. Rather, the integrity of all intellectual capital is jeopardized if digital knowledge is viewed as unworthy of payment and protection.

REFERENCES

Angus, J. and S. Boyd. 2000. "KM Revolution from an Unlikely Direction." Web Site of Lotus Development Corp., *www.lotus.com*, accessed 1 December, 2000.

Barlow, J. P. 1993. "Selling Wine Without Bottles: The Economy of Mind on the Global Net." Electronic Frontier Web Site, *www.eff.org*, accessed 14 February, 2001.

Bontis, N. 2001. "Assessing Knowledge Assets: A review of the models used to measure intellectual capital." *International Journal of Management Reviews* 3, 1: 41–60.

Choi, S.-Y., D. O. Stahl, and A. B. Whinston. 1997. *The Electronics of Electronic Commerce*. Indianapolis: Macmillan Technical Publishing.

De Long, J. B. and A. M. Froomkin. 1997. "The Next Economy?", University of Miami Law School Web Site, *www.law.miami.edu*, accessed 13 February, 2001.

MacKie-Mason, J. K. and J. F. Riveros. 1997. "Economics and Electronic Access to Scholarly Information." University of Michigan Web Site, *www.umich.edu*, accessed 12 February, 2001.

MacKie-Mason, J. K., Riveros, and R. S. Gazzale. 1999. "Pricing and Bundling of Electronic Information Goods: Field Evidence." University of Michigan Web Site, *www.umich.edu*, accessed 12 February, 2001.

Shapiro, C. and H. R. Varian. 1999. *Information Rules, A Strategic Guide to the Networked Economy*. Boston: Harvard Business School Press.

Shirky, C. 2001. "Where Napster is Taking the Publishing World." *Harvard Business Review*. Boston: Harvard Business School Press.

4

THE POWER OF KNOWLEDGE-PATTERN RECOGNITION

Bryan Davis
The Kaieteur Institute for Knowledge Management, Toronto, Canada
bdavis@kikm.org

ABSTRACT

Pattern recognition has proven to be a powerful tool in many disciplines. It is useful as an interpretive, communication, and explanatory heuristic. In the knowledge management field to-date, there is hardly any focus on knowledge patterns. An argument is made for a deeper appreciation of the potential usefulness of knowledge-pattern recognition. An attempt is made to develop a working taxonomy of knowledge patterns.

The resulting array of available knowledge patterns then provides a basis for developing strategy, conducting audits, making adept decisions, and as a guide to raising the bar on smart knowledge performance. Knowledge-pattern recognition should become an ever more critical skill and core competency as the knowledge-based economy advances.

INTRODUCTION

Given the fast-changing and ever-increasingly complex nature of the world, gaining insight into how patterns are forming and structures are developing represents the most powerful way of managing in the new economy (Farrel 1998). In the rapidly emerging knowledge-based

72

economy, knowledge is a fundamental factor input, and it is big. Knowledge is an awesome new resource for value creation. Accordingly, we have begun to pay more attention to knowledge as a fuel. It is now too precious to waste, too important to leave to ad hoc management. A new discipline, knowledge management, related to the methods, tools, and strategies for harnessing knowledge, intellectual capital, and intangible assets, has begun to evolve. Many schools of thought exist in relation to how knowledge can be successfully harnessed for productive uses. The problem is that, with all the hype, the clamor and the noise, how does one make sense of the dissonance and begin to clearly understand the tested and proven pathways to successful knowledge? We think that growing an understanding of knowledge patterns, and internalizing the inner logic of these frameworks, is a great way to move forward. Phil Jackson, the famous basketball coach, gets it right when he observes: "The idea was to code the image of a successful move into my visual memory so that when a similar situation emerged in a game it would seem, to paraphrase Yogi Berra, like déjà vu all over again" (Jackson and Delahanty 1995). We have come to the conclusion from our research that knowledge-pattern recognition is an especially critical and requisite skill for smart, innovative knowledge-strategy. This is a key approach for making better sense of the growing knowledge puzzle.

Pattern Recognition

Pattern recognition has proven itself to be a seriously powerful tool for guiding action in many other fields. In the military domain, pattern recognition can be used to identify enemy submarines by their acoustic signature—the particular pattern made by their propulsion systems. In the Gulf War, we saw vivid pictures of the Tomahawk cruise missile in action. Its guidance system is programmed with an image map of the target. It locks onto this pattern in the precise delivery of its payload. In fish farms, pattern recognition is used to sort fish by type. In some plywood manufacturing plants, sheets of board are graded and sorted by their pattern. Financial services companies use software equipped with pattern-recognition technology to spot anomalous trends and thereby intercept impending fraud. Other typical applications are automatic sorting of bank bills, recognition of a speaker by his or her speech, recognition of abnormal electrocardiogram signals, optical reading of written documents, and visual inspection of manufactured products for quality control.

Pattern recognition, therefore, has had a proven efficacy across a wide spectrum of human activities.

The double-helix of DNA is a pattern that we have decoded and now plays a major role as we map the intricate secrets of the human genome. In the knowledge management field, it is our contention that there is a great future for using such an approach. With it, one can decode a specific business context and deliver the appropriate application precisely on target. We now use just such a framework for conducting knowledge assessments and assisting our clients with the crafting of innovative knowledge strategy.

ARE PATTERNS REALLY ALL THAT IMPORTANT?

In the quotes below, you can see evidence of the fact that, in the minds of leading thinkers and practitioners today, patterns are extremely important. (This is our argument from authority.) Here are a few favorite examples:

- "Recent research on cognition shows that our minds rarely make strictly logical deductions. Instead we rely on patterns— and on feelings associated with those patterns," says W. Brian Arthur, a leading economist from the Santa Fe Institute (Arthur 1998).
- "Anyone can learn to juggle. It's about breaking down complex patterns and maneuvers into simple tasks. Juggling is a system of tosses and throws, of different patterns, that once broken down, understood and mastered can be put together to create something magical," says Micheal Moschen, one of the world's greatest jugglers (Moschen 1997).
- "The most important lesson I've ever learned is to understand and to trust abstractions. If you can learn both to see and to believe in life's underlying patterns, you can make highly informed decisions every day. For example, everyone in high tech is familiar with Moore's Law, which states that computer-processing power will double every 18 months. Now, Moore's Law isn't a law in any physical sense, but it has driven and will continue to drive our industry's development. Yet very few people and very few companies really take this law to heart—because really embracing it leads to seemingly nonsensical projections. Five years ago, when I told people that we'd have the processing power that we have

today, lots of them—even those who said they believed in Moore's Law—thought I was being ridiculous," says Nathan Myhrvold, former Chief Technology Officer, Microsoft Corp (Myhrvold 1998).

- "The third revolution is rooted in biology and self-organizing systems—the search for a sense of pattern," says James Bailey (Bailey 1996).
- "In any stream of ideas, some kind of pattern will be evident. The trick is to look for patterns," says Gary Hamel, Management Strategist (Hamel 2000).

Knowledge patterns, therefore, are pathways we should take more seriously. It is amazing that, in the knowledge field today, there has been such a lack of focus on the development of knowledge-pattern recognition as a core competency.

THE BENEFITS OF PATTERN RECOGNITION

One of the additional virtues of pattern recognition is the ability to communicate complex moves with tremendous simplicity, clarity, speed, and power. For example, I may tell you about companies that are "built to last," "built to scale," or "built to flip." With a few words, I can communicate to you pictures of three different strategic approaches. These patterns are packed with meaning and yet are communicated succinctly with great resolution and economy. They are packed with meaning, because a discernable business model is contained in the description. The same would be true if we spoke about leasing, time-sharing, and outsourcing as business models. In a few words, the action-purpose is also implicit. Therefore, as a diagnostic and assessment tool, as a training tool, as a planning tool, as an alignment tool, as a communications tool, as a tool for growing awareness, and as a guide for action, patterns can have tremendous operative value.

PATTERN RECOGNITION AND DECISION-MAKING

Pattern recognition also supports effective and rapid decision-making. And one thing is a given about the knowledge-based economy. The velocity of change is increasing amid greater complexity and chaos. So, possession of a deep understanding of knowledge patterns can enable critical decision-making whenever knowledge mobilization is an urgent issue. Gary Klein is a cognitive psychologist. He has been described as a cartographer of the human mind. He has spent a lifetime studying how people such as firefighters make split-second life-and-death decisions. He tells a story of a fire-fighting commander who suddenly ordered his men out of an inferno they were battling. Klein says, "this incident helped us understand that firefighters make decisions by recognizing when a typical situation is developing. In this case, the events were not typical. The *pattern* of the fire didn't fit with anything in the commander's experience. That made him uneasy, so he ordered his men out of the building" (Klein 2000).

In this particular case, just as the crew reached the street, the living room floor of the house in which they had been caved in. Had they not evacuated, the firefighters would have been trapped in the basement. In an increasingly changing, chaotic, and complex business environment, understanding and internalizing knowledge patterns is vital for helping us to make safe, rapid, and effective knowledge-supported decisions.

Cognitive scientist Andy Carr of Washington University calls people fast pattern completers. "We are really wonderful as humans at completing *patterns*. We get a hint and then fill in the rest. We see a black tail swishing around a corner and we assume it is a cat. We get a whiff of water upwind and we assume there is a spring nearby." "Our very survival depends on this way of thinking," says Winslow Farrell (1998). Carl Bereiter and Marlene Scardamalia are leading educational researchers at the Ontario Institute for Studies in Education. Their research (Bereiter and Scardamalia 1993) into what makes an expert an expert points similarly to pattern recognition and learned procedures as key to increasing efficiency in solving problems.

WHAT KNOWLEDGE PATTERNS ARE THERE?

One big question, then, is: What are some of the more fundamental patterns used in playing the knowledge game? At the Kaieteur Institute for Knowledge Management, we have been asking this question for some time. What patterns can we discern through the smart prism of a knowledge lens? We have derived initial answers from three credible sources. On the one hand, we have analyzed many application case histories with a view to trying to decode the knowledge pattern in use. On the other hand, we have analyzed knowledge-enabling software, which in our view is congealed intelligence pertaining to the "know how" for various functions. A third source of pattern idea, is the many "schools of thought," each with their own approach to knowledge application. What we have extracted from these combined sources, we believe, is most instructive. It forms the basis of this paper. In summary, we view best-knowledge practices in business applications, knowledge-enabling software, and "knowledge schools of thought" as providing important clues about knowledge patterns in use. This means also that the taxonomy we have developed as a consequence is grounded in theory as well as practice.

EVOLVING THE META-KNOWLEDGE PLAYBOOK

Our categories, then, are real living patterns in use, and not concepts derived just from a theoretical point of view. Together they constitute a sort of meta-knowledge playbook. We have begun to integrate this understanding we have achieved of knowledge patterns into our strategy and practice playbook. As we do so, it will undoubtedly raise the way we play the knowledge game to a higher level. After all, in sports such as basketball, famous coaches such as Phil Jackson, formerly of the Chicago Bulls and now achieving success with the LA Lakers, use playbooks in their strategic masterminding of on-court action. These playbooks represent codified knowledge of the various discrete moves that can be run. Players rehearse the pattern sequence over and over to achieve a high degree of coordination and fluidity when it comes to rapidly and smoothly implementing one of these plays. The Bulls, for example, were famous for their triangle offense. Again, as Phil Jackson tells us, "the triangle offense is best described as five-man *tai chi*. The basic idea is to orchestrate the flow of movement in order to lure the defense off balance and create a myriad of openings on the floor. The system gets its name from one of the most common patterns of movement: the sideline triangle" (Jackson and Delahanty 1995). This is a sequence of play that has a characteristic pattern to it. It became a hallmark of the Jordan-era Chicago Bulls' winning performance.

PATTERNS MUST FIT THE CONTEXT

In Formula I motor sport, Ferrari has recently been recognized as being very clever about their use of fuel strategy. Depending on the track, the competitive lineup at the start of the race, and other related factors, cars may be put on a one-, two-, or three-stop strategy for refueling. A car may be placed on a one-stop fuel pattern. However, if developments and changing conditions during the race warrant it, this may be replaced with a two-stop pattern. The main point here is that, in real-world changing conditions, the appropriate pattern must be adapted to suit the context. If one's repertoire and understanding of knowledge patterns is limited, it will be hard to readily sense and adapt to changing circumstances of knowledge. In a game, the actual formulation of intelligent strategy is frequently the call of the coach masterminding the game plan. This has to be clearly and effectively communicated to the active players who will be executing in the field. The process is a dynamic interaction, and requires a multi-dimensional harnessing of experience, judgment, and tacit knowledge. In the game of golf, different clubs are carried in the bag, depending on the hole you need to reach and the situation you are in. So, similarly in the knowledge game, knowledge patterns are, in our view, the key "clubs" one must have in one's bag to learn to play. And it will take a lifetime of playing and practice to truly master all dimensions of the game and to learn to play all available approach shots. So we are not suggesting that applying patterns, in practice, is an automatic, static, or exact science. Rather, one has to have a "feel" for knowledge patterns and internalize an understanding of them, so that knowledge-pattern recognition is fast, fluid, and adaptive. When one has achieved mastery of knowledge patterns, one will have truly become wise about knowledge. The opposite is also true. Without such mastery, one is not seriously playing the game, but only fooling around.

THE LIMITATIONS OF AUTOMATED PATTERN RECOGNITION

It is interesting that, even in the sports arena today, software is playing a supporting role involving pattern analysis. There was, for example, a recent article in *Strategy & Business* about the attempt by the New York Knicks basketball team to use a new software developed by IBM named Scout. This software is deployed in order to analyze players' patterns of play. If you can determine that every time player X goes to the basket, he uses his right hand, then that's a pattern of play that could be very useful to know about. The logic of developing a meta-knowledge playbook based on well-understood knowledge patterns, therefore, makes sense and has exciting application potential. Yet, at the end of the day, the players on the court still must play the game and execute plays well. The Knicks may have used Scout. However, the technology can only enable and assist performance. Insights have to be treated as suggestive, not definitive. Using pattern recognition, therefore, will never be the whole story to the achievement of championship-level operational performance. However, it can clearly be a highly potent contributor to winning.

KNOWLEDGE PROFIT PATTERNS

There has been a recent argument about pattern recognition in business as a key to learning and profitability. The book, *Profit Patterns* by Slywotzy, Morrison, Moser, Mundt, and Quella, makes this case in a very compelling way. They argue that "the art of identifying, understanding, and exploiting patterns needs to become part of the mental process of every decision maker interested in creating sustained profit growth" (Slywotzy, Morrison, Moser, Mundt, and Quella 1999).

This we would entirely agree with. They also decipher and discuss three forms of knowledge profit patterns. While these are very useful, knowledge patterns are not their main focus. The three knowledge patterns they cite are:

- Product-to-customer knowledge—my product business teaches me about my customer
- Operations to knowledge—assets to essence
- Knowledge to product—expertise crystallized

Their analysis does beg for a more exhaustive treatment. Their contribution is nevertheless valuable and insightful. For the purposes of our present discussion, let us simply note and agree that there can be a powerful link between the ability to recognize knowledge patterns and profitability. So this gives us all the more reason and incentive to pay active attention to the mapping and application of knowledge patterns to business. A fuller discussion of knowledge profit patterns will be an exploration for a subsequent paper.

THE KNOWLEDGE-PATTERN TAXONOMY

We now present the fundamental, underlying knowledge patterns that we have decoded. These categories are not final or exhaustive. We fully expect the list to grow, morph, and evolve as more patterns are decoded and added to the list or as we find better ways to frame them. There is no ranking or priority to the list. The category descriptions are mere sketches and brief descriptions. The main point of the taxonomy is to demonstrate the range and cross section of patterns in use. Its purpose is suggestive and illustrative. The power of such a simple taxonomy is that a meta-array of strategic choices are clearly available for deployment, depending on the appropriateness of the context. Our current working core taxonomy of knowledge patterns therefore are as follows:

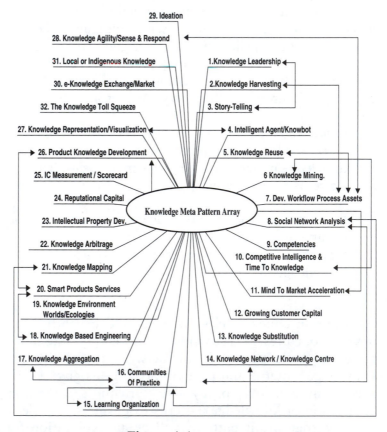

Figure 4-1

DESCRIPTION OF KNOWLEDGE PATTERNS

The thirty-two elements are described as follows:

(1) Knowledge Leadership

This attends to the development of teams of highly capable knowledge leaders. It could involve the development of a wide range of positions such chief knowledge officer, knowledge architect, knowledge steward, and so on (Mitchell and Bontis 2000; Bontis 2001). It could also involve the nurturing of grassroots knowledge activists and champions.

(2) Knowledge-harvesting

This approach is one of eliciting knowledge from knowledge workers, so that it can be recorded and codified as a corporate asset. It usually can involve interviewing and observing a knowledge subject and making explicit the know-how about a task that is currently undocumented. A sub-pattern of this technique is called *after-action-review* and is used by the U.S. military and others to extract lessons learned from actions carried out in the field.

(3) Storytelling

Storytelling is an ancient communication art. We have used it to share knowledge with others throughout history. It is used, as Moliere says, to simultaneously please, instruct, and educate. As a tool for the socialization and externalization of all aspects of knowledge, it can be most effective. David Snowden, from IBM's Institute for Knowledge Management, is a leading proponent of the use of storytelling. He suggests that the combination in stories of the use of metaphors, pictures, and images is a more enduring way to build common understanding and focus thinking in a knowledge-management program than other linear and literal communication methods. Steve Denning has also championed the use of storytelling with great effectiveness at the World Bank.

(4) Intelligent Agents/Knowbots

This involves the use of artificially intelligent software agents as surrogate knowledge agents. There are many types of agents available for use.

(5) Knowledge Reuse

This is an approach whereby knowledge is codified, shared, and made available for reuse. The benefit to an organization is that time can be saved by not having to reinvent the wheel. It eliminates redundancy. It can also be used to lift competencies across the organization by spreading know-how from where it is strong to areas where capabilities could be strengthened. Examples of organizations with application case histories where this has proven to be effective would be Texas Instruments and IBM. At Texas Instruments, over 80 percent of the software code written was reported as being reused. At IBM, templates for responding to requests for proposals cut down dramatically on the time and resources needed for salespeople to respond to potential customers.

(6) Knowledge-mining

Knowledge-mining is the analysis of large amounts of transaction data and information contained in knowledge bases for the extraction of useful insight in the form of developing trends, patterns, exploitable opportunities, or anomalies. A British supermarket, for example, is reported to have discovered a counterintuitive development that, on certain days, fathers come into their stores to pick up beer and diapers. Co-locating these items was more prospective for sales.

(7) Developing Workflow-process Assets

This would involve the mapping and embedding in software of rules, roles, and routing paths associated with a particular process. This process knowledge then becomes a process asset, a production script that is a part of an organization's infrastructural capital.

(8) Social-network Analysis

This approach is based on insights drawn from the field of anthropology. It is predicated on the notion that there are informal social networks through which much important peer-to-peer knowledge-sharing occurs. Attempts are made to understand the trusted networks and lines of influence that are normally hidden from view. This is important for nurturing change that does not run afoul of these hidden networks. A leading proponent of this technique is Karen Stephenson of Imperial College, London. There is also beginning to emerge complimentary social-network analysis software, which can be used to assist analysts in such a project.

(9) Competencies

Competency management is another tactic that has been used to address the question of what knowledge we have or need. In this approach, job positions are profiled in terms of the knowledge requirements for various positions. This can very useful for recruitment purposes. You can have a better basis for matching people with required skill sets. Internally, it can be used to locate people who have knowledge that can be useful to other areas of the enterprise. It can pinpoint corporate knowledge strengths and magnify gaps that exist. It can be used to help plan for meeting future needs. It can also give a clearer idea of areas where training should be funded and encouraged. Increasingly, ERP software systems such as SAP, PeopleSoft, JD Edwards, and Meta4 offer functionality to help HR units to do competency management.

(10) Competitive Intelligence

Competitive Intelligence has been described as one of the fast-growing new departments among the Fortune 500. Competitive Intelligence is growing as a discipline and as a profession, according to the Society of Competitive Intelligence Professionals (www.scip.org). It is ultimately centered on effective knowledge acquisition. It focuses on scanning a company's competitive landscape for threats, opportunities, risks, and advantages. Information is gathered in a coherent fashion, analyzed, and interpreted in a way that will support strategic decision-making. There is special use-software developed for assisting this function, such as Knowledge X (which was purchased by IBM), Cipher's Knowledge Assist, and Wincite Systems, Wincite. There is also special software being developed to support the building of war rooms, storyboarding, and the running of simulations. Larry Kahaner's book *Competitive Intelligence* is a basic primer covering this field (Kahaner 1996).

The following **Radar Chart** gives an example of how an organization's knowledge pattern capabilities can be represented graphically.

Figure 4-2

(11) Mind-to-market Acceleration

This approach works on streamlining and innovating, if not revolutionizing, the paths by which ideas go from concept to product or service and on to the customer.

(12) Growing Customer Capital

Knowledge of customers is now being recognized as a key to maintaining loyalty and meeting their ongoing needs. Unique customer knowledge and insight can be tremendously valuable. Don Peppers and Martha Rogers have successfully argued that having 1-to-1 knowledge of the customer can be golden (Peppers and Rogers 1993, 1997). Customer knowledge is not only about anticipating and serving their existing needs, but it can also be the foundation for capturing insight into future needs for goods and services. Moreover, if one has a high degree of customer interaction and intimacy, the customer may be willing to lend their knowledge to the project of co-creation of new products. So, from the standpoint of continuous improvement and innovation, there can be a significant competitive advantage to having the customer within your business web. Customer relationship management software, which has been evolving rapidly, can be harnessed to the project of growing customer knowledge capital.

(13) Knowledge Substitution

Knowledge substitution would, for example, attempt to swap smart logistics for physical-product storage. By knowing the timing required to service an operation, one can choreograph a movement of goods or services to minimize holding patterns.

(14) Knowledge Network, or Knowledge Center

This type of knowledge pattern usually is found in professional services firms. The idea is to have centralized repositories, or pointers to knowledge resources, so that the firm can harness all it knows in response to client needs. It is an integrating-technology network, usually supported by an intranet or portal. It functions as a clearinghouse for connecting knowledge seekers with knowledge providers. Approaches used, methodologies, case histories, and lessons learned are collated, so that they may be readily available to all members of the firm.

(15) The Learning Organization

The stock of knowledge in the world is now doubling every three years or less, according to some experts (Bontis 1999). Every organization is being challenged to ensure that its people learn continuously in order to keep up and stay ahead of the competition. A learning organization strategy is one where leadership is assigned responsibility for coordinating learning efforts. Every attempt is made to foster a culture of active learning and to provide learners with the technology, financial resources, and time to engage in learning that supports the mission of the company. Every effort is made to ensure that acquisition of new knowledge and knowledge-sharing are appropriately enabled and supported. The learning organization can mean two things: it can mean an organization that learns and/or an organization that encourages learning in its people. It should ultimately mean both.

(16) Communities of Practice

These are informal peer networks of knowledge workers who connect around shared group needs and goals. The idea is to cultivate a culture where learning is socialized and tacit plus explicit knowledge can be exchanged in a trusted community network. The World Bank, for example, has deliberately nurtured the spawning of such communities in recognition of their ability to socialize knowledge. Inherent in the idea of communities of practice are the principles of self-organization, networking, and learning.

(17) Knowledge Aggregation

Knowledge aggregation involves the building of a deep knowledge base that can serve to attract, serve, and sustain members of an online community. Amazon.com, for example, began by aggregating and organizing knowledge about books, including where they could be found and what members thought about particular books.

(18) Knowledge-based Engineering

This type of knowledge approach is mostly to be found in manufacturing environments. Knowledge about engineering design and what was done on a particular project are documented in a knowledge base, so that this knowledge is not lost when people leave. It is basically the codification of specialized and complex engineering knowledge in shareable repositories.

(19) Knowledge Environments–Ecologies–Worlds

This approach focuses on surrounding the knowledge worker with environments that are conducive and supportive to doing knowledge work.

(20) Smart Products and Services

A smart product or service is one that is intelligent, it contains congealed know-how. There is a wide spectrum of such products and services. A bookseller who uses a permission-based approach to profile customers, and then alerts them when a new book on their favorite topic, might be described as pursuing a smart-service strategy. A product such as an Otis elevator equipped with self-diagnostics, which represent the best knowledge the company has available, and which dials out to request service help well before on-site facilities management people are even aware of a developing problem. That might be classed as a smart product. Products that are designed to adapt and learn and to give the user feedback using neural network technology might also be deemed to be intelligent. This is a

Figure 4-3

strategy that can be used for varying purposes. Maintaining customer loyalty, better adapting and fitting customer needs, learning from customers, differentiating one's product from those of competitors, and achieving higher degrees of reliability—these are among the possible benefits.

(20a) Service and Support—Sub-pattern

This approach essentially involves enabling front-line knowledge workers to have the right answers for internal or external customers. This may involve the use of diagnostic knowledge bases where the accumulated knowledge about problems is stored for easy retrieval. It could encompass, at a more sophisticated level, the use of performance support and buddy systems. The latter are directories to experts who may have the answers to help the knowledge worker resolve a question they are unable to answer on their own.

(21) Knowledge-mapping

Knowledge-mapping can be a very powerful technique. We view the *Human Genome Project,* whereby all the known genes in the human body are being mapped, as a knowledge-mapping project writ large. Making maps of what knowledge exists in the organization, and where it is, can be very a very powerful and useful resource. It can facilitate understanding, navigation, and matching of knowledge-seeking with content and content providers. Allied with the use of knowledge portal, workflow, and document-management software, or other related types of enablers, the creation of yellow pages, directories, and corporate taxonomies make it easier to identify, locate, and reach corporate knowledge resources. This can save time, reduce cost, and enhance the quality of knowledge performance. In London, England, taxi drivers have a guidebook called "The Knowledge" that is a compendium of knowledge about their city and a time-honoured navigational reference resource.

(22) Knowledge Arbitrage

"Global firms, on the other hand, form multicultural teams that work across borders and within product lines in order to gain economies of scale and scope. They also engage in what is best called *knowledge arbitrage*: the efficient sourcing and distribution of ideas and products drawing on the best ideas and lowest priced inputs from around the globe. This means looking at the world as one economic unit, not a matrix of business divisions focused on countries and regions," says John Thornton, Chairman of Goldman Sachs Asia and choice as a Global Leader for Tomorrow by the World Economic Forum in 1993.

(23) Developing Intellectual Property Assets

The best case where this applies is where companies hold, or are generating, significant intellectual property assets. Dow Chemical is a well-known example of a company that has an extensive patent portfolio. By better identification, organization, classification, valuation, and management of its intellectual capital assets, it was able to use them to create more value than existed previously. Essentially, an intellectual property strategy is one involving paying more critical attention to intellectual property assets from creation to disposition. It involves taking steps to protect and extract latent value from such assets. There are software vendors, such as Aurigin Systems, who are highly focused on developing enablers to facilitate the management of such assets. The CEO of Aurigin recently co-authored, with David Kline, a relevant book on the subject called *Rembrandts in the Attic* (Rivette and Kline 2000).

(24) Reputational Capital

This is an approach in which attention is focused on ensuring that the image, brand, and reputation of the firm is carefully developed, enhanced, and maintained.

(25) Intellectual Capital Measurement–scorecard

The balanced scorecard is an approach articulated by Kaplan and Norton. It is one performance-measurement approach that moves beyond the gap that results when only traditional indicators are used. In this scheme, knowledge is included as a factor in organizational metrics. It is based on the concept that what is measured gets done. Therefore, by having a measurement system for organizations that also takes into account their effectiveness in terms of their use of intellectual and human capital, it is designed to ensure that there is a consistent alignment in the way attention is paid to harnessing knowledge, along with other factor inputs. Several vendors have developed software to help companies monitor their business performance using a balanced-scorecard approach. Examples are Gentia and Corvu.

(26) Knowledge Discovery and Innovation

Knowledge discovery involves the generation and production of new knowledge from R and D explorations or from synthesizing new lessons from business performance in one domain that can be ported to another knowledge domain.

(27) Knowledge Representation and/or Visualization

We increasingly face challenges where the data-set we are trying to analyze is too large (or small) and complex for us to readily make a meaning of it. Interpretation and navigation can often be facilitated by having information in a knowledge base presented in a visually more meaningful way. With software from Visible Decisions, Inc., for example, you may be able to dynamically "helicopter" through a report and get a better understanding of its implications than if it was viewed literally.

(28) Knowledge Agility—Sensing and Responding

Because of the chaotic and fast-changing nature of many markets, some organizations are being designed based on an agility paradigm.

They are equipped with a flexible, sense-and-respond, adaptable metabolism. To be able to quickly and fluidly process incoming knowledge from customers and the business environment, the enterprise is enveloped in a smart-technology matrix.

"Patterns of interaction between companies and their customers are changing profoundly, and the interpenetration or overlap is becoming ubiquitous. This requires an agility of thought in seeing the new patterns, responding to ever-changing conditions, and in being able to discard a successful product, service, or way of working to make room for the new." —Dr. Charles Savage.

(29) Ideation

Ideation is the label we give to a group of approaches that have in common—peering into the future. This involves imagineering, running scenarios, and conceptualizing future states and how the company will be able to anticipate, prepare, and exploit emerging developments. Scandia, for example, under the leadership of Leif Edvinsson, set up Scandia Future Centres. These were playgrounds for testing ideas about how the future might evolve and for conceptualizing how the organization could better anticipate, visualize, get ready for, and create an advantage in the marketplace by knowing more and seeing more clearly. It is a combination of effective knowledge creation and knowledge acquisition. Software for mind-mapping, mind-scaping, visualization, modeling, and simulation is increasingly available to assist such efforts.

(30) E-knowledge Markets

The e-knowledge market approach explicitly recognizes that there is a de facto marketplace for knowledge and ideas. It is a way of better organizing and supporting the trade or commerce in knowledge and intellectual capital. It is the "e-Bay for ideas" model. There are many variations on the knowledge market theme. Sub-patterns include such models as the knowledge store, the e-learning exchange, the question-and-answer exchange and/or experts exchange, the intellectual property exchange, the talent exchange, the knowledge auction, the investment knowledge exchange, and the community-knowledge or social-capital exchange. These approaches are so potentially revolutionary in their significance that they may yet come to represent a disruptive technology innovation in relation to the future management of knowledge. This rapidly evolv-

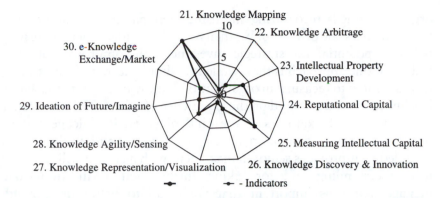

Figure 4-4

ing domain is profiled at our "Meta Portal to e-Knowledge Markets" at http://www.kikm.org.

(31) Local or Indigenous Knowledge

This is the conservation, extraction, and harnessing of intimate knowledge of the local environment or culture that could be extremely valuable. Ethnobotanists are frequently focused on this realm.

(32) The Knowledge Toll–knowledge Squeeze

This is a pattern whereby a company tries to hold a monopolistic or dominant position in a field of knowledge and to extract a fee for access to, and use of, this knowledge. It is akin to a utility business model.

CONCLUSIONS

These are, therefore, some of the fundamental patterns we have observed in our research. They encapsulate major intellectual capital strategy choices in playing the knowledge game. We have argued that these patterns can be very powerful for aiding understanding, communication, training, and alignment. However, they can also be very powerful as a diagnostic and assessment tool. This is what we work with in completing our knowledge assessments and knowledge-strategy assessment for clients. In our audits, we ask how adept a particular organization is at recognizing and using these patterns. Each question is scored on a scale of 1 to 10. We then have a clear idea where there may be great potential for strategic investment and improvement. The beauty of this approach is that, while it is simple, fast, and easy to use, it is calibrated to measure an organization's knowledge-strengths where it is known to count, based on the experience of others. The three radar charts above are examples of the kind of visual knowledge-pattern profiling we produce of an organization's strengths and weaknesses in knowledge. It provides senior management with a clear baseline metric for understanding and for taking further action. In knowledge management it is important that we begin to better understand, recognize, internalize, and harness the fundamental knowledge patterns applicable to the game. Knowledge-pattern recognition is now a critical skill-set and a core competency.

REFERENCES

Arthur, B. 1998. *Fast Company* 18: 93.

Bailey, J. 1996. *After Thought—The Computer Challenge To Human Intelligence.* New York: Basic Books.

Bereiter, C. and M. Scardamalia. 1993. *Surpassing Ourselves.* Chicago: Open Court.

Bontis, N. 2001. "CKO Wanted—Evangelical Skills Necessary: A Review of the Chief Knowledge Officer Position," *Knowledge and Process Management* 8, 1: 29–38.

Bontis, N. 1999. "Managing Organizational Knowledge by Diagnosing Intellectual Capital: Framing and Advancing the State of the Field," *International Journal of Technology Management* 18, 5/6/7/8: 433–62.

Farrell, W. 1998. *How Hits Happen.* New York: Harper Collins.

Hamel, G. 2000. *Leading The Revolution.* Boston: Harvard Business School Press.

Kahaner, L. 1996. *Competitive Intelligence.* New York: Simon and Schuster.

Kline,G. 2000. *Fast Company* 38: 296.

Jackson, P. and H. Delahanty. 1995. *Sacred Hoops.* New York: Hyperion.

Mitchell M. and N. Bontis. 2000. "Aligning Human Capital with Business Strategy: Foreign Bank and Luxury Retail.," In L*eading Knowledge Management and Learning,* ed. D. Bonner. Alexandria, Va.: ASTD.

Moschen, M. 1997. *Fast Company* 11: 174.

Myhrvold, N. 1998. *Fast Company* 15: 83.

Peppers, D. and M. Rogers. 1993. *The One To One Future*. New York: Currency Doubleday.

Peppers, D. and M. Rogers. 1997. *Enterprise One To One*. New York: Currency Doubleday.

Rivette, K and D. Kline. 2000. *Rembrandts In The Attic*. Boston: Harvard Business School Press.

Slywotzy, Morrison, Moser, Mundt, and Quella. 1999. *Profit Patterns*. New York: Times Business–Random House.

5

COMPETITIVE CAPITAL:

A FOURTH PILLAR OF INTELLECTUAL CAPITAL?

Helen N. Rothberg
School of Management, Marist College, Poughkeepsie, U.S.A.
HNRothberg@aol.com

and

G. Scott Erickson
Division of Economics and Business, SUNY College at Oneonta, New York, U.S.A.
erickss@oneonta.edu

ABSTRACT

This chapter considers the similarities between intellectual capital management systems and competitive intelligence systems. Each concerns itself with collecting scattered knowledge from within and without the organization, codifying that knowledge, analyzing it, and redistributing it, as appropriate. By applying intellectual capital principles to competitive intelligence, its management can likely be improved. Similarly, intellectual capital managers may have something to learn from intelligence professionals.

INTRODUCTION

Intellectual capital (IC), also referred to in knowledge management (KM) theory and practice, has developed rapidly over the past decade. Scholars generally discuss three major areas comprising intellectual capital: human capital, structural capital, and collaborative/relational capital.

This chapter proposes to add a fourth area to the KM structure, that is, competitive capital. Competitive capital is generated through activities in competitive intelligence (CI) systems (Rothberg and Erickson 1999) that are conceptually and practically similar to intellectual capital management processes (Rothberg and Erickson 1998). As CI deals with matters outside the organization but not with friendly collaborators, it does not fit neatly into the current KM paradigm (Davenport, De Long, and Beers 1998; Erickson and Rothberg 1999; Rothberg and Erickson 1998).

The organization of the chapter will include a review of the IC-KM literature and practice. A review of competitive intelligence concepts and practice, with an emphasis on the similarities between the two fields, will follow. Competitive intelligence techniques, as well as the layers of competitive advantage that can be obtained from CI programs, will be covered. Finally, some implications for intellectual capital, given the presence of CI activities, will be discussed.

INTELLECTUAL CAPITAL

Intellectual capital theory developed out of practice, as firms increasingly recognized the value of soft or intangible assets. As firms with few hard assets, such as Microsoft, obtained incredible market capitalizations and as substantial amounts of knowledge walked out the door during the layoffs of the early 1990s, observers and scholars attempted to define and measure these knowledge assets.

Knowledge management (KM) has become an often-used synonym for intellectual capital, and we will use the KM acronym to avoid confusion between the similar CI and IC abbreviations. Knowledge management, evolving as a topic of concern for business, developed in the early 1990s. Interestingly, and unlike many contemporary management trends, KM came more from practice than from academia. As noted above, part of this was because of the corporate managers' awareness of unmeasured assets within their organizations that would benefit from recognition and active management.

Skandia (1996) and Leif Edvinsson (Edvinsson and Malone 1997) are often credited with the first substantive attempts to measure, manage, and report on intellectual capital, and Thomas Stewart (1991; 1997) of *Fortune* was instrumental in creating interest in the business press. Nonaka and Takeuchi (1995) developed a scholarly framework for the discipline that has since received attention in a number of the major academic journals (Davenport, DeLong, and Beers 1998; Nahapiet and Ghoshal 1998; Hansen, Nohria, and Tierney 1999).

Theorists (Bontis 1998, 1999; Davenport and Prusak 1998) suggest that employees throughout the organization possess individual knowledge about aspects of their jobs that are often difficult to express or communicate to others. This personal know-how is termed *tacit knowledge*. The goal of organizations is to identify tacit knowledge throughout the firm, capture it from individuals, systematize it in an organizational knowledge base, and use it to improve performance of individuals throughout the firm. If tacit knowledge can be codified in this way, it can become explicit knowledge, an intellectual asset of the firm. In fully exploiting this asset, the firm will want to redistribute the knowledge back to individuals. In leveraging the knowledge in this way, each individual in the organization could theoretically have access to the entire know-how of all other employees throughout the firm.

Intellectual capital is typically grouped into three categories: human, structural, and relational-collaborative capital. *Human capital* refers to individual knowledge about how to perform a particular function. From the assembly line worker who knows how to order or perform required activities to the research scientist who understands how to bring a concept to prototype, individuals throughout the organization possess tacit knowledge about how to accomplish their jobs.

Structural capital refers to the systems in place that support the human capital. Knowledge about how to organize and utilize capital equipment, labor (including human capital), processes, and so on, can also be of value. Managers within the firm who know how to best arrange and exploit firm resources are also a knowledge asset.

Finally, *relational* or *collaborative capital* refers to knowledge about dealing with those outside of the organization. Originally conceptualized as customer capital, the idea has been extended in successive permutations to include dealing with all outside entities, not just customers. So the salesperson who understands how to stroke a particular customer, the procurement specialist who knows how to deal with a particular supplier, and the operations manager who can coordinate with a collaborator all possess relational capital that makes such outside-the-firm activities operate more efficiently.

Managing intellectual capital, of course, involves discovering, collecting, and dispersing this knowledge. Special concerns include obtaining cooperation from individuals who associate knowledge with power and developing systems to manage knowledge codification and sharing. But even if difficulties are apparent, there can be little doubt that most organizations can dramatically improve their knowledge management activities, thus improving their own competitiveness.

COMPETITIVE INTELLIGENCE

Competitive intelligence has also grown apace over the past decade. *Competitive intelligence* refers to any information-gathering activities, pursuing knowledge inside and outside the organization, or reflecting on competitive activities and strategies (Gilad 1994; Levinthal and Myatt 1994; Bonthous 1995; Prescott 1995). Although some firms and individuals may cross the line, most CI activity is both legal and ethical. The Society of Competitive Intelligence Professionals (SCIP) maintains a code of ethics that stresses the use of appropriate techniques adhering more to aspects of intelligence than espionage.

Thus competitive intelligence, as commonly understood within the discipline, includes monitoring public information sources, collecting competitive knowledge possessed by employees, and actively seeking out information concerning particular competitors. In terms of secondary sources, common activities include monitoring patent and trademark activity, financial filings, Internet activity, and media reports. Competitors discerned, for example, that Amazon.com was moving into greeting cards when the company registered the domain names amazongreetings.com and amazoncard.com (Nelson and Anders 1999). Similarly, a recent patent procedure involving Amgen was notable for the number of interested industry observers in the gallery (Bennett and Mantz 2000).

Often the best sources for information on competitors are a firm's own employees. Employees can overhear conversations on flights and in airports, can gather information at trade shows, or can pick up tidbits by talking to suppliers or customers. One particularly popular method for obtaining competitive information in high-technology fields is simply hiring employees who have knowledge concerning a competitor. While noncompetition agreements can get in the way of such strategies (as can accusations of poaching employees), the practice is widespread and includes such high-profile examples as Amazon.com-Wal-Mart (Nelson and Anders 1999) and Cisco-Lucent (Solomon and Thurm 2000).

Firms can also aggressively gather information on competitors, purposely setting employees or consultants to the task of monitoring competitive activities. Palm, for example, planted an employee at a session that Microsoft had organized to demonstrate Windows CE to "enthusiasts" (Tam 2000). This aggressiveness can sometimes straddle the ethical line as well, as in the celebrated Oracle-Microsoft dumpster-diving incident (Bridis, Simpson, and Mangalindan 2000).

Seeking to organize their competitive intelligence operations, firms will set up systems to gather relevant competitive knowledge within the firm while collecting any available or obtainable information outside the firm. Motorola, one of the pioneers of competitive intelligence, established an intelligence unit in the early 1980s that provides information to the highest decision-making levels (King and Bravin 2000). The point of the unit is to gather and analyze the information, providing intelligence for upper management upon which it may take action.

In addition to information about competitors, competitive intelligence units have evolved to further integrate economic, political, social, and psychological information (Eells and Nehemkis 1984). Competitive intelligence systems (CIS) have taken this practice a step farther by integrating with knowledge management systems. A CIS creates the structure around which information flows into and through a firm (Gilad 1994). Figure 5-1 portrays a typical CIS system. This four-ring model is fueled by an organization's grassroots—employees who contribute information and insight. The second ring is a structured network of "expert analysts" who offer their technical skill, knowledge, and personal information, and contribute to and conduct analyses. These experts are primarily firm employees as well as a composite of outside consultants.

The third ring is a convergence point for information: the CI facilitator (CIF). The CIF is the "decoder of market signals" (Gilad 1994) and is responsive to senior decision-makers such as the firm CEO or Strategic Business Unit President, the fourth ring. The CIF pieces together contributions from the firm's competitive knowledge network, that is, its grassroots data-gathering system, its expert ring

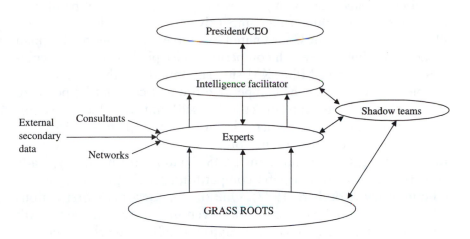

Figure 5-1

reports, and its cadre of outside sources. As part of the executive cabinet, the CIF ensures that objective, impartial information and analysis are available when strategic issues are discussed and courses of action are orchestrated (Erickson and Rothberg 1998). If the CIF does not have access to the fourth ring, or executive management, then the utility of his or her activities will never be realized, and executive management may not access essential intelligence for their decision processes.

Human capital is the heart of the CIS. Through individuals submitting information or experts applying their specialized knowledge and networks, IC contributes information and generates competitive knowledge. By creating special CI units or "shadow teams," a CIS can transform IC into competitive capital—competitive knowledge assets arising from institutionalized market-driven intelligence and analysis created by structurally embedded intelligence teams (Rothberg and Erickson 1999).

COMPETITIVE CAPITAL

This type of competitive intelligence system should begin to look familiar to intellectual capital scholars and practitioners. Information is available throughout the organization (as well as outside it), and firms seek to gather it together, organizing it into a useful knowledge bank. As appropriate, it can then be further leveraged by distributing back out to employees in the field who may be able to make use of it in countering competitive efforts. Consider an example. A saleswoman for Coordinated Resources, a reseller for Herman Miller, was able to research competitive sales pitches regarding cubicles. At the Herman Miller KM site, she found out that other salespeople had noted that the competitive product couldn't be powered (i.e., nothing plugged into the cubicle itself) and was able to use this competitive information in her sales presentation (Peterson 1999).

The similarities grow even more evident with the application of the shadow team technique in a CIS. Shadow teams are typically constructed around a specific competitor, specific product, or specific industry (Rothberg 1997). One of Lou Gerstner's first actions when he came in was to construct "venture teams" around IBM's core product areas (Behnke and Slyton 1998). Similarly, Microsoft maintains a shadow team that monitors Linux (Gomes 1999).

The shadow team is established as a central body that gathers and analyzes all available knowledge concerning the targeted company or other concern. As with any CI effort, public sources are monitored, employees are solicited, and other information is pursued by appropriate means. The shadow team, with its specialized background, is enjoined to codify and analyze all this knowledge, providing intelligence to decision-makers upon which they may take action. As with other CI techniques, the shadow team's knowledge can be leveraged by redistribution back out to employees in the field.

One interesting aspect of shadow teams that can inform other KM areas is the layering of expertise that can develop. On one level, the shadow team can uncover competitive activities, including particular processes along the value chain. In particular, processes kept hidden by competitors may be discovered by the shadow team, through previous employees of the competitor, patent filings, or other typical CI techniques. In such situations, the firm can copy or counter processes and activities that might pose a competitive threat to it.

On a second level, however, the shadow team may have the expertise to put together the various pieces of information and discern not just proprietary processes and activities but also the underlying strategies of the competitor. One firm in the cereal industry, for example, based on reports from an employee of a new facility being built by a competitor, explored sources of information within its own firm as to the nature of the building. From these internal sources, the firm was able to identify the facility as a test-and-production location for the introduction of a new product. Armed with knowledge of this strategic intent of its competitor, the firm was able to take steps to counter the introduction. An effective shadow team can develop a capacity to really understand its competitor(s), enabling it to think in the manner of those competitors.

Ideally, this understanding can pass to an even higher level, as the shadow team not only uncovers current strategies of its competitor(s) but develops a capacity to think in their manner. Sufficient time spent in observing and studying the activities and strategies of a target firm can allow the shadow team to develop an empathetic understanding of the way the competitor thinks and acts. Such empathy can allow the shadow team to anticipate strategies and actions before they even occur.

Competitive capital is a product of this type of shadow team activity. Shadow teams are charged with integrating and analyzing information that ultimately influences the strategy development processes of the firm. Similarly, the competitive capital they create can have a significant impact on competitive advantage. Because shadow team activities are created and sanctioned by the firm, with proper documentation, their products (as is the case with other intellectual capital) may be protected under the U.S. Economic Espionage Act of 1996 (Erickson and Rothberg 1998).

Shadow teams, through the CIS, potentially can become a core competence of the firm, and thus assist in identifying and sustaining "layers of competitive advantage" (Gilad 1996) or in creating the "organizational advantage" (Nahapiet and Ghoshal 1998) necessary for success in the current hypercompetitive, knowledge-intensive climate. With the added advantage of creating identifiable knowledge assets, competitive capital generated by shadow teams may be protected by law.

CONCLUSIONS

Intellectual capital managers should consider whether the competitive intelligence function should be part of their responsibilities. Given the similarities between the systems, much of the work that has gone into developing knowledge management could conceivably be transferred to competitive intelligence activities as well. Further, as long as tacit knowledge is being collected throughout the organization, why not structure the process to obtain competitiveness in knowledge in addition to that in the other areas?

Competitive capital can benefit an organization in many of the same ways as other forms of intellectual capital. Simply by capturing the full information of the firm regarding competitors and processing it for future use, a competitive intelligence system can gain many of the same efficiency advantages as may be seen in other areas. But even more important, competitive capital offers opportunities for success in the marketplace because of superior strategies. At its highest levels, firms can anticipate and outmaneuver competitors, allowing sustainable competitive advantage going beyond process advantages.

REFERENCES

Behnke, L. and P. Slyton. 1998. Shaping a corporate intelligence function at IBM. *Competitive Intelligence Review* 9, 2: 4–9.

Bennet, J. and B. Mantz. 2000. Amgen's patent infringement trial draws rivals' lawyers in search of data. *Wall Street Journal* (26 June): A43A.

Bonthous, J. M. 1995. Intelligence as learning. *Competitive Intelligence Review* 6, 1: 4–14.

Bontis, N. 1998. Intellectual capital: an exploratory study that develops measures and models. *Management Decision* 36: 2, 63–76.

Bontis, N. 1999. Managing Organizational Knowledge by Diagnosing Intellectual Capital: Framing and Advancing the State of the Field. *International Journal of Technology Management* 18, 5/6/7/8: 433–62.

Bridis, T., G. Simpson, and Mylene Mangalindan. 2000. When Microsoft's spin got too good, Oracle hired private investigators. *Wall Street Journal* (29 June): 1.

Davenport, T. H., D. W. De Long, and M. C. Beers. 1998. Successful knowledge management projects. *Sloan Management Review* Winter: 43–57.

Davenport, T. H. and Prusak, L. 1998. *Working Knowledge.* Boston: Harvard Business School Press.

Edvinsson, L. and M. Malone. 1997. *Intellectual Capital: Realizing Your Company's True Value by Finding Its Hidden Brain Power.* New York: Harper Collins.

Eells, R. and P. Nehemkis. 1984. *Corporate Intelligence and Espionage.* New York: Macmillan.

Erickson, G. S. and H. N. Rothberg. 1998. Protecting intellectual capital in a competitive intelligence world. *Annual Research Volume, American Society for Competitiveness Annual Conference.* Boston, Mass., 22–24 October: 346–56.

Gilad, B. 1994. *Business Blindspots.* Chicago: Probus Publishing Company.

Gilad, B. 1996. Strategic intent and strategic intelligence. In *The Art and Science of Business Intelligence,* eds. B. Gilad and P. Herring. Greenwich, Conn.: JAI Press.

Gomes, L. 1999. Upstart Linux draws a Microsoft attack team. *Wall Street Journal* (21 May): B1, B9.

Hansen, M., N. Nohria, and T. Tierney. 1999. What's your strategy for managing knowledge? *Harvard Business Review* March/April: 106–116.

King, Jr., N. and J. Bravin. 2000. Call it mission impossible inc.—corporate spying firms thrive. *Wall Street Journal* (3 July): B1, B4.

Levinthal, D. and J. Myatt. 1994. Co-evolution of capabilities and industries: the evolution of mutual fund processing. *Strategic Management Journal* 15: 45–62.

Naphapiet, J. and S. Ghoshal. 1998. Social capital, intellectual capital, and the organizational advantage. *Academy of Management Review* 23, 2: 242–66.

Nelson, E. and G. Anders. 1999. Wal-mart, Amazon.com settle fight over recruitment and trade secrets. *Wall Street Journal* (6 April): A3.

Nonaka, I. and H. Takeuchi. 1995. *The Knowledge-Creating Company: How Japanese Companies Create the Dynamics of Innovation.* New York: Oxford University Press.

Peterson, A. 1999. Making the sale. *Wall Street Journal* (15 November): R16.

Prescott, J. 1995. Competitive intelligence as a core capability. *SCIP Europe Spring Conference* (30–31 March) Copenhagen.

Rothberg, H. 1997. Fortifying competitive intelligence systems with shadow teams. *Competitive Intelligence Review* 8, 2: 3–11.

Rothberg, H. N. and G. S. Erickson. 1999. Competitive capital: a sustainable source of competitive advantage. *American Society for Competitiveness Annual Conference* (5–7 October) Atlanta, Ga.

Skandia. 1996. Power of Innovation, Intellectual Capital. *Interim Annual Report Supplement.*

Solomon, D. and S. Thurm. 2000. Lucent files suit to keep ex-employees from disclosing sensitive data to Cisco. *Wall Street Journal* (21 June): B5.

Stewart, T. A. 1997. *Intellectual Capital: The New Wealth of Organizations.* New York: Doubleday.

Stewart, T. A. 1991. Brainpower. *Fortune* (3 June): 44–57.

Tam, P. 2000. Palm puts up its fists as Microsoft attacks hand-held pc market. *Wall Street Journal* (8 August): A1, A14.

6

STRATEGIC KNOWLEDGE SOURCING, INTEGRATION, AND ASSIMILATION:

A CAPABILITIES-PORTFOLIO PERSPECTIVE

George Tovstiga
ABB Business Services Ltd., Business Consulting, Baden, Switzerland
George.tovstiga@ch.abb.com

and

David W. Birchall
Henley Management College, Greenlands, Henley-on-Thames, Oxford-shire, U.K.
Davidbi@henleymc.ac.uk

ABSTRACT

Strategic management has a key role in managing the firm's internal and external portfolio of knowledge-driven capabilities to match the changing nature of opportunities and challenges in the competitive environment. In order to make the most of its knowledge, a firm must master at least three steps. First, its managers need to "know what the firm knows." Then, if that knowledge is strategically relevant and valuable, it needs to be exploited. Finally, new knowledge streams need to be sourced and successfully integrated into the firm's existing portfolio of capabilities.

The authors present a methodology that can be used to identify key capabilities and also the knowledge internalization trajectory that describes (1) the sourcing, (2) the internalization of new knowledge streams and, ultimately, (3) the reconfiguration of existing knowledge in the firm for maximum impact. Entirely new capabilities need to be developed and implemented for each of the three stages. We explore implications of these in the context of the organization's culture, its management structures, and practices. The paper closes with a case illustration of how the capabilities might be established that enable a "new economy" firm to derive competitive impact from its strategic knowledge sourcing capabilities.

INTRODUCTION

Leading enterprises consistently succeed in demonstrating responsiveness with rapid and flexible innovation. Innovation, ultimately, is the key driver for new value generation. Firms that succeed at creating better value to increasingly multiple stakeholders have the competitive edge over their competitors. Traditionally, this has simply meant bringing new and better products and services to the marketplace in less time or at lower cost. A continuous stream of incremental innovations has been sufficient for many businesses to maintain their competitive position in the face of their traditional competition. But in the new economy, challenges to the old order are such that organizations must constantly seek what Hamel (2000) describes as *business concept innovation*. This is innovation not only in product, processes, and management systems but also in the more fundamental business model. In order for the firm to maintain competitiveness, experimentation with these new business models must keep pace with the speed at which the new economy is moving and must be seen as an ongoing necessity.

Much has been written about the concept of core capabilities. These are defined as those capabilities that give the firm its competitive advantage; they have been accumulated over time and they are not easily replicated or imitated (Hamel 1994). In an earlier paper, the authors distinguished the range from "hard" to "soft" capabilities, identifying those embedded within technology and systems that might be classified as "hard" contrasted with aspects of the organization's culture and unwritten ways of working that are "soft." Innovation in organizations is the result of the application of capabilities in acquiring and integrating new knowledge into the organization's functioning. Clearly, organizations do not need control over all the necessary capabilities in order to develop innovative solutions, but the lower the degree of organizational control, the less likely that sustainable advantage will result (Birchall and Tovstiga 2000).

Innovation occurs at the interface of planes representing new knowledge; it feeds on new streams of knowledge and appropriate capabilities (which in themselves, by definition, are manifestations of organizational knowledge). Firms need to either generate or attract new knowledge in order to capitalize on innovation. However, firms can be innovative only if they succeed in creating the requisite, new organizational space for assimilating, integrating, and, ultimately, nurturing the new knowledge. Firms can source new knowledge in various ways (Christensen and Overdorf 2000; Halleloid and Simonin 1994; Van Rossum and Omta 1998):

1. **Internal Development.** New organizational structures are created within the organization's existing boundaries in which new knowledge is created on the basis of existing internal capabilities. This has traditionally been the mode of choice for most firms.
2. **Assisted Internal Development.** Other firms, or external consultants, are employed to assist in the acquisition of a firm's development of capabilities.
3. **Direct Market Procurement.** Firm purchases bundles of specific information or capabilities in the marketplace. The real return on the investment occurs only when the acquiring firm succeeds in converting the purchased "information" into "actionable knowledge."
4. **Strategic Alliances and Joint Ventures.** Firm cooperates with another firm to acquire, build, and internalize new knowledge and capabilities, but maintains its own identity. Cross-cultural aspects become increasingly important.
5. **Merger and Acquisition.** Firm acquires an external organization whose knowledge and capabilities closely match the requirements of the new task.
6. **Networked, Virtual Organizations.** Multiple firms create flexible linkages to attain common or complementary linkages in a boundaryless virtual web. As we move into the new economy,

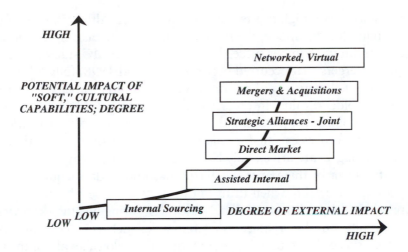

Figure 6-1 *Different modes of knowledge acquisition; Degree of external impact and potential impact of "soft," cultural capabilities*

knowledge flows and transactions within networks are becoming the imperative for rapid access to new capabilities.

Arguably, as we move down the list of acquisition modes, the degree of organizational control over the resources and processes, the complexity of integration, and the potential impact of "soft," cultural-related capabilities on the likelihood of success increases exponentially, along with the degree of potential for external impact, as suggested schematically in Figure 6-1.

Indeed, as we move into the new economy, we find both pioneering and traditional firms in the midst of fundamental change—from monolithic and rigid organizational entities geared for repetitive transactions and routine activities toward flexible and agile organizational forms that can readily accommodate innovation, novelty, and change. This new organizational form has been referred to as the *fluid, networked organization* (see, for example, Birchall and Lyons 1995 and Maira and Thomas 1998). We argue that, as firms move toward forms of knowledge acquisition with significant potential external impact, complex, "soft" capabilities become more important.

Consider also that in today's technology-driven economy, speed is increasingly becoming a key competitive differentiator. Firms need rapid access to new knowledge, technologies, markets—and fresh talent. They can no longer wait, nor can they afford, to develop all their capabilities internally. Hence, we find more and more firms opting for the modes of acquisitions with high degrees of external impact. Although many firms are opting for this mode, the number failing at the task is substantially greater than the number succeeding. In a recent KPMG study of the 700 biggest mergers that occurred between 1996 and 1998, fully 83 percent of the studied mergers did not improve the acquirer's ability to increase its shareholders' value. In other words, these mergers failed to achieve the stated objectives justifying the exercise (Rigdon 2000). Knowledge-acquisition processes fail for many different reasons. Often they fail when managers are driven only by immediate, short-term benefits of the targeted firm. In this paper we allege that knowledge-acquisition processes fail invariably when firms fail to invest sufficient effort in developing key organizational capabilities for bringing the knowledge successfully into the organization. Companies such as Cisco, which consistently succeed in sourcing new, external technology, go about the task in a very deliberate and planned way. They rely on carefully nurtured integration capabilities to make the new acquisition a success.

In this paper we build on earlier work in which we propose a three-stage knowledge-acquisition trajectory against the backdrop of the organization's portfolio of existing capabilities (Birchall and Tovstiga 2000). In this paper we deepen the discussion on the nature and scope of the organizational capabilities required for each of the three stages of the trajectory: (1) sourcing, (2) integrating, and (3) assimilation of new knowledge in the firm.

ORGANIZATIONAL KNOWLEDGE AND CAPABILITIES

Competitive advantage is gained through the deliberate and purposeful management of the firm's stock of knowledge. For the most part, this knowledge will be embedded in the firm's portfolio of key or core capabilities. We understand capabilities to be bundles of constituent skills and technologies—rather than single discrete skills or technologies—that create disproportionate value for the customer, differentiate its owner from competitors, and allow entrance to new markets (Hamel 1994). The value perspective is very important when talking about capabilities. We argue that capabilities are interesting from a competitive perspective only if they contribute to the creation and delivery of better value for the firm's customers and other stakeholders.

Capabilities represent an accumulation of learning over time. They reflect a deep understanding that is advanced compared to other competitors in the industry, or they may be a unique ability in an important area of business. Either way, the notion of a capability encompasses the *"ability to do"* and to actively apply knowledge to a task and thereby to generate *"actionable knowledge."* Capabilities, in particular the firm's core capabilities, constitute the building blocks of the firm's core competencies.

Hamel identifies three key classes of capabilities that emerge from the firm's collective set of knowledge-based skills and technologies:

1. **Process-related Capabilities**—Competencies such as quality, cycle-time management, and just-in-time management: these allow the firm to do things more quickly, flexibly, and with a higher degree of reliability than competitors.
2. **Market-interface Capabilities**—Where the term *marketing* is used to embrace management of product/brand development, pricing, communication, sales, distribution, and service: in short, these constitute the market interface knowledge-based competencies that are nontechnical in nature.
3. **Functionality-related Capabilities**—Skills and technologies that enable the firm to integrate into its services and products unique functionality, resulting, in turn, in distinctive customer benefits.

A well-managed portfolio of knowledge-based capabilities is a prerequisite for building a strong and sustainable competitive advantage. Key competitive knowledge—primarily tacit knowledge embedded in complex organizational routines and evolving from experience over time—tends to be unique and difficult to replicate, imitate, and transfer (Birchall and Tovstiga 1999; Zack 1999). These features of a capability carry a number of important implications for competitive differentiation. One of these has to do with the ease with which a capability can be replicated, transferred, or lost to a competitor. For example, a high *degree of tacitness* can be an effective barrier to diffusion of knowledge. From the external perspective, this represents a protective mechanism; for internal operations, this represents a challenge to be overcome, that is, firms must maintain mechanisms for consciously and deliberately managing their stock of tacit knowledge. Tacit knowledge, we argue, plays an increasingly important role as we move to higher levels of external impact (Figure 6-1) since it is very difficult to transfer between firm boundaries.

In this paper, we posit that Hamel's three categories of capabilities will not suffice to build a position of competitive strength and high impact for the firm over time. Why? A firm's capabilities are neither stable over time nor uniform at any point in time (Bogner and Thomas 1994). In rapidly shifting competitive environments, firms are required to exploit their current portfolio of knowledge-based capabilities, all the while seeking to create a new competitive basis. Successful players in the global market place, Teece and Pisano (1998) point out, need to clearly go beyond simply managing their current portfolio of capabilities; they must demonstrate timely responsiveness, rapid and flexible innovation, and the management capability to continually source and deploy new external capabilities. Knowledge brought in from the external environment is the key factor in building a sustained new competitive basis.

We propose adding a fourth complementary set of capabilities for supporting the management of strategic relationships with external partners and the process of internalizing new knowledge sourced in the external environment of the firm. This new set of capabilities ranges from managing strategic relationships in the firm's external network to ultimately adapting, integrating, linking, and reconfiguring internal and external knowledge-based competencies in response to shifts in the firm's competitive environment. The capabilities consist of clusters of both hard and soft skills. We argue that they need to be an integral part of the firm's existing portfolio of capabilities. In this paper we examine the nature of these capabilities and the key function they fulfill in maximizing the strategic impact of the firm's portfolio of knowledge-based capabilities.

We take the notion of a capability further, however. For this, we borrow two concepts concerning the nature of capabilities from Leonard-Barton (1995).

Strategic Impact of Capabilities. First, we recognize that a firm's capabilities may vary in their strategic impact. Every firm will have capabilities that are simply supportive or supplemental; they fulfill only a marginally important role and can often be outsourced. Enabling capabilities are important to the firm, since they constitute a minimum basis of competitiveness in the industry—on a "qualifier" level, so to speak. By themselves, however, they convey no competitive advantage. Core capabilities are those on which the firm stakes its competitive edge; these set the firm apart from its competitors.

Dimensions of a Capability. Leonard-Barton puts forward the notion that core capabilities can be broken down into at least four interdependent dimensions, two of which are knowledge competence repositories—(1) people-embodied knowledge and skills, and (2) physical technical systems—and two of which are organizational knowledge-control and -channeling mechanisms—(3) managerial systems, and (4) organizational culture, values, and norms.

1. **People-Embodied Knowledge and Skills.** In addition to knowledge of techniques specific to the firm, this dimension includes industry-specific, as well as scientific and professional, knowledge. The knowledge within the capability is both in-depth and broad, in that there is a deep understanding in narrow areas, but enough understanding of the interfaces between the specific and the general to make it possible to relate the in-depth knowledge to its wider application and thus cultivate new or improved applications. The firm's specific knowledge is generally the least codified and therefore the most difficult to replicate and hence transfer.

2. **Physical Technical Systems.** People-embodied knowledge gets embedded into processes such as manufacturing layouts and configurations software. This embedded knowledge remains even after the originators have moved on. The rationale for the system may well be forgotten and become tacit in nature as a result. But it remains accessible to the organization as a result of it having been embedded into systems.

3. **Managerial Systems.** Managerial systems can include formalized procedures, for example, for decision-making. But they also include the many implicit ways of managing organizations that seem to be part of the fabric and are learned over time by working within the firm and being passed on from one group to another.

4. **Culture, Values, and Norms.** The dominant values and norms can be seen as the glue that underpins the organization and determines how it functions. No two organizations are alike. Often the dominant culture was set by the founders of the business and in many organizations has been enduring. Even when organizations are envied for the particular characteristics of their culture, it is impossible to copy and replicate them. Some organizations clearly have a culture that fosters innovation—typified by encouraging experimentation, openness, 'no-blame,' and learning from experience. We all recognize that it is extremely difficult to transform an organization that has always been a follower, a 'me too,' into an industry leader.

When we use the term *technological capability*, for example, we need to understand that we are really referring to the entire system of activities, including knowledge embedded in physical-technical systems (probably the most obvious), but also managerial systems, people-embodied knowledge, and, probably least obvious, the firm's cultural attributes and mechanisms.

FRAMEWORK FOR STRATEGIC KNOWLEDGE SOURCING, INTEGRATION, AND ASSIMILATION

In an earlier paper the authors proposed a three-stage trajectory for tracking the acquisition of knowledge into the firm's existing portfolio of capabilities. Figure 6-2 illustrates the three stages of *sourcing, internalization,* and *assimilation.* Each capability is positioned on the matrix according to its likely or actual competitive impact and also the degree of control exercised by the firm, hence determining its competitive position and future significance for the firm.

Capability C^1_{int} is a strategically important capability for the firm and one over which it has considerable control. It is "emerging" in that it is supporting products and services that are just becoming important in the market place and hence are leading edge. C^2_{int}, on the other hand, is a capability that is supporting products and services that have been turned into a commodity and therefore are readily replicated by other firms. K_{ext}, in contrast, is a knowledge domain that is emerging and has a strong likelihood of impacting on the products or services offered by the firm in the future. It is an area where mastery is expected to become important for competitive positioning, and therefore greater control is desirable. The potential offered for integration with existing capabilities and for assimilation with other capabilities to form recombinations that address new market needs is shown in Figure 6-2, where C^3_{new} represents a capability over which the firm has now secured a

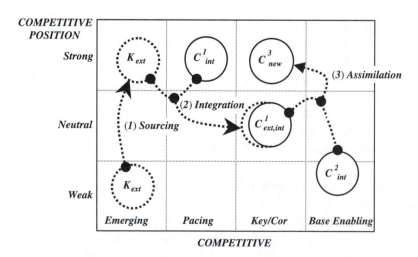

Figure 6-2   *The Knowledge Internalization Trajectory*

high degree of control built on a strong capability, which had over time become weak in terms of market position.

For the firm to better understand its needs in relation to the sourcing, integration, and assimilation of new knowledge, we propose a mapping of capabilities in a matrix as shown in Table 6-1. This enables the firm to identify its own strengths and weaknesses and areas where it needs to focus attention in order to improve its performance in the process. By mapping in this way, the firm can answer some key questions about its capabilities. Examples: Which characteristics of the capability (tacit versus explicit) come to bear most in the sourcing stage? As we proceed along the acquisition trajectory, does the nature of the capability become increasingly more tacit (leaning toward organizational culture and people-embodied knowledge) and thus more difficult to define, develop, and also replicate? How vulnerable is the firm to the loss of key personnel who contribute significantly to the key capabilities?

To illustrate the process of completion of an exercise to identify key capabilities, we have considered one case, that of Cisco Systems. We chose this firm for the study because it is recognized as an industry leader in its own particular strategy for knowledge acquisition, that of acquiring energetic, established, but recent, start-ups with technologies that expand their own service ranges in areas where customer needs have been identified. We have used secondary sources for information gathering and then content analysis to establish the key factors for success in their strategy. We started by identifying what we consider to be key steps in the business processes (the vertical dimensions in the matrix). We then completed the matrix from our own interpretation of the information from the content analysis. Having identified key components of capability, it would now be possible for speculation on the degree to which these capabilities are present and for a search for answers to the questions posed earlier. The approach illustrated could be undertaken by members of the firm, by a group representing the firm and target companies, or by external analysts or other stakeholder groups as a means of better understanding the strengths and weaknesses of Cisco's, or any other firm's, capabilities in knowledge acquisition.

Much information can be gleaned from books such as Bunnell (2000) and from reports of interviews with executives such as John Chambers, CEO (Internetweek 1998), Michael Volpi, Vice-president of Business Development at Cisco Systems (Drexage 1999), and Tim Merrifield, Manager of Cisco's IT Acquisition Integration team

(Reardon 2000), and from more general articles about the acquisition strategy (e.g., Goldblatt 1999).

A number of key features of Cisco's organization and preferred acquisition route that are believed to explain their success emerge from the literature:

1. An acquisition approach that is well understood both internally and externally
2. Target smaller firms that excel in specific areas
3. An understanding of customer's technology needs
4. Constant scanning of markets for potential competitors and technology trends
5. Target firms with a good momentum that have a track record and finished and tested product, but are still in an early stage of development and have not yet taken the product to market
6. A similar market perspective—seeking technological leadership, a desire to excel, and a focus on customer needs
7. Early attention in the appraisal process to the cultural fit
8. Seeking talent in the depth and quality of management (management that has made a big mistake but learned lessons from it and a management team that acts in support of each other)
9. Geographic proximity
10. A rising stock valuation and purchase via shares rather than cash
11. Speedy acquisition process, concentrating on the macro-issues and avoiding getting bogged down in the details
12. A well-planned and swift integration process involving Business Development, HR (maximum 30-day expectation), and IT (maximum 60-day expectation)
13. Financial engineering expertise
14. A strong research and development effort
15. An ability to integrate acquisitions into a cohesive organization

These features enable speculation as to the underpinning capabilities. This has resulted in the detailed analysis shown in Table 6-1. We would expect that readers may well take a different view as to the key capabilities, just as within any group analyzing the situation there would be a divergence of views. This richness of opinion undoubtedly results in a richer view of the key capabilities and new insights into what makes Cisco such a success at knowledge-sourcing through acquisition.

Table 6-1
An analysis of capabilities

	Dimensions of Capability			
Capability/Skill Area	ORG. Culture	People-Embodied Knowledge and Skills	Managerial Systems	Technical, Physical Systems
		Features		
	• Behaviors • Values • Norms	• Experiential Knowledge	• Incentives • Management Practices • Structures • Communities of Practice	• Technology • Physical Networks • Hard & Software
	Dimensional Mapping of Capability (Weighting Distribution)			

1. *Knowledge Sourcing*

Capability/Skill Area	ORG. Culture	People-Embodied Knowledge and Skills	Managerial Systems	Technical, Physical Systems
Strategy Processes • Strategic roadmapping • Capability gap analysis • Defining capability requirements • Planning matrix	Valuing foresight Outward looking Questioning	Analytical	Systematic processes Networked to key customers	
Market Scanning & Intelligence • Monitoring of external technology • Scouting and external networking	Curiosity Valuing new technologies that challenge the status quo	Technology expertise Strategic perspectives Insight	Visioning Maintenance of focus	
Identifying Acquisition Targets • Screening (Cisco's "5 principles") • Due diligence process • HR screen—cultural matchmaking(Cisco)	Team working valued Risk taking	Integration of disparate functions Attention to appropriate detail Responsiveness	Networked to industry Defined processes A good sense of timing	

Table 6-1
An analysis of capabilities (*Continued*)

	Dimensions of Capability			
2. Knowledge Integration				
"Docking to the mother ship"	Openness to new opportunities	Financial engineering	Decisiveness	IT integration
• Technology integration and compatabilisation (establishment of common networking code—Cisco)	An 'embracing' culture	Multi-disciplinary working	Expertise in managing clearly defined processes	
• Transition Teams		Problem-solving	Speedy response in solving problems	
• Leadership			Managing customer interfaces—any discontent or animosity quickly surfaced and responded to	
• Developing communications strategy & platform				
3. Knowledge Assimilation				
• Grafting new capabilities into existing ones	A motivational environment rewarding entrepreneurial approaches	Spotting opportunities and making the case	Motivation and retention of key staff	
• Employee retention	Thirsty for change	Absorption of new ideas through interaction and learning	Integration of new technologies into company overall	
• "Impedance matching"(Cisco)	A strong 'ante not invented here' culture		Optimization in deployment of new resources	
• Performance metrics			Demonstrating success in integration	
			Demonstrating on-going security to acquired talent	
			Maintaining market focus	

CONCLUSIONS

In this article we have used the case of Cisco to illustrate how the capabilities needed to be successful in a strategy for knowledge acquisition can be identified. We see this as an important process for any firm seeking to improve its knowledge-sourcing activities. First, it is clearly necessary to relate to a particular strategy whether internal sourcing, alliances, mergers and acquisition, or networking. The next stage is then to map out the process in detail. Against each step in this process, capabilities can be identified using a breakdown into the four components of organizational culture: people-embodied knowledge and skills, managerial systems, and technical and physical systems.

As the strategy progresses along the trajectory shown in Figure 6-1, we anticipate that, for the strategy to be a success, there will be increasing emphasis on the need for strength in the soft skills, cultural ones in particular.

Innovation is becoming paramount as companies strive to remain competitive and improve their situation. Innovation is dependent upon new knowledge streams that need to be sourced and successfully integrated into the firm's existing portfolio of capabilities. As we move into the era of the extended, boundaryless, networked knowledge enterprise, this last step is becoming ever more important. Entirely new sets of predominantly soft capabilities are required to achieve this integration of new knowledge streams. A methodology for assessing the firm's capabilities needs can offer a means for targeting development as well as enabling a better fit between knowledge sourcing strategy and organizational capability.

REFERENCES

Birchall, D. W. and L. Lyons. 1995. *Creating Tomorrow's Organization.* London: F. T. Pitman.

Birchall, D. W. and G. Tovstiga. 1999. Knowledge Is Priceless. *Henley Manager* 3 (Autumn): 6–7.

Birchall, D. W. and G. Tovstiga. 2000. The Strategic Potential of a Firm's Knowledge Portfolio. In *The Financial Times Handbook of Management*, eds. S. Crainer and L. Dearlove, second edition. London: Pearson Education.

Bogner, W. C. and H. Thomas. 1994. Core Competence and Competitive Advantage: A Model and Illustrative Evidence from the Pharmaceutical

Industry. In *Competence-Based Competition,* eds. G. Hamel and A. Heene. 111 London: John Wiley and Sons.

Bunnell, D. 2000. *Making the Cisco Connection.* New York: John Wiley and Sons.

Christensen, C. M. and M. Overdorf. 2000. Meeting the Challenge of Disruptive Change. *Harvard Business Review* (March–April): 67.

Drexhage, G. 1999. How Cisco Bought Its Way to the Top. *Corporate Finance.* (May). London.

Goldblatt, H. 1999. Cisco's Secrets, *Fortune* (Nov. 8).

Halleloid, D. and B. Simonin. 1994. Organizational Learning and a Firm's Core Competence. In *Competence-Based Competition.* eds. G. Hamel and A. Heene. 214 London: John Wiley and Sons.

Hamel G. 1994. The Concept of Core Competence. In *Competence-Based Competition,* eds. G. Hamel and A. Heene. London: John Wiley and Sons.

Hamel, G. 2000. *Leading the Revolution,* Boston: Harvard Business School Press.

———1998. "The InternetWeek Interview—John Chambers, President and CEO, Cisco," *Internetweek* (Aug. 31).

Leonard-Barton, D. 1995. *Wellsprings of Knowledge.* Cambridge: Harvard Business School Press.

Maira, A. N. and R. J. Thomas. 1998. Organizing on the Edge: Meeting the Demand for Innovation and Efficiency, *Prism* (third quarter).

Reardon, M. 2000. IT Takes Starring Role in Cisco's Acquisitions Adventures. *Informationweek* (Feb. 28).

Rigdon, J. I. 2000. The Integration Game. *Red Herring* (July): 356.

Teece, D. and G. Pisano. 1998. The Dynamic Capabilities of Firms: An Introduction. In *Technology, Organization and Competitiveness,* eds. D. Teece and Chytry. Oxford. pp. 193–212.

Van Rossum, W. and O. S. W. F. Omta. 1998. A Five-Step Model to Successful Technological Collaboration, Faculty of Management and Organization Working Paper, University of Groningen (Netherlands).

Willett, S. 1998. John Chambers, *Computer Reseller News* (Nov. 16).

Zack, M. 1999. Developing a Knowledge Strategy, *California Management Review9* vol. 41, no. 3 (Spring).

7

Integrating Organizational Learning and Knowledge Management:

A Case Study

Susana Pérez López
Faculty of Economics, University of Oviedo, Spain
sperez@econo.uniovi.es

José Manuel Montes Peón
Faculty of Economics, University of Oviedo, Spain
jmmontes@econo.uniovi.es

and

Camilo José Vázquez Ordás
Faculty of Economics, University of Oviedo, Spain
cvazquez@econo.uniovi.es

Abstract

Recently, a wide body of scientific literature has appeared, aiming to explain the process linking collective knowledge with individual knowledge and the intraorganizational learning process. This collective knowledge will become the main foundation of the organization, of its growth, and of its rent-generation strategy. In this

119

chapter, we try to set a link between organizational learning and knowledge management. We identify two sets of variables that are key to developing an effective organizational learning capability on which managers should focus their attention. Through case study analysis we analyze the experience of seven Spanish firms in knowledge management, and we offer some hints to improve their operational knowledge management strategy.

INTRODUCTION

The achievement of a competitive advantage in a business environment characterized by complexity, globalization, and dynamism, demands firms have the ability to adapt and foresee changes in their markets, thus developing their learning capability. Today, it is widely recognized in the management literature that organizational learning is a lasting process linked to the acquisition of knowledge and to the improvement in business performance (Bontis et al. 2002). The purpose of this chapter is to analyze and link the organization's capacity to learn knowledge management, thus setting a reference framework for strategic business action. First, we will analyze the organizational learning process, which will lead us to the conclusion that, in order to learn, organizations must encourage the exchange of mental models and then they must institutionalize them in their operational structure, thus modifying the decision-making processes that control their behavior. Second, we will analyze the key elements supporting the learning process in order to manage them explicitly. Finally, we will make an in-depth case-study analysis of seven firms that are leaders in their economic sector. We will describe their current situation as far as knowledge management is concerned, and we will outline several patterns of their behavior that could be changed in order to improve their knowledge management practices.

ORGANIZATIONAL LEARNING

Recently, strategic literature has placed special emphasis on the importance of knowledge as a determining factor in entrepreneurial competitiveness, basically for two reasons: first, knowledge explains a large part of an organization's added value; and second, the barriers to its transfer and imitation give it an important strategic relevance. Within this focus, one of the main factors of heterogeneity is found in an organization's potential for learning. Therefore, the competitive advantage rests mainly on how the knowledge itself is nurtured and developed. Organized learning is a collective phenomenon, although it is true that the firm can learn only through its members. Therefore, one of the main aspects dealt with in the literature is related to the level, whether individual or organizational, at which learning is produced. However, few studies analyze the existing relationship between these levels that, in our view, constitute a fundamental aspect in understanding how learning and knowledge-generation are produced.

Individual learning is generated when individuals develop a new mentality, change their manner of understanding things, and face difficulties in a new way. Nonetheless, in this process we must take into account the feedback mechanisms that start in an individual's mental model and end in its reinforcement. Ideas for improvement depend directly on people's volume of knowledge in such a way that the greater their initial knowledge endowment, the greater the capability of an individual to understand the organizational environment and, consequently, the introduction of new decision-making processes. It may, therefore, be concluded that new concepts, relationships, rules for decision-making, and activities that increase the capacity to make effective decisions and entertain feedback learning are developed as a result of individual learning processes.

However, organizational learning does not consist of a simple collection of individual experiences; rather, it is a much more complex and dynamic process. Individual learning must be communicated, shared, and integrated into the routines in order to be considered organizational. Crossan, Lane, and White (1999) offer a model that may be useful to understand this process. These authors start from the differentiation between individual, group, and organizational learning levels and consider four types of learning processes—intuition, interpretation, integration, and institutionalization—that allow for the analysis of interactions between the different levels. The intuition process presupposes the subconscious recognition on the part of the individual of different models and possibilities inherent to past experiences. Interpretation links the individual and group levels by developing through language the cognitive maps of the individuals referring to the distinctive domains in which they operate. Integration, which serves as a nexus between the group and organizational levels, consists of the development of a shared understanding and coordinated decision-making. Finally, the institutionalization process makes reference to the integration of new knowledge and capacities in organizational routines.

Thus, the key to organizational learning resides in the exchange of mental models and their institutionalization in a firm's operational structure by transforming the rules for decision that, until then, have dominated its behavior, thus enabling it to carry out more effective actions.

A Model for Knowledge Management

We argue that the design and implementation of policies that allow for the management of activities directly related to knowledge creation, transformation, and utilization within the firm are the responsibility of the Board of Directors. From this perspective, we define *knowledge management* as a set of policies and managerial decisions whose objective it is to promote learning processes that generate knowledge, in accordance with the objectives of the organization.

Based on the learning process described in the previous section, and with the support of an ample revision of the relevant literature, we identify two groups of key variables for the development of effective learning, on which we believe that managers must center their interest: (1) support instruments, and (2) organizational design factors.

Support Instruments for the Learning Process

Support instruments must act directly on the knowledge generation process, defining the effectiveness of both individual and organizational learning. In this model, we set forward eight instruments: the firm and conscious commitment of the entire organization, autonomy, creative chaos, dialog, shared vision, an unlearning capability, documentation practices, and environmental surveillance.

The firm and conscious commitment of the entire organization, especially that of its leaders, with generative learning at all levels, is the first requirement for the success of any knowledge management initiative. It is necessary to recognize explicitly that learning is a process that must be managed and to which all types of resources must be committed.

Organizations must allow their personnel to act as freely as possible, as this could increase the possibility of developing innovations, creations, or ideas representing new opportunities. Therefore, autonomy fosters and gives meaning to personal commitment, which must be managed in the organization (Nonaka 1994; Ghoshal and Barlett 1994). Self-organized teams are a powerful tool for giving individuals the opportunity to act autonomously as a group or collective, working together on the creation of new concepts; first sharing their perspectives and later articulating the agreed-upon concept.

Creative chaos may be defined as a state that possesses an inherent force capable of activating and fostering the firm's evolutionary processes and, specifically, the creative processes for organizational knowledge (Nonaka 1994; Nonaka and Takeuchi 1995). This increases the tension within the organization, directing it toward the search for development and not merely toward environmental adaptation (Zimmerman 1993). However, highly elevated objectives can create a sense of frustration that limits learning. This idea is important for the assignment of tasks to the workers, since tasks must be assigned to individuals whose qualifications place the goal in the ideal position for learning to take place (Muñoz-Seca and Riverola 1997).

Dialog must be defined as the capability to listen and communicate ideas. It allows for the development of a common language that creates the foundation for a fast transfer of ideas and viewpoints, thus clarifying the confusing situations and the learning process. In many organizational contexts, it may be enough to totally transfer a learning experience.

Shared vision aims to bring sensations to individuals that will presumably affect their mental model. It therefore allows individuals to share and integrate aspects of their knowledge that had not been commonly held among them, thus attaining a shared vision. We can point out three fundamental instruments for the construction of experiences: (1) developing interfunctional or interdepartmental teams in which individuals work together in the development of a product or new project in an undefined or overlapping division of labor, (2) the development of rotation strategies for personnel in different functional areas, favoring the interdisciplinary perspective and fluidity of knowledge and, therefore, making it much easier to put the knowledge generated into practice, (3) the creation of microclimates or learning laboratories, which enable their participants to experiment actively and question the manner in which things are seen and the way that other group members act, as well as simulation techniques that bring out the consequences of certain actions throughout a period of time.

Unlearning implies discarding knowledge that has become obsolete. This activity is fundamental for a correct shared interpretation, as the effort to maintain previous viewpoints may lead to information being interpreted within a very limited domain. This would result in a collective myopia that impedes the detection of new opportunities. The difficulty that organizations with a successful history have in discarding manners of acting that were productive in the past is a case in point. This resistance probably has its origin in the reticence of experienced people to abandon the knowledge and manners of operating that were acquired through the years and that constitute their only capital.

Documentation is an essential step in the transformation process from individual to organizational knowledge. It confers a certain degree of permanence on knowledge that prevents it from existing only in people's minds. Its objective is to make knowledge explicit, easy to understand, and accessible to all who need it. For this reason, knowledge must be given a structure, a format in which it can be stored, shared, and combined in multiple manners. The main difficulty in this process is to avoid the loss of distinctive properties and thus convert knowledge into information of little relevance or simple data.

Finally, *environmental surveillance* is a process of measurement and diagnosis. Its objective is to prepare the organization to face any changes that may affect it and thus to anticipate its adaptation. Companies are not passive receptors of the information on their environment, but rather, with their behavior, they can change its image and create a less ambivalent operational model (Daft and Weick 1984). When the environment is dynamic, many of the aspects defining it and explaining its behavior vary. In agreement with Ashby's principle of "relative variety," the more unstable the environment and the greater the dependence the organization has on it, the greater the need for information. In situations of instability, a passive performance on the part of an organization's members with respect to the collection of data on the environment can impede the comprehension of its functioning in the organization's action. To avoid a lack of data blocking a firm's knowledge development, it must remain active in information collection and establish surveillance mechanisms that enable it to be in a continuous state of alert (Fahey, King, and Narayanan 1981).

Organizational Design Factors Conditioning Learning

Organizational design factors delimit the domain in which support instruments act and therefore determine the capacity to carry out effective organizational learning. In this model, five conditioning elements for learning are identified: leadership, organizational culture, personnel management, strategy, and organizational structure.

Leadership is understood as a collection of managerial roles and abilities. It is a key element within the organization because the Board of Director's decisions and behavior condition the management, culture, and manner of operating the organization. The demand for new knowledge and innovation has provoked the resurgence of a new type of leader, whose basic role is to coordinate the knowledge possessed by the organization's personnel, supporting them in the process of finding answers. The main obstacle to implementation of this new style of leadership is the unwillingness to discard the established cultural norms and habits that essentially stipulate that everything must be under management's control. Learning not only invalidates such control but also entails the recognition of errors as a valuable part of the process.

The Board of Directors must find a balance between intuition and reason when making decisions. Intuition, which is appropriate when no model exists to explain how facts and data are related, requires critical thought and an unconscious application of experience and learning. However, reason, which is the application of logical, linear thought, responds to the existence of a mental model explaining a given situation (Revilla 1996).

Culture expresses a collection of beliefs and manners of thinking and acting that, as manifested through a series of symbols, attitudes, rituals, and values, serve as a point of reference in the interpretation of experiences and generation of actions. Learning development requires a new cultural domain. The power to make decisions is granted to the worker, holder of much of a firm's knowledge. The reason for this delegation stems from the impossibility of finding tools that allow the control of creative work, given that such work is not only new and unpredictable but also possesses productivity levels that are difficult to measure, as its objectives are frequently redefined.

The implementation of a learning culture within a company requires the assumption of this type of behavior. For this reason, it is essential to create a climate of confidence and security that may promote innovation, experimentation, and risk, motivating the worker to develop learning capacity while becoming familiar with the new changes at work. Therefore, a complete commitment to this idea is necessary, both on the part of management to delegate authority and on the part of company members, for the assumption of responsibility. On the one hand, it requires an acceptance of loss of managerial power. On the other hand, the employees should be able to accept the new challenges and responsibilities that are demanded, while having a share of both the successes and failures of the firm or project. Human resource policy must be aligned with the new company culture in such a way that it may reinforce behavior and undertakings in accordance with the needs of the learning process.

Personnel selection continues to be an influential factor in the definition of entrepreneurial policies that aspire to improve management. To simply contract the best and the brightest makes little sense in these circumstances. The organization must have a clear idea of its integral aspirations and the competence necessary to attain them, being thus in a condition to require certain types and levels of knowledge, ability, and attitudes of the professionals and employees that it wishes to hire. Moreover, it must utilize the mentoring possibilities within the firm to socialize new members and reduce the time they need to get used to the existing culture (Ulrich 1998).

Training must be linked to the strategy of the firm and directed toward the promotion and development of the core competencies within the organization. Its main objective is to achieve a change in learners' behavior, strengthening the workers' cooperative attitude, so that they may gain in confidence and teamwork. At the same time, the compensation systems may provide workers with incentives to improve their job training and remain within the firm for the long term. Career promotion must be associated with aspects related to an employee's learning capacity and ability to transfer knowledge. The organization should reward, with economic benefits or some other type of social recognition, those workers who, having developed new knowledge, transfer it or suggest how to manage it within the organization. Some compensation schemes try to enhance employees' involvement in the company through the concession of stock options or the sale of shares at a discount. When employees are at the same time proprietors of the firm, they identify themselves more intensely with it, which increases their motivation and contributes to reducing the conflict between capital and labor.

Job stability facilitates the willingness to acquire new knowledge and skills, and increases commitment with the company (Pfeffer 1998). Companies tend to be reticent to invest resources in a careful selection and training of personnel if they are not going to remain in the firm long enough to recoup the investment. In the same way, the delegation of authority and the fact of sharing strategic information demands mutual confidence between the company and employee, necessitating a long-term commitment.

With respect to strategy, its main goal is the articulation of the firm's future orientation, positioning the company with respect to the competition, customers, regulators, technological changes, and investors. It is conceivably possible to differentiate strategy formulation from its implantation. This requires the organization to have the necessary capacities at its disposal for its development in accordance with the initial plan. That is to say, a company should possess the capacity to utilize the totality of resources at its disposal, which entails the development of given models of interaction between them that materialize in a series of organizational routines (Nelson and Winter 1982). The consideration of a strategy from a dynamic perspective reveals that the fundamental problem that the entire organization faces consists of finding the optimum combination between the exploitation of existing resource and capacities and the exploration of new alternatives.

Finally, organizational structure is one of the most important elements, as it gives support to all the previous ones by specifying the interactions between individuals and groups within an organization. The challenge to achieve an effective knowledge management depends on the consideration of its most important elements: the combination of knowledge, lateral communication, and temporal and flexible structures with relatively stable groups. Therefore, organizational structure, rather than locking the organization into a determined state of equilibrium, must learn to dynamically synchronize the movement of its activities, phases, procedures, and values in accordance with the demands of the transformation process and knowledge materialization.

Brown and Duguid (1998) have shown that the traditional work organization characterized by the division of labor and hierarchic control is ineffective for the attainment of organizational learning. This is due to the fact that this organization is directed toward *segmentalism,* assuming that problems can be solved individually by assigning them to experts. The main difficulty lies in the fact that people neither share this mental model nor are decisions made by taking multiple perspectives into account. Such a focus does not contemplate need, derived from interdependent relationships, to perform continuous adjustments and redefinitions in the procedures and activities that converge in product development.

As a result of this criticism, organizations have moved toward more organic structures that favor learning and are characterized by a reduced formalization, scarce centralization in decision-making, and more participative planning and control. These characteristics allow the experimentation, the confrontation of mental models, the integration of new knowledge, and, in short, the development of double-loop or generative organizational learning. This shifts the conception of the worker from a mere executor of tasks to an individual submitted to creative tension.

ANALYSIS AND DISCUSSION OF THE CASE STUDY

In order to examine knowledge management closely in the entrepreneurial reality of our area, an exploratory study was carried out on seven companies in September 2000. The analysis was oriented toward measuring the degree of development of each firm in the different elements of the model presented in the previous section. In this way, a starting point may be described, enabling an advance to take place in the exposition of new policies and instruments for the improvement of knowledge management.

For reasons of confidentiality, the identity of the firms studied will not be revealed, and we will identify them through their entrepreneurial activity: engineering and electronic assembly, transportation, computer technology, consulting, finance, anticorrosive protection, and metallurgy. In all of them, capital entitlement is private and their individual market share surpasses 30 percent. Thus, we believe that their level of management excellence is above average. The study was carried out by means of personal interviews with the General Director, or Director of Human Resources, and complemented with a questionnaire. The questions had to be answered on a Likert-type scale, oriented toward evaluating the degree of development in the model's different elements.

The results are structured in two sections. First, the companies' situations are described in relation to the support instruments. Second, the results are presented referring to the organizational design variables.

Support Instruments

First, the high level of consciousness shown by the directors regarding the need to manage learning is noteworthy. They all declare that their companies grant primary importance to learning, recognizing the value of individuals in entrepreneurial management.

With respect to autonomy, the directors interviewed recognized it as a central point in their companies, although a proactive focus on people is not being clearly favored. However, it is worth pointing out the difference that is appreciated in the most learning-intensive companies—computer technology, consulting, and finance—that have positively assessed the opportunity that individuals and teams have in fixing their own objectives for learning and being responsible for their accomplishment.

To detect the presence of creative chaos, we designed several questions intended to discover, first, whether management is attempting to evoke a sense of crisis among the organization's members by establishing important challenges. These questions are also meant to find whether organizational changes are being introduced, such as the elimination of the most routine aspects from jobs, or the reassignment of workers' tasks. The challenges being assumed by the firms are ambitious with respect to the current situation, as well as being dynamic and transformational. However, it is not so clear that these challenges are being transmitted to the rest of the organization, generating a tense atmosphere. This must be due to the fact that they are in the first stage of the process and have not yet introduced the necessary organizational elements to transfer these challenges in an operative way to all the individuals, groups, and work units.

Capacity for dialog was positively evaluated by all the directors in the sample. Moreover, practices intended to favor it, such as discussion groups, were set in motion in some of the firms, although the ability to dialog is not an essentially technical problem but rather is closely linked to specific cultural values and leadership styles, configuring a favorable learning atmosphere.

We aimed to infer the existence of a shared vision through a series of questions intended to assess the degree to which individuals perceive the same aims, as well as the development of the proposed mechanisms for their construction (interfunctional work teams, personnel rotation, etc.). First, individual commitment to a common goal was positively assessed. In like manner, the responses obtained reveal that work in interfunctional teams is a basic mechanism for the achievement of a shared vision. These teams are created not only for new product development but also to undertake habitual tasks related to a company's habitual activity. However, the relatively low valuation that the directors granted to the capacity of employees to abandon their respective departments when working in a team must be pointed out. The majority of organizations develop internal job rotation programs in order to provide the personnel with a greater understanding of the function and problems of other departments.

Furthermore, the predisposition and capacity to unlearn was also positively assessed. The ability to abandon obsolete knowledge is a prerequisite for learning and appears to be influenced by the size of the organization. The relatively lowest assessments were made by the largest companies, those belonging to the computer technology and metallurgy sectors and employing more than five thousand workers.

The directors in the sample also positively evaluate the mechanisms that their companies possess for storing and re-utilizing existing knowledge within the organization. However, in five of the seven firms it is recognized that the loss of personnel entails a loss of important knowledge and skills, which is due to the impossibility in many cases of codifying the tacit knowledge of individuals. In fact, people are rarely aware of all that they know, as this is the result of all that is learned explicitly and absorbed implicitly. Therefore, it will be necessary to develop complementary mechanisms in order to incorporate into the collective work routines and patterns the tacit knowledge of individuals.

Finally, with respect to environmental surveillance, a low level of external opening was observed. The majority of the companies hardly relate themselves at all to the competition, and connote a scarce capacity to learn through interorganizational collaboration. Nevertheless, four of them acquire knowledge by means of benchmarking practices, introduced with the object of improving total quality management. This was fostered by the need to satisfy customer demands and attain processes of continuous improvement. These data may be considered to be of concern, given that, in an environment that is increasingly complex and interrelated, the closed nature of an organization may become a competitive disadvantage.

Organizational Design Factors

The leadership style reflected in the interviews may be defined as open and accessible, although three weaknesses can be pointed out:

1. The limited capacity to create an atmosphere in which all personnel contribute to the maximum of their capabilities

2. The insufficient support given to employees in their search for answers
3. The limited capacity to learn from errors and to review past experiences

This may be owing to the difficulty in breaking with the norms and cultural habits that have been traditionally established, which, as we have seen, imply that everything must be under management control and all answers must come from there. Moreover, this last aspect reflects to a certain extent an underestimation on the part of the directors of the need to continue learning, arguing for the need to be present in the day-to-day operations.

With respect to organizational culture, it was observed that the companies under study consider change to be natural and necessary. Moreover, the directors perceive a respectful climate for the diversity of opinions, although it must be pointed out the relatively low score that four of the seven companies granted to risk assumption on the part of individuals and the discussion of problems without searching for scapegoats. This leads us to believe that, although a certain sensitivity does exist as to the importance of creating a climate of confidence to motivate change and risk assumption, these practices and manners of operation have not yet been institutionalized in order to achieve this objective. In this aspect, the most knowledge-intensive firms present a profile most akin to "intelligent organizations."

For its part, strategy may be considered, in agreement with the sample results, as proactive, flexible, oriented toward the future, and the result of a continuous process. However, the control systems used are essentially based on short-term results, which produce a contradiction between strategic orientation and what is really valued. In like manner, the negligible degree to which the formulation of strategy is shared by the personnel must also be pointed out. Despite the fact that all firms in the sample design their strategies in collaboration with the managers and experts responsible for the different implied areas, only two of them involve the rest of the individuals in this process. Therefore, the challenge remains of making the maximum number of people in the organization participants in it, guaranteeing that they focus their energy in a synergetic manner. Once again, the most knowledge-intensive companies show the most positive evaluations with respect to this question.

With respect to the system of personnel management, according to the perception of the directors interviewed, it is not oriented to learning in all its dimensions. The results show an orientation of the criteria of selection and promotion toward teamwork and continuous training. However, the remuneration systems do not consider this type of factor. Therefore, in the majority of cases, these types of factors are revealed as ineffective and the cause of problems of salary unfairness, which affect the performance of their duties. This is one of the most difficult points to solve, not only for the conflicts that the implantation of certain mechanisms could generate but also for the difficulty of knowing the individual contribution of each employee, given the inherent social complexity of tacit knowledge and the impossibility of being observed.

Finally, in relation to the organizational structure, the results do not show the dominant profile clearly. Most of the directors state that their company's organizational structures do not have excessive hierarchical levels and that communication is fluid. In the same way, they consider that the job descriptions avoid the separation between the function of thinking and doing. However, it was worth stressing the fairly high grades (three and four on the scale) that they give to the formalization of tasks and the centralization of decision-making. This can be due to the fact that the majority of them are still undergoing a process of transition toward more flexible structures and have not yet managed to do away with certain practices and ways of performance that are deeply rooted in the organization and that lead to obtaining high levels of efficiency.

CONCLUSION

The strategic consideration of knowledge as a key business asset and the capability of creating knowledge as a core competence of the organization have contributed in an important manner to the evolution of the strategic management paradigm. From the case study analysis made, we can conclude that the participating firms are really concerned with the importance of knowledge and with the need to develop a business climate that promotes their learning capabilities. Despite business requirements linked to total quality management, client orientation and benchmarking are perceived by these firms as strategic and have been implemented; the business practices leading to organizational learning have not yet been institutionalized. Even though there are some informal practices toward taking them into account, there is still a lack of specific knowledge management procedures that take a global approach in the analysis of the elements involved in the learning capability of an organization. Therefore, they do not yet form part of a reference framework within the organization. However, it is still necessary to institutionalize in the daily operative behavior of the firm, the transformation process of ideas into learning, and their fast diffusion and embodiment in the organization. Real change and knowledge management implementation will not occur until individuals redesign their roles and relationships.

The theoretical foundations to implement knowledge management that are presented in this paper have a double outcome. On the one hand, they set the general framework of reference for a coherent strategy about knowledge management and, on the other hand, they also provide a set of practices and recommendations needed to put this strategy into practice. However, we must still pursue this research, trying to obtain additional empirical evidence to corroborate the link between organizational learning and the management of those assets that enhance learning, its role on value creation, and the achievement of a sustainable competitive advantage.

References

Bontis, Nick, M. Crossan, and J. Hulland. 2002. Managing an Organizational Learning System by Aligning Stocks and Flows, *Journal of Management Studies* 39, 4 (forthcoming).

Brown, J. S. and P. Duguid. 1998. Organizing Knowledge. *California Management Review* 40, 3: 90–111.

Crossan, M. M., H. W. Lane, and R. E. White. 1999. An Organizational Learning Framework: From Intuition to Institution. *Academy of Management Review* 24, 3: 522–37.

Daft, R. L. and K. E. Weick. 1984. Toward a Model of Organizations as Interpretation Systems. *Academy of Management Review* 9, 2: 284–95.

Fahey, L. W., W. R. King, and V. K. Narayanan. 1981. Environmental Scanning and Forecasting in Strategic Planning: The State of the Art. *Long Range Planning* 14, 1: 32–39.

Ghoshal, S. and C. Bartlett. 1994. Linking Organizational Context and Managerial Action: The Dimensions of Quality of Management, *Strategic Management Journal* 15, 2 (special issue, summer): 91–112.

Muñoz-Seca, B. and J. Riverola. 1997. *Gestión del Conocimiento*. Barcelona: Folio.

Nelson, R. and S. Winter. 1982. *An Evolutionary Theory of Economic Change*. Cambridge: Harvard University Press.

Nonaka, I. 1994. A Dynamic Theory of Organizational Knowledge Management, *Organization Science* 5, 1: 14–37.

Nonaka, I. and H. Takeuchi. 1995. *The Knowledge-Creating Company.* New York: Oxford University Press.

Pfeffer, J. 1998. Seven Practices of Successful Organizations, *California Management Review* 40, 2: 96–124.

Revilla, E. 1996. *Factores determinantes del aprendizaje organizativo. Un modelo de desarrollo de productos.* Madrid: Club Gestión de Calidad.

Ulrich, D. 1998. Intellectual Capital = Competence × Commitment, *Sloan Management Review* 39, 2: 15–26.

Zimmerman, B. 1993. The Inherent Drive Towards Chaos. In *Implementing Strategic Processes: Change, Learning and Co-operation,* eds. P. Lorange, B. Chakravarthy, J. Roos, and A. van de Ven. Cambridge, Mass.: Blackwell. 373–94.

8

INTELLECTUAL CAPITAL DISCLOSURES IN SWEDISH ANNUAL REPORTS

Philip R. Beaulieu
Faculty of Management, University of Calgary, Calgary, Canada
pbeaulie@ucalgary.ca

S. Mitchell Williams
Faculty of Management, University of Calgary, Calgary, Canada
mwilliams@mgmt.ucalgary.ca

and

Michael E. Wright
Faculty of Management, University of Calgary, Calgary, Canada
wright@mgmt.ucalgary.ca

ABSTRACT

The purpose of this chapter is to determine the extent of intellectual capital disclosure practices in Swedish corporate annual reports. We develop an intellectual capital disclosure index based on the model of intellectual capital created by Brooking (1996) and using a scoring system similar to that utilized by Wiseman (1982) to measure environmental disclosures. We then measure the intellectual capital disclosure for a sample of thirty publicly listed companies from Sweden. Three independent variables thought to affect the level

135

of intellectual capital disclosures are also measured: size, profitability, and industry classification based on research and development intensity. The empirical results indicate that only size is significantly associated with the intellectual capital disclosure index. Further analysis of the data indicates some interaction effect between size and research and development intensity on the disclosure index. The companies that disclosed the most were large companies with high research and development intensity whereas the companies that disclosed the least were small companies with high research and development intensity.

INTRODUCTION

The traditional accounting model and its associated measures of corporate performance, such as net income and rate of return, developed during the last two centuries, in which physical capital was a predominant input factor. However, the new economy is dominated by intellectual capital. As Pulic and Bornemann (1999: 1) wrote, "[in] this new economy . . . intellectual capital has become the one and only competitive advantage" of a firm. Stakeholders will require that they be provided with information relevant to the intellectual capital of a firm. The traditional accounting model is not designed for this new economy; consequently, either the accounting model itself will need to change or companies will need to provide supplemental disclosures in their annual reports. In this chapter, we examine the extent to which a sample of thirty Swedish companies chose the latter route and provide supplemental information concerning intellectual capital in their annual reports.

To date there has been limited empirical research of intellectual capital disclosures in annual reports (e.g., Guthrie and Petty 2000; Brennan 1999). This study involves a larger sample size and a broader measure of disclosure than previous studies. Our intellectual capital disclosure index utilizes five subcategories of intellectual capital, rather than relying on an overall measure of intellectual capital. Cowen, Ferreri, and Parker (1987) argue that an examination of total disclosure without considering subcategories may hide valuable insights into disclosure practices. In addition to measuring intellectual capital disclosure, we examine three factors that are likely to affect disclosure practices: corporate size, profitability, and industry type as measured by research and development intensity.

INTELLECTUAL CAPITAL AND ITS DISCLOSURE

Definition of Intellectual Capital

Although there is agreement among intellectual capital scholars as to the importance of intellectual capital (Bontis 1999), there is no agreement about its definition. Stewart (1997: ix–x) defines it in the Foreword to his book as, "the sum of everything everybody in a company knows that gives it a competitive edge. Unlike the assets with which business people and accountants are familiar—land, factories, equipment, cash—intellectual capital is intangible." He goes on to say more precisely that "intellectual capital is intellectual material— knowledge, information, intellectual property, experience—that can be put to use to create wealth" (p. x). Brooking (1996: 12) defines intellectual capital as "the combined intangible assets which enable the company to function."

Brooking (1996) suggests that intellectual capital is a function of four major asset types: (1) intellectual property assets, (2) infrastructure assets, (3) human-centered assets, and (4) market assets. SMAC (1998) adapts Brooking's classification system. We also define intellectual capital in terms of asset types, but in order to capture the information we found in annual reports accurately and consistently, we use five asset types: human resources, customers, information technology, processes, and intellectual property.

Disclosure of Intellectual Capital

Steven W. H. Wallman, Commissioner of the SEC, predicts that the disclosure of intellectual capital–related information would one day become the most central emphasis of a firm's annual report (Edvinsson and Malone 1997: 5). A number of surveys report an increasing interest and demand amongst investors for companies to report on intellectual capital and related nonfinancial matters. A report from Taylor and Associates (1999) finds, based on a 200-item proprietary disclosure index drawn from criteria established by the world's most influential money managers, that investors rank the disclosure of information on intellectual capital in the top ten of their information needs. Taylor and associates state, "institutional investors have, more than ever before, recognized the role of such intangibles as intellectual capital in determining future profit potential. Companies that fail to communicate concrete strategies and tactics for the future seriously jeopardize investor confidence, future financial performance and ultimately share price" (1999: 1).

Some companies have recognized the potential benefits of voluntarily disclosing intellectual capital in their annual reports or other supportive publications. Skandia AFS, for example, was one of the first corporate proponents for reporting on intellectual capital. Apart from the disclosure on intellectual capital in their annual report, Skandia AFS supplemented these details by providing in 1994 (and since) a separate report entitled "Visualizing Intellectual Capital in Skandia" (Skandia 1995). Skandia AFS's underlying justification for the reporting on intellectual capital is that the traditional financial reporting model only presents the past financial information about the firm. Additional information on Skandia AFS's intellectual capital is needed for investors to understand both an organization's current and future capabilities (Luthy 1998). Other leading companies voluntarily reporting on intellectual capital include Swedish companies such as Telia and Consultus, Canadian companies such as Canadian Imperial Bank of Commerce, and U.S. companies such as U.S. West, Buckman Labs, and Hughes Space and Communications.

Generally speaking, there is both a deficiency and inconsistency in current reporting practices of a corporation's intellectual capital (Abdolmohammadi, Greenlay, and Poole 1999). It is likely that the disclosure of intellectual capital will intensify in the future. In the next subsection we discuss three potential factors at the organizational level that may explain the amount of intellectual capital disclosures in corporate annual reports. Although other factors, such as social and governmental regulations, would no doubt affect disclosure, they are beyond the scope of this study.

Potential Determinants of Intellectual Capital Disclosure

Prior research has developed a considerable body of literature regarding the relationship between organizational characteristics and the extent of disclosure in corporate annual reports (e.g., Singhvi and Desai 1971; Firth 1979; Cooke 1991; Marston and Robson 1997). A review of prior international research by Marston and Shrives (1991) and Ahmed and Courtis (1999) suggests that corporate size and profitability are among a list of five organizational level factors that are most commonly examined in relation to the extent of disclosure in corporate annual reports.[1] Though not on the lists compiled by Marston and Shrives (1991) or Ahmed and Courtis (1999), another organizational factor that has received attention is the effect of a firm's industry classification.

To develop a better understanding of intellectual capital disclosure practices, the association between the extent of intellectual capital disclosure and three organizational level factors, namely, organizational size, profitability, and industry type, must be investigated.

Size

Whether measured by total book-value of assets, market capitalization, total sales, number of employees, or the number of shareholders, prior empirical research consistently indicates a significant and positive association between size and the extent of disclosure in corporate annual reports (e.g., Courtis 1979; Inchausti 1997). We measure size by the book value of total assets, the most common measure of size in prior research (Ahmed and Courtis 1999). Data on the firm's book value of total assets were obtained from the corporate annual reports. The log of total assets was used in the statistical analysis.

With respect to the amount of intellectual capital disclosure, larger firms may have incentives to disclose more information than smaller firms. They face closer scrutiny by analysts and the media, and have stronger incentives to manage the interpretation of their earnings through intellectual capital disclosures. Simply by virtue of their size, the gap between their market and book values is larger, and again there is an incentive to explain this discrepancy in terms of intellectual capital. On the other hand, smaller firms may be especially keen to indicate their growth potential to capital markets, and intellectual capital disclosure is one means of accomplishing this. Following this line of reasoning, one could expect to see more disclosure by small firms. A significant factor affecting the disclosure decision is the competitive advantages or disadvantages associated

---

[1]The other remaining organizational level factors on this list were listing status, leverage, and size of the audit firm. This chapter acknowledges the possible association between these three organizational level factors and the extent of disclosure of intellectual capital information in the annual report of publicly listed companies in Sweden. The influence of these factors was not examined in this study, however, due to a lack of variation among the survey companies and/or needed information. For example, in relation to listing status of the companies surveyed the vast majority were domestically listed only, or their listing concentration was on the A-listing of the Stockholm Stock Exchange.

with disclosure. For example, firms could raise apparent barriers to entry by describing in detail their investment in intellectual capital— thus, they may see a competitive advantage in disclosure. Alternatively, any detailed process-oriented intellectual capital information released by firms could be used other firms to copy these processes, resulting in a competitive disadvantage. We expect the amount of intellectual capital disclosures to be related to firm size, but ex ante we cannot predict the direction of this relationship.

Profitability

We measure profitability as the *return on capital employed* (ROCE). This measure was selected for two reasons. First, ROCE has received considerable attention in the financial press and recent academic studies as an acceptable measure of profitability. Second, this measure of profitability is commonly referred to within the Swedish business environment. Consistent with the understanding of ROCE in the Swedish business environment, this measure of profitability was defined as operating income, financial revenues, and net participations in associated companies, as a percentage of average capital employed. *Capital employed* is defined as visible shareholders' equity plus interest-bearing liabilities. Data were obtained from the corporate annual report.

Prior researchers generally hypothesized a positive relationship between profitability and the extent of disclosure levels in corporate annual reports (e.g., Singhvi and Desai 1971; Cooke 1991; Wallace, Naser, and Mora 1994; Wallace and Naser 1995). Empirical results, however, have been somewhat mixed. Singhvi and Desai (1971) and Wallace, Naser, and Mora (1994) find a significant positive relationship. Conversely, Belkaoui and Kahl (1978) and Wallace and Naser (1995) find a significant negative relationship between disclosure levels and profitability. Finally, some studies have found no evidence of a statistical association (e.g., Raffournier 1995).

Given the mixed prior empirical results, it is unclear whether a firm's profitability will have a positive or negative impact on the extent of disclosure of intellectual capital–related information in the annual reports of publicly listed companies. There would be a positive relationship between the two variables if (1) firms active in the management of intellectual capital tended to be more profitable, even though some of the returns to investment in intellectual capital may lag recognition in the financial accounts, and (2) these firms were to choose to disclose information about intellectual capital. Disclosures could be used to signal barriers to entry and in that case we would expect to observe greater disclosure among highly profitable firms. Alternatively, disclosure could help other firms that are unprofitable learn how to leverage their intellectual capital, and therefore, the profitable firms may refrain from disclosing intellectual capital. A negative relationship between firm profitability and disclosure would also be observed if unprofitable firms find it especially important to signal their prospects for improved profits by disclosing their activities in intellectual capital–related activities. We expect the amount of disclosures to be related to profitability, but as with firm size we cannot predict the direction of this relationship.

Industry Type—Research and Development Intensity

Prior research suggests that companies in specific industries may have a greater incentive to disclose certain kinds of information. For example, in the case of environmental disclosures, it has been suggested (e.g., Patten 1991; Walden and Schwartz 1997) that firms in environmentally sensitive industries, such as the chemical, petroleum, forestry, and consumer products provide more disclosure on this issue than companies in other industries. Firms in environmentally sensitive industries have an incentive to provide more disclosure, so as to reduce the scrutiny from special interest groups, avoid regulatory intervention, and protect its own self-interests and image.

There is as yet no clear evidence from the prior literature to suggest what particular industry feature may determine which industries are more sensitive to the disclosure of intellectual capital information. Nonetheless, some studies emphasize the importance of research and development expenditures to the creation of intellectual capital assets (e.g., OECD 2000; Harris 2000). For our study, therefore, the intensity of research and development undertaken by a firm is considered a relevant proxy for industry type. We define *research and development intensity* as the ratio of reported research and development expenses to total assets, consistent with prior empirical studies (Sanders and Carpenter 1998). Research and development intensity is a financial-statement measure of investment in intellectual assets not included in our intellectual capital disclosure index.

Our definition of research and development intensity enables us to examine the linkage between conventional financial statement disclosure of knowledge-producing activity and the voluntary disclosures of intellectual capital in our index. We assume that firms reporting higher levels of research and development are more likely to engage in the intellectual capital activities captured in our index; they are knowledge-intensive firms in a general sense. However, it is still each firm's choice whether to disclose these other activities to the public, and there are associated competitive advantages and disadvantages. As in the previous discussion of firm size, high-intensity research and development firms may wish to signal barriers to entry through intellectual capital disclosures, or they may not want to be emulated by low-intensity research and development firms and decide not to disclose.

Research Design

Sample Selection

We selected Swedish companies for this study for two important reasons. First, the literature indicates that companies in Sweden are leaders in the management of intellectual capital. However, there has been no research on their intellectual capital disclosure practices. It is of interest, therefore, to determine if companies in Sweden, apart from actively managing intellectual capital, provide discretionary disclosures related to this concept. Second, the Swedish economy has undergone considerable transformation in the last few decades. Sweden has shifted from a reliance on traditional commodities and manufacturing toward wealth creation that utilizes information technology and knowledge as primary factors of production. As a consequence of this transformation, there is likely to be a variety of stakeholder groups interested in the provision of intellectual capital information.

Thirty companies were randomly selected from among the ninety-three publicly listed companies from Sweden with 1998 annual reports available on the World Wide Web in English. An underlying assumption of this study is that the annual report is a firm's principal mechanism for communicating intellectual capital–related information to stakeholders; this assumption is supported by prior research (Gray, Kouhy, and Lavers 1995; Tilt 1994).

Measure of Intellectual Capital Disclosure

Measurement of the independent variables (size, profitability, and research and development intensity) was described previously. We measured the dependent variable, intellectual capital disclosure, by constructing a disclosure index similar to that of Hossain, Tan, and Adams (1994). Brooking (1996) was selected as the basis of the disclosure index comprising fifty-three discretionary intellectual capital disclosure items. Items contained in the disclosure index were then categorized into five major components (or subcategories) of intellectual capital in:

(a) Human Resources—Covers statements about the employees' qualifications, the management system's handling of the human resource development task, and the employees' satisfaction

(b) Customers—Covers statements about the composition of customers, the company's efforts to develop the customer relationship, and customer satisfaction and loyalty (repeat business and long-term relations)

(c) Information Technology—Covers the scope and availability of IT systems and, for example, investments in research and development

(d) Process—Relates to the activity-oriented expression of a number of business activities especially favored by the company (for example, lead time, economy, and productivity of administrative processes). "Processes" are also an expression of quality, error rate, and waiting time toward the surroundings of the company

(e) Intellectual Property—covers statements by a company on its investment into and development of creative ideas and items to which rights have been assigned. The term covers such items as used to refer to that group of rights that include patents, trade marks, copyrights, industrial designs, trade secrets, and confidential information

Finally, to limit ambiguity, we analyzed intellectual capital disclosures on a sentence basis. We selected sentences as the unit of analysis because a "sentence is easily identified, is less subject to interjudge variation than phrases, clauses or themes, and has been evaluated as an appropriate unit in previous research" (Ingram and Frazier 1980: 617). We evaluated each sentence in the annual report as to whether it addresses one of the fifty-three intellectual capital concepts, and the concept was then assigned a score based on the following classification:

(a) Quantitative/Monetary—If the disclosure item was clearly defined in monetary terms or actual physical quantities, then a score of four (4) was assigned.

(b) Descriptive—If the disclosure item was discussed, showing clearly its impact on the company or its policies, then a score of three (3) was assigned.

(c) Obscure—If the disclosure item is discussed in limited passing or vague comments while discussing other topics and themes, then a score of two (2)was assigned.

(d) Immaterial—If the company states that the disclosure item is immaterial to the financial well-being and results of the firm, then a score of one (1) was assigned.

(e) Non-disclosure—If the disclosure item does not appear in the annual report, then a score of zero (0) was assigned.

Each of the fifty-three concepts would be assigned a single score based on the highest number awarded to the sentences concerning that concept. For example, if one sentence dealing with customer loyalty was awarded a score of two, and another sentence in the same section of the annual report dealing with customer loyalty was awarded a score of three, customer loyalty would be awarded a score of three for that section of the annual report. The scores are then combined to provide totals for each company for: (i) each specific subcategory of intellectual capital, and (ii) the total disclosure index.

Results

Table 8-1 provides some descriptive statistics for the sample of Swedish publicly listed companies included in our study. Relative to other disclosure studies of Swedish listed companies, such as Cooke (1991), our sample companies are generally larger, whether measured in terms of total assets, market capitalization, or sales. The differences in corporate size are not significant, given the passage of time between our study and the prior work. The profitability of our sample companies is consistent with prior studies. Research and development costs have not been reported in previous studies, so we cannot evaluate how our sample compares to previous studies.

The intellectual capital disclosure index is reported in Table 8-2. The Table provides both the average total index score and the average score for each of the five major subcategories. The subcategory with the highest average score is human resources at 21.00, but this may be in part a reflection of the construction of the index. This subcategory has fourteen items that can be scored, compared to ten items for the customer subcategory (whose score was second at

Table 8-1
Descriptive statistics of survey sample

Organizational Level Characteristic	Mean	Standard Deviation
Total Assets at End 1998 (Millions of Swedish Kroner)	60,524.44	163,304.17
Total Liabilities at End of 1998 (Millions of Swedish Kroner)	50,521.18	156,720.57
Total Sales for Period Ended 1998 (Millions of Swedish Kroner)	19,474.99	26,526.72
Research and Development Costs 1998 (Millions of Swedish Kroner)	486.83	1,933.61
Market Capitalization at End of 1998 (Millions of Swedish Kroner)	27,474.47	54,466.76
Return on Capital Employed (ROCE)	12.38%	10.72%

14.43). If we consider the score per item within the subcategories, we get 1.5 per item for the human resources subcategory and 1.44 per item for the customer subcategory. The remaining subcategories each had ten items per subcategory.

Table 8-3 shows the Pearson-correlation results between size, profitability, and research and development–intensity, and the total intellectual capital disclosure and each of the five major subcategories. The only significant correlation with total intellectual capital disclosure is with respect to size (0.407, p = 0.027). Profitability is essentially uncorrelated with total intellectual capital disclosure (.057), whereas research and development–intensity is negatively correlated with total intellectual disclosure (–.189), though not significantly. There are three significant correlations with the five subcategories of intellectual capital. Size was positively correlated to the amount of human resources disclosure. Conversely, research

Table 8-2
Total disclosure index and category averages

Major Category of Intellectual Capital Disclosure					
Total Disclosure	Human Resources	Customers	Information Technology	Processes	Intellectual Property
59.07	21.00	14.43	8.90	7.60	7.13
(18.07)α^*	(10.11)	(4.67)	(6.43)	(5.32)	(8.37)

$^*\alpha$ = Standard deviation is in parenthesis

Table 8-3
Pearson correlations between dependent and independent variables

Pearson Correlations Between Dependent and Independent Variables			
Dependent Variable	**Independent Variable**		
	Organizational Size (LogTA)$^\beta$	Profitability (ROCE)$^\chi$	R&D Intensity (RDI)$^\delta$
Total Intellectual Disclosure (TID)	0.407*	0.057	–0.189
Human Resource Disclosure	0.417*	0.007	–0.409*
Customer Disclosure	0.304	0.239	–0.244
Information Technology Disclosure	0.311	–0.164	–0.164
Processes Disclosure	0.256	0.010	–0.121
Intellectual Property	–0.195	0.099	0.515**

Legend:

α: TID = Proxy measure for a firm's "Total Intellectual Disclosure"—sum of intellectual capital disclosures by company's in their 1998 annual report to total possible disclosure score.

β: LogTA = Proxy measure of a firm's "Size"—natural log of the total assets of the firm at the end of 1998.

χ: ROCE = Proxy measure of a firm's "Profitability"—return on capital employed.

δ: RDI = Proxy measure of a firm's "R&D Intensity"—ratio of the firm's level of research and development expenditure to total assets.

* = Correlation is significant at the 5% significance level (2—tailed).

** = Correlation is significant at the 1% significance level (2—tailed).

and development–intensity was negatively correlated with the amount of disclosure regarding human resources. Finally, research and development–intensity was positively correlated with the amount of disclosure related to intellectual property. Stepwise regression results, not reported here, produced results consistent with the correlation analysis.

The positive association between intellectual capital disclosure and size is consistent with most of the previous disclosure studies. This suggests that smaller firms are not more inclined to disclose more information to demonstrate their growth potential to the market. The positive correlation would also indicate that larger firms are not more concerned than smaller firms about disclosing potentially competitive information.

To further analyze the potential association between the independent variables and the amount of intellectual capital disclosure, we segregated the sample companies into high and low groupings on each independent variable. For example, the sample was segregated into "large companies" and "small companies" based on the median size. The sample was similarly segregated into "high profitability companies" and "low profitability companies," and into "high research and development–intensity companies" and "low research and development–intensity companies" based on median values. This analytical approach is consistent with prior research such as Adams, Hill, and Roberts (1998).

Table 8-4 panels A, B, and C report index scores by the segregated independent variables. Panel A shows that the total intellectual capital disclosure index for small companies is 51.60 and for large companies it is 66.53. Independent t-test results indicate that this is a significant difference. Among the five major subcategories of the intellectual capital disclosure index, there is a significant difference by company size for the amount of disclosure for information technology and for processes. The results in panel B suggest there is no significant difference in the total intellectual capital disclosure index by level of research and development–intensity. If we consider the subcategories, we see some interesting results. The average amount of disclosure on human resource issues is significantly higher for low research and development-intensity companies compared to high research and development-intensity companies, whereas, conversely, the average amount of disclosure on intellectual property issues is significantly lower for low research and development–intensity companies compared to high research and development–intensity companies.

Finally, results in Table 8-4 panel C show that the average amount of total intellectual disclosure does not differ between firms classified as low profitability and those classified as high profitability. Neither does the average amount of disclosure for the five different subcategories of intellectual capital differ significantly by profitability-grouping.

The results reported in Table 8-4 considered the possible effects of size, research and development–intensity, and size, separately. Such an examination, however, may be insufficient due to possible interaction effects between the three variables. For instance, the effects of profitability may differ across companies of various size

Table 8-4

Total disclosure index and major category averages by organizational level characteristics

| | Total Disclosure | Major Category of Intellectual Capital Disclosure | | | | |
		Human Resources	Customers	Information Technology	Processes	Intellectual Property
Panel A – Size						
Smallest Companies	51.60 (18.32)	18.00 (10.83)	13.53 (3.76)	6.47 (5.95)	5.67 (3.99)	7.93 (8.54)
Largest Companies	66.53 (16.76)	24.00 (8.16)	15.33 (5.31)	11.33 (6.41)	9.53 (6.02)	6.33 (9.36)
Independent t-tests	2.451 [0.021]β*	1.676 [0.105]	1.059 [0.300]	2.207 [0.036]*	2.104 [0.044]*	-0.517 [0.609]
Panel B - R&D Intensity						
Low R&D Intensity	61.53 (18.91)	25.47 (9.80)	15.33 (4.95)	10.53 (6.93)	6.67 (4.43)	3.53 (5.15)
High R&D Intensity	56.60 (16.73)	16.53 (8.12)	13.53 (4.36)	7.27 (5.34)	8.53 (6.02)	10.73 (9.75)
Independent t-tests	-0.742 [0.464]	-2.663 [0.013]*	-1.059 [0.299]	-1.415 [0.168]	0.959 [0.346]	2.573 [0.016]*
Panel C - Profitability						
Low ROCE	60.07 (19.33)	23.00 (10.40)	13.60 (4.22)	10.53 (6.29)	8.07 (5.57)	4.87 (7.77)
High ROCE	58.07 (17.95)	19.00 (9.40)	15.27 (4.95)	7.27 (6.28)	7.13 (5.10)	9.40 (9.97)
Independent t-tests	-0.298 [0.768]	-1.087 [0.286]	0.977 [0.337]	-1.415 [0.168]	-0.474 [0.639]	1.515 [0.141]

Legend:

α: = Standard deviation is in parenthesis; β = Significance of t-value in parenthesis; * = Significant 5% level; ** = Significant 10% level.

and research and development–intensity, and vice versa. Therefore, to explore the relationship among the three variables of interest, we must further analyze the total disclosure index. The results are shown in Table 8-5, panels A, B, and C, respectively.

Results in Table 8-5 panel A suggest some interaction between the size of a company and the extent of research and development–intensity on the total intellectual capital disclosure index scores. For larger companies, the extent of research and development-intensity appears to have little or no impact on the level of total intellectual capital disclosure; whereas for smaller companies, research and development–intensity

Table 8-5
Cross-sectional effects of organizational level factors on total disclosure scores

Panel A – Size and R&D Intensity		
	Low R&D Intensity	High R&D Intensity
Small Companies	60.333	45.778
Large Companies	62.333	72.833

ANOVA Test Results:
F-value = 3.700; Significance = 0.024*

Panel B – Size and Profitability		
	Low ROCE	High ROCE
Small Companies	54.556	47.167
Large Companies	62.571	70.000

ANOVA Test Results:
F-value = 2.433; Significance = 0.088**

Panel C – R&D Intensity and Profitability		
	Low ROCE	High ROCE
Low R&D Intensity	61.250	61.857
High R&D Intensity	58.714	54.750

ANOVA Test Results:
F-value = 0.228; Significance = 0.876

Legend: * = Significant 5% level; ** = Significant 10% level.

does seem to impact the level of disclosure. The highest disclosure index is reported for large companies that are research and development intensive. However, as shown in Table 8-5 panels B and C, there is no significant interaction between size and profitability, and profitability and research and development–intensity, respectively.

Discussion

There is considerable variation in the extent of intellectual capital–related information disclosed by Swedish publicly listed companies in their corporate annual reports. This finding is consistent with some prior research of studies in other countries and regions of the world (e.g., Guthrie and Petty 2000). As an advance over the prior literature, however, our study indicates that the disclosure of intellectual capital information is not evenly spread among the major subcategories of this concept. For example, the average amount of intellectual capital disclosure related to human resource capital is significantly greater than that for processes. This finding demonstrates that aggregating the amount of intellectual capital disclosure in a single index, rather than considering the relevant major subcategories, may lead to valuable insights and conclusions being overlooked.

There is a positive relationship between the size of Swedish publicly listed companies and the total amount of intellectual capital disclosure provided in the corporation's annual report. Size also affects the amount of disclosure specifically related to information technology, processes, and, to a limited extent, human resources. There is no evidence to indicate what is the cause of this relationship. We can speculate, however, that the lack of disclosure among smaller companies on matters of intellectual capital may be due to threats of competitive disadvantage. Prior research indicates that intellectual capital assets, such as key employees or products designs, are highly mobile in their nature, not only at a national level but also globally. Smaller companies may decline to disclose information on the intellectual capital assets they possess, for fear that the mobility of human assets may entice competitors to lure them away. Being smaller, such companies may not be able to replace the loss of its human capital as well as can larger companies.

Research and development–intensity is negatively correlated with total intellectual capital disclosure, although not strongly. This raises a question about the effect of research and development–intensity upon disclosure—why might incentives to disclose, such as competitive advantage or disadvantage, work in opposite directions for firm size and research and development–intensity?

One possibility is that the effect of research and development–intensity is signed differently for the five disclosure subcategories in the total intellectual disclosure measure. There are significant correlations between research and development–intensity and the subcategories of human resource disclosure (–.409) and intellectual property (.515), and these correlations have opposite signs. The correlations with the other three subcategories are negative but not significant. Irrespective of the willingness of firms to disclose intellectual capital, research and development–intensive firms may invest in intellectual property instead of, or in preference to, making human resource investments, such as training. Another way of stating this is that firms may choose to either develop intellectual capital through research and development–spending and investing in specific intellectual property projects, or develop overall human resource potential that cannot be traced to individual projects. Our speculation here is that the effect of research and development–intensity upon total intellectual disclosure depends on the actual allocation of investment across the five dimensions of intellectual capital.

Our empirical results fail to discern any significant association between profitability and the total amount of intellectual capital disclosure. Neither is profitability a significant determinant of the amount of disclosure related to the five major subcategories of intellectual capital. Profitability appears to be only of influence when this factor is considered in conjunction with the size of the firm. Of the two, size appears to be the major factor behind any differences in the amount of total intellectual disclosure, rather than profitability.

The lack of an association between profitability and the amount of intellectual capital disclosure is consistent with prior research on disclosure practices in general (e.g., Raffournier 1995). Based on our findings, two conclusions can be reached with respect to the influence of profitability on disclosure practices. First, if profitability does affect disclosure practices, the effect is only marginal. Second, profitability cannot be used as a predictor of future intellectual capital disclosure practices, should intellectual capital grow in importance as the pivotal item for wealth creation of a company. Our measure of profitability, ROCE, is essentially a traditional accounting model measure of profit and accordingly is a reflection of a company's physical, rather than intellectual, capital. There may, therefore, be little association between this measure of profitability and the amount of intellectual capital activities and hence, the disclosure of those activities.

Finally, we should comment on the significant interrelationships between size and research and development–intensity, and between size and profitability. Our findings, reported in Table 8-5, suggest that, regardless of size, firms that are not research and development–intensive are likely to report similar amounts of information on intellectual capital (60.333 for small low-intensity companies and 62.333 for large low-intensity companies). The least inclined to report on intellectual capital are smaller firms that are high in research and development–intensity and smaller firms that have a high level of profitability (45.778 and 47.167, respectively). Smaller firms that are not research and development-intensive and smaller firms that have a low level of profitability may feel these conditions fail to draw the attention of competitors, and so the size of the entity becomes secondary in the disclosure decision. In contrast, firms that are both high research and development–intensive and have high profits may think such properties will draw the attention of their competitors and accordingly they choose to disclose less (see panel C: 54.750). Due to a greater size, larger firms may not perceive a threat from competitors as they have the resources to survive any such scrutiny. Therefore, large companies that are highly research and development–intensive will disclose more than small companies that are highly research and development–intensive, and large companies that have a high level of profitability will disclose more than small companies that have a high level of profitability.

Conclusion

The major objectives and contributions of this chapter are twofold. First, our study examines the intellectual capital disclosure practices of companies from Sweden, which, although known as a leader in the development of the concept of intellectual capital, has not received much attention. Second, prior research on intellectual capital disclosure practices, generally speaking, have been largely descriptive in nature and have not examined the underlying determinants of disclosure practices. Our study seeks to overcome, in part, this gap in the literature by examining empirically the influence of three organizational-level factors on intellectual capital disclosure practices: corporate size, profitability, and industry type, as measured by research and development–intensity. Our empirical results indicate significant variations in the amount of intellectual disclosure among listed companies in Sweden. The size of the company, and to a limited degree the level of research and development pursued by the company, has a positive impact on the amount and type of intellectual capital information disclosed. Profitability, however, does not affect intellectual capital disclosure. Regardless of the contribution of our findings, further research is required in order to develop a complete understanding of intellectual capital disclosure practices.

REFERENCES

Abdolmohammadi, M. J., L. Greenlay, and D. V. Poole. 1999. Accounting Methods for Measuring Intellectual Capital. http://www.round.table.com/scholars/articles/acctg-intellectual-capital.html, accessed 1 November 2000.

Adams, C. A., W. Y. Hill, and C. B. Roberts. 1998. Corporate Social Reporting Practices in Western Europe: Legitimating corporate behaviour? *The British Accounting Review* 30, 1: 1–21.

Ahmed, K. and J. K. Courtis. 1999. Associations Between Corporate Characteristics and Disclosure Levels in Annual Reports: A Meta Analysis, *The British Accounting Review* 31: 35–61.

Belkaoui, A. and A. Kahl. 1978. *Corporate Financial Disclosure in Canada*. Research Monograph no. 1. Vancouver, Canada: Canadian Certified General Accountants Association.

Bontis, N. 1999. Managing Organizational Knowledge by Diagnosing Intellectual Capital: Framing and Advancing the State of the Field, *International Journal of Technology Management* 18, 5/6/7/8: 433–62.

Brennan, N. 1999. Reporting and Managing Intellectual Capital: Evidence from Ireland. Paper presented at the International Symposium Measuring and Reporting Intellectual Capital: Experiences, Issues and Prospects, June, Amsterdam, Netherlands: OCED.

Brooking, A. 1996. *Intellectual Capital: Core Assets for the Third Millennium Enterprise*. London: Thomson Business Press.

Cooke, T. E. 1991. An Assessment of Voluntary Disclosure in the Annual Reports of Japanese Corporations, *The International Journal of Accounting* 26, 2: 174–89.

Courtis, J. K. 1979. Annual Report Disclosure in New Zealand: Analysis of Selected Corporate Attributes. Research Study no. 8. Armidale, New South Wales, Australia: University of New England.

Cowen, S. C., L. B. Ferreri, and L. D. Parker. 1987. The Impact of Corporate Characteristics on Social Responsibility Disclosure: A Typology and Frequency-Based Analysis, *Accounting, Organizations and Society* 12, 2: 111–22.

Edvinsson, L. and M. S. Malone. 1997. *Intellectual Capital: Realizing Your Company's True Value by Finding its Hidden Brain Power.* New York: Harper Business.

Firth, M. 1979. The Impact of Size, Stock Market Listing and Auditors on Voluntary Disclosure in Corporate Annual Reports, *Accounting and Business Research* 9 (Autumn): 273–80.

Gray, R., R. Kouhy, and S. Lavers. 1995. Corporate Social and Environmental Reporting: A Review of the Literature and a Longitudinal Study of U.K. Disclosure, *Accounting, Auditing and Accountability* 8, 2: 47–77.

Guthrie, J. and R. Petty. 2000. Intellectual Capital: Australian Annual Reporting Practices, *Journal of Intellectual Capital* 1, 3: 241–51.

Harris, R. 2000. The Knowledge-Based Economy: Facts and Theories. Working paper: Queen's Management Research Centre for Knowledge-Based Enterprises, http://www.business.queensu.ca/kbe, accessed 1 June 2000.

Hossain, M., L. M. Tan, and M. Adams. 1994. Voluntary Disclosure in an Emerging Market: Some Empirical Evidence from Companies Listed on the Kuala Lumpur Stock Exchange, *The International Journal of Accounting Education and Research* 29, 3: 334–51.

Inchausti, B. G. 1997. The Influence of Company Characteristics and Accounting Regulation on Information Disclosed by Spanish Firms, *The European Accounting Review* 6, 1: 45–68.

Ingram, R. and K. Frazier. 1980. Environmental Performance and Corporate Disclosure, *Journal of Accounting Research* 18 (Autumn): 614–22.

Luthy, D. H. 1998. Intellectual Capital and Its Measurement. http://www3.bus.osaka-cu.ac.jp/apira98/archives/htmls/25.htm, accessed 1 November 2000.

Marston, C. L. and P. Robson. 1997. Financial Reporting in India: Changes in Disclosure over the Period 1982–1990, *Asia-Pacific Journal of Accounting* 4, 1: 109–39.

Marston, C. L. and P. J. Shrives. 1991. The Use of Disclosure Indices in Accounting Research: A Review Article. *The British Accounting Review* 25: 195–210.

Organization for Economic Cooperation and Development (OECD). 2000. *Final Report: Measuring and Reporting Intellectual Capital: Experience, Issues and Prospects.* Paris: OCED.

Patten, D. 1991. Exposure, Legitimacy and Social Disclosure, *Journal of Accounting and Public Policy* 10, 4: 297–308.

Pulic, A. and M. Bornemann. 1999. The Physical and Intellectual Capital of Austrian Banks. http://www.measuring-ip.at/English/papers.html, accessed October 8, 2001.

Raffournier, B. 1995. The Determinants of Voluntary Financial Disclosure by Swiss Listed Companies, *The European Accounting Review* 4, 2: 261–80.

Sanders, W. G. and M. A. Carperter. 1998. Internationalization and Firm Governance: The Roles of CEO Compensation, Top Team Composition and Board Structure, *Academy of Management Journal* 41, 2: 158–78.

Singhvi, S. S. and H. B. Desai. 1971. An Empirical Analysis of the Quality of Corporate Financial Disclosure, *The Accounting Review* 46, 1: 120–38.

Skandia Insurance Company. 1995. *Visualizing Intellectual Capital in Skandia: Supplement to Skandia Annual Report 1994.* Stockholm: Skandia Insurance Company.

Stewart, T. A. 1997. *Intellectual Capital: The New Wealth of Organizations.* New York: Doubleday/Currency.

Taylor, S. and Associates. 1999. *Full Disclosure 1998.* London: Shelley Taylor.

The Society of Management Accountants of Canada. 1998. The Management of Intellectual Capital: The Issues and the Practice, Issues Paper no. 16. Hamilton, Canada: The Society of Management Accountants of Canada.

Tilt, C. A. 1994. The Influence of External Pressure Groups on Corporate Social Disclosure: Some Empirical Evidence, *Accounting, Auditing and Accountability Journal* 7, 4: 47–72.

Walden, W. D. and B. N. Schwartz. 1997. Environmental Disclosures and Public Policy Pressure, *Journal of Accounting and Public Policy* 16, 2: 125–54.

Wallace, R. S. O. and K. Naser. 1995. Firm-Specific Determinants of Comprehensiveness of Mandatory Disclosure in the Corporate Annual Reports of Firms on the Stock Exchange of Hong Kong, *Journal of Accounting and Public Policy* 14: 311–68.

Wallace, R. S. O., K. Naser, and A. Mora. 1994. The Relationship Between Comprehensiveness of Corporate Annual Reports and Firm Characteristics in Spain. *Accounting and Business Research* 25, 97: 41–53.

Wiseman, J. 1982. An Evaluation of Environmental Disclosures Made in Corporate Annual Reports, *Accounting, Organisations and Society* 7, 6: 553–63.

9

RELEVANT EXPERIENCES IN MEASURING AND REPORTING INTELLECTUAL CAPITAL IN EUROPEAN PIONEERING FIRMS

Patricia Ordóñez de Pablos
Faculty of Economics, University of Oviedo, Spain
patricia@econo.uniovi.es

ABSTRACT

This study reports both the results of a survey among Danish firms and the empirical examination of their annual reporting of intellectual capital. A section with a general view of IC-reporting in Spain is also provided. The findings suggest that a three-stage path is clearly evident in how leading firms take their first steps in the intellectual capital field. Generally, these firms begin their journey in the intellectual capital world by implementing a knowledge management model. Later ad hoc, nonfinancial metrics are introduced to grasp the value of intangible resources that are not recorded in the book value. Finally, in order to generate internal and external benefits, firms initiate the disclosure of their intellectual capital metrics. In conclusion, Danish firms are playing a leading role in the field of intellectual capital reports. Even if other firms, such as Spanish ones, are trying to catch up with the Danish "first movers," it is not an easy task. Organizational knowledge gathered through the process of the development of intellectual capital reports impede imitation because of causal ambiguity and time-compression diseconomies.

INTRODUCTION

This study examines the proposition that intellectual capital–reporting is a key element in a firm's sustainable competitive advantage. This relevance will be reflected by way of disclosure of intellectual capital in the annual report or intellectual capital report. The disclosure of organizational intellectual capital contributes to the formation of a more detailed picture of the organization. It clearly signals organizational competencies in key elements—human capital, relational capital, and organizational capital—that form the "invisible" roots of the organizational value. However, intellectual capital measurement tools and intellectual capital reports contribute to make visible these hidden roots. Firms that have responded to the challenge of measuring and reporting intellectual capital are able to visualize their intellectual capital, and with this strategic view, they are able to compete and gain a sustainable competitive advantage.

THE STRATEGIC IMPORTANCE OF KNOWLEDGE MANAGEMENT

From the resource-based view of the firm to the knowledge-based view of the firm, it is clear that a particular intangible resource has become the cornerstone of sustainable competitive advantage (Barney 1986; Foss 1996; Penrose 1959; Ventura 1996). This resource is organizational knowledge. According to Peteraf's framework (1993: 186), "four conditions must be met for a firm to enjoy sustained above-normal returns. Resource heterogeneity creates Ricardian or monopoly rents. Ex post limits to competition prevent the rents from being competed away. Imperfect factor mobility ensures that valuable factors remain with the firm and that the rents are shared. Ex ante limits to competition keep costs from offsetting the rents."

Undoubtedly, organizational knowledge qualifies as "the key resource" in today's competitive environment.

However, knowledge management is a slippery concept. Knowledge management is a fast-moving field that has been created by the collision of several other—human resources, organizational development, change management, information technology, brand and reputation management, performance measurement, and valuation (Bukowitz and Williams 2000). Knowledge management is especially important for business in terms of gaining a competitive advantage and increasing profits. So far, KM has gone through at least three phases. As Sveiby (2000) states, the first phase was from around 1985 to 1990. In this phase, researchers took their inspiration from philosophers such as Wittgenstein and Polanyi, and they explored the value created by leveraging the competence and skills of people and knowledge creation. The second phase was around 1991–1997. The information technology (IT) revolution and the Internet started driving change in organizations. It was all about reusing existing knowledge and how to avoid reinventing the wheel. In this second phase, knowledge management and intellectual capital terms became the highlights of conferences and publications in both Europe and the United States. These terms were seen basically as means to increase organizational efficiency. Since 1998 we are living in the third phase of KM and IC management. The hot topics are organizational-knowledge creation and innovation knowledge management. More and more managers realize the importance of creating suitable environments where employees feel comfortable to collaborate, create, diffuse, and share their individual knowledge (Sveiby 2000).

KNOWLEDGE MANAGEMENT AT THE OPERATIONAL AND STRATEGIC LEVELS

According to the Cranfield University's survey on the state of the art of knowledge management in Europe, "around 85% of companies believe a value can be attached to business knowledge and over 90% claim to have plans to acquire and exploit it. Cross analysis with other answers shows a pattern of increasing awareness of the need to address knowledge management in a more formal way than at present." Undoubtedly, knowledge management has become the buzz word in business today. However, the majority of firms following this trend are approaching it in a truly operational way. So let us have a look at the concepts of operational knowledge management and strategic knowledge management.

Companies already aware of the need to distribute information throughout the organization are making use of a variety of operational knowledge management techniques. Their main concern is to connect people to the system being used for the distribution and transfer of knowledge. Although this may be a good start, companies have found—more often than not—that this tends to become costly, ineffective, and nonproductive. Strategic knowledge management gives balance by linking the building of your company's knowledge to your business strategy (Tissen et al. 1998: 25).

Strategic knowledge management turns out to be very valuable for managing important intrafirm relationships and setting an ad hoc scenario for collaboration between knowledge workers. According to Tissen et al. (1998: 31), "the first prerequisite for collaboration is to create direction and a shared understanding of goals and opportunities. A knowledge strategy will guide the creation of knowledge that can be turned into market value." The critical success factor is not only the number of new ideas but more so their implementation. This can be facilitated by having the right company culture, leadership, and infrastructure (Skandia 1996: 4).

The intelligent organization focuses knowledge flows and relationships to achieve sustained growth in value. In such an organization, knowledge growth is a two-way process. It is an organization that both collects and rapidly shares knowledge. Knowledge is a kind of capital that is not depleted when applied. On the contrary, it is capital that grows in value when applied for the benefit of employees, customers, or business partners. In the industrial economy, returns on capital diminish progressively over time. The knowledge economy is governed by the law of increasing marginal utility. In the knowledge economy, when knowledge is shared and applied by an ever greater number of users, its value is increased (Skandia 1996: 20).

Knowledge Management Strategy: Sharing versus Hoarding

Knowledge-sharing strategy is a cornerstone of the competitive strategy of the firm. The most cited elements in the knowledge sharing strategy are "best practices, knowledge and process agents, and mentorships": for example, in Systematic. Generally, firms record their "best practices" and make them available on the intranet. The employees should be able to draw on the stored knowledge and exchange it with the help of information technologies. Knowledge- and process-agent roles consist of employees with particular knowledge of a relevant specific organizational field. Her or his role is to convey this valuable knowledge to other members of the firm. Finally, mentorship activities are helpful for young employees to acquire relevant working knowledge that is not normally taught at an University.

Cowi (1999: 12) states that "the production apparatus in COWI is the staff; its fuel is knowledge. Therefore we do not own our production plant—but we do own an organization that creates the working conditions and opportunities for the staff which, used properly, given the chance to maintain, build on and share knowledge . . . By improving the condition on knowledge sharing across organizational boundaries through a 'Best Practice' system, we make best use of strength that comes from size. Today, we have 612 'Best Practices,' all available on the intranet."

Knowledge-hoarding strategies are characteristic of firms in which the concept of individual knowledge is equivalent to individual power. Much of the cultural resistance to create a knowledge culture is based on the idea that knowledge is power. People who know are more powerful than people who do not know. Knowledge is used as a weapon for internal one-upmanship—not for the greater good of the company. However, replacing such a mentality with one of "power is in sharing knowledge" cannot happen overnight. Yet many firms are becoming aware of the need to do just that (Tissen et al. 1998).

Undoubtedly, strategic knowledge resources must be protected against unwanted permeability and diffusion that could deteriorate a firm's competitive advantage. As Tissen et al. (1998: 53) put it "the security and protection of knowledge is therefore becoming critical in any company's strategy. Knowledge can simply get up and walk out of the door." However, sharing organizational knowledge is not a zero-sum game. So, to maximize organizational knowledge potential, employees must share and put in use their individual knowledge and through this action at individual level, the organizational spiral of knowledge creation starts (Nonaka and Takeuchi 1995). The ultimate scarce organizational resource in a knowledge-based economy is an organization's ability to create new knowledge (Sveiby 2000).

Among the most-cited organizational benefits from KM are the following items: improved efficiency and increased learning skills, increased competitiveness, and fast access to relevant knowledge.

A FIRM'S JOURNEY TO KM AND IC

It is true that firms have different histories, goals, and visions as well as different endowments of organizational resources. These factors contribute to what the organization is today and to its success and development. At the same time the historical organizational path and decisions as well as the resource endowments can be the cause of organizational inertia and therefore the source of organizational-core rigidities. In this sense, knowledge-intensive firms tend to complement their knowledge management strategy with the implementation of intellectual capital–measuring and –reporting initiatives.

Generally, firms start their intellectual capital journeys by setting up a company model (see Fig. 9-1) in which organizational foundation (organizational vision, values and goals), efforts (people, processes, infrastructure, etc.), and results ("soft" results related to employees, customers, etc., and financial results) connect.

Sometimes they also include a knowledge management model underlying the most strategic areas for the company's success. Knowledge management covers all activities that are aimed at generating, sharing, utilising, conveying, and measuring organizational knowledge. Firms allocate special emphasis on increasing learning capabilities and sharing knowledge as well as experience of technologies and processes.

Related to knowledge management is the concept of an intellectual capital report. As Larsen et al. (1999: 15) argue, "more precisely, knowledge management activities are the object that intellectual capital statements attempt to illuminate." So the next section is devoted to the strategic analysis of intellectual capital and intellectual capital reports.

INTELLECTUAL CAPITAL

Stewart (1997) defines intellectual capital as "the intellectual material—knowledge, information, intellectual property, experience—that can be put to use to create wealth." The concept of intellectual capital helps one understand why organizational book-value differs from market value (Joia 2000). However, as Gormsen et al. (2000: 17) recall, "the market value of the company is determined by the expectations as regards to future earnings." In this sense, the objective of this empirical study is to explore the concept of intellectual capital and the development of intellectual capital reports that could help both

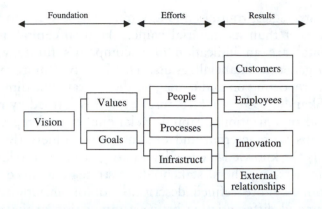

Source: Systematic's Intellectual Capital Report (2000: 8)

Figure 9-1 *Company Model*

academics and practitioners more readily understand the importance of intellectual capital reports and their impact on organizational results in today's competitive environment.

Prior to continuing the dissertation on the strategic relevance of intellectual capital reports, it may be helpful to conceptualize what are the components of intellectual capital. Although definitions and conceptualizations are not entirely identical, the field is starting to see a convergence of what IC encompasses (Bontis 1998; Bontis 1999; Bontis, Chua, and Richardson 2000). Generally, literature has identified three subphenomena that constitute the concept of intellectual capital: human capital, relational capital, and organizational capital.

Quite simply, human capital represents the individual knowledge stock of an organization as represented by its employees (Bontis et al. 2002). It is the accumulated value of investments in employee training, competence, and future (Skandia 1996). Human capital is important because it is a source of innovation and strategic renewal. . . . The essence of human capital is the sheer intelligence of the organizational member (Bontis 1998: 65–66).

The concept of structural capital refers to the value of what is left when the human capital—the employees—has gone home: databases, customer lists, manuals, trademarks, and organizational structures, to give a few examples (Skandia 1996). According to Bontis, Chua, and Richardson (2000: 88), structural capital "includes all the non-human storehouses of knowledge in organizations which include the databases, organizational charts, process manuals, strategies, routines and anything whose value to the company is higher than its material value." Human capital and structural capital are an indication of a company's future value and ability to generate financial results. This is why a more systematic method of reporting on and managing these intangible dimensions is needed (Skandia 1996: 6). Structural capital is formed by relational capital and organizational capital. Relational capital represents the relationships with internal and external stakeholders (Roos et al. 1998). It is the knowledge embedded in organizational relationships with customers, suppliers, stakeholders, strategic alliance partners, and so on. A more refined description of organizational capital would demand differentiating between innovation capital and process capital. Skandia (1996) declares that

> Innovation capital refers to the explicit, packaged result of innovation, in the form of protected commercial rights, intellectual property, and other intangible assets and values. Harnessing this power of innovation requires a more dynamic perspective and a synchronized focus on human and structural capital for renewal. Thus the power of innovation is found in the border zone between human capital and structural capital. The goal is to achieve a multiplicative effect in order to enhance rapid knowledge sharing and develop new business applications. In doing so, new value is created. . . . (Skandia 1996: 4).

Intellectual capital provides firms with a huge diversity of organizational value such as profit generation, strategic positioning (market share, leadership, name recognition, etc.), acquisition of innovations from other firms, customer loyalty, cost reductions, improved productivity, and more (Harrison and Sullivan 2000). Sucessful firms are those which routinely maximize the value from their intellectual capital.

INTELLECTUAL CAPITAL MEASUREMENT

The measurement of intellectual capital has become an important element in a firm's strategy. Several major research studies are currently examining aspects of intellectual capital in Europe. One of these projects is MERITUM Project—measuring intangibles to understand and improve innovation management—funded by the Targeted Socio-Economic Research (TSER) program of the European Union. The following European countries are participating: Finland, France, Denmark, Norway, Spain, and Sweden. Its objective is to produce guidelines to measure and disclose intangible resources. These guidelines are expected to have both internal and external benefits, helping firm's managers and stakeholders to visualize a holistic picture of the organizational value.

The measurement of intangible resources should be considered a key element in a firm's strategy. As Harrison and Harrison (2000) state, "calculating the value of intangibles companies based on their ability to develop and maintain cash flows by converting their ideas and innovations into revenue streams is fundamental to adequately assessing and quantifying the value of these firms." Different methods have been developed. Among the most well-known methods for intellectual capital measurement is Skandia Navigator (Edvisson and Malone 1997), Intangible Assets Monitor (Sveiby 1997), Technology Broker (Brooking 1996), and the Competence-based Strategic Management Model (Bueno 1998).

INTELLECTUAL CAPITAL REPORT

What is an intellectual capital statement? The object of an intellectual capital statement is to give a picture of the corporate effort to build up, develop, and streamline its resources and competencies in relation to its employees, customers, technology, and processes. The intellectual capital statement underpins the development of the future value of the company and consequently its competitiveness in the knowledge economy (Danish Agency for Trade and Industry 2000: 4).

Intellectual capital statements are "complex forms of measuring, reporting and acting at the same time . . . the 'object' to be illuminated and managed via intellectual capital statements is knowledge management activities rather than knowledge itself" (Larsen et al. 1999). As Meku (2000: 23) states, "intellectual capital account has become a useful management tool, made by us for us." However, today the number of firms that publish intellectual capital reports is small (Mouritsen 1998).

IC REPORT VERSUS TRADITIONAL ANNUAL FINANCIAL REPORT

Leading European pioneer firms publish two types of reports: the intellectual capital report and the financial report. Some firms elaborate and publish the intellectual capital report separately from the financial report. However, both types of reports are complementary and offer a more holistic view of the firm.

The IC report is aimed at providing a holistic picture of the firm on the basis of chosen strategies, actions taken, and current challenges. Rather than on financial resources, this report is focused on "softer" resources, such as intellectual capital. In essence it is a supplement to the financial accounts as well as a valuable strategic management tool. Most of the participating firms in this research recognize that the objective of the intellectual capital accounts is to deal with all major knowledge-related activities in the firm. In fact, according to Cowi (1999), "it is a tool to help us measure the results of knowledge management at all levels of the organization. The accounts show whether we are on the right track in implementing our strategies and policies."

Cowi is a special case due to its decentralized intellectual capital report. They compile a decentralized intellectual capital report of each department and division of the organization. This decentralization has two major objectives: first, the intellectual capital report can be used as a landmark for decentralized planning and secondly as a guide for evaluating to what extent a manager lives up to the values that are not expressed in the financial accounts. The intellectual capital report is a dynamic report that shows the direction in which the firm's intellectual capital is being developed.

APPLICATIONS OF THE IC REPORT

The intellectual capital report serves to make the organizational intangible resources visible and to measure them. The report could be prepared for the purpose of giving external partners relevant information supplementary to the other parts of the annual report and/or for using it as an ad hoc management tool for the development of the organization. Although the primary target group of the intellectual capital report is existing and potential customers and employees, it also catches the attention of capital investors, the press, and the university community.

Although substantial investments are made today in intellectual capital, the payoff and value will not be visible in the financial accounting until some time later. Through systematic accounting of developments in various areas—such as the customer base, staff competence and processes—an earlier indication of the company's future performance can be obtained (Skandia 1994: 6).

ACCOUNTING POLICIES

Intellectual capital does not appear in the traditional financial report. The explanation is the following. An asset—under International Accounting Standard Committee (IASC) literature—is a resource controlled by an enterprise as a result of past events and from which future economic benefits are expected to flow to the enterprise. According to International Accounting Standard (IAS) 38, the list of items that will not make it onto the balance sheet includes expenditures on the following items: (1) research, starting-up a business, training and advertising; and (2) generating internally customer lists, brand names, mastheads, customer loyalty, customer relationships, human capital, structural capital and publishing titles. These items will not meet the definition of an intangible asset and the recognition criteria. Expenditures on these items will therefore be expended when incurred (Rivat and Nulty 1998).

As there are no generally accepted accounting policies for the presentation of the intellectual capital accounts, this is a field currently under development, in which everything is left to be done in the following years. Additionally, as there are no standards and/or generally accepted accounting policies for the intellectual capital accounts, the reliability of intellectual capital accounts depends "on quality data and accumulation methods, and we have therefore chosen to draw up accounting policies, which explain how Carl Bro data is obtained" (Carl Bro 1999).

AUDITOR'S REVIEW OF THE INTELLECTUAL CAPITAL REPORT

Generally, the auditor's report on intellectual capital is formed by two sections: basis of opinion and opinion. The basis of opinion section declares that the intellectual capital reports are a new reporting format and have not yet been regulated by legislation or recognized requirements regarding contents and methods of statement (Systematic 2000). So the general purpose of the auditor's review is to verify that all data in the intellectual capital report is reliable and presented in accordance with the guidelines specified previously on the intellectual capital report (inter alia: the work of the auditors includes accounting analyses, reviews of data and underlying documentation material, and checks on the test-basis). An audit would require the existence of generally accepted accounting principles regarding the contents, methods of valuation, and so on, of the intellectual capital accounts, requirements that unfortunately are not currently established.

The opinion section declares whether, in the opinion of the auditors, the intellectual capital report is supported by accurately collected data and presented in accordance with the guidelines specified in the report (Systematic 2000). In some cases the auditors state specific proposals for future improvement, such as increased integration between the intellectual capital report and the financial report, and further development of supporting recording and reporting procedures, to ensure completeness and accuracy. We now turn to our empirical research on intellectual capital–measuring and –reporting in European pioneer firms, underlying the strategic importance of nonfinancial metrics.

THE STATE OF THE ART OF THE DEVELOPMENT OF INTELLECTUAL CAPITAL REPORTS IN DENMARK

Data Collection

The intellectual capital and knowledge management questionnaire was developed by the author of this paper and administered to nineteen Danish firms. The respondents were all members of firms that are collaborating on the development of intellectual capital reports with the Danish Agency for Development of Trade and Industry. Both of these firms and the Danish Agency for Trade and Industry wish to develop a set of guidelines for the development and publication of intellectual capital statements. The choice of this sample provides an excellent chance to observe which steps world pioneer firms take in the development of intellectual capital reports.

The questionnaire was designed in an easy-to-read booklet format that contained questions covering different areas—knowledge management strategy, intellectual capital measuring and reporting, and organizational performance. Many of the total design method (TDM) recommendations suggested by Dillman (1978) were adopted. The questionnaire was two pages in length and was accompanied by a cover letter in which the purpose of the survey was fully explained. Additionally, an in-depth case analysis of the intellectual capital reports of the participating firms was performed.

The findings showed that all respondents were from service industries: consultancy (four firms), information technologies (three firms), software development (one firm), hotel (one firm), telecommunications (one firm), finance sector (one firm), legal services (one firm), health services (one firm), and other services (two firms). The Danish firms that finally agreed to participate in this research are shown in Table 9-1.

Table 9-1
Sample of participating firms

Agency.com
Atp
Carl Bro Gruppen
Coloplast A/S
Cowi
Dansk Shell A/S
Hofman-Bang A/S
Hotel Impala A/S
Kommunedata A/S
Nellemann Konsulenterne (NIRAS)
Rungstedgaard A/S
Systematic Software Engineering
Tele & Data
Rambøll Informatik
Pls Rambøll

The Findings for Knowledge Management and Intellectual Capital Reports in Danish Firms

What are the problems involved in the development of a system for measurement of intellectual capital? The success of intellectual capital accounts depends deeply on the interest of the senior management. There is a difference in the function heading the work with intellectual capital accounts. In most cases (40 percent), intellectual capital work is organized through the managing director. In other cases (20 percent), there is a chief knowledge officer (CKO) leading the work with intellectual capital (Bontis 2001). In the rest of the cases, the work with intellectual capital report is headed by the human resource function (13.3 percent), the knowledge management consultant (13.3 percent), the intellectual capital report director (6.7 percent), or the financial function (6.7 percent).

Three groups of firms could be differentiated on the basis of the number of employees. The vast majority of the firms have less than two hundred employees (nine firms). In particular, there are firms with two, thirty, forty-five, and eighty employees, respectively

(Teledata, Hotel Impala, Nelleman, and Rungstedgaard). Another group has approximately five hundred employees (two firms) and the third group ranges from twenty-one hundred to three thousand employees (four firms).

Knowledge Management Strategy

Most of the firms surveyed (86.7 percent) have developed and implemented a knowledge management strategy. A majority of them recognized they had an explicit knowledge-sharing strategy (73.3 percent), whereas 26.7 percent of firms pointed out the existence or coexistence of a knowledge-hoarding strategy. Most of the firms with a knowledge management strategy and a knowledge-sharing strategy have less than 250 employees. Most firms have one or two knowledge management projects on the way (40 percent), whereas 20 percent have from three to five projects and another 20 percent of firms are working on from six to ten projects.

Intellectual Capital and the Intellectual Capital Report

A majority (86.7 percent) of the firms measure intellectual capital and 93.3 percent of this figure publish an intellectual capital report. This report includes nonfinancial metrics that complement the information stated in the traditional financial accounts. The intellectual capital report is a *special* report, because, in addition to the organizational, nonfinancial metrics, a *narrative* section accompanies each group of nonfinancial metrics. In the intellectual capital report, firms state their own process of development and implementation of knowledge management activities as well as key data on intellectual capital.

Verification of the intellectual capital report by an external and independent auditor was reported in 46.7 percent of firms that publish intellectual capital reports. The auditor does not perform strictly traditional auditing, but rather a check of all compiled data in accordance with the principles described in the intellectual capital report. Auditing firms such as PricewaterhouseCoopers, Deloitte and Touche, and KPMG C. JESPERSEN reviewed the intellectual capital report of these firms.

Most firms (six firms) started their intellectual capital measurement in 1999, whereas there is a pioneer group of firms (three firms) that entered the intellectual capital field in 1997. Most of these pioneer firms published their intellectual capital accounts for the first time one year later in 1998. The first group published their first intellectual capital accounts the same year they initiated their measurement activities (1999).

The number of people working on the elaboration of the intellectual capital statement differs across the firms. Most firms (60 percent) have one or two individuals working on the elaboration of this statement, whereas others have three, four, or five firm members working on it (20 percent).

Intellectual Capital Value

Firms were also asked about their impact on intellectual capital value. The following responses were mentioned: strategic positioning (market share, leadership, standard setting, name recognition) (92.9 percent), profit generation (income products or services and income from intellectual capital itself) (64.3 percent), customer loyalty (64.3 percent), improved productivity (57.1 percent), acquiring the innovation of others (35.7 percent), cost reductions (21.4 percent), and others (28.6 percent).

Areas Grasped in the Intellectual Capital Report

An *employee* area was included in all intellectual capital reports, whereas a *process* area was only in 86.7 percent of the cases, and a *customer* area and *technology* area in 73.3 percent of the cases. These firms have developed their own nonfinancial measures to visualize the "hidden" roots of organizational value. In particular, their nonfinancial measures are indicators designed to measure the subphenomena that constitute intellectual capital. They offer an X-ray of employees, customers, technologies, and processes.

In the firms we have studied, employee skills are the competitive muscle of organizations, thus differentiating the firm from competitors. The development and use of human potential and a learning organization constitutes the firm's bridge to long-term success. So a key element in organizational human capital strategy is the development of the employee to foster common goals, vision, and mission. *Continuous learning* by individuals, groups, and the organization as a whole is a clear need for organizational strategic survival in dynamic environments.

After elaborating these reports, firms differ in the interest they generated from four core-target groups: customer, employees, process, and technology. Customers and employees showed great interest in intellectual capital reports.

However, no participating firms reported investors as a core-target group, although they mentioned in their intellectual capital report that this report attracts great attention from investors as well as the press and the university community.

Impact of Intellectual Capital Reports

Eighty percent of firms said that the intellectual capital report had a considerable impact on attracting new staff. This fact confirms what the Danish Agency states in its report: "Intellectual capital statements have had a considerable impact when it comes to attracting new staff. Here the companies report increased interest and an improved basis of recruiting. Many Danish companies say that they attach great importance to adult and continuing education and vocational training, but companies who set up intellectual capital statements can prove it!" (2000: 5).

In this sense, Cowi's personnel policy states that "the employees are the company's most important resource. We make great demands on staff and managers in terms of business acumen, professional competence, human skills and the ability to adapt and develop" (Cowi 1999: 10). Through its intellectual capital report, Cowi proves this commitment. In conclusion, Table 9-2 summarizes the major steps toward the development of intellectual capital reports.

Table 9-2
Major steps in the development of intellectual capital reports

☑ Mission, vision, and values

☑ Organizational excellence model

☑ Knowledge management model and organizational intellectual capital structure

☑ Intellectual capital accounts and reports

☑ Auditing intellectual capital accounts

☑ Dynamic review of intellectual capital indicators included in intellectual capital accounts + building intellectual capital account standards

The State of the Art of the Development of Intellectual Capital Reports in Spain

After discussing the results of our survey on knowledge management and intellectual capital–measuring and –reporting in leading firms at the international level (Danish firms), now we turn to look at the situation in Spain and offer a comparative perspective. Although these hot topics attract high levels of attention from different fields—such as academic researchers, the business and financial world, and so on (Cañibaño et al. 1999; Ordóñez 1999, 2000; Sánchez et al. 2000)—the state of the art in knowledge management and intellectual capital reports is in an embryonic stage in Spain. However, a group of Spanish "first mover" firms are learning from the intellectual capital reports presented by Danish leading firms and trying to close the gap with them.

In Spain a small group of firms are just beginning to incorporate the intellectual capital report into their annual reports. In this pioneering group of firms is Bankinter (1998), BBV Group (1998), Indra (1999), Mekalki (1998), and Repsol (1998)—just to name a few examples. Let us move through the examination of the intellectual capital report in firms of different sizes. Though the intellectual capital model of BBV Group is based on the Intellect Project (Bueno 1998)—in line with the Skandia Navigator—Mekalki has chosen to use the popular intellectual capital framework developed by Sveiby (1997).

Mekalki S. Coop

Mekalki S. Coop is located in Oñate, Gipuzcoa (Spain). It is a small-sized firm (thirty-seven employees)—working on mechanized integral services—that published its first intellectual capital report in 1998. In particular Mekalki differentiates among human capital (number of employees, level of employee education, number of training hours per year, employee loyalty and satisfaction, etc.), structural capital (organizational culture and structure, leadership style, strategy, information technology, and staff management), and relational capital (customer satisfaction, number of new clients, perceived value, relational marketing, etc.). An outstanding finding is that Mekalki's intellectual capital report includes comparative data on metallurgic sector and industry. This provides a good mirror to visualize the competitive position in its sector and industry in Spain. Finally, the last paragraph of its intellectual capital report states that "this report does not specify a measure to analyze the goodness and quality of intellectual capital reports at Mekalki. We will look forward to develop a measurement system with the aim of diagnosing intangible measurements such as individual and organizational learning" (1998: 9).

BBV Group

Now let us examine BBV Group, a larger-sized firm. BBV Group's intellectual capital and knowledge management model includes the identification and measurement of value-creating intangible resources in order to make visible these strategic resources. It also incorporates the management of intellectual capital's growing process. Its objective is to transform the existing intellectual capital into a more valuable resource. In BBV Group's model, intellectual capital is structured into three parts: human capital, structural capital, and relational capital. According to BBV Group (1998: 5) "intellectual capital measurement is a key element in order to provide information to third parties on the value of the firm (external perspective). The intellectual capital model aims to give information on a firm's intangible resource structure and its value generating capability. Additionally intellectual capital measurement has a strategic role in intra-firm management (internal perspective)." So BBV Group considers a double objective for its intellectual capital report. From the internal perspective, it provides strategic information for internal management, and from the external perspective, it supplies rich information for investors, analysts, auditors, and so on, that helps them to assess the invisible roots of organizational value.

Since 1997, BBV Group has started the publication of internal management system indices on intangible resources in its Annual Report. It could be said that BBV Group has a pioneering role in intellectual capital reports in Spain. However, BBV Group underlines the urgent need to converge to standard guidelines. One of its objectives is to produce relevant information that could be compared with information from other firms.

CONCLUSIONS

In summary, the main findings from this exploratory study are as follows. First, those firms that have decided to implement knowledge management strategies and publish intellectual capital statements are taking this challenge seriously. Second, intellectual capital accounts are more than just nonfinancial metrics. Although these metrics represent an important part of the intellectual capital report, a "narrative" section is also included in the intellectual capital report. This section explains a firm's experience in development and implementation of knowledge management and intellectual capital reports. Intellectual capital reports are presented in an easy-to-read format, with special emphasis on attracting the reader's attention (with figures, "vivid" examples, and so forth). In sum, Danish intellectual capital reports are an important step toward the development and publication of intellectual capital, but they are also "eye-catching."

Third, with the publication of intellectual capital reports, firms send clear signals to the market regarding their commitment to the development of their intellectual capital. Especially, they devote a specific section to their human capital. The strategic importance of this intangible resource is clearly stated there; even if it is not owned by the firm, it clearly provides organizational value. This statement was empirically validated by the results of the survey. However, no firm declared investors as their target group.

Another conclusion is that pioneering firms basically report their intellectual capital within the Skandia Navigator or Sveiby's Intangible Assets Monitor framework. However, the study has concluded that there is no established mutually agreed-upon framework for which particular intellectual capital indicators should appear in each area of the intellectual capital report.

Finally, firms developed nonfinancial metrics as indicators of their intellectual capital (number of staff, staff age distribution, staff satisfaction, education, customer satisfaction and loyalty, IT costs per employee, innovation activity per employee, etc.). However, in the analyzed reports, there is no single measure at aggregate level that summarizes the human capital, relational capital and organizational capital, and intellectual capital as a whole. In this sense, it is noteworthy recalling the work of Edvinsson and Malone (1997). An intellectual capital formula is proposed by these authors in order to obtain a figure corresponding to the intellectual capital in the firm. This formula states that intellectual capital is the result of multiplying "C" (the monetary value of intellectual capital) by "i" (the efficiency coefficient on intellectual capital utilization). These authors also propose indicators that constitute each subphenomenon of intellectual capital. But once again, empirical evidences show that intellectual capital guidelines are really needed at the international level. These guidelines should cover different aspects from which particular areas should appear in the intellectual capital report to which specific metrics should be included in each area, among others.

REFERENCES

Barney, J. B. 1986. Organizational culture: can it be a source of competitive advantage? *Academy of Management Review* 1: 656–65.

BBV. 1998. *Intellectual Capital Report 1998.*

Bontis, Nick. 1999. "Managing Organizational Knowledge by Diagnosing Intellectual Capital: Framing and Advancing the State of the Field." *International Journal of Technology Management* 18, 5/6/7/8: 433–62.

Bontis, N. 1998. Intellectual capital: an exploratory study that develops measures and models. *Management Decision* 36, 2: 63–76.

Bontis, N. 2001. "CKO Wanted—Evangelical Skills Necessary: A Review of the Chief Knowledge Officer Position." *Knowledge and Process Management* 8, 1: 29–38.

Bontis, N., W. Chua, and S. Richardson. 2000. "Intellectual Capital and the Nature of Business in Malaysia." *Journal of Intellectual Capital* 1, 1: 85–100.

Bontis, N., M. Crossan, and J. Hulland. 2002. "Managing an Organizational Learning System by Aligning Stocks and Flows." *Journal of Management Studies.*

Brooking, A. 1996. *Intellectual Capital. Core Asset for the Third Millennium Enterprise.* London: International Thomson Business Press.

Bueno, E. 1998. El capital intangible como clave estratégica en la competencia actual. *Boletín de Estudios Económicos* 13 (Agosto): 207–29.

Bukh, P. N., H. T. Larsen, and J. Mouritsen. (Forthcoming). Constructing intellectual capital statements. *Scandinavian Journal of Management.*

Bukowitz, W. R. and R. L. Williams. 2000. *The Knowledge Management Fieldbook.* London: Financial Times, Prentice Hall.

Cañibaño, L., M. Garcia-Ayuso, and P. Sanchez. 1999. *The value relevance and managerial implications of intangibles: a literature review.* Paper presented at the International Symposium Measuring and Reporting Intellectual Capital: Experiences, Issues, and Prospects, June, Amsterdam: OECD.

Cowi. 1999. *Intellectual Capital Report 1999.*

Chong, C. W., T. Holden, P. Wilhelmij, and R. A. Schmidt. 2000. Where does knowledge management add value? *Journal of Intellectual Capital* 1, 4.

Danish Agency for Development of Trade and Industry. 1997. *Intellectual Capital Accounts. Reporting and Managing Intellectual Capital.*

Danish Agency for Development of Trade and Industry. 2000. *Intellectual Capital Statement—Towards a Guideline.*

Dillman, D. A. 1978. *Mail and Telephone Surveys: The Total Design Method.* New York: Wiley and Sons, Inc.

Edvinsson, L. and M. S. Malone. 1997. *Intellectual Capital. Realizing Your Company's True Value by Finding Its Hidden Brainpower.* New York: Harper Collins Publishers.

Foss, N. J. 1996. Knowledge-based approaches to the theory of the firm: Some critical comments. *Organization Science* 7, 5 (September-October).

Gormsen, P., P. N. D. Bukh, and J. Mouritsen. 2000. *When knowledge is introduced on the stock exchange.* In *Intellectual Capital Statement—Towards a Guideline.* Danish Agency for Development of Trade and Industry.

Harrison, S. and P. Sullivan. 2000. Profiting from intellectual capital: Learning from leading companies. *Journal of Intellectual Capital* 1, 1: 33–46.

IAS. 1998. *Intangible Assets* 38 (September). IASC.

Joia, L. A. 2000. Measuring intangible corporate assets: Linking business strategy with intellectual capital. *Journal of Intellectual Capital* 1, 1: 68–84.

Larsen, H. T., P. N. D. Bukh, and J. Mouritsen. 1999. Intellectual capital statements and knowledge management: 'measuring', 'reporting' and 'acting.' *Australian Accounting Review* 9, 3.

Mekalki. 1998. *Intellectual Capital Report 1998.*

Meku. 1999. *Intellectual Capital Report 1999.*

Mouritsen, J. 1998. Driving growth: economics value added versus intellectual capital. *Management Accounting Research* 4 (December).

Mouritsen, J. 1999. *Valuing Expressive Organisations: Intellectual Capital and the Visualisation of Value Creation.* Copenhagen: Copenhagen Business School.

Nonaka, I. and H. Takeuchi. 1995. *The Knowledge-Creating Company.* Oxford: Oxford University Press.

Ordóñez de Pablos, P. 2000. Herramientas estratégicas para medir el capital intelectual organizativo (Strategic tools to measure organizational intellectual capital). *Revista de Estudios Empresariales* 102 (Junio). (In Spanish.)

Penrose, E. T. 1959. *The Theory of the Growth of the Firm*. New York: John Wiley and Sons.

Peteraf, M. A. 1993. The cornerstone of competitive advantage: A resource based-view. *Strategic Management Journal* 14: 179–91.

Rivat, L. and K. Nulty. 1998. Accounting for intangible assets. *Boletín de Estudios Economicos* 13: 251–64.

Roberts, H. 1999. *Classification of Intellectual Capital*. Sandvika: Norwegian School of Management.

Roos, G., J. Roos, L. Edvinsson, and N. C. Dragonetti. 1998. *Intellectual Capital—Navigating in the New Business Landscape*. New York: New York University Press.

Stewart, T. A. 1997. *Intellectual Capital: The New Wealth of Organizations*. New York: Double/Currency.

Sullivan, P. and P. Sullivan. 2000. Valuing intangibles companies—An intellectual capital approach. *Journal of Intellectual Capital* 1, 4.

Sánchez, M. P., C. Chaminade, and M. Olea. 2000. Management of intangibles: an attempt to build a theory. *Journal of Intellectual Capital* 1, 4.

Skandia. 1996. *Supplement to the Annual Report. Customer Value.*

Sveiby, K. E. 1997. *The New Organizational Wealth: Managing and Measuring Knowledge Based Assets*. San Francisco: Berrett Kohler.

Sveiby, K. E. 2000. http://www.sveiby.com.au/vikings.htm#three, accessed on 15 November 2000.

Systematic. 1999. *Intellectual Capital Report 1999*.

Systematic. 2000. *Intellectual Capital Report 2000*.

Tissen, R., D. Andriessen, and F. L. Deprez. 1998. *Creating The 21st Century Company: Knowledge Intensive, People Rich. Value-Based Knowledge Management*. Netherlands: Addison Wesley Lingman.

Ventura Victoria, J. 1996. *Analisis Dinamico de la Estrategia Empresarial: Un Ensayo Interdisciplinar (Dynamic Analysis of Firm's Strategy: An Interdisciplinary Essay)*. Servicio de Publicaciones, Universidad de Oviedo. (In Spanish.)

Vickery, G. 1999. Accounting for intangibles: issues and prospects. In *Intangibles and Competitiveness: An Empirical Approach*. Northampton: Edward Elgar Publishing.

10

Understanding Intellectual Capital Statements: Designing and Communicating Knowledge Management Strategies

Jan Mouritsen
Copenhagen Business School, Denmark
jm.om@cbs.dk

Heine Thorsgaard Larsen
Copenhagen Business School, Denmark
htl.om@cbs.dk

and

Per Nikolaj Bukh
Aarhus School of Business, Denmark
pndb@asb.dk

Abstract

The objective of this chapter is to review the intellectual capital reporting systems of two Danish organizations. Dator (www.dator.dk) is a small Danish IT company and Carl Bro (www.carlbro.dk) is a Danish engineering company. The analysis of these two firms illustrates that their respective structure of intellectual capital indicators varies in ways that are in accordance with their knowledge management strategies. One focuses on people management and the other on systems management, even as both attempt to construct an integrated, capable firm.

Introduction

Often, when authors write about intellectual capital statements, they do so in a very general way, as they often analyze "new forms" of reporting systems that include "nonfinancial" indicators (e.g., Bontis et al. 1999; Bontis 2001; Erhvervs Udviklingsrådet 1997; Guthrie 2001; Guthrie and Petty 2000; Harvey and Lusch 1999; Johanson et al. 1998, 1999; Larsen et al. 1999; Mouritsen 1998; Sánchez et al. 2000). Rarely, however, were these reporting systems specifically developed as intellectual capital statements. This is why the object of intellectual capital statements is often ill-specified. In contrast, in this paper we set out to analyze intellectual capital statements that, from the outset, were intended to be about a firm's intellectual resources and that explicitly connected the statement with knowledge management. This research shows that there is more to an intellectual capital statement than indicators and numbers; there is also a grand knowledge management narrative and a set of bold visualizations. Guthrie and Petty's (2000) survey of the structure of indicators uses the three-way breakdown of intellectual capital into human capital, organizational capital, and customer capital (Bontis 1996; Edvinsson 1997; Edvinsson and Malone 1997; Roos et al. 1997; Stewart 1997; Sullivan 1998). They suggest that the indicators used in statements spread across the three forms of intellectual capital as 30 percent human capital, 30 percent organizational capital (internal structure), and 40 percent customer capital (external structure). It is thus possible to count the number of indicators. It is also possible to aggregate them. Roos et al. (1997: 83 ff) create an indicator for each of the three forms of intellectual capital, and an aggregated one. Weights have to be assigned to the actual value of each indicator, and then the weighed IC index can be produced. The problem here is to find the weights. It is even possible to simulate and present the indicators in complex graphs. Edvinsson et al. (2000) show how an IC landscape can describe the intellectual capital components in three-dimensional representations, illustrate the effects of simulations, and use them as forecast information.

Whether the indicators are weighed or not, and whether they are simulated and visualized or not, however, the three-way model is limited; it tends to draw the indicators away from their contexts (Mouritsen et al. 2001). There is more to an intellectual capital statement than the indicators. Reading an intellectual capital statement is different from reading a financial statement, because the intellectual capital statement does not have the institutions that make certain readings conventional, as in the case of the financial statement. The financial statement is an institutionalized reading of, for example, profitability, liquidity, and solidity. Throughout history, capital markets have increasingly refined this reading, taking into account industry-specific influence, firm-specific variance, and the effect of the general economic climate. This is located in strong institutional contexts.

The intellectual capital statement does not have such institutions. This is why the indicators in the intellectual capital statement typically cannot be read as directly and easily as the ones in financial statements. The logic of reading the indicators can, therefore, not be "outside" the document but it has to be made part of it. Roos et al. (1997: 6–7) say that the measurement of the intellectual capital and the management of knowledge and information go hand in hand: "Intellectual capital is concerned with how better to manage and measure knowledge and other intangibles in the company." Measurement and management are related. If measurement does not make management—or intervention—possible, there is no need for it. Therefore, the measurement system needed to probe into intellectual capital must be part of an idea of intervention. This intervention is argued in the intellectual capital literature to be orientated toward managing knowledge (Allee 1997: Baxter and Chua 1999; Bukh et al. 2001; Birkitt 1995; Larsen et al. 1999; Roos 1998; Ross and Roos 1997; Sveiby 1997; Sullivan 1998).

In effect, an intellectual capital statement must be about a firm's knowledge management activities. How is this possible? How can this be read from an intellectual capital statement? In this paper an approach that expands on the three-way model, includes knowledge management explicitly, and considers presentation and communication is offered as a means of understanding what intel-lectual capital statements communicate.

WORKING WITH IC STATEMENTS— DANISH EXPERIENCES

The approach is one of the outcomes of a three-year research and development project organized by the Danish Agency for Develop-ment of Trade and Industry in collaboration with researchers (the authors of this paper), a consulting firm, and seventeen Danish firms. The Agency wished to develop a set of guidelines for the development and publication of intellectual capital statements in an act of national industrial policy to promote a knowledgeable society. The seventeen firms had agreed to develop and publish at least two intellectual capital statements. All but two of the firms participating in the project were service companies, and half of them were from the IT business, making it by no means a representative sample of Danish firms (see www.efs.dk/icaccounts). In the different firms, the discourse of intellectual capital mobilized a set of different, albeit overlapping, themes of interest. Figure 10-1 illustrates the impor-tance of different motives pointed out by the firms.

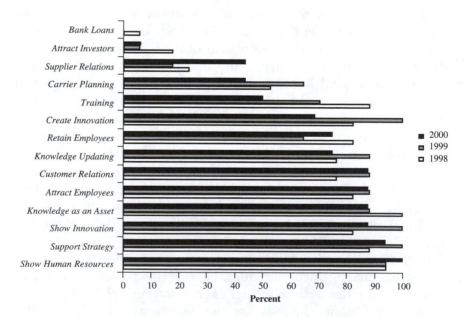

Figure 10-1 *Interests in intellectual capital*

BUSINESS REPLY MAIL

FIRST-CLASS MAIL   PERMIT NO. 78   WOBURN MA

POSTAGE WILL BE PAID BY ADDRESSEE

DIRECT MAIL DEPARTMENT
Butterworth-Heinemann
225 WILDWOOD AVE
PO BOX 4500
WOBURN MA 01888-9930

Keep up-to-date with the latest books in your field!

Complete this postage-paid reply card and return it to us now! We will notify you of upcoming titles and special offers. Visit our website and check out information on our newest releases.

What title have you purchased? _____

_____

How did you hear about it? _____

Where was the purchase made? _____

Name _____

Job Title _____

Institution _____

Address _____

City _____ State _____

Zip/Postcode _____

Country _____

Telephone _____

Email _____

(FOR OFFICE USE ONLY)

BUTTERWORTH
HEINEMANN

www.bh.com

BRC2001

Figure 10-1 shows the responses to a selected set of questions. It shows the percentage of the responses given as 4s and 5s on a 5-point Likert-type scale. It is clear that, in this sample, the interest in intellectual capital is internal to the firm and oriented toward creating and implementing certain kinds of organizational strategies. Financial resources, as in access to new financial capital, are not the reason to be concerned with intellectual capital for these firms. This is a management-oriented theme, rather than a financial one. Interviews with the seventeen firms provide some interpretation of Figure 10-1, and one or more variations of the following explanations about the expected and desired effects of their work with intellectual capital would come up. One effect is to see intellectual statements as *knowledge management* tools to be used internally in order to "manage knowledge and competencies" as well as to improve knowledge-sharing or as a supplement to other knowledge management activities. A second effect is to use intellectual capital statements as media for *communication* to be used to identify, support, and disseminate a corporate identity in relation, for instance, to values and ways of working. This could be relevant both in relation to *recruitment* of new employees and *attraction* of new customers. Firms experience increased competition both in the "factor" market and in the "product" market. A third desired effect of intellectual capital is the provision of a framework for *human resource development*. From this perspective, attention is on outlining current employee competencies as well as competencies needed in order to develop a map of competence-gaps, which would provide the links from the training and education programs to the intellectual capital statement. For a few of the firms, intellectual capital statements were interesting for their potential ability to illustrate the *value* of the company, in order to inform potential investors of the "true" value of the firm. Another aspect of this is the potential role as a *marketing* mechanism, demonstrating the knowledge or competencies of the firm.

These different explanations show why firms are interested in managing knowledge. These are some of the translations made to make intellectual capital statements fit into an organizational system where the objects for management control are being reinvented. Figure 10-2 helps illustrate that this is a corporate-wide agenda, as the people working with the development of intellectual capital statements are drawn from many sectors of the firm.

Figure 10-2 illustrates that top management's interest is both impressive and rising and that the accounting and the HR

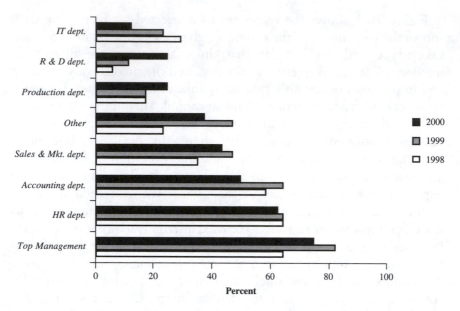

Figure 10-2 *The participants of the intellectual capital projects*

departments have been heavily involved in the projects. This suggests that the intellectual capital statement is not easily located in an existing organizational function. Intellectual capital tends to work across organizational boundaries and crafts new organizational agendas. The spread of parties involved in the project and the massive interest of top management suggest that a new organizational theme is being formed.

The results of the work also vary dramatically between the firms. The first set of published reports was produced in spring 1998. The details of the reports are impossible to capture in a paper, but it can be noted that the number of indicators used ranges from five to more than fifty. Explanations of this difference must be cautious, given that the firms are still experimenting with the format of their intellectual capital statement.

UNDERSTANDING INTELLECTUAL CAPITAL STATEMENTS —BEYOND THE "THREE WAY SPLIT"

When reading intellectual capital statements, the impression is one of diversity. They do not have a set model, but they all somehow are organized along three dimensions. First, they offer a form of knowledge management vision—a scenario that is a story line of the capabilities of the firm and thus of how it is good at doing something. The knowledge management vision is a presentation of the firm's knowledge resources focusing on how they interact and allow the firm to be capable at doing certain things for external users. It thus has both a proposition of the firm's "production function" and of the value proposition supplied to users. Second, intellectual capital statements identify a set of knowledge management challenges that are the efforts management puts in place to develop and condition the firm's knowledge resources. These management challenges are related to the knowledge management vision, as they seek to identify and implement activities that help realize the vision. Third, there is a report that combines numbers, visualization, and the vision in a composition designed to show the development of the firm's knowledge resources.

The commonalties between firms are illustrated in Figure 10-3. It illustrates how the *indicators* are defined and connected with a set of *management challenges* and how they in turn together connect with a knowledge management *vision* or *strategy* that makes them relevant. These three elements are tightly coupled, although in very different ways among the firms.

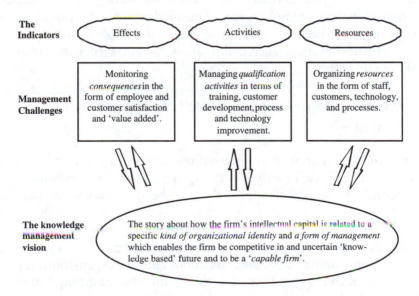

Figure 10-3 *The idea of the intellectual account*

Following Figure 10-3, intellectual capital statements connect specific numbers, management challenges represented by these numbers, and the knowledge management vision that guides the development of the intellectual capital.

The Knowledge Management Vision—Strategies of Knowledge Management

Figure 10-3 suggests that the knowledge management vision is one that specifies the identity of the *"capable firm"* located in a "knowledge-based" world. This general story is then translated in each firm into a set of management challenges that show the mechanisms that managers use to enhance the knowledge management vision. When reading an intellectual capital statement along these lines, the concern is to establish the firm's unique aspiration to be a capable firm. In this way the intellectual capital statement is about the knowledge management strategy of the firm, and it defines what the firm is to be able to accomplish. The knowledge management vision is a guiding aspiration that connects the user and the firm's capabilities. It shows how the firm is to be capable and why. It also illustrates the specific translations from the knowledge management vision to a set of management challenges, which are corporate-wide concerns often focusing on issues that are cross-organizational. It also shows that numbers can be attached to the management challenges to show how they are implemented. The numbers do not show the financial value of intellectual capital. They show the implementation of the management challenges suggested to allow the knowledge management vision to flourish.

Structuring the Indicators of the Intellectual Capital Statement

The three-way split of intellectual resources is inadequate because it does not lend itself easily to descriptive analysis and possible prescription. An analytical approach may be metaphorically parallel to—if different from—reading a financial accounting statement. A financial accounting statement has some domains (transactions about revenues, costs, assets, and liabilities) and the model proposed also has some domains (statements about employees, customers, processes, and technology). Likewise, the financial accounting statement allows three prescriptive readings: one of solidity, one of liquidity, and one of profitability. The intellectual capital statements may be read for portfolio management activities about the firm's knowledge resources, for its qualifying activities, when resources are improved, and for its monitoring of productivity, when effects are surveyed. These parallels obviously should not be taken too far, but the possibility that broader insights can be read from the intellectual capital statement than the individual number itself allows a reader to form some intelligent evaluation of the attempts to make knowledge management activities important management issues.

The indicators developed in the seventeen firms can be classified according to the model presented in Figure 10-4.

The arguments for this model have empirical support from the larger project involving seventeen firms. Through interviews, the dimensions of the model became clear as respondents made their uses of the intellectual capital statement problematic. The management agenda arose out of the discussion of how to make implications from the information contained in intellectual capital statements. This model has a *vertical* dimension indicating domains

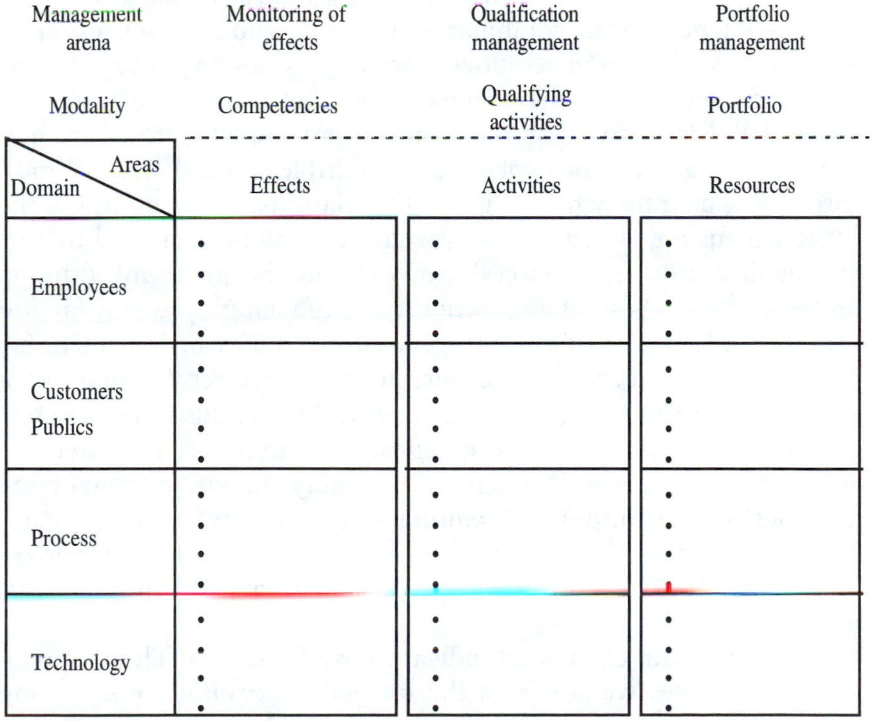

Management arena	Monitoring of effects	Qualification management	Portfolio management
Modality	Competencies	Qualifying activities	Portfolio
Domain \ Areas	Effects	Activities	Resources
Employees	• • • •	• • • •	• • •
Customers Publics	• • •	• • •	• • •
Process	• • • •	• • • •	• • • •
Technology	• • • •	• • •	• • •

Figure 10-4 *Analyzing intellectual capital indicators*

for knowledge resources and competencies and a *horizontal* dimension indicating three possible types of management activities that can be performed on knowledge resources and competencies. The vertical part consists of four objects for intervention, employees, customers, processes, and technology, and the horizontal part consists of three types of prescriptions.

The indicators in the "resources" column addresses the question, "what is the (right) portfolio of resources?" *Resource* indicators concern the firm's stock of relatively stable objects such as a customer, an employee, a computer, and a process. Such indicators show how large, how diversified, how complex and how related resources are. The indicators in the "qualifying activities" column is the answer to the question, "do managers undertake qualifying activities?" *Activity* indicators describe activities undertaken to upgrade, develop, or improve the resources. They show what is done in the firm to change resources through objects such as training, investments in process improvement, activities undertaken to attract customers, and so on. Finally, the "effects" column addresses the question, "does what we do work?" *Effect* indicators illustrate overall consequences of the combination of the decisions about resources and about qualification activities. Such effects can be put together by any combination of the elements of the model illustrated in Figure 10-4. It is not a simple input-output model. Effects are network effects and can be explained by multiple constellations of indicators. It is a strategy to point out this relation and act on it. On the other dimension, statements on *employees* may be indicated by formal qualifications ("resources"), investments in on-the-job training and education ("qualifying activities") and employee satisfaction ("effects"). Likewise, statements on *customers* may be indicated, for instance, as number of large customers ("resources"), marketing efforts per customer ("qualifying activities"), and customer satisfaction ("effects"). Statements on *processes* may be indicated by resources per process ("resources"), quality activities ("qualifying activities"), and output-and-waiting time ("effects"). Lastly, statements on *technology* may be indicated PCs per employee ("resources"), IT investments ("qualifying activities"), and IT certificates ("effects").

This model can classify all indicators we have seen. These categories are the ones we see from the intellectual capital reports being published by the Danish companies, but note here that the research is carried out primarily around service and consulting firms, meaning that other categories, for instance, suppliers, might be important for other kind of companies, for instance, manufacturing ones. It is noteworthy that indicators sometimes advocated in the literature and among practitioners are not visible here. Innovation, flexibility, learning, and customer orientation are not here. This is because they convey strategy rather than transactions. For example, "innovation" may be indicated in some firms by the number of new patents ("effects, processes"), other firms present revenues from new products ("effects, customers"), and yet others from aggregate number of patents ("resources, processes") or number of Ph.D.s ("resources, employees"). Innovation is not an indicator but a strategy that can be laid out in different ways. As suggested by the examples shown, innovation can be made relevant to the firm in various ways. It does not exist per se and it is therefore not a category in an accounting system of intellectual capital. Classifying some numbers may be more difficult than others. Therefore, there is a need for rules-of-thumb, or accounting standards. As an example, involvement by customers and employees in training programs can be seen as improving both the qualifications of the customers and the qualifications of the employees—and it could also be an activity to upgrade the firm's image. Another example could be employees that were trained in process optimization. This could be seen as qualifying act in relation to the employees but also in relation to the process dimension. In these cases it will be necessary to apply rules-of-thumb to classify the indicator. Should it be placed according to the domain that is mentioned first in the definition of the indicator? Or should it be classified according to the most "important" part of the indicator? And then, what will the most important part be?

Many types of indicators are possible. Some intellectual capital statements focus on a selected set of indicators, whereas others have a much broader scope. For all indicators, relevance is determined by their ability to support the firm's identity story. The indicators' relevance and usefulness depend on the ideals of the knowledge management vision, and, as a consequence, indicators in intellectual capital statements vary.

Using the model analytically, Table 10-1 shows the spread of indicators used by the seventeen firms.

Table 10-1 shows that, generally, the model can capture indicators used by the seventeen firms. Most of the indicators are about employees, typically in the form of resources, and numbers about the composition of the workforce are frequent. There

Table 10-1
Stratified number of indicators in intellectual capital statements

	Effects	*Activities*	*Resources*
Employees	9%	17%	23%
Customers	11%	4%	9%
Processes	8%	5%	5%
Technology	2%	4%	4%

are also many numbers about qualifying employees often in the form of training, and there are effects measures, for instance, in the form of employee satisfaction.[1] The stratification of these indicators suggests that, on average, there are numerous ways in which numbers have been attached to organizational knowledge management activities, and thus the precise way in which this may be done requires more detailed analysis of cases. To illustrate these complexities, two examples will be presented below. They illustrate two knowledge management contexts that they help illuminate and explain.

Two Cases of Intellectual Capital: Dator and Carl Bro

There is much more to an intellectual capital statement than the indicators. There is also an interpretation that connects the knowledge management activities to a story line, because, per se, there is little connection between knowledge and the numbers. They are made relevant not because they are logical in a strictly mathematical sense (as is the case with financial key-ratio analysis) but because they connect to a broad story about the capabilities and identity of the firm. This knowledge management vision is seen to thrive when the collectivity is supported by new or strengthened relationships between employees, customers, technologies, and

---

[1] It should be noted that this is a presentation of the stratification of the numbers. This does not mean that their function can always be limited to their position in the classification. Sometimes certain indicators carry several possible categories such as, for instance, employee training in technology or customer satisfaction with employees' service. For such numbers, accounting standards have to be developed. Here, training on technology is a statement on technology and customer satisfaction with employee service is a statement on customers. Likewise, employee training must have an object; it is often about technology, processes, or customer relations.

processes, and when people's "psychical energy," or motivation, is directed to identifying and solving the firm's problems at large. There is, in the discourse of intellectual capital statements, a scenario of an organizational identity where some measure of empowerment is in place because new markets and more heterogeneous customers must be served. There is talk about an increasingly "individualized firm" (Bartlett and Ghoshal 1997; Johansen and Swigart 1994; Reich 1991; Sveiby 1997).

Therefore, the intellectual capital statement is not only a set of numbers. There is more: namely, visualizations and narratives. Together, numbers, visualizations, and narratives form a network that constitutes the report. The numbers show that management is serious about intellectual capital and can be held accountable to its words and espoused aspirations. The visualizations construct identity and the story creates coherence and ambition.

The general explanation of intellectual capital provided above discusses the conditions of variation, but does not exemplify it. Therefore, in this section, two cases are presented that connect the individual firm's knowledge management vision, its management challenges, and its constellation of numbers in two different ways.

Dator

In the case of Dator (www.dator.dk), a small Danish IT company, there is a knowledge management vision of a firm working to integrate employees' "hearts and minds." Case 1 of Dator shows a three-way interaction between a quotation about the knowledge management problems of the firm, a sketch that shows the boundaries of what intellectual capital is about in this particular firm, and the set of numbers that is reported in the intellectual capital statement. The firm presents its competencies as follows:

> Dator's technical solutions are produced in project groups, which are assembled differently from project to project. Employees' knowledge can be distinguished in professional knowledge and application knowledge. The professional knowledge is knowledge about programming, software and hardware. Application knowledge covers knowledge about customers' processes and needs.

Case 1: Dator's indicators

Category\Form	Effect indicators	Activity indicators	Resource indicators
Employees		* Average training investment/employee/year * Training investment (% of total salaries) * Average hours of on-the-job training * Average hours	* Number of staff * Number of women vs. men * Intake of new employees (last year) * Resignations (last year) * Staff distribution (development/operation vs. other) * Average seniority * Average age of staff * Educational profile * List of different education's of employees
Customers			
Processes			
Technology			

In Dator, all the indicators are constructed around employees. Its management challenges concern how high professional capabilities can be combined with personal qualities, "psychical" competencies, so that the employee is able to act as a responsible project leader. Here is a "capable" organization performed through people. As they suggest at Dator:

> We normally say that this place is characterised by 'hard fun.' It has to be fun to be here. This is what we want, and this is precisely what young people want. Work has to be developing and fun at the same time. We have a reputation that says that you can only be an employee here if you have top grades, but we try hard to say that this is not the only kind of knowledge we want. It is true that a person has to be professionally very able, but his or her personal competencies are just as important. This is important since we have lots of project leaders who alone can get the responsibility that an airport system in China actually works. This requires an intelligent engineer from the IT business, but it also requires a person who can co-operate and manage processes etc. This is the agenda: We say that we want the knowledge of a whole person—even if this sounds a bit too popular.

The idea of a "whole" person is a humanistic project but not that only. It is also a resource requirement for a firm where employment is low (about sixty people) and where, at the same time, jobs are conducted all over the world. Here, there is little room for division of labor, and the individual has to be able to understand the business of the firm intuitively. This is also why Dator works directly with corporate culture:

> We have to start with mission and vision, i.e., how we want to work. We say that we want to make the employee a strategic partner, and this will be the point of departure for our intellectual capital statement. This combines strategy and reporting, and obviously the employees have to be part of this process.

There is a relationship between the knowledge management vision and the intellectual capital statement that points out elements in the management agenda. Employees must understand what the business is about and how it is to solve problems. Therefore, the mechanics of management is organized around the acquisition of people, their training, and their enrollment into the organizational machine and ways of working. The individual employee must "have fun," as it was suggested, but he or she also must accept responsibility to co-produce the business and not expect to be managed, but to sort out the problem for him- or herself.

> We are very focussed on the timing of when we can make people project leaders. We are very concerned that they are "psychically" robust for the job and we tell people that we have to make them strong and robust, be active "go-getters" . . . Dator's unique way to conduct its business is the learning organisation, i.e., open offices, get the individual to seize responsibility, and an open culture.

Here, there is a concern to make intellectual capital a matter of heart and brain, which must be in concert. Knowledge management activities are concerned to attract and retain the best people from both a professional perspective and a personal perspective. The competencies needed are not only academic but also social. This is particularly important because most of the employees work independently as project leaders in collaboration with customers, and, being a small firm, employees in Dator must be able to manage things on their own.

Dator's intellectual capital statements single out heart and brain as two parameters for managing the firm. The associated management challenges suggest that the primary levers of knowledge management are the in-house testing of people's psychical robustness and ability to handle technical and organisational problems on a job far away from the help of the firm. Knowledge management rests in the management of academic knowledge, which is a question of acquisition, and personal skills, which is the upbringing set in motion to persuade the individual to be part of a team and to suggest that the firm is more than a platform to mobilize the employment market. Lots of things go on within the firm to align people with each other. This can be documented by the numbers preferred by Dator and published in its statement: they concern people and their entry and development in the firm. It is not so much about their results, because these are said to be much too complex and ambiguous to be part of a long-term strategy to develop organizational competencies. Dator's employees own a portion of the firm's shares, and it underlines that the intellectual capital statement must make the "person-centered" strategy realistic:

> It is important that the HR management is in charge of the intellectual capital statement. One objective is to show that we mean it seriously when we say that we centre our employees and their knowledge, and it is a way to signal that we are a very young firm. . . . We have to show that this is more than "fancy words." There is a mental hurdle to accept that the expenses we spend [on HR development] are not only philanthropy, and that building good relations with each other really improves the bottom line. We must have a coherent group of people and a culture, which says: Well we may spend money for social activities here, but this is not merely a waste of money. It is a mental attitude and one has to understand the house to really appreciate the power of this.

The intellectual capital statement is part of a wider scheme of believing that resources and competencies are important. It is a 'belief' that employment markets cannot provide the skills and competencies needed for the firm to thrive. It is also, however, an indication that, even if the individual is centered, he or she cannot work sensibly without the support of the culture or the connections that make everyday life not a thing-in-isolation but indeed part of a collective community of practice.

Carl Bro

Carl Bro (www.carlbro.dk), a Danish engineering company, in case 2 tells a story of intelligent solutions that is a metaphoric statement of what intellectual capital is to produce. The model that organizes the numbers is a breakdown of intellectual capital into components that results in six different forms of capital to be reported: human capital, customer capital, image capital, innovation capital, process capital, and IT capital. The firm presents its capabilities as follows:

> Our national and international services require innovation and cultural sensitivity. Our employees strengthen their abilities by representing Carl Bro group locally and internationally. This makes it easy to work across boarders and cultures. The Carl Bro group delivers intelligent solutions by constantly being one step ahead strategically and professionally. This requires a broad spectrum of expertise. Therefore the firm has a continuously increasing number of employees with different backgrounds. Through co-operation across these backgrounds we reach our common goal—intelligent solutions.

Case 2: Carl Bro's indicators

Category\Form	Effect numbers	Activity numbers	Resource numbers
Employees	* Share of satisfied employees	* Investment in training (employee/year) * Share of employees with updated development plan	* Number of staff * Number of women vs. men * Distribution of age * Educational profile * Percentage of staff working abroad
Customers	* Customer satisfaction * Image amongst managers of other firms * Image amongst students (percentage seeing Carl Bro as an ideal vs. potential future employer)		* Distribution of turnover public vs. private sector customers * Distribution of turnover on centres of expertise * Five largest customers share of turnover * Ten largest customers share of turnover
Processes	* Share of employees satisfied with the administrative system * Total number of first-time sales on new concepts/ products	* Total number of innovation projects * Number of innovation projects per employee	* Number of projects involving different sectors of the company * Share of interdisciplinary projects of all projects

Case 2: Carl Bro's indicators (Continued)

Category\Form	Effect numbers	Activity numbers	Resource numbers
	* Number of first-time sales on new concepts/products per employee		* Share of projects involving different business units * Share of turnover from projects involving different business units
Technology		* Investment in IT per employee	* Percentage of employees with the possibility of teleworking * Size of shared knowledge data base in gigabytes * Number of shared knowledge documents on Intranet

Carl Bro's indicators focus on portfolio indicators and on effect indicators. This is a model of a balance sheet of intellectual capital where its elements are treated as separable assets that can be grouped in the six categories (human, customer, image, innovation, process, and IT capital) each constituting a form of closed description. The model does not describe the output process, but rather it singles out the types of resources that constitute the resources of the firm.

Carl Bro's knowledge management vision is about the capabilities to create "intelligent solutions." This is a complex story of interlinked resources and capabilities, so that any user can get access to a spectrum of expertises who can cooperate toward a solution for a user. The complexities of intelligent solutions rely on multiple and interdependent resources. Carl Bro's management challenges are concerned with the organization of competence centers, which are groups of people who debate certain professional issues pertaining to the professional and scientific basis of their practices. Here, the "capable organization" is one in which employees have the ability to collaborate with customers and colleagues to provide intelligent solutions. On the one hand, the individual employee, by virtue of membership in one or more competence centers, has professional knowledge. On the other hand, by certain employee development programs, the employee is encouraged to move into relations characterized by interdisciplinary thinking, creativity, and inventive attitudes. For example, it was stated at Carl Bro:

What do we think the intellectual capital statement says about us? Primarily that we are willing to think and to change, that there is no final story about the firm. Our story is that we would like to be society's advisors. A place, a house, where you go if you have a large and complex problem, and so we can work with good ethics and social understanding. This is our story, and the intellectual capital statement supports this, but does not in itself tell it. . . . When I say intelligent solutions, it is about giving the customer the best solution, and it is about having an appropriate basis for it. It is partly about mission, values and vision, and intelligent solutions are ethical—and then we construct all this by having good IT infrastructures, etc.

Carl Bro here explains that there is a whole infrastructure to an intellectual capital statement. First of all, the statement itself does not tell all the details of the firm's story, which is nuanced, complex, and often metaphorical: "intelligent solutions." Yet it helps create certain seriousness about the story of intelligent solutions. The story itself plays out different levels of understanding and makes an array of justifications of the relevance of the firm, which is presented as a social asset helping society to solve its problems. The firm also has missions, values, and visions that help employees to grow, and its solutions are said to be intelligent. The idea of intelligence is a substitute for a complex description of the engineering craft, and its justification is found in appeals to social benefits. The last part of the quotation explains that, in order to be able to do this, there must be a good supply of infrastructural assets. IT has to be in place, organizational-competence centers must be in place, and—to read from the front again—employees must be outgoing and interested in mingling with society.

The intellectual capital statement helps this more outgoing type of person to be realized. For example, it helps changing language toward one that is more modern:

Let us take an example, for example in the area of innovation. We have a strategy that our innovation activities have to be very visible internally and externally. We make innovation an asset by counting it so that it is pushed into the area of attention. However, the particular work in innovation is much more detailed than the indicators, which are one set of tools among others here. This is also what we have to do, just as in the financial area we use a lot of concepts, which are in the financial accounts, but also a lot that are not included.

Such a language game may help the firm change its reputation, primarily internally but then, in turn, also externally:

> The intellectual capital statement helps us to change the reputation of the firm. I almost could say that when I came to this firm it was extremely "dusty" and "old." To me, the intellectual capital statement has been a tool to change this. Similarly, our work with mission, values and vision were "gibberish" and difficult to communicate. Terminology and language are very different among departments in this firm because it is quite clear that certain departments are very innovative without using this word to characterise their activities. They may have managers who do not use the word innovation, and who therefore do not really motivate their employees by engaging them, e.g., by saying: "Come on, hear this, this is so interesting, and we will be doing all this new stuff!" From the perspective of recruitment and retention of employees, it is harmful not to say this, and this is where the intellectual capital statement comes in because its role is to change reality and not only register it.

Here, the intellectual capital statement changes language games. New concepts are invented for processes already in place, but by assigning new words to these processes they change. They change meaning and suddenly it is possible to create psychical energy and motivation that influence the object to which they are directed. Therefore, Carl Bro's management challenge is about organizing spaces of expertise that create the foundation for innovative and independent people who are full of initiative. It is a capable organization that performs such individuals who—when they engage in specific relations to customers—manufacture intelligent solutions based on interdisciplinary work, creativity, and innovation.

CONCLUSION—COMMUNICATING KNOWLEDGE MANAGEMENT STRATEGIES

Intellectual capital is no ordinary accounting concept. It is a new concept often carried more by huge market-to-book ratios than by its own work. In this paper, its own work has been analyzed on the basis of empirical evidence from seventeen firms and more specific evidence from two of these firms. The analysis indicates that intellectual capital is in search of a referent. To merely say that it somehow reflects the difference between market values and book values of a firm is inadequate. When firms talk about intellectual capital statements, they are expressing their interests in controlling and managing the firm. Therefore, as a practice, intellectual capital concerns the activities that managers can put in motion in the name of knowledge. These activities turn out often to be about employee development, restructuring organizations, and developing marketing activities.

Such activities, however, do not carry a lot of power per se. Therefore, the firms express in stories and narratives how ordinary daily life is interesting, compelling, and future-oriented. To do this, ordinary daily life must be related to grand narratives of innovation, the information society and "we-live-from-knowledge" claims. For this story to be communicable, it has to be drawn up. There is a challenge to create a persuasive intellectual capital statement, and therefore it consists not merely of numbers but also of narratives and visualization that allow a series of translations to take place. The story communicates the firm's functioning, the sketch creates identity and boundaries around the theme termed *intellectual capital,* and the indicators relate to the sketch certain numbers and create a form of seriousness as the story can be "audited." The numbers are loosely coupled, and they cohere for their relationship to the story and the sketch. It is not a bottom-line in itself. They are part of a vision in which they grant some form of credibility to it, so that it helps promote the story and avoid contradicting it. This reading takes intellectual capital to the local stories and strategies, it is set in action to explicate and defend.

The broad types of managerial actions made possible through intellectual capital statements are closely related to its numbers, which inscribe and monitor management's efforts. This is why there is also a broad set of classifications more directly linked to the discourse of management than to the local assembly of stories, numbers, and sketches in the statement. This broad classification of management actions has, as domains for intervention, only four separate types: employees, customers, organizational processes, and technology. These are the objects that management can influence in the name of knowledge. The classification also suggests that intervention can be accomplished through portfolio management, qualification management, and productivity management. When combining the domains and the ways of intervening in an analytical model, broad statements can be made about firms' management activities across the domains that can be read out of the indicators actually being used in the intellectual capital statement. For the seventeen firms, it is clear that the indicators used to illustrate the work to enhance knowledge management cover several possible combinations of the domains and the ways of intervening. The two firms—Dator and Carl Bro—illustrate that different firms' knowledge management strategies differ and that the structure of the indicators varies in ways that are in accordance with their knowledge management strategies. One focuses on people-management and the other on systems-management, even if both attempt to construct an integrated capable firm.

REFERENCES

Allee, V. 1997. *The Knowledge Evolution: Expanding Organizational Intelligence*. Boston: Butterworth-Heinemann.

Bartlett, C. A. and S. Ghoshal. 1997. *The Individualized Firm*. New York: Harper Business.

Baxter, J. and W. F. Chua. 1999. Forum on Knowledge Management: Now and the Future, *Australian Accounting Review* 9, 3: 3–14.

Birkitt, W. F. 1995. Management Accounting and Knowledge Management. *Management Accounting* 7, 55: 44–48.

Bontis, N., N. C. Dragonetti, K. Jacobsen, and G. Roos. 1999. The Knowledge Toolbox: a Review of the Tools Available to Measure and Manage Intangible Resources, *European Management Journal* 17, 4: 391–402.

Bontis, N. 2001. Assessing Knowledge Assets: A Review of the Models Used to Measure Intellectual Capital, *International Journal of Management Reviews* 3, 1: 41–60.

Bontis, N. 1996. There's a Price on Your Head: Managing Intellectual Capital Strategically, *Business Quarterly* Summer: 40–47.

Bukh, P. N. D., H. T. Larsen, and J. Mouritsen. 2001. Constructing Intellectual Capital Statements. *Scandinavian Journal of Management* 17, no. 1: 87–108.

Edvinsson, L. 1997. Developing Intellectual Capital at Skandia, *Long Range Planning* 30, 3: 266–373.

Edvinsson, L. and M. S. Malone. 1997. *Intellectual Capital*. London: Piatkus.

Edvinsson, L., B. Kitts, and T. Bedling. 2000. The Next Generation of IC Measurement—the Digital IC-Landscape, *Journal of Intellectual Capital* 1, 3: 263–73

Erhvervs Udviklingsrådet. 1997. *Intellectual Capital Accounts—Reporting and Managing Intellectual Capital.* Copenhagen: Agency for Trade and Industry. http://www.efs.dk/publikationer/rapporter/engvidenregn/.

Guthrie, J. 2001. The Management, Measurement and Reporting of Intellectual Capital, *Journal of Intellectual Capital* 2, 1: 27–41.

Guthrie, J. and R. Petty. 2000. Intellectual Capital: Australian Annual Reporting Practices, *Journal of Intellectual Capital* 1, 3: 241–51.

Harvey, M. G. and R. F. Lusch. 1999. Balancing the Intellectual Capital Books: Intangible Liabilities, *European Management Journal* 17, 1: 85–92.

Johansen, R. and R. Swigart. 1994. *Upsizing the Individual in the Downsized Organization.* London: Century.

Johanson, U., M. Ekelöv, M. Holmgren, and M. Mårtensson. 1998. Human Resource Costing and Accounting Versus the Balanced Scorecard: A Literature Survey of Experiences with the Concept. Working paper, School of Business, Stockholm University.

Johanson, U., M. Mårtensson, and M. Skoog. 1999. Measuring to Understand Intangible Performance Drivers. Working paper, School of Business, Stockholm University.

Larsen, H. T., J. Mouritsen, and P. N. D. Bukh. 1999. Intellectual Capital Statements and Knowledge Management: Measuring, Reporting and Acting, *Australian Accounting Review* 9, 3: 15–26.

Mouritsen, J. 1998. Driving Growth: Economic Value Added Versus Intellectual Capital, *Management Accounting Research* 9, 4: 461–83.

Mouritsen, J., H. T. Larsen, P. N. D. Bukh, and M. R. Johansen. 2000. Reading an Intellectual Capital Statement: Describing and Prescribing Knowledge Management Strategies, *Journal of Intellectual Capital* 2, 4.

Reich, R. B. 1991. *The Work of Nations.* New York: Vintage Books.

Ross, J. 1998. Exploring the Concept of Intellectual Capital (IC), *Long Range Planning* 31, 1: 150–53.

Roos, G. and J. Roos. 1997. Measuring Your Company's Intellectual Performance, *Long Range Planning* 30, 3: 413–26.

Roos, G., G. Ross, L. Edvinsson, and N. C. Dragonetti. 1997. *Intellectual Capital: Navigating in the New Business Landscape.* Houndsmils: Macmillan Business.

Sánchez, P., C. Chaminade, and M. Olea. 2000. Management of Intangibles. An Attempt to Build a Theory, *Journal of Intellectual Capital* 1, 4: 312–27.

Stewart, T. A. 1997. *Intellectual Capital*. London: Nicholas Brealey Publishing.

Sullivan, P. H., ed. 1998. *Profiting from Intellectual Capital: Extracting Value from Innovation*. London: Wiley and Sons.

Sveiby, K. E. 1997. *The New Organizational Wealth: Managing and Measuring Knowledge-Based Assets*. San Francisco: Berrett-Koehler.

11

THE LEARNING CAPACITY INDEX

A MEASUREMENT SYSTEM FOR LINKING CAPACITY TO LEARN AND FINANCIAL PERFORMANCE

Karen McGraw
Cognitive Technologies, Marietta, Georgia, U.S.A.
kmcgraw@mindspring.com

Laurie Bassi
Human Capital Dynamics, Chevy Chase, Maryland, U.S.A.
lbassi@hcdynamics.com

and

Daniel P. McMurrer
Human Capital Dynamics, Chevy Chase, Maryland, U.S.A.
dmcmurrer@hcdynamics.com

ABSTRACT

This chapter reports on Saba's learning capacity index (LCI), which was designed and launched as a part of an effort to improve the state of measurement with regard to organizational learning. Literature from the fields of business, organizational learning, training and development, and knowledge management was reviewed to identify six factors that appear to influence an organization's learning capacity and capability. The LCI was constructed as a self-assessment survey instrument that consists of a total of thirty-nine questions. The instrument covers six major factor areas from the research: vision and mission, structure and governance, culture, strategies, education and training function processes, and training technology infrastructure. It also captures demographic information on the enterprise. A pilot version of this tool has been used to gather initial data and help refine the LCI. Although the LCI database is not yet large enough to draw definitive conclusions, it is already evident that there are clear patterns in the learning capacities of organizations, with some practices generally far more advanced than others.

Introduction

The wisdom of the adage that "what gets measured gets managed" suggests that most organizations' efforts to promote learning are seriously undermanaged. As learning has become an increasingly important source of competitive advantage, the capacity to measure it, value it, and run it in a business-like manner has lagged far behind the need to do so.

An emerging body of research has demonstrated that the magnitude of firms' investments in education and training creates a wide variety of benefits, including improved retention of key employees, greater customer satisfaction and retention, enhanced capacity to innovate, improved financial outcomes, and higher total stockholder return (Bassi, Copeman, and McMurrer 2000). In other words, money matters. Unfortunately, much less is known on a systematic, rigorous, and quantitative basis about what—beyond money—matters most. Although there is no shortage of theoretical speculation about what distinguishes effective from ineffective strategies to promote organizational learning, hard evidence in support of the theory is in extremely short supply. Consequently, despite the large number of enterprises that are striving to become "learning organizations," few have any way of measuring their success (or lack thereof) in doing so.

This chapter reports on Saba's learning capacity index (LCI), which was designed and launched as a part of an effort to improve the state of measurement with regard to organizational learning. The first section of the chapter provides a review of the literature on organizational learning and summarizes the attributes that a wide variety of authors have identified as being likely to determine the effectiveness of learning strategies. The second section describes the intent of Saba's LCI and how it reflects the literature that precedes it. The third section provides additional detail on how the LCI was constructed. The fourth section summarizes the preliminary empirical findings that have emerged from a pilot test of the LCI, and the final section summarizes our initial conclusions and planned next steps.

LITERATURE REVIEW

Literature in the fields of business, organizational learning, training and development, and knowledge management was reviewed to identify factors that appear to influence an organization's learning capacity and capability. The review revealed that the following factors are believed to have an impact on the ability of an organization not only to learn but also to achieve business success:

- Alignment of the training and development function's vision and mission with organizational strategy and goals, and organizational members' perceptions of this vision and mission
- Strategies for managing competencies, learning, and "knowledge assets"
- Structure and governance of the training and development or learning function within the organization
- Strength of the culture's support for learning
- Training and development processes that produce desired outcomes
- Technological infrastructure for training-development and how technology is used to manage learning and human knowledge assets throughout the enterprise

The sections that follow summarize key research findings and principles related to each factor.

Vision and Mission

Numerous authors have documented the impact of vision and mission clarity on business success. Ulrich and Lake (1990) report that a shared understanding of, and commitment to, vision and mission is a critical element for enhanced organizational capability. The *Towers Perrin Workplace Index* (1997) includes items that measure employees' understanding of the workplace. Responses to this index indicate that commitment to organizational goals and vision shows a clear, positive relationship with commitment to help the organization succeed. Extensive research conducted by Gallup (Buckingham and Coffman 2000) reveals a strong correlation between the extent to which individuals throughout the enterprise have a shared mindset about the organization's goals and their commitment to helping achieve those goals. Similarly, Davenport (2000) notes that employees must be able to connect with strategy and see how what they do contributes to business success.

In light of this research, it is reasonable to assume that individuals within training and development and/or learning functions should be able to discern answers to these questions:

- What is our role in executing business strategy?
- How do our capabilities contribute to the firm's success?
- Do our investments clearly support achievement of business strategy?
- Do we have the information we need to make intelligent decisions about which learning interventions we develop and support, and the strategies we use to help the organization learn?

It is not enough, however, that employees within the training and development function have a clear mission and vision that aligns with corporate strategy and goals. People throughout the enterprise (i.e., their constituents and customers) should have a clear understanding of the vision, mission, and role of the training and development function in helping organizational members succeed in meeting business goals.

Strategies for Managing Competencies, Learning, and Knowledge Assets

What does the organization do to ensure that it can produce desired business results? The answers should describe the strategies it employs to manage competencies, learning, and knowledge assets. According to Nonaka and Takeuchi (1995), the new economy approach to strategy, competitiveness, and business success is "resource-based"; competencies, capabilities, skills, and human assets have become the primary source of sustainable competitive advantage of an organization (Korn/Ferry 1999; Davenport 2000). Teece, Pisano, and Shuen (1991) identify the dynamic capabilities of an organization (e.g., the ability of an organization to learn and change) as a key determinant for business success. In the new economy, competitive success depends on managing knowledge assets (Davenport 2000) by:

- Hiring people with the right abilities
- Creating an environment that encourages people to contribute what they know toward continual learning
- Developing people's human capital through formal and informal learning
- Sustaining and maintaining people's competencies by keeping them committed and engaged and by motivating them to learn continually

Hiring. Yeung, Ulrich, Nason, and Von Glinow (1999) have shown that organizations can generate ideas and attain new competencies in many ways: by hiring the competency from the outside, developing people internally, partnering, and/or benchmarking. Ulrich and Lake (1990) suggest that interviewing and hiring is *the* single greatest determinant of organizational effectiveness. Numerous researchers (Ulrich and Lake 1990; Wayland and Cole 1997) argue that the selection process within an organization is critical because it ensures that the firm hires employees with competencies required to meet present and future needs. Wood and Payne (1998) describe benefits of a competency-based recruitment and selection process as:

- Improving accuracy in assessing someone's suitability for a job
- Facilitating a closer match between a person's skills and interests and the demands of the job
- Enabling interviewers to make judgments based on characteristics that are relevant to the job rather than on "gut" instinct

Developing. Developing competencies can have a profound impact on productivity and business success. Increasing worker knowledge through learning improves productivity by as much as 16 percent (Lynch and Black 1995). Davenport (2000) reports that competency-based hiring and development-learning has been linked to business success; a specialty home-products retailer was able to link human capital applications (hiring, development, performance assessment) to enable them to generate growth in net sales from $440M to $933M over a four-year period. To produce results such as this, Wayland and Cole (1997) argue that organizations must identify critical competencies and knowledge required to meet customer expectations and assist employees in acquiring them.

Sustaining and Maintaining. Once competence is hired or otherwise acquired, organizations should address the issue of sustaining and maintaining workplace competence. This requires performance feedback, reward and recognition, and general management support. Yeung, Ulrich, Nason, and Von Glinow (1999) argue that managers should have frequent interaction with employees to discuss performance, growth, and goals, rather than just the once-a-year performance review that is commonplace in most organizations. Numerous researchers (Ulrich and Lake 1990; Sherriton and Stern 1997; Buckingham and Coffman 1999) agree that employees should receive frequent feedback about how well their performance meets established standards. Ulrich and Lake (1990) and Harlow and Hanke (1975) contend that good managers should define, and make sure employees understand, performance outcomes, clearly communicating performance expectations to individuals and teams.

Successful organizations also employ a performance-based development process to ensure that individuals can produce required job outputs faster, with better quality, and with less "time to competence." However, less than 20 percent of workers responding to a California survey say they receive any formal training from their employers (Field Institute and Future of Work and Health 1996). And whereas about 70 percent of organizations surveyed train their middle managers, executives, and supervisors, only 37 percent of organizations surveyed train nonmanagerial, production, or customer service workers (Marshall and Tucker 1992).

Research done by the Center for Workforce Development (1998) indicates that support for competence-building is a key organizational value. When it is present, people do not wait until they enter a classroom to start acquiring skills and knowledge. Consequently, firms should create an environment that supports both formal and informal learning. Examples include blended-learning solutions composed of Web-based training, an instructor-led course, a downloadable job aid, and one-on-one coaching.

Finally, learning initiatives to develop and maintain competence should be targeted to enable the performance required for a job. A recent Forrester report predicts that "one size fits all" learning—offerings and catalogs of generic content—will be less useful over the next two years as learners select more customizable (i.e., in terms of learning strategy, content, and depth) solutions (Dalton 2000).

Structure and Governance

Effective firms have organizational structures in place that support management processes and strategy. Executives increasingly believe that a firm's "knowledge assets" will be critical in achieving its business strategy (Korn/Ferry 1999). If this is the case, organizations must examine how the firm is structured to make best use of these assets. This includes examining how key business units are organized and how the training and development functions are organized to support the business units. An investigation of nearly two hundred organizations concluded that organizations seeking competitive advantage and superior performance from their human capital resources must design and configure the organization's structure to maximize performance (Dess and Picken 1999).

Traditional organizational structures have proven less than effective in developing and managing knowledge assets (Nonaka and Takeuchi 1995). The primary organizational structure for the last several decades has been a bureaucratic, formalized, highly centralized structure. Bureaucratic structures work well when conditions are stable, since they emphasize control and predictability. The "task force" model is a newer, more dynamic, flexible, and decentralized structure. However, this model is often ineffective in transmitting and sharing new learning quickly. The task force structure and its variations support the empowerment of people, emphasize the importance of competencies, and recognize knowledge as a leverageable asset. Nonaka and Takeuchi (1995) argue that organizational structures should help a firm exploit its competencies and knowledge assets, as well as accumulate and share new learning quickly. Consequently, some combination of centralized bureaucratic structure and decentralized task force structure is needed to provide a solid base for optimal knowledge creation and ongoing learning.

Another variable that impacts learning capacity is governance—the guidelines, procedures, and rules related to training and learning. These may be written or unwritten, formal rules or just "norms." They dictate who gets training, how much training they get, and the percentage of formal versus informal training. They influence the role the training function plays in managing learning and the process through which one goes to request or identify new training needs. Governance may exhibit itself as a stated average of training-hours-per-employee that are allowed (or required) per year. It may also be illustrated in the organization's commitment of budget for employee development and learning.

Learning Culture

A learning organization is one that views learning and development as a strategic investment; its management is willing to invest in the process of enabling learning and knowledge creation (Senge, et al. 1999; Quinn 1992). It is one that recognizes that "ability to compete" is based on the organization's ability to learn and continually create and use knowledge (Leonard 1998). It requires a culture that not only values and recognizes the strategic nature of learning but also includes incentives and rewards to encourage learning and knowledge creation (Leonard 1998).

One way to determine how an organization values learning and development is to examine whether the training function is viewed as a cost or as a strategic investment. Another factor is whether the organization makes time available for learning: for example, enabling anytime-anywhere learning, scheduling time for focus and concentration, and trusting people to control their own use of time (Senge et al. 1999). Another variable is how the organization *typically* learns. Some organizations "learn" by making strategic acquisitions of other firms with the needed competence or hiring from the outside; others spend time to invest in and develop individuals and teams, while still others learn by benchmarking. A final variable is the availability of learning throughout the enterprise. Stalk, Evans, and Shulman (1992) contend that Honda's ability to train and support not only its employees but also its dealer network is as important to their success as their innovative product design.

Training and Development Processes

The literature on quality highlights the importance of having, effectively using, and evaluating the impact of formal processes for getting work done (Hodgetts, Luthans, and Lee 1994; Payne 1993). For a formal process to be "good," researchers (Hammer and Champy 1993; Hodgetts, Luthans, and Lee 1994) suggest it should have the following characteristics:

- Processes should be customer-driven and supportive of executive strategy.

- Processes should be broken into logical tasks and should evidence control and accountability.
- As few people as possible should be involved in the performance of a process.
- The process should be documented.
- Individuals within the organization should be trained in how to work within the process.
- Processes should be linked to rewards; there should be incentives that motivate individuals to work within the process.

Good, formal processes help people work effectively only when people know that they exist, why they are important, and how to use them. People must be motivated to use them consistently and in appropriate ways. Additionally, people must be able to continually improve and update them dynamically as needs and strategies change. Furthermore, the processes must not be so complex that individuals within the training and learning function cannot be responsive to customer needs.

Finally, measurement and evaluation of processes and training and development products is the key to continual improvement. Leading-edge training and development-functions recognize that the success of their business depends on demonstrating the value of the investment in learning, maximizing value for training dollars spent, and continually satisfying customers (Sharpe 1999). Organizations should use measurement to learn and continually improve products and services, however, not just to "produce reports" (Phillips 1996). To run training like a business, learning interventions should have measurable outputs. This enables the organization to determine not only how enjoyable a learning intervention was but also whether it helped the participant learn and produce the desired business results. Consequently, assessment and measurement goals and strategies should be developed through partnership with executive leaders and, thus, tied closely to the organization's strategic goals (Senge et al. 1999).

Technological Infrastructure

Business-planning activities should identify the potential impact of any new technology on specific business functions. Changes in technologies of products upon which the business function depends affects the value-adding activities of operations within that function

(Porter 1985). Firms and functions within firms must carefully identify the probable direction of technological change, focusing on the impact of these changes on competitiveness. They also must carefully select and integrate technology strategies, such that they reinforce the firm's overall competitive strategy (Porter 1985; Betz 1987).

Today, training and development functions find themselves in the midst of widespread technological change. Presentation and distribution methods now present a wide array of choices and require extensive technical infrastructure. According to *ASTD's 1999 State of the Industry Report,* there are seven types of presentation methods: computer-based training (CBT), multimedia, interactive television, teleconferencing, groupware, virtual reality, and the Electronic Performance Support System (EPSS). Of these seven methods, multimedia, teleconferencing, and CBT are the most widely used (Bassi and Van Buren 1999). ASTD also identified twelve distribution methods for learning technologies: cable television, CD-ROMs, e-mail, extranets, the Internet, intranets, LANs, satellite television, simulators, voicemail, wide-area networks (WANs), and the World Wide Web. Of these twelve methods, CD-ROMs, the World Wide Web, intranets, and the Internet are the most widely used for training distribution (Bassi and Van Buren 1999). A learner now can learn anyplace, anytime, and on his or her own schedule, while simultaneously receiving the most up-to-date training materials by downloading them through Web-based technologies (Boies, Peck, and Warren 2000).

Another critical function for organizations is their ability to track an employee's training efforts and accomplishments. For example, if an employee enrolls in a corporate class, a system can track and identify an employee's skills, so this information can be tied to the human resources hiring processes. In fact, the trend is to combine distance learning and learning-management technologies to meet customer-learner needs and, thus, performance goals for the business. However, if technology-supported learning is to meet its promise, key factors must be addressed, including:

- Equal access by all employees to the technology they need for delivery of technology-based learning
- Training for learners that ensures they can operate the technology required for delivery of learning interventions
- Commitment of IT resources to the training-learning function to ensure that the function receives the support it needs to

select, implement, troubleshoot, and maintain technology, networks, and presentation-delivery software

- Selection of learning products and technologies that are compliant with emerging standards (e.g., AICC, IMS) to ensure interoperability
- Replacement of numerous "homegrown" tools that vary from one business unit or function to another, with a standardized, scaleable system for managing learning processes (i.e., scheduling, registration, marketing, learning development plans, assessment, access to learning products, etc.) across the enterprise

THE PURPOSE OF THE LEARNING CAPACITY INDEX

The learning capacity index has been constructed by incorporating and building upon the insights from the literature outlined above. The LCI is a self-assessment survey instrument that consists of a total of thirty-nine questions. The instrument covers seven major areas: demographic information on the enterprise, vision and mission, structure and governance, culture, strategies, education and training function processes, and training technology infrastructure.

From the Participant's Perspective

The LCI service is designed to provide an enterprise with free, high-quality, objective information on where it stands with regard to its overall capacity to learn, as well as specific diagnostic information on the strengths and weaknesses of its learning capacity.

Those enterprises that fill out the LCI survey are given a free, customized report that provides them with an assessment of their organizations' overall capacity for learning, specific areas of strength and weakness, and recommendations for improvement. The report serves as an objective, authoritative source of information that enterprises can use to determine how they can and should alter their policies, strategies, and investments in learning, so as to promote organizational performance.

The Research Purpose

The ultimate intent of the LCI is to provide a foundation for a systematic, rigorous, empirical exploration of what aspects of organizational learning strategies are most critical in driving organizational performance. We expect to use the LCI to collect data on a large number of organizations, which will enable us to identify trends in learning capacity and maturity, correlation of learning capacity and maturity with organizational demographics such as size and industry, and those factors that consistently inhibit an organization's learning capacity. For those publicly traded organizations that submit LCI data, it will be possible to merge their data with publicly reported information on a wide range of measures of financial performance. Ultimately, as the database grows, we expect to be able to determine which aspects (if any) of organizational learning are systematically linked to financial performance.

In addition to this long-term objective, we will also be using the LCI to systematically explore a range of currently unanswered empirical questions, such as the following:

- Of the attributes that have been identified by students of organizational learning, which ones are typically the areas of greatest strength and weakness?
- Do the areas of strength and weakness vary across geographic regions or industrial sector?
- Are there significant differences between the for-profit, not-for-profit, and governmental sectors?

The Construction of the Learning Capacity Index

The factors identified in the literature as the determinants of an organization's learning capacity and capability were grouped and normalized (i.e., common labels applied to ideas that were similar). Next, principles related to each factor were identified. Then, content of the LCI was developed from these factors and principles, using the following categories:

- Vision and mission
- Structure and governance
- Organizational culture
- Strategies
- Education and training function processes
- Training technology infrastructure

Defining Data-Use and Target Audience Population

The target audience-population includes individuals operating at senior management–director level and above to whom employee performance and learning is important, who have knowledge about the way their organization learns, develops, and manages learning.

Survey Methodology

The body of the survey consisted of two main sections: a demographic data section with nine items and a learning capacity item section of thirty items chunked into six groupings. The survey methodology is based on use of a rating scale with descriptive items, ranging from a null- or low-maturity response to high-maturity responses. Items were presented in groups based on the factor or determinant to which they related. The first three groupings (vision and mission, structure and governance, and organizational culture) were more conceptual or general, and the final three groupings (strategies, education and training function processes, and training technology infrastructure) were more concrete and specific.

Each item was constructed in a format similar to the following question: "To what extent do managers demonstrate a sincere commitment to making time available during work for their employees to learn?" followed by five response options. The survey reflected a 5-point scale (0 to 4) because there is considerable evidence to suggest that anything over a 5-point scale is irrelevant. (Although 7- to 10-point scales may seem to gather more discriminating information, there is debate as to whether respondents actually discriminate carefully enough when filling out a questionnaire to make these scales valuable. Also, these scales are often collapsed into 3- or 5-point scales for reporting purposes.)

The response options ranged from a null or negative response to a highly positive response. To guard against habituation (always choosing the same response), we varied the response labels. Sometimes the median response was generic (e.g., "to some extent"), whereas in other cases it was more specific (e.g., "20–29 hours per year"). Though the literature suggests some tendency to pick the choices nearest the start of a list when reading from a computer screen, we believe this is balanced by the slightly positive skewing of data that may occur when using a 5-point scale.

Item Development and Presentation

Items were developed using protocol and standard format. A table of factors-determinants and possible questions to address each factor-determinant were constructed. Items were then refined to achieve the following goals:

- Eliminate redundancy
- Ensure that each item truly reflected the factor with which it was associated
- Ensure items were structured in a similar format
- Improve readability

The resulting question bank, grouped by factor-determinant, was circulated to other researchers and suggestions for refinement collected. Next, a preliminary survey was created and refined to ensure that item stems and response options were understandable, easy to respond to, nonredundant, and would provide the details needed about the factor-determinant. Finally, surface-level design was addressed to ensure that the survey used a large enough point size and adequate white space and enabled respondents to easily select desired options using the computer-based form.

Validity

According to the American Psychological Association, validity "refers to the appropriateness, meaningfulness, and usefulness of the specific inferences made from test scores" (Standards for Psychological and Educational Testing 1999 : 9). The LCI survey has strong content validity (i.e., survey items are representative of the topic being measured) because its content is based on research in organizational learning and factors that appear to impact an organization's capacity to learn (see Section 11.2). Both the factors-determinants and the individual items are representative of the topic and adequately cover primary aspects of it. Criterion-related validation involves calculating a "validity coefficient" by correlating the survey items with another measure (criterion) already known to be related to other aspects of the attribute. Our intent is to subject the LCI to the ultimate validity test—that is to say, does it predict organizational performance? Construct-validation attempts to understand what is being measured by examining the relationship between constructs (abstract ideas used as an explanatory concept). Construct-validation involves understanding why items are related by examining the underlying concepts.

Piloting the Survey

A pilot version of the Saba LCI data collection instrument was distributed to twelve selected individuals in eight organizations, including organizations with which Saba was working in some capacity, as well as other interested parties. These organizations are fairly typical of the types of firms that we expect will respond to the LCI questionnaire once it is broadly released.

PRELIMINARY FINDINGS

Twelve organizations or organizational subunits submitted full learning-capacity data to Saba in the pilot phase of this research. Five of the subunits represented the five global regions of the same worldwide organization. Thus, the data were received from a total of eight different parent organizations.

Although the resulting database is too small to draw definitive conclusions, it nevertheless represents a useful first look at patterns of responses, as well as identifying some areas in which participating organizations displayed particularly strong or weak capacities for learning.

As noted previously, scores are based on a 5-point scale ranging from 0 to 4. The midpoint, 2.0, is generally intended to represent "average" organizational capacity for each specific question, with higher scores reflecting a stronger capacity and lower ones a weaker capacity.

Six category scores were calculated for each organization, each one based on the mean of the individual factors that make up one of the six broad learning-capacity categories. A summary score was also calculated for the organization as a whole (the summary score represents the average of the six category scores, ensuring that each category is weighted equally).

All reporting units were included in the preliminary analysis that follows. Examination of the effects of the multiple units from the single parent organization revealed that they had little effect on the overall results. Means for each question were similar (in only 20 percent of the individual questions was there more than a 10 percent difference in average score, if the organization had been treated as a single organization, rather than five separate ones). Interestingly, analysis of standard deviations indicates that learning capacities in the five subunits generally differed from one another on a similar scale to differences across the unrelated organizations.

Overall Results

Average category scores (see Figure 11-1) for the six broad categories were higher than the midpoint (of 2.0) in five of the six categories, with only one (training and development processes) slightly below the midpoint (1.97). The highest average summary category scores were in the vision and mission area (2.79), with structure and governance also scoring high at 2.69. These two average scores were statistically significantly different (at the .10 level) from the two lowest average scores (which were in education-training processes and strategies).

Measured by standard deviation, differences in category scores across organizations were fairly similar in most categories, with summary scores slightly more similar in the strategies and culture sections, and more different in the vision-mission and training technology infrastructure sections.

At 2.4, the average summary score was above the midpoint, with the summary scores ranging from a high of 3.3 to a low of 1.4. Only two of the twelve organizations scored below the midpoint (of 2.0), whereas only one scored above a 3.0.

Demographics

The pilot database does not contain demographic information on all responding organizations, although most of the parent organizations did submit such information. The demographic data suggest that the organizations in the database are generally large, established, global organizations. The vast majority are for-profit organizations. Each has at least 1000 employees (and many have significantly more), and at least four have $100 million or more in annual revenue.

Vision-Mission

As noted above, vision-mission received the highest average category scores across the organizations, suggesting that this is an area

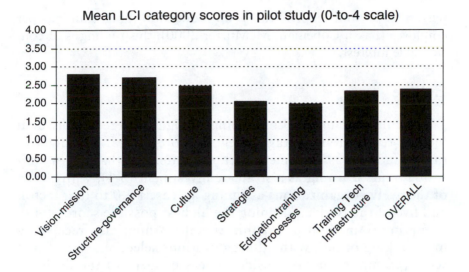

Figure 11-1 *Mean LCI Category Scores*

of clear relative learning capacity strength for the organizations in the sample. All twelve of the organizations rated the alignment between training function and business mission and goals at least at the 2.0 level (nine of the twelve rated it at least 3.0). Ten of the twelve organizations also rated the extent to which employees understood the vision and goals of the education-training function at the 2.0 level or higher.

Structure-Governance

Structure-governance also received relatively high scores from the twelve organizations. Rated most highly of the four separate factors in this category were the extent to which organizations had a centralized mechanism for handling broad-reaching educational and training needs across the organization (3.2 average) and the extent to which there was a mechanism for handling unit-specific needs (3.0 average). Both factors were ranked at 2.0 or higher by eleven of the twelve organizations. Budgetary commitment to education and training received the lowest score (2.0 average), with no organizations ranking the commitment at the 4.0 level and only a slim majority (seven of twelve) ranking the commitment at the 2.0 or higher. Given the research that points to a significant link between financial performance and expenditures on education and training per employee (Bassi, Copeman, McMurrer 2000), this finding is of considerable interest.

Culture

The culture category, comprising of eight different individual factors, received an average category score of 2.5. The highest-ranked factor was agreement with the statement that the organization treats learning as a strategic investment (3.1), with eleven of the twelve organizations assigning at least a 2.0 to that factor, and five of the twelve assigning the highest possible score of 4.0. The primary method of organizational learning also received a high ranking of 3.0, with all organizations selecting exactly that score (prompting us to consider a reassessment of the different types of responses available for that factor). The lowest-ranked factor was the extent to which the organization shares knowledge through communities of practice or best practices (1.9). Only two of the twelve organizations ranked this factor above 2.0. Also ranked relatively low were the extent to which learning is enabled through an organization's extended enterprise (customers, suppliers, etc.) (2.0) and the extent to which the organization creates formal mechanisms to reinforce the importance of learning (2.2).

Strategies

The strategies factor received a relatively low average category score of 2.1, with four organizations scoring below the 2.0 midpoint, and only one organization scoring above 2.3. As noted above, of the nine individual factors in this category, three received an average score of 1.3 (the lowest score of factors in any category)—the extent to which the organization measures the quality of learning interventions for purposes of continuous improvement, the extent to which the effectiveness of learning interventions is evaluated, and the extent to which learning interventions are customized to individual needs. In each of these three factors, only one of twelve organizations ranked above 2.0. The highest-ranking strategy factors were the extent to which learning-development opportunities are discussed with new hires (2.8) and the extent to which the organization provides a variety of different types of learning interventions to meet learning needs (2.8). A majority of organizations scored above 2.0 for each of these two factors.

Training-and-Development Processes

The three-factor training-and-development-processes category received the lowest overall category score (1.97). The only one of the three factors that scored above 2.0 was the extent to which the organization's training department follows formal processes (2.5). The other two, the extent to which formal processes allow the education and training organization to meet customer needs more effectively (1.8) and the extent to which the organization measures the effectiveness of its formal processes (1.6), both scored below 2.0. In terms of the latter factor, measuring effectiveness of formal processes, no organization scored above 2.0, and only seven of twelve scored at the 2.0 level.

Training-Technology Infrastructure

The organizations in the sample scored an average of 2.3 in the four-factor training-technology-infrastructure category. There was a significant gap across the various factors in the category, with organizations scoring a high average of 3.4 for the scope of individual learners' access to technology-based training (with eleven of twelve organizations scoring 3.0 or better), but an average of only 1.7 for the extensiveness of their training or learning management "system" (with only three organizations scoring 3.0 or better).

Summary

Although the LCI database is not yet large enough to draw definitive conclusions, it is already evident that there are clear patterns in the learning capacities of organizations, with some practices generally far more advanced than others. With regard to the six broad categories covered in the Saba LCI, the organizations in the pilot database are less advanced in the areas of strategies and processes (and to a lesser extent, infrastructure), whereas they have progressed further in areas related to vision-mission and structure-governance (and to a lesser extent, culture).

The three highest-ranked *individual* factors were the:

- Scope of individual learners' access to technology-based training (3.4)
- Alignment between training function and business mission and goals (3.3)
- Existence of a centralized mechanism for handling broad-reaching education and training needs across the organization (3.2)

The three individual factors that received the lowest rankings were all in the strategies category:

- The extent to which the organization measures the quality of learning interventions for purposes of continuous improvement
- The extent to which the effectiveness of learning interventions is evaluated
- The extent to which learning interventions are customized to individual needs (each was at 1.3)

CONCLUSIONS

If learning is really a strategic investment that provides competitive advantage and distinguishes excellent from mediocre performance, then it must be measured as though it matters. The Saba Learning Capacity Index represents a step toward improving the state of measurement with regard to organizational learning. By building upon and incorporating the insights from the existing learning-organization literature into a quantitative tool, we have laid a foundation for ongoing empirical work. Our ultimate intent is to develop a sufficiently large database on publicly traded firms to enable us to determine systematically and rigorously what aspects of an enterprise's learning strategy, processes, and infrastructure are essential to driving financial performance.

Although it will take us some time to achieve this goal, the initial pilot phase of the analysis has already produced some interesting insights. With regard to the six broad categories covered in the Saba LCI, the organizations in the pilot database are less advanced in the areas of strategies and processes (and to a lesser extent, infrastructure), whereas they have progressed further in areas related to vision-mission and structure-governance (and to a lesser extent, culture).

One interpretation of this is that the glass is half-full; it is encouraging that, at least for this sample of enterprises, there does appear to be a fairly strong organizational commitment to learning (in terms of vision-mission, structure-governance, and culture). The other interpretation is that the glass is half-empty, since reality (as measured by strategy, processes, and infrastructure) appears to be lagging behind the commitment.

It remains to be seen, of course, whether these findings will be replicated in a larger sample of organizations. And even within a larger sample of firms, repeated measurement over time will be required to identify the trends that will enable us to determine whether the glass is, indeed, half-empty or half-full.

In the interim, however, it is noteworthy that one area of weakness is budgetary commitment to education and training, which previous research has shown to be a significant determinant of organizations' financial performance. Other areas of particular weakness include evaluation of learning effectiveness, customization to individual needs, learning-management infrastructure, and sharing of knowledge across the organization. Although it is still too early for our research to shed empirical light on which particular factors matter most in terms of driving organizational performance, it seems probable that these areas of weakness are likely to be important barriers if learning is, indeed, to become a strategic investment.

These are among the issues that we ultimately intend to pursue as the Saba LCI database grows in size. The immediate next steps of this research will consist of the following:

- Revising the Saba LCI, based on what has been learned from the initial pilot phase of the project
- Developing a Web version of the LCI, with an automated mechanism for providing the customized reports back to respondents
- Creating a benchmarking capacity as the database grows, so that the reports provided back to respondents assess not only strengths and weaknesses, but also provide actual benchmarking data

REFERENCES

Bassi, L. and M. E. Van Buren. 1999. *The 1999 ASTD State of the Industry Report.* Alexandria, Va.: American Society for Training and Development.

Bassi, L., D. Copeman, and D. McMurrer. 2000. *The Business of Learning.* Redwood Shores, Calif.: Saba.

Betz, F. 1987. *Managing Technology: Competing Through New Ventures, Innovation, and Corporate Research.* Englewood Cliffs, N.J.: Prentice Hall.

Boies, T., D. Peck, and J. Warren. 2000. Distance Learning Primer. http://www.fedtraining.org.

Buckingham, M., and C. Coffman. 1999. *First, Break All the Rules: What the World's Greatest Managers Do Differently.* New York: Simon and Schuster.

Dalton, J. 2000. Online Training Needs a New Course, *The Forrester Report.* Cambridge, Mass.: Forrester Research, Inc.

Davenport, T. 2000. *Human Capital: What It Is and Why People Invest in It.* San Francisco: Jossey-Bass.

Dess, G. and J. Picken. 1999. *Beyond Productivity: How Leading Companies Achieve Superior Performance by Leveraging Their Human Capital.* New York: American Management Association.

Hammer, M. and J. Champy. 1991. *Reengineering the Corporation.* New York: Harper Business.

Harlow, D. and J. Hanke. 1975. *Behavior in Organizations.* New York: Little Brown.

Hodgetts, R., F. Luthans, and S. Lee. 1994. New Paradigm Organizations: From Total Quality to Learning to World Class, *Organizational Dynamics* 23, 3 (Winter): 4.

Leonard, D. 1998. *Wellsprings of Knowledge: Building and Sustaining the Sources of Innovation.* Boston: Harvard Business School Press.

Lynch, L. M. and S. E. Black. 1995. Beyond the Incidence of Training: Evidence from a National Employers Survey, Working paper no. 5231. National Bureau of Economic Research. Cambridge, Mass..

Marshall, R. and M. Tucker. 1992. *Thinking for a Living: Education and the Wealth of Nations.* New York: Basis Books.

Nonaka, I. and H. Takeuchi. 1995. *The Knowledge-Creating Company.* Oxford: Oxford University Press.

Payne, T. 1993. Let's Call It Quality this Time, *Canadian Manager* 18, 3: 25.

Phillips, J. 1996. How Much Is the Training Worth? *Training and Development* (April): 20.

Porter, M. 1985. *Competitive Advantage.* New York: Free Press.

Quinn, J. 1992. *Intelligent Enterprise: A Knowledge and Service-Based Paradigm for Industry.* New York: Free Press.

Senge, P., A. Kleiner, C. Roberts, et. al. 1999. *The Dance of Change: The Challenges to Sustaining Momentum in Learning Organizations.* New York: Doubleday.

Sharpe, C. 1999. *Info-line Guide to Training Evaluation. Info-line Collection for Training & Performance Professionals.* Alexandria, Va.: ASTD.

Sherriton, J. and J. Stern. 1997. *Corporate Culture/Team Culture: Removing the Hidden Barriers to Team Success.* New York: American Management Association.

Stalk, G., P. Evans, and L. Shulman. 1992. Competing on Capabilities: The New Rules of Corporate Strategy, *Harvard Business Review* 57 (March-April).

Teece, D. J., G. Pisano, and A. Shuen. 1991. *Dynamic Capabilities and Strategic Management.* Center for Research in Management. Berkeley, Calif.: University of California Press.

Towers Perrin. 1997. *The 1997 Towers Perrin Workplace Index.* New York: Towers Perrin.

Ulrich, D. and D. Lake. 1990. *Organizational Capability: Competing from the Inside Out.* New York: John Wiley.

Ulrich, D., J. Zenger, and N. Smallwood. 1999. *Results-Based Leadership.* Boston: Harvard Business School Press.

Wayland, R. and P. Cole. 1997. *Customer Connections: New Strategies for Growth.* Boston: Harvard Business School Press.

Wood, R. and T. Payne. 1998. *Competency-Based Recruitment and Selection: A Practical Guide.* New York: Wiley and Sons.

Yeung, A., D. Ulrich, S. Nason, and M. Von Glinow. 1999. *Organizational Learning Capability.* New York: Oxford University Press.

———— 1996. *Job Skills Training in the California Workforce.* San Francisco: Field Institute and Future of Work and Health.

————1998. *The Teaching Firm: Where Productive Work and Learning Converge.* Newton, Mass.: Center for Workforce Development, Education Development Center.

———— 1999. Executive Insights, second edition. Los Angeles: Korn/Ferry International.

————1999. Standards for Psychological and Educational Testing, Washington, D.C.: American Educational Research Association.

12

DEVELOPING A MEASURE OF KNOWLEDGE MANAGEMENT

Jenny Darroch
Department of Marketing, University of Otago, Dunedin, New Zealand
jdarroch@commerce.otago.ac.nz

and

Rod McNaughton
Eyton Chair in Entrepreneurship, University of Waterloo, Waterloo, Canada
rmcnaugh@engmail.uwaterloo.ca

ABSTRACT

The purpose of this chapter is to discuss the conceptual development of an instrument developed to measure knowledge management. The instrument is based on the Kohli-Jaworski market-orientation instrument that was developed to measure a firm's ability to acquire, disseminate, and use market information. However, it includes more than just market information and uses Nonaka and Takeuchi's knowledge creation spiral to expand the section on information dissemination. By using the knowledge management instrument, future research can be conducted that expands our understanding of the knowledge management discipline by, for example, quantifying a firm's knowledge management orientation or looking for links between knowledge management and consequences such as innovation and firm performance.

INTRODUCTION

The study of knowledge as a concept is not new, but there is renewed emphasis on effective knowledge management as firms seek to compete effectively in knowledge-based economies (Capon, Farley, Lehmann, and Hulbert 1992; Chiesa, Coughlan, and Voss 1996), which are characterized by the rapid accumulation and diffusion of knowledge (Arundel, Smith, Patel, and Sirilli 1998). As a consequence, knowledge management and the related concepts of organizational learning (Nonaka and Takeuchi 1995) and organizational agility (Dove 1999) are now prevalent themes in both academic and management discourse.

Knowledge management, however, is still very much a new discipline (Preiss 1999; Shariq 1998), and it seems that very little is known about what effective knowledge management really means (Nonaka and Takeuchi 1995). As Despres and Chauvel (1999: 110) suggest, "knowledge management is clearly on the slippery slope of being intuitively important but intellectually elusive." Knowledge management is important because "a company's value derives not from things, but from knowledge, know-how, intellectual assets, competencies—all of it embedded in people" (Hamel and Prahalad 1996: 241). However, it is elusive because definitions of knowledge seem abstract and sweeping (Alvesson 1993), which makes knowledge hard to quantify, analyze, and connect to company performance (Preiss 1999). Knowledge management is a good example of a new discipline in which practices are established before methods for analyzing and understanding the new reality (Preiss 1999). "The need now is for analytical methods that can be used in this new discipline, so that management may add a quantitative dimension to qualitative [knowledge management] approaches" (Preiss 1999: 39).

WHAT IS KNOWLEDGE MANAGEMENT?

In an earlier paper by Darroch and McNaughton (2000: 4), knowledge is defined as follows:

> Knowledge comprises two types: tacit and explicit. Tacit knowledge is highly people dependent and is created when insights or experiences are added to information. Tacit knowledge resides within individuals or becomes embedded in organizational

routines and procedures. It is non-verbal and so is difficult to articulate, codify, measure, spread and store.

Explicit knowledge is less dependent on people and can be codified, measured, spread or stored. Information is data that has had context or meaning added. Data are a collection of records or facts. Together, information and data make up explicit knowledge.

In the same paper, and following a thorough review of literature and discussions with senior managers, Darroch and McNaughton (2000: 6) offer a definition of knowledge management. Knowledge management is:

The management function that creates or locates knowledge, manages the flow of knowledge within the organization and ensures that knowledge is used effectively and efficiently for the long-term benefit of the organization.

Various studies have reported consequences of effective knowledge management. For example, effective knowledge management:

- Creates some kind of competitive advantage (Connor and Prahalad 1996; Hall 1993; Powell and Dent-Micallef 1997; Rumisen 1998)
- Enhances performance (Bassie 1997; Teece 1998; Bontis et al. 2002; Wiig 1999)
- Enables a firm to be more innovative (Antonelli 1999; Carneiro 2000; Dove 1999; Nonaka and Takeuchi 1995)
- Allows a firm to anticipate problems better (Carneiro 2000)
- Enables a firm to analyze and evaluate information better (Carneiro 2000)

To date, few empirical studies have examined the consequences of effective knowledge management. Thus, the purpose of this paper is to develop an instrument to measure knowledge management, thereby enabling future research to empirically test the link between knowledge management and consequences such as innovation and firm performance. The following section outlines the conceptual development of the instrument.

WHAT IS A KNOWLEDGE MANAGEMENT ORIENTATION?

A *knowledge management–oriented firm* is defined as one that demonstrates superior skills in creating or locating knowledge, managing the flow of knowledge within the organization, and ensuring that knowledge is used effectively and efficiently for the long-term benefit of the organization (Darroch and McNaughton 2000). There are strong parallels between this definition and an earlier definition of a market-oriented firm. Here, a *market-oriented firm* is defined as one that exhibits three organizational behaviors: an organization-wide generation of market intelligence pertaining to current and future customer needs, the dissemination of intelligence across departments, and an organization-wide responsiveness to that intelligence (Kohli and Jaworksi 1990). The Kohli-Jaworski instrument for measuring a market orientation has been operationalized (Kohli, Jaworski, and Kumar 1993) and antecedents and consequences of a market orientation identified (Jaworksi and Kohli 1993).

The following diagram illustrates the definition of a knowledge management–oriented firm.

Figure 12-1 describes a knowledge management–oriented firm. It shows that information from both internal and external sources flows into a firm. Information is then disseminated throughout the firm. As information is disseminated, knowledge is created and converted. The organization then responds to the information and new knowledge—a responsive organization is considered agile (Dove 1999). Outcomes of a knowledge management orientation might include innovation, performance, and organizational learning (Bontis, Crossan, and Hulland 2002).

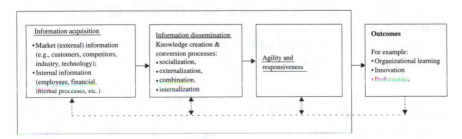

Figure 12-1 *A knowledge management-orientation*

Though the definitions of a market orientation and a knowledge management orientation appear similar, there are several differences. First, a market-oriented firm confines its inputs to information about customers' needs and wants. This means that a market-oriented firm will collect customer information and information on other external events that might affect customers' needs and wants. By contrast, a knowledge management–oriented firm will collect a wider range of external information as well as internal information, such as financial information, employee information, and technical information.

Another key difference between the two orientations is that a knowledge management–oriented firm will focus on internal processes that facilitate information dissemination, thereby allowing knowledge to be created and converted as it flows around the organization. Knowledge creation processes that enable information dissemination have not been featured in instruments developed to measure a market orientation (e.g., Kohli et al. 1993; Narver and Slater 1990; Ruekert 1992). This omission might reflect the fact that there has been very little work done to refine the instruments presented in seminal market orientation studies. In fact, the main emphasis in the stream of market orientation research has been to identify the antecedents and consequences of following a market orientation (Hart and Rolender 1999).

The final difference between a market orientation and a knowledge management orientation is that none of the consequences listed earlier have been tested empirically. By contrast, the consequences of a market orientation have been established empirically. For example, a market-oriented firm should perform better. Performance has been operationalized in various ways. For example, Jaworksi and Kohli (1993) simply asked respondents to note whether the firm had improved its overall performance last year. Their findings suggested that firms did perform better by following a market orientation. Narver and Slater (1990) showed that having a market orientation improves return on assets. The group of studies linking market orientation and performance has been ably reviewed in Gray, Matear, Boshoff, and Matheson (1998). Other studies have measured the link between a market orientation and innovation (Atuahene-Gima 1996; Gatignon and Xuereb 1997; Han, Kim, and Srivastava 1998). In addition, some researchers (Desphande 1999; Slater and Narver 1995) have hypothesized a link between a market-oriented firm and a learning organization.

There are also established links between various outcomes of a market orientation. For example, innovation has been linked to performances in several studies (e.g., Daniel and Tomkin 1999; Han et al. 1998; Li and Calantone 1998; Slater and Narver 1994). So, although the consequences of a knowledge management orientation have not been empirically tested, one can look to the parallel stream of market orientation literature for clues as to what might result from having a knowledge management orientation.

DEVELOPING A MEASURE OF A KNOWLEDGE MANAGEMENT ORIENTATION

The purpose of this chapter is to discuss the conceptual development of an instrument intended to measure knowledge management. The instrument is based on the Kohli-Jaworski market orientation instrument (Kohli et al. 1993) that was developed to measure a firm's ability to acquire, disseminate, and use market information. However, along with including a wider range of information, we suggest that any study of knowledge management should have an expanded measure of information dissemination. In the context of knowledge management, this means capturing the processes that enhance the creation, conversion, and use of knowledge within an organization. These processes are said to have more impact on the long-term benefits to the firm (Day 1994; Fahey and Prusak 1998; Teece 1998) since one could argue that all firms more or less have access to the same types of information.

To examine the creation, conversion, and use of knowledge management, the contribution of Nonaka and Takeuchi (1995) is incorporated. Nonaka and Takeuchi (1995) developed a knowledge-creating spiral, often referred to as *the SECI model,* that identifies four categories of knowledge flow. Essentially, an organization's knowledge capacity can be increased as knowledge moves along a spiral that sees it being converted from tacit knowledge to explicit knowledge to tacit knowledge and so forth (Nonaka and Takeuchi 1995). Each category of knowledge flow is discussed below and, under each heading, the knowledge management practices that belong to each category of knowledge flow are noted.

1. *Socialization*—where tacit knowledge interacts with tacit knowledge. In this case, individuals share knowledge and experiences with others.

Examples of socialization processes include:

(a) Developing shared mental models (Nonaka and Takeuchi 1995)

(b) Mentoring, coaching, apprenticeships, and other forms of on-the-job training (Beijerse 1999; Geisler 1999; Nonaka and Takeuchi 1995)

(c) Hiring smart people and letting them talk to one another (Davenport and Prusak 1998b)

(d) Establishing communities of practice (Bennett and Gabriel 1999)

(e) Imitating (Beijerse 1999)

(f) Brainstorming (Beijerse 1999; Nonaka and Takeuchi 1995)

(g) Quality circles (Nonaka and Takeuchi 1995)

(h) Meetings or networking among organizational members and customers (Beijerse 1999; Nonaka and Takeuchi 1995)

(i) Debriefing after attending a conference, seminar, or important meetings with clients, suppliers, or regulators, after concluding a significant sales agreement, or shortly before being transferred or promoted (Geisler 1999)

(j) Running internal seminars led by managers who share their experiences (Bennett and Gabriel 1999)

2. *Externalization*—where tacit knowledge converts to explicit knowledge. That is, the processes that enable knowledge to be articulated and translated into forms that can be understood by others.

Examples of externalization processes include:

(a) Creating metaphors and analogies (Nonaka and Takeuchi 1995)

(b) Translating customer requirements into an agenda for a new product or process development (Ballantyne 2000)

(c) Training and education (Galvin 1996)

(d) Capturing the experiences of employees by asking questions such as, "What do you know about?" "What do you think about?" "Who in this company has done this?" (Geisler 1999: 18)

(e) Capturing best practices (Bennett and Gabriel 1999)

(f) Developing a knowledge map that shows who has what knowledge and where to find those with knowledge

(Bennett and Gabriel 1999; Davenport and Prusak, 1998a)

(g) Developing an organizational memory. This requires the codification of tacit knowledge, which is then stored as one might store explicit knowledge (Davenport and Prusak 1998a; Moorman and Miner 1997). Nonaka and Takeuchi (1995) suggest that an organizational memory should include case studies related to various company activities.

3. *Combination*—where explicit knowledge is converted into other sets of explicit knowledge.

Examples:

Combination is typical in information processing situations and might include reconfiguring existing knowledge bases through sorting, adding, combining, and categorizing explicit knowledge (Pérez-Bustamante 1999). Therefore, combination will make heavy use of databases and computerized communication networks, as these will make the capturing, storing, retrieving, and transmitting of codified knowledge easier (Fahey and Prusak 1998).

Nonaka and Takeuchi (1995) include documents, meetings, phone calls, education, and training as examples of combination techniques. It should be noted that education and training have already appeared in the previous section on externalization. It is possible that examples of other knowledge management conversion processes might also appear in other categories, depending on the nature of the knowledge transfer.

4. *Internalization*—where newly created explicit knowledge is converted into tacit knowledge.

Examples of internalization include:

(a) Learning by doing (Nonaka and Takeuchi 1995)
(b) Documenting knowledge into manuals, oral traditions, diagrams, papers, case notes or the organization's culture (Nonaka and Takeuchi 1995)
(c) Having access to technical libraries (Bennett and Gabriel 1999)

Ballantyne (2000) considers this stage essential in diffusing or circulating knowledge. Thus, although developing an organization's memory might fall into externalization, calling upon that organizational memory would become internalization. This is indicative of the spiral nature of Nonaka and Takeuchi's (1995) knowledge conversion process.

Based on the research above, a measure of knowledge management orientation is proposed and included as an Appendix.

CONCLUSIONS

This chapter discussed the theoretical development of an instrument to measure a firm's knowledge management orientation. In particular, the instrument focuses on measuring a firm's ability to acquire, disseminate, and use information and develop knowledge. It contributes to our understanding of knowledge management in two ways: first, it proposes an instrument to measure a firm's knowledge management orientation, and, second, it operationalizes Nonaka and Takeuchi's (1995) work for the first time.

Once data is collected using this instrument, our understanding of knowledge management can be enhanced further. For example, we can confirm whether various knowledge management processes fit within each category of Nonaka and Takeuchi's (1995) knowledge creation spiral. We can also establish the consequences of having a knowledge management orientation. Identifying the consequences of a knowledge management orientation is an area requiring substantial future research, since many of the links between knowledge management and proposed consequences, such as innovation and performance, are either hypothetical or consider only a small part of the knowledge management spectrum. For example, Brand (1998) attests that tacit–tacit knowledge flows are more important for innovation at 3M. Barczak (1991) found that tacit–tacit knowledge flows are the most effective between a team leader and his or her new product development team. Madhavan and Grover (1998) took a slightly different perspective by suggesting that, in order to develop new products, knowledge embedded in people needs to become embodied in products; this is a form of tacit–tacit knowledge flow. Preiss (1999) suggests that innovation will follow when tacit knowledge is converted into explicit knowledge (i.e., externalization) or when explicit knowledge is converted into explicit knowledge (i.e., combination). Clearly, there is room for more research in this area.

REFERENCES

Alvesson, M. 1993. Organizations as Rhetoric: Knowledge-Intensive Firms and the Struggle with Ambiguity, *Journal of Management Studies* 30, 6.

Antonelli, C. 1999. The Evolution of the Industrial Organization of the Production of Knowledge, *Cambridge Journal of Economics* 23: 243–60.

Arundel, A., K. Smith, P. Patel, and G. Sirilli. 1998. *The Future of Innovation Measurement in Europe*. Europe: Step Group.

Atuahene-Gima, K. 1996. Market Orientation and Innovation. *Journal of Business Research* 35: 93–103.

Ballantyne, D. 2000. Reframing Internal Marketing. Paper presented at the Australasian Services Research Workshop, February), Melbourne.

Barczak, G. 1991. Communications Patterns of New Product Development Team Leader, *IEEE Transactions on Engineering Management* 38, 2: 101–09.

Bassie, L. J. 1997. Harnessing the Power of Intellectual Capital, *Training & Development* 51, 12: 25–30.

Beijerse, R. P. 1999. Questions in Knowledge Management: Defining and Conceptualizing a Phenomenon, *Journal of Knowledge Management* 3, 2.

Bennett, R. and H. Gabriel. 1999. Organizational Factors and Knowledge Management Within Large Marketing Departments: An Empirical Study, *Journal of Knowledge Management* 3, 3: 212–25.

Bontis, Nick, M. Crossan, and J. Hulland. 2002 (forthcoming). Managing an Organizational Learning System by Aligning Stocks and Flows, *Journal of Management Studies* 39, 4.

Brand, A. 1998. Knowledge Management and Innovation at 3M, *Journal of Knowledge Management* 2, 1: 17–22.

Capon, N., J. U. Farley, D. R. Lehmann, and J. M. Hulbert. 1992. Profiles of Product Innovators Among Large U.S. Manufacturers. *Management Science* 38, 2: 57–168.

Carneiro, A. 2000. How Does Knowledge Management Influence Innovation and Competitiveness? *Journal of Knowledge Management* 4, 2: 87–98.

Chiesa, V., P. Coughlan, and C. A. Voss. 1996. Development of a Technical Innovation Audit. *Journal of Product Innovation Marketing* 13: 105–36.

Connor, K. R. and C. K. Prahalad. 1996. A Resource-Based Theory of the Firm: Knowledge Versus Opportunism, *Organization Science* 7, 5: 477–501.

Daniel, E. and N. Tomkin. 1999. Firm-Level Benefits of Radical Innovation, *Journal of General Management* 24, 4: 38–52.

Darroch, J. and R. McNaughton. 2000. *Knowledge and Knowledge Management Practices*. Dunedin: Marketing Performance Centre, University of Otago.

Davenport, T. and L. Prusak. 1998a. *Working Knowledge. Executive Excellence* 15, 9–10. Cambridge, Mass.: Harvard University Press.

————1998b. *Working Knowledge Executive Excellence* 15. Cambridge, Mass.: Harvard University Press.

Day, G. 1994. The Capabilities of Market-Driven Organizations, *Journal of Marketing* 58: 37–52.

Desphande, R. ed. 1999. *Developing a Market Orientation*. Calif.: Sage.

Despres, C. and D. Chauvel. 1999. Knowledge Management(s), *Journal of Knowledge Management* 3, 2: 110–20.

Dove, R. 1999. Knowledge Management, Response Ability, and the Agile Enterprise, *Journal of Knowledge Management* 3, 1: 18–35.

Fahey, L. and L. Prusak. 1998. The Eleven Deadliest Sins of Knowledge Management, *California Management Review* 40, 3: 265–76.

Galvin, R. 1996. Managing Knowledge Towards Wisdom, *European Management Journal* 14, 4: 374–78.

Gatignon, H. and J. M. Xuereb. 1997. Strategic Orientation of the Firm and New Product Performance, *Journal of Marketing Research* 34: 77–90.

Geisler, E. 1999. Harnessing the Value of Experience in the Knowledge-Driven Firm, *Business Horizons* (May-June): 18–26.

Gray, B., S. Matear, C. Boshoff, and P. Matheson. 1998. Developing a Better Measure of Market Orientation, *European Journal of Marketing* 32, 9/10: 864–903.

Hall, R. 1993. A Framework Linking Intangible Resources and Capabilities to Sustainable Competitive Advantage, *Strategic Management Journal* 14: 607–18.

Hamel, G. and C. K. Prahalad. 1996. Competing in the New Economy: Managing Out of Bounds. *Strategic Management Journal* 17: 237–42.

Han, J. K., N. Kim, and R. K. Srivastava. 1998. Market Orientation and Organizational Performance: Is Innovation a Missing Link? *Journal of Marketing* 62: 30–45.

Hart, S. and R. Rolender. 1999. *Working with the Enemy: Target Cost Management and the Search for Market Orientation*. Glasgow: University of Strathclyde.

Jaworksi, B. J., and A. K. Kohli. 1993. Market Orientation: Antecedents and Consequences, *Journal of Marketing* 57: 53–70.

Kohli, A. K. and B. J. Jaworksi. 1990. Market Orientation: The Construct, Research Propositions and Managerial Implications, *Journal of Marketing* 54: 1–18.

Kohli, A. K., B. J. Jaworski, and A. Kumar. 1993. MARKOR: A Measure of Market Orientation, *Journal of Marketing Research* 30: 467–77.

Li, T. and R. J. Calantone. 1998. The Impact of Market Knowledge Competence on New Product Advantage: Conceptualization and Empirical Examination, *Journal of Marketing* 62: 13–29.

Madhavan, R. and R. Grover. 1998. From Embedded Knowledge to Embodied Knowledge: New Product Development as Knowledge Management, *Journal of Marketing* 62: 1–12.

Moorman, C. and A. S. Miner. 1997. The Impact of Organizational Memory on New Product Performance and Creativity, *Journal of Marketing Research* 34: 91–106.

Narver, J. C. and S. F. Slater. 1990. The Effect of a Market Orientation on Business Profitability, *Journal of Marketing* 54: 20–35.

Nonaka, I. and H. Takeuchi. 1995. *The Knowledge-Creating Company*. New York: Oxford University Press.

Pérez-Bustamante, G. 1999. Knowledge Management in Agile Innovation Organizations, *Journal of Knowledge Management* 3, 1: 6–17.

Powell, T. C. and A. Dent-Micallef. 1997. Information Technology as Competitive Advantage: The Role of Human, Business, and Technology Resources, *Strategic Management Journal* 18, 5: 375–405.

Preiss, K. 1999. Modeling of Knowledge Flows and Their Impact, *Journal of Knowledge Management* 3, 1: 36–46.

Ruekert, R. W. 1992. Developing a Market Orientation: An Organizational Strategy Perspective, *International Journal of Research in Marketing* 9: 225–45.

Rumizen, M. C. 1998. Report on the Second Comparative Study of Knowledge Creation Conference, *Journal of Knowledge Management* 2, 1: 77–81.

Shariq, S. Z. 1998. Sense-Making Artifacts: An Exploration into the Role of Tools in Knowledge Management, *Journal of Knowledge Management* 2, 2: 10–19.

Slater, S. F. and J. C. Narver. 1994. Does Competitive Environment Moderate the Market Orientation–Performance Relationship? *Journal of Marketing* 58: 46–55.

Slater, S. F. and J. C. Narver. 1995. Market Orientation and the Learning Organization, *Journal of Marketing* 59: 63–74.

Teece, D. J. 1998. Capturing Value from Knowledge Assets: The New Economy, Markets for Know-How and Intangible Assets, *California Management Review* 40, 3: 55–79.

Wiig, K. M. 1999. What Future Knowledge Management Users May Expect, *Journal of Knowledge Management* 3, 2: 155–65.

APPENDIX: A MEASURE OF KNOWLEDGE MANAGEMENT ORIENTATION

Knowledge Acquisition
Information input—customers We meet with customers at least once a year to find out what products or services they will need in the future (KJ[1]). People, other than those in the marketing department, interact directly with customers to learn how to serve them better (KJ). Our organization does a lot of market research (KJ). We are quick to detect changes in our customers' preferences (KJ). We survey end-users at least once a year to assess the quality of our products and services (KJ). We often acquire new ideas through export activities. Market research rather than technological advances usually drives our business direction (KJ). Real market needs rather than internal politics usually drive new product development (KJ).
Information input—competitors Information about our competitors is collected by more than one department within our organization (KJ).
Information input—industry We often collect industry information by informal means (e.g., lunch with industry friends, talks with trade partners) (KJ).

[1]KJ denotes that a similar question appeared in the Kohli-Jaworski market-orientation instrument. However, some have been placed differently relative to placements in the Kohli-Jaworski instrument.

Information input—financial
We know exactly how much each of our products or services costs us.
We often analyze the financial contribution of our products or services.
We know exactly how much it costs us to service each customer.
We know who our most profitable customers are.
We have good financial information on our organization.

Information input—employee
We have regular staff meetings with employees.
Managers frequently try to find out employees' true feelings about
their jobs.
We survey employees regularly to assess their attitudes toward work.
We have regular staff appraisals in which we discuss employees' needs.

Information input—technology
We manage to keep up to date with technological developments that
could affect our business.
We periodically review the likely effect of changes in technology on our
customers.
We regularly benchmark ourselves against industry best practices.

Information inputs—collaboration
We prefer to seek growth through acquisitions rather than spend money
on internal R&D activities.
We prefer to use ideas developed by overseas organizations rather than
spend money on internal R&D activities.
We prefer to use ideas developed by other New Zealand organizations
rather than spend money on internal R&D activities.
We often acquire new ideas through strategic alliances.
We often acquire new ideas through equity joint ventures.
We acquire new ideas through corporate venture funds.

Knowledge Dissemination

Socialization
We encourage job rotation within our organization.
We successfully attract employees trained in math, science, technology,
information technology, or engineering.
We successfully attract employees trained in sales and marketing.
We have a large number of people employed here who are trained in
math, science, technology, information technology, or engineering.
Many of our employees have worked for our organization for a long time.
We encourage employees to take time to think about our business.
We always seem to have people traveling overseas on business matters.
Employees often have informal discussions (e.g., around water coolers,
in hallways, over coffee) about our business (KJ).
Our workspace is set up to make it easy for people to talk to each other.
Each department has regular formal meetings.

There are regular meetings between departments to discuss market trends and developments (KJ).

Marketing people in our organization frequently spend time discussing customers' future needs with people in technical departments (KJ). We often use video-conferencing within our organization.

We often use teleconferencing within our organization.

We encourage people with similar interests to work together to solve a problem.

We frequently use techniques such as brainstorming in our organization.

We frequently use techniques such as quality circles in our organization.

Employees are expected to provide feedback to others whenever they attend conferences, seminars, or exhibitions.

Our organization actively encourages mentoring or coaching.

Our managers often give seminars or presentations to other staff.

We frequently step back and reflect on what went well or did not go well in aspects of our business.

Discussions on the latest scientific inventions are common here.

There is cooperation among employees to get things done.

Externalization

Employees are encouraged to attend training seminars and conferences.

Employees are encouraged to undertake university or polytechnic courses.

Employees are encouraged to take the time to read publications to which our organization subscribes.

Our organization subscribes to a wide range of publications.

We frequently use the Internet as a source of ideas.

When people in our organization need information about marketing issues they know exactly who to ask.

When people in our organization need information about technical issues they know exactly who to ask.

We make good use of Intranets to share information on products and processes within the organization.

We make good use of GroupWare, such as Lotus Notes, to share information on products and processes within the organization.

Combination

We periodically circulate documents (e.g., reports and newsletters) about our business to external stakeholders (KJ).

We keep a database of customer information that is easy to access.

Internalization

We encourage learning by doing in our organization.

We frequently update policy and procedure manuals.

Information about customer satisfaction is disseminated to all levels of our organization on a regular basis (KJ).

A large number of written reports circulate within our organization.

We often write case notes on successful and unsuccessful products and processes.

We often record internal best practices.

We often develop metaphors and analogies to describe what we know.

Responsiveness

Responsive to customers; changes to marketing

When something important happens to a major customer the whole organization knows about it quickly (KJ).

We usually respond to changes in our customers' product or service needs (KJ).

Our customers like us to provide them with something new all the time.

Our organization periodically reviews its product development efforts to ensure that they are in line with what customers want (KJ).

We are quick to respond to customer complaints (KJ).

When we find our customers are unhappy with the quality of our services, we act immediately (KJ).

When we find that a customer would like us to modify a product or service, the departments involved make a concerted effort to do so (KJ).

We frequently change our marketing strategies.

We often change the range of products or services that we offer.

Most changes to products or processes have occurred as the result of a crisis.

Our organization seems to be able to implement marketing plans quickly (KJ).

Our organization seems to be able to implement marketing plans effectively.

Responsive to competitors

When something important happens to a competitor the whole organization knows about it quickly (KJ).

We are quick to decide how to respond to competitors' initiatives (KJ).

If a major competitor launches an intensive campaign targeted at our customers, we would implement a response immediately (KJ).

We are quick to implement strategies in response to significant changes in our competitors' pricing structures (KJ).

Responsive to technology

Information about new technological developments that might affect our business is circulated quickly.

We are quick to decide how to respond to changes in technology.

We frequently change our technical strategies.

Responsive to industry

We are quick to detect fundamental shifts in our industry (KJ).

Responsive to environment

Several departments within our organization get together periodically to plan a response to changes taking place in our business environment (KJ).

Responsive to financial information

We will readily delete unprofitable products or services.

We often look for ways to reduce the costs of the products or services we sell.

We frequently look for ways to improve the cost effectiveness of our selling and promotional activities.

We will put fewer resources into customers that become financially unattractive.

We are quick to respond to changes in the organization's financial position.

Responsive to employees

We are quick to respond to concerns raised by employees.

We are very receptive to ideas contributed by employees.

Responsive—implementation

We often change our procedures for doing things.

The activities of the different departments within our organization are well coordinated (KJ).

13

INNOVATION CAPABILITY– BENCHMARKING SYSTEM (ICBS)

José María Viedma Marti
Polytechnic University of Catalonia and ESADE, Barcelona, Spain
icms.viedma@terra.es

ABSTRACT

The Innovation Capability–Benchmarking System (ICBS) is both a new management method and a new management tool that allows companies to benchmark their core innovation capabilities against the world-class competitors in their sector. It is a framework built around the key factors and criteria that determine competitiveness in innovation within the context of global markets. The factors considered are: emerging needs, project objectives, new products and services, new processes, new core capabilities, new professional core capabilities, company innovation, and infrastructure financial results. ICBS identifies the specific innovation and competitiveness factors that are relevant in a given business sector. ICBS identifies, audits, and benchmarks the core capabilities or key intellectual capital that the company needs to develop to reach its future goals and successfully compete with "best in class" competitors. When using ICBS in a systematic way, companies produce innovation competitiveness balance sheets that complement financial balance sheets and enable companies to leverage their innovation-related intellectual capital. The system

243

has been successfully piloted in more than ten European small- and medium-sized enterprises.

Introduction

Most industry analysts agree that innovation is the key to successful competition in the information society. At the same time, researchers in the areas of sustainable competitive advantage have come to the conclusion that the only things that give an organization a sustainable edge are what it knows, how it uses what it knows, and how fast it can learn new things. However, although there is general agreement on the key role of knowledge as a source of competitive advantage, few in the industry know how to manage intellectual capital to produce value in an efficient way. This lack of expertise is especially relevant when dealing with the acquisition of new knowledge, which is one of the key drivers of the innovation process. ICBS identifies, audits, and benchmarks the core capabilities or key intellectual capital that the company needs to develop to reach its future goals and successfully compete with "best in class" competitors.

The Internationalization of the Economy and the Globalization of Markets

It is no secret that over the last few years an extraordinarily important socio-economic phenomenon has changed the world we live in. This phenomenon consists of an unstoppable globalization of the economy and markets. Advances in transportation, communications, electronics, data processing, telecommunications, and new materials have converted the world into a global village, whose inhabitants are getting to know each other much better and in which consumption patterns and production methods and techniques are becoming increasingly uniform. The very same McDonald's, Burger King, Body Shop, Ermenegildo Zegna, and multinationals, such as IBM, Samsung, Sanyo, Seiko, and Nestle, are found in all the built-up areas of the industrialized and developed countries. As a result, similar appliances and utensils (washing machines, videos, refrigerators, and PCs, for example) can be found in many homes, and the same occurs in offices and companies (fax, electronic mail, PCs, and Windows 95). Multinational companies encourage this process and also promote strategic alliances, franchises, and cooperative agreements (Brilman 1995).

The following is a list of factors that encourage the internationalization of markets and competition.

- Opening up of frontiers (U.S.A., NAFTA, Mercosur, etc.)

  - The circulation of products: international products
  - The increase in the number of new companies and the acquisition of companies
  - Greater number of multinationals
  - Increase in the number of business trips
  - International services for companies: banking, transportation, consulting, auditing, and so on

- Communications

  - Worldwide telecommunications networks
  - The circulation of images
  - The rapid spreading of fashions: the "snob" effect
  - Internationalization of tastes
  - Transnational segments of clients: teenagers, yuppies, and businessmen
  - World products
  - World brand names
  - Universal messages
  - Satellite communications

- World products

  - The cost of technology, the profitability of research and development and investments
  - Manufacturing with a worldwide perspective
  - International supplying and purchases from beyond national borders
  - Internationalization of components and equipment
  - Internationalization of suppliers and outsourcing

- Worldwide distribution

  - Rapid international transportation
  - Data transmission networks
  - Telecommunications equipment
  - World standards
  - Internationalization of services

- Tourist Travel
  - Client-traveler
  - Discovery of products in other countries
  - The need for products to be present in other countries
  - Worldwide quality standards
  - Internationalization of services for travelers
  - Internationalization of hotels, banks, travel agencies, etc.

COMPANY COMPETITIVENESS IN THE NEW INTERNATIONALIZED GLOBAL ENVIRONMENT

All companies in the context we have described above are obliged to develop their activities in a highly competitive and increasingly international environment, regardless of their size and the country they are located in.

If they are to be successful in formulating strategies and making decisions, all companies operating in this environment require systematic and up-to-date information on the following subjects:

- The competitive environment of their specific business activity
- The competitive gap between them and the international market leaders
- Knowledge of the causes of the competitive gap

Figure 13-1 below illustrates the concepts discussed in Section 13.2.

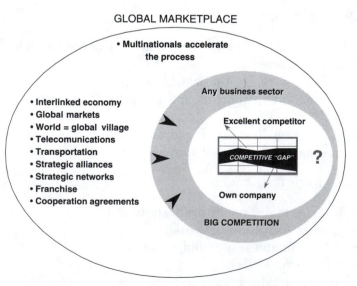

Figure 13-1 *Global marketplace*

Filling and Reversing the Competitive Gap

Knowledge and Intellectual Capital as the Only Sources of Sustainable Competitive Advantages

Laurence Prusak (1996) stated the following: "Researchers in the areas of sustainable competitive advantages have come to the conclusion that the only thing that gives an organization a competitive edge, the only thing that is sustainable, is what it knows, how it uses what it knows, and how fast it can know something new." So, in other words, he gives the answer to the fundamental question, which are the causes of the competitive gap? The answer obviously is knowledge. But what does Prusak mean by knowledge? His clear definition is (Davenport and Prusak 1998: 5): "*Knowledge* is a fluid mix of framed experience, values, contextual information, and expert insight that provides a framework for evaluating and incorporating new experiences and information. It originates and is applied in the minds of knowers. In organizations, it often becomes embedded not only in documents or repositories, but also in organizational routines, processes, practices and norms."

Nevertheless, before going ahead, we consider that it is important to establish a clear distinction between the concept of knowledge management and the concept of intellectual capital management. In accordance with Kark M. Wiig (1997: 339), "Intellectual Capital Management (ICM) focuses on building and governing intellectual assets from strategic and enterprise governance perspectives with some focus on tactics. Its function is to take overall care of the enterprise's intellectual capital." And "Knowledge Management (KM) has tactical and operational perspectives, KM is more detailed and focuses on facilitating and managing knowledge related activities such as creation, capture, transformation, and use. Its function is to plan, implement, operate, and monitor all the knowledge-related activities and programs required for effective intellectual capital management."

So, summarizing, we can say that *IC* refers to the intellectual assets from a strategic and global perspective and *knowledge* refers to the components of the intellectual assets from a tactical, or operational, perspective. In fact both concepts overlap, and they are in practice the same thing taken from different perspectives. Concluding, the answer to the question that we put before on which are the causes of the competitive gap, these could be either knowledge or intellectual capital, but because the causes in that case are obviously global and strategic, we think that IC is definitely the more appropriate answer.

The Need to Benchmark: What to Benchmark?

Each specific business activity has the specific and relevant intellectual capital that explains the competitive gap. Once determined, the specific intellectual capital is used as a comparison basis in order to benchmark the world's best competitors in the same business activity. If we are, for example, in the fast food sandwiches industry and we consider McDonald's as the international best-in-class company, the relevant core competencies or the relevant knowledge, or the relevant intellectual capital of McDonald's, will be the model's constituents to benchmark. In this particular case the answer to the question what to benchmark is the core competencies of McDonald's.

Nevertheless, in order to be more specific about the core competencies to benchmark, we need to consider how value is created in the internal business process value chain. The business process value chain could be divided into two big groups: the innovation process and the operations process. The innovation process is made up of product design and product development, and the operations process is made up of manufacturing, marketing, and post-sales service. Figure 13-2 illustrates the business process value chain.

The traditional perspective focused on the operations process. This short wave of value creation begins with the receipt of an order from an existing customer for an existing product or service and ends with the delivery of the product to the customer (Kaplan 1996). In this case, value is created through operations core competencies, or operations intellectual capital.

But the innovation process, the long wave of value creation, is for many companies a more powerful driver of future financial performance than the short-term operations process. If this is the case, they may require an organization to create entirely new products and services that

Business process value chain

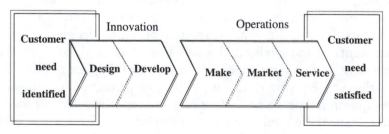

Figure 13-2 *Adapted from Kaplan (1996)*

will meet the emerging needs of current and future customers. For many companies, their ability to manage successfully a multiyear, product development process or to develop a capability to reach entirely new categories of customers may be more critical for future economic success than for managing existing operations efficiently, consistently, and responsively. In this specific case, value will be created through innovation core capabilities, or innovation intellectual capital.

The paper that I presented at the Third World Congress on Intellectual Capital and Innovation (Viedma 1999) was mainly focused on operations core competencies or operations intellectual capital. This chapter, entitled "Innovation Capability–Benchmarking System (ICBS)," is mainly focused on the innovation core capabilities, or the innovation intellectual capital.

So going back to the previous question, what to benchmark, the answer in this particular case will be the innovation core capabilities or the innovation intellectual capital of McDonald's. These core capabilities are the ones that will guarantee long-term excellence or long-term success.

The ICBS Framework

ICBS is a framework that focuses on the innovation process of the business process value chain. We have said that innovation process represents the long wave of value creation, and it is the main powerful driver of future financial results. In that sense, competing successfully in the long run means innovating, and innovating entails building new competencies, new capabilities, and new knowledge. When companies compete for the future (Hamel 1994), they compete on building and deploying the right core competencies and capabilities in a consistent way. We assume that core competencies and core capabilities are substantially the same thing. Stalk and others (1992: 57) underline the following differences: "But whereas core competence emphasizes technological and production expertise at specific points along the value chain, capabilities are more broadly based, encompassing the entire value chain. In this respect competencies are visible to the customer in a way core capabilities rarely are." Consistency depends first of all on a deep consensus about which competencies to build and support and second on the stability of the management teams charged with competence development. Such consistency is unlikely unless senior managers agree on what new competencies should be built. Without such a consensus, a company may well fragment its competence-building efforts, as various business units pursue their independent competence-building agenda, or the firm may simply fail to build new competencies (Hamel 1994).

We conclude that companies do not compete on products and services. They really compete on the underlying capabilities that make the products and services possible. Accordingly, competing for the future will be competing for the future capabilities (source of new processes, products, and services) against the world-class future capabilities of the best future competitors.

ICBS framework evaluates or assesses the innovation capabilities that make possible the realization of new projects that will lead to new products and services through the appropriate processes. ICBS also assesses the innovation infrastructure that supports all the new projects that the company has started or is going to start in the near future.

The assessment process is carried out in a two-fold fashion. On one side, we take as reference benchmarks the innovative project objectives and goals; on the other side, we take as a reference benchmark the equivalent innovative project of the best world competitor. See Figure 13-3 for a better comprehension of the above explanation.

BUILDING THE ICBS FRAMEWORK

The modern theory of management provides the paradigms for the competitive or excellent company in the context of the global markets.

The following are some, but by no means all, of the most meaningful paradigms:

• *The intelligent enterprise*	James Brian Quinn (1992)
• *Innovation explosion*	James Brian Quinn (1997)
	Jordan J. Baruch
	Karen Anne Zien
• *The knowledge-creating company*	Ikujiro Nonaka
	and Hirotaka Takeuchi
	(1995)
• *The living company*	Arie de Geus (1997)
• *The learning organization*	Peter Senge (1990)
• *The change masters*	Rosabeth Moss Kanter
	(1983)
• *When giants learn to dance*	Rosabeth Moss Kanter
	(1989)
• *World class*	Rosabeth Moss Kanter
	(1995)
• *Innovation and entrepreneurship*	Peter Drucker (1985)

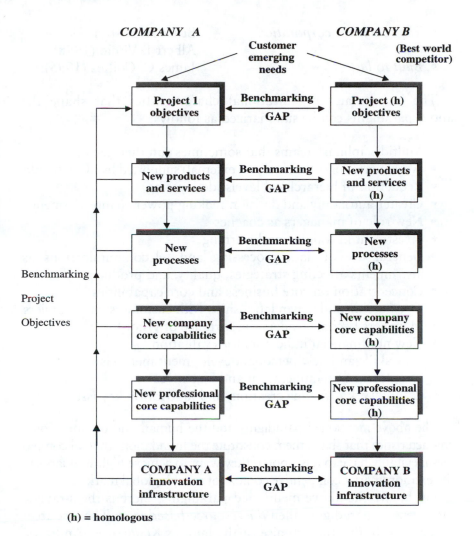

Figure 13-3 *The ICBS framework*

- *Competing for the future*   Gary Hamel and
                                      K. C. Prahalad (1994)
- *Mastering the dynamics*   James M. Utterback (1994)
  of innovation
- *Intellectual capital*   Leif Edvinson and
                                      Michael Malone(1997)
- *The balanced scorecard*   Robert S. Kaplan and
                                      David P. Norton (1996)
- *The new organizational wealth*   Karl Erik Sveiby (1997)

- *The centerless corporation*   Bruce A. Posternack and
                                    Albert J. Viscio (1998)
- *Built to last*   James C. Collins (1995)

The human and organizational characteristics that shape the above paradigms can be summarized as follows:

- Multidisciplinary teams that sometimes run themselves
- Work in networks (internal and external) supported by PC networks
- Reduction of hierarchical levels (de-layering)
- Greater autonomy and decision-making powers (empowerment)
- New role of managers as coaches
- Investment in training and learning
- General use of data processing and telecommunications as instruments affecting strategies, quality, and productivity
- Concentration on core business and core capabilities
- Outsourcing and new relationships with customers and suppliers
- Managers become leaders (importance of vision)
- New nonfinancial indicators for evaluation
- New skills and new personal development methods
- New forms of remuneration and incentives
- Creativity, knowledge creation, and innovation key issues

The above-mentioned paradigms and the human and organizational characteristics that shape them constitute the foundations that all companies inevitably have to rely upon if they want to achieve high standards in the extraordinarily competitive context of today's global markets.

But before the above-mentioned paradigms, there is the strategic management paradigm called *the resource-based view*. The resource-based view fulfills the promise of the famous Kenneth R. Andrews' strategy framework that defined *strategy* as the match between what a company can do (organizational strengths and weaknesses) within the universe of what it might do (environmental opportunities and threats). The resource-based view acknowledges the importance of company-specific resources (tangible and intangible) and competencies, yet it does so in the context of the competitive environment (Collins 1990). It sees capabilities and resources as the heart of a company's competitive position, subject to the interplay of the three fundamental market forces: demand (does it meet customers needs and is it competitively superior?), scarcity (is it imitable or substitutable and is it durable?), and appropriability (who owns the profits?).

Put another way, these paradigms and the concepts, principles, theories, and techniques they contain constitute the current sources of inspiration for achieving entrepreneurial success.

We have included in the brief bibliography some of the most meaningful books written on the formulation of today's theory of entrepreneurial excellence. We think it useful to complement the above explanations, stressing the fact that nowadays the management theorists are wrestling with the problem of how organizations can continually adapt, change, innovate, create, and network to survive and succeed in market environments that are quickly becoming more unpredictable, with technologies that are becoming more pervasive and integrative with organizations that have become pliable and porous, and with people who are questioning, assertive, and independent. In other words, to be viable in the changing and demanding business environment of today, organizations must be able to improve themselves continually as part of their normal functioning; to be intelligent, critical, and open, and to be creative and capable of eternally transforming themselves, while sustaining a sense of purpose and direction (Clarke 1998).

Finally, we would like to point out the fact that creativity, knowledge, creation, and innovation are the key issues. In this way Zangwill (1993: 5) asserts: "For more than twenty years, my work has probed the characteristics that distinguish the top companies from the mediocre. Above all, one characteristic stands out: no firm stays on the top long unless it is highly innovative. Especially with technologically related companies, whatever their country, the companies that stay in the lead continually innovate new products that customers want."

The ICBS General Framework

The paradigms of the competitive or excellent company, in the context of the global markets and especially the innovative-company paradigm, provide us with bases for constructing the ICBS general framework.

The framework is articulated around the following eight factors: (see Figures 13-4, 13-5, and 13-6)

1. *Emerging needs.* Potential or emerging customer-segment needs that the company expects to cover through the project.
2. *Project objectives.* The project is the innovation business unit that leads to new products and services through new processes, using company and professional core capabilities and company

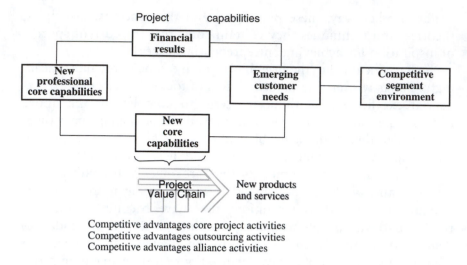

Figure 13-4 *Project capabilities*

innovation infrastructure. The ultimate objectives of the projects are the expected financial results.

3. *New products and services.* New products and services with their attributes and characteristics and functions.

4. *New processes.* Primary and support value chain activities that produce the project's new products and services. These activities

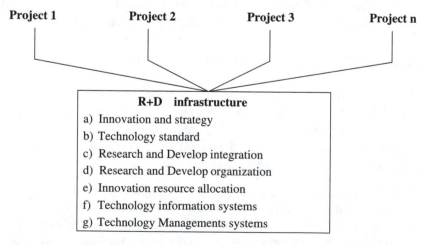

Figure 13-5 *Common research and development infrastructure*

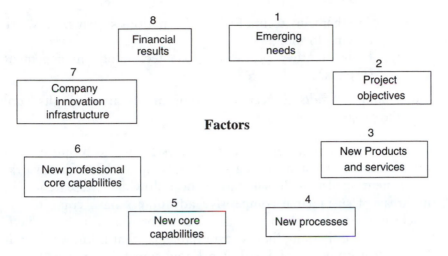

Figure 13-6 *The eight-factors framework*

are made up of core project activities, outsourcing activities, and strategic alliances and cooperation agreement activities. Competitive advantages will be generated mainly in the different value chain core project activities.

5. *New company core capabilities.* Essential knowledge or core capabilities that will make it possible and will give way to competitive advantages, new processes, and new products and services within the project.

6. *New professional core capabilities.* Professionals, managers, and support staff capabilities that will generate and perfect core capabilities and core competencies.

7. *Company innovation infrastructure.* Research and development infrastructure (tangible and intangible assets) that the company has and that is for the use of the different projects.

The company innovation infrastructure covers the following issues:

(a) Is technology innovation part of the business strategy?
(b) What is the company's knowledge and technology standard?
(c) Is the research and development department working together with the other main departments?
(d) How well organised is the research and development department?
(e) How many resources are allocated to the innovation function?

(f) Are there any technologies informations systems? How are they performing?

(g) How are they performing the technology management systems?

8. *Financial results.* Expected economic and financial results from the project.

Figure 13-7 complements and completes Figure 13-3 and gives a full overview of the main elements that make up the ICBS framework.

We mentioned that Prusak stated the following: "Researchers in the areas of sustainable competitive advantages have come to the conclusion that the only thing that gives an organization a competitive edge, the only thing that is sustainable, is what it knows, how it uses what it knows, how fast it can know something new." We are now in the case of new essential knowledge, new core competencies, new core capabilities, or new intellectual capital.

The eight-factors framework that we have already described is, in fact, a flexible framework that allows the core capabilities, or intellectual capital, identification, and evaluation within each particular factor. By the same token the different components of intellectual capital (human capital, structural capital, and relational capital) can be assessed and appraised. The eight-factors framework explains how sustainable competitive advantages are achieved in the new products and new services that come out of the processes and operations. Briefly, they can be achieved in the following way. Companies, if they want to compete successfully in the future, need to innovate in a systematic way. The way to innovate is through projects that have the clear objective of satisfying emerging customer needs. Customer-needs satisfaction is accomplished through the project's new products and services. Nevertheless, competitive products and services are not easily achieved; a lot of work is needed to gradually establish competitive advantages in the different core activities of the value chain process. Core competencies and core capabilities in the core project activities of the value chain produce new products and services with competitive advantages and high knowledge or intellectual content. In addition, the company innovation infrastructure, or company research and development department, gives the necessary support to the whole process.

Finally, the acquisitions of core capabilities and the accomplishment of all those competitive advantages is only possible by means of the actions of the different project leaders who decide on and carry out objectives and strategies and then shape business culture with their ways and methods.

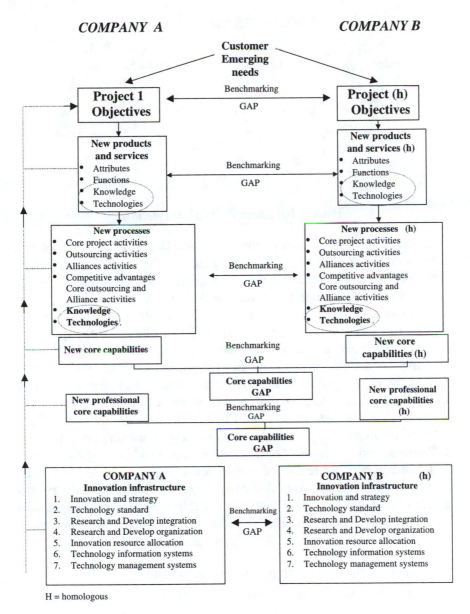

Figure 13-7 *General ICBS framework*

From the General to the Specific ICBS Framework

The ICBS general framework that we have already described is a general framework that can be used to generate the specific ICBS framework suitable to a specific business context. The ICBS general

Specific ICBS framework

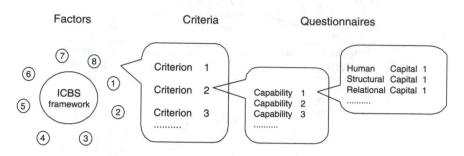

Figure 13-8 *Specific ICBS framework*

framework consists of eight factors, and each factor is composed of several criteria, and each criterion is composed at the same time of several questionnaires. We customize the ICBS general framework to a specific business context through the criteria and questionnaires or by choosing from among the criteria and questionnaires the ones that best suit the specifications of a given business design. When filling out the questionnaires, the different benchmarking teams (which are also learning teams) are able to define and evaluate the innovation core capabilities, and within the core capabilities the three main types of intellectual capital: human capital, structural capital, and relational capital.

Given that a large part of the information (above all, on the best-class-competitor project) may not be known precisely, all the questions in all the ICBS questionnaires have a "response precision" box.

By integrating the results of the response precision boxes, the ICBS method also permits us to evaluate the degree of reliability of the benchmarking and its constituent parts, to establish plans for systematically improving information acquisition, and to set up a competitive intelligence team in the company. Figure 13-8 draws the process described above.

The Key Role of Strategic Benchmarking in Framework Construction

As has been said before, ICBS is both a new management method and a new management tool that allows companies to benchmark their core innovation capabilities against the world-class competitors in their sector. Nevertheless, ICBS not only benchmarks core capabilities but also processes (value chain sources of competitive advantage) and the products and services that the execution of the project turns out. Finally, it also benchmarks innovation infrastructure.

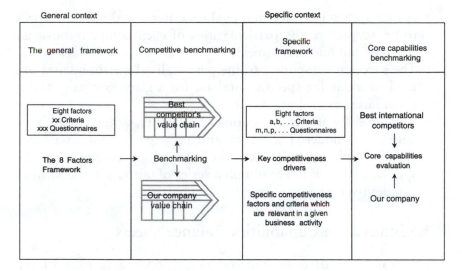

Figure 13-9 *From general framework to specific framework*

The eight-factors framework is used for moving from the general framework (general context) to the specific framework (specific business context). We customize the general framework through two types of variables: through the criteria and the questionnaires and through a benchmarking process that covers the activities of two value chains (the one that belongs to our company and the one that belongs to our best competitor). The process of competitive benchmarking allows us to determine the specific competitiveness factors and criteria that are relevant in a firm's business activity. These factors and criteria may also be termed *key competitiveness drivers*.

The questionnaires that are directly derived from the criteria allow us to evaluate and benchmark core capabilities in the specific business context. Core capabilities are at the same time made up of the three main classes of intellectual capital, that is to say, human capital, structural capital, and relational capital.

For better comprehension of the above, see Figure 13-9.

ICBS IMPLEMENTATION PROCESS

The following elements are involved in putting the ICBS method into practice:

- A general data base that contains all the possible criteria and questionnaires to be used. This means that each factor can be looked at in the greatest possible detail.

- A user-system interface that enables criteria and questionnaires to be adapted to the particularities of each company business segment and business project.
- The successive responses to the personalized questionnaires are used to create the specific database for a given company and a given business project.
- Specific software incorporating the factors, criteria, questionnaires, and underlying theory and principles of the excellence model enables us to process the information contained in the specific database and to obtain a series of outputs in the form of competitiveness figures, results, and balances.

ICBS Innovation Capabilities Balance Sheets

The processing of questionnaires corresponding to each of the company competitiveness factors provides us with the innovation capabilities results and balance sheets. These results and balance sheets can be obtained for the project as a whole or for each competitiveness factor. Some examples of balances and results are given below: (Figures 13-10, 13-11, and 13-12.)

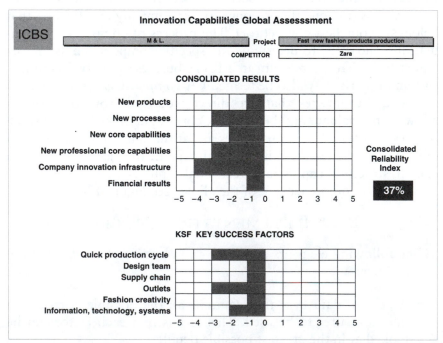

Figure 13-10 *Innovation capabilities global assessment*

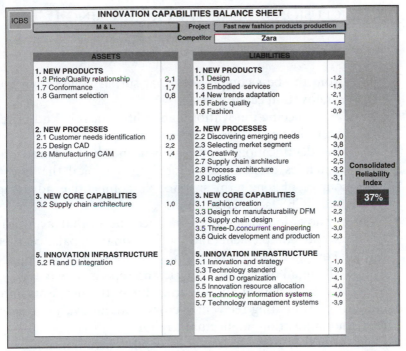

Figure 13-11 *Innovation Capabilities Balance Sheets*

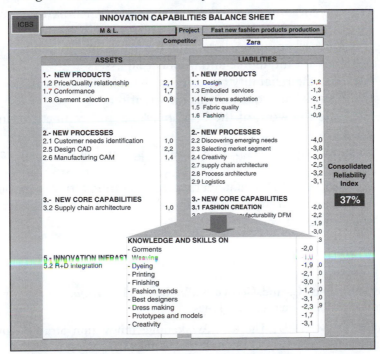

Figure 13-12 *Innovation Capabilities Balance Sheets*

CONCLUSIONS: BENEFITS FROM USING ICBS

The main benefits can be summarized in the following recommendations:

- Learn from the best competitors that surpass one's own competitive innovation capabilities
- Identify the specific innovation capabilities factors and criteria that are relevant in a given business activity
- Enable the identification, audit, and benchmark of the innovation core capabilities or innovation intellectual capital that are the main sources of long-term sustainable competitive advantages through the ICBS factors framework
- Obtain innovation capabilities balance sheets that are future-oriented and complement and perfect finance balance sheets leading companies to leverage innovation intellectual capital by using ICBS in an orderly systematic and repetitive way
- Select in a systematical and organized way the necessary information for evaluating relevant factors, core innovation capabilities, and innovation intellectual capital
- Identify the key areas in which in-depth benchmarking can be carried out in the future
- Promote organization learning through benchmarking teams, assessment teams, project teams, and strategic teams
- Introduce a common language for company managers when dealing with intangible and intellectual assets
- Measure the reliability concerning the relevant information and the progress of acquiring this information
- Facilitate the work of the benchmarking and competitive intelligence teams
- Facilitate the work of the knowledge and intellectual capital managers
- Give to the SME's managers access to innovation capabilities and innovation intellectual capital management in a systematic and organized way

REFERENCES

Abbeglen, James C. and George Stalk, Jr. 1986. *Kaisha. La corporación japonesa*. Barcelona: Plaza y Janes.

Amidon, D. M. 1997. The Ken Awakening: Innovation Strategy for the Knowledge Economy. London: Butterworth-Heinemann.

Bondell, T., L. Boulter, and J. Kelly. 1994. *Ventajas competitivas a través del Benchmarking*. Barcelona: Folio.

Boxwell, J. R. 1994. *Benchmarking para competir con ventaja*. Madrid: McGraw-Hill Management.

Brilman, J. 1995. *L'entreprise réinventée. Les éditions d'organisation*. Paris: Managinter.

Brooking, A. 1996. *Intellectual Capital. Core Asset for the Third Millennium Enterprise*. London: Thomson Business Press.

Canals, J. 1990. *El entorno económico de los negocios internacionales*. Bilbao: Deusto.

Canals, J. 1993. *La nueva economía global*. Bilbao: Deusto.

Canals, J. 1994. *La internacionalización de la empresa*. Madrid: McGraw-Hill.

Clarke, T. and S. Clegg. 1998. *Changing Paradigms*. London: HarperCollins Business.

Clifford, K., Donald, E. Jr., and Richard Cavanagh. 1985. *The Winning Performance*. London: Sidgwick and Jackson.

Collins, C. James. 1995. *Built to last*. New York: Harper Business.

Collis, D. J., and A. C. Montgomery. 1995. "Competing on Resources: Strategy in the 1990s," *Harvard Business Review* (July-August): 118–28.

Cook, S. 1995. *Practical Benchmarking*. London: Kogan Page.

Dale, N. 1998. *The Knowledge Economy*. New York: Butterworth-Heinemann.

Davenport, T. H. and L. Prusak. 1998. *Working Knowledge*. Boston: Harvard Business School Press.

Davis, S. and J. Botkin. 1994. "The Coming of Knowledge-Based Business," *Harvard Business Review* (September-October).

Davis, S. and B. Davidson. 1991. *20-20 Vision*. New York: Simon and Schuster.

De Geus, Arie. 1997. *The Living Company*. Boston: Harvard Business School Press.

Drucker, F. Peter. 1985. *Innovation and Entrepreneurship*. London: William Heinemann.

Edvinsson, L. and M. S. Malone. 1997. *Intellectual Capital*. New York: Harper Business.

Gerber, E. Michael. 1995. *The E Myth Revisited*. New York: Harper Business.

Goldsmith, Walter, and David Clutterbuck. 1985. *The Winning Streak*. London: Penguin Books.

Goldsmith, Walter and David Clutterbuck. 1985. *The Winning Streak Workout Book*. London: George Widenfield and Nicolson, Ltd.

Grant, R. 1995. *Dirección estratégica: Conceptos, técnicas aplicaciones*. Madrid, Spain: Civitas.

Hamel, G. and C. K. Prahalad. 1994. *Competing for the Future*. Boston: Harvard Business School Press.

Inkson, Kerr, Brian Henshall, Nick Marsh, and Gill Ellis. 1986. *Theory K. The Key to Excellence in New Zealand Management*. Auckland, New Zealand: David Bateman, Ltd.

Jill, P. 1993. *International Business*. London: Pitman Publishing.

Kaplan, R. S. and D. P. Norton. 1996. *The Balanced Score Card*. Boston: Harvard Business School Press.

Kennedy, P. 1993. *Preparing for the Twenty-First Century*. London: Fontana Press Harper Collins.

Klein, D. A. 1998. *The Strategic Management of Intellectual Capital*. New York: Butterworth-Heinemann.

Mc Nair, C. J. and H. J. Kathleen. 1992. *Benchmarking. A Tool for Continuous Improvement*. New York: Harper Collins.

McRae, H. 1994. *The World in 2020*. Boston: Harvard Business School Press.

Morrison, 1996. *The Second Curve*. New York: Ballantine Books.

Naisbitt, J. 1994. *Global Paradox*. London: Nicolas Brealey.

Naisbitt, J. and P. Aburdane. 1991. *Megatendances*. Paris: First Documents.

Nolan, L. Richard and C. David Croson. 1995. *Creative Destruction*. Boston: Harvard Business School Press.

Nonaka, I. and H. Takeuchi. 1995. *The Knowledge-Creating Company*. New York: Oxford University Press.

Ohmae, K. 1990. *The Borderless World*. New York: Harper Business.

Pagé, J. P., D. Turcq, M. Bailly, G. Foldès. 1987. *La Recherche de l'Excellence en France*. Paris: Bordas.

Pearson, Gordon. 1992. *The Competitive Organisation*. Maidenhead, England: McGraw-Hill.

Peteraf, M. A. 1993. "The Cornerstones of Competitive Sdvantage: A Resource-Based View," *Strategic Management Journal* 14: 179–91.

Peters, J. Thomas and H. Robert Waterman, Jr. 1982. *In Search of Excellence*. New York: Harper and Row.

Prusak, L. 1996. "The Knowledge Advantage," *Strategy and Leadership* (March-April).

Prusak, L. and T. H. Davenport. 1998. *Working Knowledge*. Boston: Harvard Business School Press.

Prusak, L. 1997. *Knowledge in Organizations*. New York: Butterworth-Heinemann.

Quinn, James Brian. 1993. *Intelligent Enterprise*. New York: The Free Press.

Slyowtzky, J. Adrian. 1996. *Value Migration*. Boston: Harvard Business School Press.

Spendolini, J. M. 1992. *The Benchmarking Book*. New York: Amacom.

Stalk, G., P. Evans and L. E. Schulman. 1992. Competing on Capabilities: The New Rules of Corporate Strategy. *Harvard Business Review* (March-April): 57–69.

Stewart, T. A. 1997. *Intellectual Capital: The New Wealth of Organizations*. New York: Currency Doubleday.

Sveiby, K. E. 1997. *The New Organizational Wealth*. San Francisco: Berett-Koehler Publishers.

Tayeb, H. M. 1992. *The Global Business Environment*. London: Sage Publications.

Taylor, J. and W. Wacker. 1997. *What Happens After What Comes Next*. New York: Harper Collins.

Valls, R. A. 1995. *Guía práctica del Benchmarking*. Barcelona: Gestión 2000.

Viedma, J. M. 1999. *ICBS Intellectual Capital Benchmarking System*. Third World Congress on Intellectual Capital and Innovation. January. Hamilton, Canada.

Viedma Marti, José M. 1992. *La Excelencia Empresarial*. Madrid: Serie de Management de McGraw Hill.

Watson, H. G. 1995. *Benchmarking Estratégico*. Buenos Aires: Javier Vergara.

Wiig, M. K. 1997. "Integrating Intellectual Capital and Knowledge Management," *Long Range Planning* 30, 3: 339.

Zangwill, W. I. 1993. *Lightning Strategies for Innovation*. London: Maxwell MacMillan International.

14

DEVELOPMENT AND IMPLEMENTATION OF AN INTELLECTUAL CAPITAL REPORT FOR A RESEARCH TECHNOLOGY ORGANIZATION

Karl-Heinz Leitner
Department for Technology Policy, Austrian Research Centers, Seibersdorf, Austria
karl-heinz.leitner@arcs.ac.at

Manfred Bornemann
Department of International Management, Karl Franzens University, Graz, Austria
manfred.bornemann@kfunigraz.ac.at

and

Ursula Schneider
Department of International Management, Karl Franzens University, Graz, Austria
ursula.schneider@kfunigraz.ac.at

ABSTRACT

In 2000, the first-ever intellectual capital report was published by the largest research technology organization (RTO) in Austria, the Austrian Research Centers Seibersdorf (ARCS). Generally, it is a great challenge for RTOs to evaluate and communicate research and business performance activities. ARCS was interested in improving the intelligibility of its intangible assets that were not supported by its traditional reporting system. With the intellectual capital report, ARCS now readily communicates the intangible value-added it has created. To implement the intellectual capital report, an integrated process model that combines corporate strategy, corporate knowledge goals, and knowledge processes with intangible results was developed and implemented. The basic model was developed in a cooperative effort between an internal team at ARCS and an external research institution, namely, the Department of International Management at Karl-Franzens University. This chapter will discuss the principles of reporting intangible assets in the context of an RTO. The chapter consists of background information, model development, and the implementation plan. Note: the 1999 intellectual capital report of ARCS can be downloaded from http://www.arcs.ac.at/publik/fulltext/wissensbilanz.

INTRODUCTION

Research technology organizations (RTOs) perform an important knowledge transfer function between the basic research at universities and the applied research and development initiatives in companies. RTOs have a broad scope of activities, which differ from universities and private firms. They are faced with three main challenges: (1) the transformation of the environment into a knowledge-based economy, (2) the transition toward more applied innovation research, and (3) the increasing competition for scarce research funds.

The emerging knowledge-based economy stresses the importance of knowledge as a new production factor. Even though knowledge creation has always been an important task for research organizations, increased investment in research and development is now of paramount importance. This entails new organizational structures and requires new forms of measurement and management. The fundamental change of companies toward knowledge-based organizations is indicated by several findings. The most important of which is the increased financial investment in intangible assets in most industrial countries. Since these investments account for a substantial part of the enterprise value, a need for a report on the performance of these intangible assets is necessary.

The transition of science is characterized by a stronger orientation toward applied and interdisciplinary research, compared to the past. This trend is sometimes labeled as *modus II of knowledge production* (Gibbons 1994). Innovation as the economic output of the research process does not only depend on the performance of firms, universities, and research organizations but also on their interaction. Intense cooperation between different actors (i.e., firms, universities, RTOs, training institutions, public agencies, etc.) is therefore necessary for the improved performance of the overall scientific community. Austerity policies of public agencies and an increasingly competitive climate within the industry of applied sciences force Austrian RTOs to raise funds via professional research contracts. However, since substantial funding from public institutions still exists, communication about its use for the public is desired.

To meet these internal and external challenges, ARCS decided to develop an intellectual capital report (IC report). ARCS wanted to communicate its research achievements and the intangible value-added it created to promote a culture of openness and transparency. The valuation and assessment of intangible assets is a serious academic task, and therefore fits perfectly into the mission of a research organization to work on new approaches and new models for further reference. The development of the IC report is highly influenced by the present research on valuing intangibles and the modern innovation theory.

In this chapter we describe the instrument and implications of IC reporting for research organizations. The IC report is based on a framework that documents and measures intangibles that are (1) strategically important for running the business of contract research organizations, (2) influential for corporate governance, and (3) necessary to increase the transparency of communication with external stakeholders.

THE ROLE OF ARCS AS RTO IN THE AUSTRIAN INNOVATION SYSTEM

Austrian Research Center, Seibersdorf (ARCS), is the largest research organization in Austria with public and private owners that operates as a private limited enterprise. ARCS was founded as a nuclear research institution at the end of the 1950s and diversified its research range during the following decades. Currently, ARCS performs research and development in the fields of information technology, material technologies and engineering, life sciences, and nuclear technology services and systems research. ARCS performs non-profit–oriented research and development services for the economy and society. More than seven hundred employees currently work on publicly funded research projects and industry-funded applied research and development projects.

Innovation is spawned by interactive contact between different players such as companies, universities, research laboratories, and educational institutions, all of which produce, combine, disseminate, and employ a wide range of knowledge. In the Austrian innovation system, ARCS assists the transfer of knowledge from universities to the economy, enhancing the quality of Austria as a research location. This means that ARCS:

- Transfers academic knowledge to practical application
- Provides an infrastructure and a platform for cooperative research projects
- Addresses the need for information and concepts that benefit society as a whole, for example, the need to develop procedures that save resources or improve consumer safety (public goods)
- Assumes the risk of innovative research in the early stage (if it seems too great for private organizations to bear)

ARCS is linked in national and international university-, industrial-, and public networks. As a network node, ARCS offers its own researchers and partners access to various pools of knowledge that they can then combine with their existing knowledge to come up with new concepts to solve technological, market-related, and general economic problems. One of ARCS's particular strengths lies in the development of new networks, for example, in the form of virtual teams involving universities, companies, and public institutions.

ARCS provides a wide variety of services to promote interaction between independent research and contract research. The spectrum ranges from publications, lectures, and testing services to expert opinions, prototypes, and software to the management of networks.

BACKGROUND ON THE VALUATION OF INTANGIBLE ASSESTS

Intangible assets are of increasing importance for the corporate value-creation processes of all kind of organizations (OECD 1999). This has severe consequences for internal and external reporting and hence for decision-making processes. Intangibles treated as resources of distinctive value should consequently be developed and allocated according to "objective" measures and according to accepted economic criteria. We are confronted with higher expectations for measuring methods and reporting tools to properly monitor investments into intangible assets. Questions about technical feasibility and cost-benefit arise but so far have not been resolved satisfactorily (OECD 2000) to the extent of defining standards or legally binding procedures.

Until recently, investments in intangible assets were usually not documented in a systematic manner. As a consequence, external reporting fell short of creating the required transparency because data was not available. Therefore, a reasonable estimate about the future performance potential of an organization could not be provided. Valuing intangibles is not a new issue for service and knowledge-intensive areas of the economy. There is a huge body of literature covering the legally protected assets, such as patents, licenses, trademarks, and copyright (see IASC E38 or Brockington 1995 for further details). But this is only a small fraction of what usually is summarized under the term *intangibles*. Besides these elements, there exists a list of legally unprotected elements of value that are already widely discussed in the intellectual capital literature (Sveiby 1997; Stewart 1997; Edvinsson and Malone 1997; Bontis 1998; Bontis et. al. 1999; Bontis 2001). Also important are the earlier works about human capital by Becker (1975) and about knowledge production by Machlup (1980), who was an instrumental pathfinder of the modern debate about valuing intangibles and knowledge assets. Furthermore, there exists literature on the valuation of technology and research and development, which is especially relevant for RTOs (Lev and Zarowin 1998).

Although we will not discuss the methods to measure and evaluate intangibles in this chapter, a list with some key terms will be provided (Leitner, Grasenik, and Haubold 2000; Canibano, Covarsi, and Sanchez 1999; Schneider 1999). There are two ways to differentiate the approaches: monetary and non-monetary measures.

1. Monetary measures:

   (a) cost approach (production cost and replacement cost)
   (b) market approach (what the market is willing to pay)
   (c) income approach (predicts the income and discounts it to present value)
   (d) real options (financial value of different strategies that alternatively could be applied in a given situation)

2. Nonmonetary measures:

   (a) structural models (e.g., Intangible Asset Monitor by Sveiby 1997 and the Skandia Navigator by Edvinsson and Malone 1997)
   (b) process models (e.g., European Foundation for Quality Management)

Investors demand valuation methods that are compatible with established tools of assessing financial value of an enterprise such as the capital asset–pricing model or price-earning multiples. From the perspective of corporate governance, there is a need for a broad and reliable information base that determines the daily decision processes of senior management. Corporate executives frequently face situations of high uncertainty, and therefore should take account of almost any information available, even if it is characterized as "soft." Ultimately, the goal of any measurement process needs to be clearly understood. Unfortunately, we have no current valuation methods that fulfill all of these requirements adequately.

THE DIFFERENCE BETWEEN ANNUAL REPORTING AND INTELLECTUAL CAPITAL REPORTING

Intangible assets as a resource can be shared among several people, which causes severe difficulties for developing and operating a new accounting system. Because of their characteristics, intangibles are not restricted to a specific location but oscillate seamlessly through the organization. The constant change of *shape* implies unspecified volume or value. Furthermore, valuing knowledge is context-specific. This makes it difficult to establish a commonly accepted methodology or standard to assess intangibles, which would be necessary if universal reporting was mandatory for organizations.

Another problem is the intrinsic logic of financial values: more equity or profit is generally rated as *good* . . . more expenses and obligations are generally rated as *bad*. This intuitive frame of reference is not valid for intangibles, as the following illustration shows. Since we cannot know *everything* on a given subject, we inevitably get locked in a learning loop and never come out of it to *act* in order to create value. Thus, we have to define exit levels where the learning progress is good enough to act upon and must be decidedly different for each situation.

As with classical balance sheets, intellectual capital reports contain comparative information and they can be reasonably interpreted only in the context of comparisons. Such comparisons may be made with historical information, they may relate to the achievement of strategic goals or represent a benchmark, indicating a position in relationship to comparable organizations. Only then do differences and deviations come to light, which prompt the ongoing modification of the company's strategy. In this context, it is particularly important to have a clear understanding of the facts and the set of circumstances for which a certain indicator supplies information.

Rationale for Intellectual Capital Reporting in RTOs

Austerity policies of public agencies and an increasingly competitive climate within the industry of applied sciences forced ARCS to raise funds via professional research contracts. In contrast, the traditional governmental funding route did not primarily demand immediate returns but rather the creation of public goods, such as technology transfer or the maintenance of public-technology policies. In the 1990s, ARCS was forced to seek out privately funded projects in order to survive. This required a new orientation of strategic goals and a focus on selected key topics in various research fields. Additionally, a new initiative to spin off new science-oriented, start-up companies was adopted.

ARCS continued to move forward with its transformation and by the mid 1990s had shed most of its historically highly diversified organizational structure. With the implementation of a process-oriented structure and the support of the active score card—a modified balanced scorecard—the management of ARCS developed a modern organizational framework that was decentralized and more fluid.

In 1991, Eccles wondered: "Would managers be willing to publish anything more than the financial information that the SEC requires?" and he concluded, "As soon as one leading company can demonstrate the long-term advantage of its superior performance on quality or innovation or any other non-financial measure, it will change the rules for all its rivals forever" (Eccles 1991: 42). ARCS took this suggestion seriously and established a vision of developing and implementing new ways of management and external reporting. ARCS decided to commit to developing an IC report for the following three reasons:

- As an RTO, ARCS depended on the proper management of its knowledge base and therefore needed to document and assess the potential and the development of its intellectual capital. Although several internal reports contained elements of the development of the intangible assets, a systematic compilation did not exist until the implementation of a balanced scorecard. Elements of this set were communicated more publicly to strengthen the internal and external awareness of their importance.
- Because substantial funding was still coming from public institutions, transparency about its use to the public was desired. ARCS wanted to communicate their scientific achievements and added value and thus create a culture of openness and transparency.
- Finally, the valuation and assessment of intangible assets was a serious academic task, and therefore it perfectly fit into the mission of a research organization working on new approaches and new models for further reference. It was a natural decision to start with ARCS as a pilot organization. Furthermore, it was one of the expected public tasks of playing a progressive role in the application of innovative forms of leadership.

CHALLENGES IN DESIGNING A MODEL

The primary challenge for designing a model for intellectual capital–reporting for ARCS was to establish the perfect fit with the given specific organizational requirements and simultaneously reflect the knowledge creation processes in an optimal way. After a rough first design, it soon turned out to be crucial to select specific indicators and process the relevant data. The indicators needed to reflect corporate strategy, conform with the process-oriented model, obey the cost-benefit criteria, and, finally, avoid revealing extremely sensitive information.

Another challenge was the alignment of the new reporting system with existing ones to avoid double efforts and thus de-motivate employees. The project team started with an evaluation of existing models to prepare its own IC report in mid 1999. After designing the model under consideration of the specifics of RTOs (Schneider

1999; Ohler and Leitner 1999), the project was implemented from January, 2000, to April, 2000. The IC report was finally published in April, 2000 (ARCS 2000). Since then, the discussion of the model has continued internally as well as externally and has resulted in a few modifications that will be documented at the end of this chapter.

THE ARCS MODEL FOR INTELLECTUAL CAPITAL–REPORTING

The ARCS IC report has been compiled to meet the following objectives; namely, to illustrate the development of intangible assets; explain the achievements of research and their benefits to stakeholders; create transparency about the use of public funds; point out future areas of promise and track the benefits they bring; reveal leverage effects and externalities that are part of the performance potential of ARCS.

The IC report is based on a model (see Figure 14-1) that reflects the cycle of knowledge within the company. One underlying principle is that knowledge in the form of human, structural, and relational capital (Bontis 1999) is always both an input and an output. With this model, which in the future will be used by all divisions of ARCS, specific combinations of intangible resources can be traced. The process of acquiring, applying, and exploiting knowledge starts with the definition of knowledge goals, which can be derived from the corporate strategy. These goals form the framework for the utilization of the intellectual capital at ARCS, which is composed of structural, human, and relational capital. Projects are carried out at the operating level and provide added value when utilized, requiring them to be constantly developed

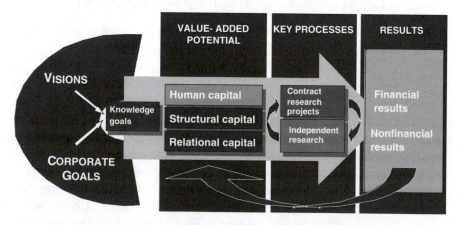

Figure 14-1 *The ARCS Intellectual Capital Report Model (ARCS 2000: 13)*

and maintained. There are numerous interactions and spill-over effects in the process, which give ARCS its unique interdisciplinary character.

A specific attribute of the ARCS model is the integration of intangible results. Intangible results are nonfinancial results with respect to economy, research, and society. In addition to these results, there are also financial returns that appear in the ARCS annual report. ARCS divides its value-added activities into independent research, which is increasingly being structured as programs, and contract projects carried out for various different customers. Whereas contract research keeps ARCS in close touch with practical applications and the market, independent research promotes continuity and creates opportunities for the production of new knowledge.

Depending on the assignment, either all three elements of intellectual capital are utilized equally or individual elements are applied selectively to projects. In general, large, long-term research projects will tend to combine all three elements. Projects are carried out for national and international customers. The results are passed on to the client and charged at the going market price. In some cases they are also published. Contract research at ARCS is self-financing. Independent research provides some initiatives for contract research and vice versa—the effect can be described as *spill-over*. Some of the services offered by ARCS are sold on the market, but some are performed as public services. Profit alone has limited value as a measure of the success of these services. The model identifies nonfinancial results that have a financial impact only at a later date or have no direct financial benefit, but instead a benefit as an externality in another area. Examples are knowledge for which other parties find an application, or ideas learned from publications or lectures and then put into practice, or the leverage effect of a research and development link between companies.

The model helps to illustrate the development of intangible assets over the past reporting-period and helps to interpret the processes. The complexity of the processes in a research institute caused by interactions can only be hinted at, since, as in a classical balance sheet, details are lost in consolidated presentation. Nevertheless, the IC report represents an important step in highlighting relations that have not been covered in the annual report.

The IC report furnishes information on the knowledge available at ARCS and on the flow of knowledge within the company. Intangible assets are represented by indicators, for each of which a frame of reference is described. For each element of the model, indicators are defined. Dependencies between indicators, developments, and especially target achievements are also described in the IC report, often in the form of best practices or examples of excellence.

LESSONS LEARNED

The experience gained by other organizations with management tools demonstrates that many new concepts, methods, or tools are overestimated or miss their mark and are thus often turned down after a certain time. Some solutions rarely deliver as much as they promise and turn out to be only quick-fix solutions. There is no doubt that the development and publication of an IC report is expected to have benefits for an organization. However, if the process of development and implementation is not well managed, the results will be inferior. In the following section the experiences with development and implementation of the IC report at ARCS are systematically reflected. The aim is to identify the main factors for a successful implementation for other organizations.

In order to analyze the process of development and implementation, the following aspects were considered as crucial:

- Organizational goals and strategies as framework for implementing the IC report
- The definition of indicators and gathering of data
- The implementation of an IC report system as process and management innovation, project management, and organizational aspects
- The IC report system as a medium of communication

One essential task when implementing an IC report is the discussion of corporate aims and strategies. In contrast to the traditional balance sheet, the development of an IC report requires the explicit formulation of goals of the organization. The discussion of goals and strategies forces senior management to concentrate on the essential value-creating processes that must then be measured, documented, and communicated. This explicit goal-orientation is one of the significant differences between these two reporting-systems. The formulation of corporate goals is necessary for the second step of the process, that is, to define the indicators for the IC report.

This task of pinning down the goals of an organization is not always trivial, and the articulated goals and strategies are often too abstract or vague to fulfil the job of defining indicators. In the past few years, European RTOs with a focus on carrying out contract research have changed their strategic orientation considerably and have had to find their (new) position between the university sector and the private sector. Whereas private firms aim to maximize their profits, nonprofit contract research organizations do not.

Goals of ARCS are the transfer of technologies to the industry and/or to develop new technological solutions in an interdisciplinary manner. After defining the framework for the strategic direction of the organization, it was possible to formulate knowledge goals. Knowledge goals define the areas where specific skills, structures, and relationships should be built up or improved to ensure that the corporate strategy can be put to work. They are in line with the company's long-term goals and provide, together with financial goals, the framework for corporate development. Knowledge goals form the framework for the utilization of the intellectual capital of ARCS. Their linkage to corporate objectives is to ensure strategic relevance of all knowledge management activities resulting from the report.

After defining the knowledge goals, the project team started to formulate the indicators for the IC report. Apart from the knowledge goals that served as the foundation for this project-step, the existing data in the firm were another element of reference. The aim was to formulate valid indicators for every category of the underlying model: intellectual capital, key processes, and results. The ideal way of defining indicators derived from goals was not always possible. Sometimes information and indicators that existed in different departments had to be evaluated on their relevance for the task of valuing intangibles. The development of the indicators was a combination of top-down and bottom-up processes. Sometimes indicators were developed in expectation that afterward the picture of the essentials and priorities of the firm would be more precise. However, it is not possible to define indicators without an exact idea of the intended development of the organization. During the formulation of goals and indicators, it was also necessary to develop hypotheses for the business. These hypotheses could be interpreted as strategic constructs that show important relations of the business model. During the strategic discourse, driving forces of competition, market, and technology were brought into the model. It was important to find out the implicit rules for the research process and research competition. In addition, data-gathering had to be kept economically feasible. A common database of core data should be established to serve several reports.

This interactive process between the project team and the top management demonstrates that the preparation of an IC report is a medium of communication that helps to get a better idea of fundamental values, priorities, and goals of the company and helps whenever discrepancy between various strategies or aims arise. Therefore the IC report is a strategic management tool to a higher degree than the traditional balance sheet and helps to operationalize the corporate goals and strategies.

One of the biggest dangers when developing an IC report is to define too many goals or indicators. If neither the picture of the company development nor the important intangible resources required are clear, people or organizations tend to want *everything*. However, strategic thinking entails setting priorities. Although strategic discussions are crucial for such a project, it is also important to be able to stop the strategic discourse at a certain point in the process, as otherwise it might be possible that successive interventions harm the development or lead to a permanent modification of the model.

After the definition and selection of the indicators, relevant data needed to be gathered. In some cases, the data already existed; in other cases, different departments had to prepare it. Furthermore, some indicators that were used within the active scorecard were also published in the IC report. When selecting indicators, a priority must be to define them as exactly and as transparently as possible. During the implementation process in ARCS, the project team had to decide whether the indicator really measured the phenomenon that it wanted to express and whether the measurement was possible and not too expensive. A further complicating element was that IC indicators measured different things, and sometimes similar resources and results. An example would be the indicator "number of lectures per scientific employee," which is a measurement of knowledge-transfer to students, a measurement of the value of the opportunities for networking or recruiting, and even a measure for competence enhancement of the lecturer. When defining the indicators, the project team also tried to use indicators that were used internationally in other firms or had already been published in the literature. The aim was to create conditions for a sustainable international benchmarking of indicators.

During the data collection process, it was very important to continually motivate the employees for the task and convince them of the benefits of an IC report. In recent years a lot of projects had been initiated, such as total-quality management, management of information systems, business reengineering, and new forms of activity-based cost-accounting. Due to these earlier efforts, many structures, procedures, reports, and indicators had been implemented in the whole organization. The aim for ARCS was to avoid the same information being gathered twice. The list of all used indicators can be found in Table 14-1.

Table 14-1
ARCS Intellectual Capital Report Indicators

Human capital

Human resources

New staff total

research staff

Total staff fluctuation

Total staff leaving

research staff, total

of whom aged 25-35

of whom aged 25-35 within 2 years

of whom aged 35-45

of whom aged 45-59

of whom retired

Total retirement

Average seniority (in years)

Percentage of research staff

Number of awards

Training

Days training per employee, total

Days training per employee: communication and management

Days training per employee: computer literacy

Days training per employee: technical

Training cost in % of salary, per employee

Structural capital

IT infrastructure

IT expense per employee in ATS

Processes: project schedule adherence

Success ratio for EU research programs (projects won/ submitted)

Success ratio for national research programs/competence centers (projects won/submitted)

Knowledge-based infrastructure

Number of databases to which ARCS has access

Accreditation and certifications

Table 14-1 ARCS Intellectual Capital Report Indicators (*Continued*)

Relational capital

Project cooperation and networking

EU projects and Kplus (as a % of all new projects)

In-house collaboration (as a % of all new projects)

Research activities abroad in man years

Number of international research scientists (as a % of research workers)

Dissemination and networking

Number of conferences attended, total (per research worker)

Lectures at scientific conferences (per research worker)

Referees: journals and evaluation panels, number of people (per research worker)

Involvement on boards: scientific, industrial, political (per research worker)

Teaching assignments (per research worker)

Customers, image, and stakeholders

First-time customers (as a % of all new projects)

New stakeholders

"Response indicator" (name ARCS mentioned in the media)

Independent research

Number of project categories

Percentage of independent research in total expenditure

Percentage of international projects

Contract research projects

Number of customer projects (not including small projects)

Revenue from customer projects incl. small projects (orders received) in ATS million

Revenue per project (not incl. small projects)

Customers

Average size of small projects in ATS

Table 14-1 ARCS Intellectual Capital Report Indicators (*Continued*)

Results

Financial results

Total turnover in million ATS

Growth in turnover compared to the previous year*

Percentage of financing from own resources

Economy-oriented results

Number of new contract projects with customers

Number of new customers in %

Number of projects for private customers

Number of new EU contract projects

Research co-ordination and network management

EU, competence centers, cluster initiatives (prime contractor)

Authorizations and certifications

Number of spin-offs

Number of customers–training

Research-oriented results

Publications: scientific journals

Publications: trade journals, conference proceedings, books

Presentations at scientific conferences

Patents

Teaching assignments

Completed theses and dissertations

Society-oriented results

Involvement in scientific, technical, or business boards

Policy consulting projects

"Response indicator" (name ARCS mentioned in the media)

The IC report of ARCS has been developed for the whole company, therefore the indicators for the different departments have been aggregated. The aggregation of indicators has the disadvantage that the specifics of the individual departments cannot be considered. It was crucial to use the IC report not as a tool to exercise control over single domains of a company but as a tool to communicate with each other and to evaluate the performance systematically and holistically.

Apart from the engagement of middle management, the commitment of top management is usually a crucial prerequisite for implementing an innovative new project. The most important promoter for the project was the Managing Director of ARCS for Science and Technology himself, Professor G. Koch. He was the main initiator concerning the implementation of the IC report for the organization.

One central conclusion of the project experience is the importance of coordinating the process of implementation with other activities and projects within ARCS. If this is not guaranteed, tons of data are collected and aggregated into reports, but nobody uses them because of redundancy or the "not-invented-here" syndrome. In ARCS this process of alignment was quite successful, but there is still room for further improvement.

The project management structure was as simple as necessary and started in the fall of 1999. The whole process of implementation lasted four months. Preliminary work and the experience of the team allowed the project to be implemented within this short period of time.

After defining the indicators, the last step of the project was to interpret the data and write the IC report. The main part of the IC report consists of the model that is activated through the interpreted indicators. Nearly all data are interpreted and, if possible, compared with other benchmarks or with corporate aims. However, as there are always certain kinds of intangibles as well as relations between different elements of the model that cannot be sufficiently operationalized by indicators, text is used to value them. We believe that, in the near future, it will be necessary to evaluate intangibles on the basis of qualitative criteria, too. In the last phase of the process, the team cooperated with an external layout team.

The first IC report in the history of ARCS was finished in April, 2000, and then presented and discussed internally and externally. One of the main tasks when publishing an IC report is to initiate a discussion process with different stakeholders. For the interpretation of the indicators it is essential to find a common language, which means that all stakeholders refer to the same framework. Assessments can be made on the basis of the development over time, by comparing them with the formulated goals, or by benchmarking them with similar research organizations.

We think that the development and implementation of an IC report system is an innovative challenge and the task could be interpreted as a process innovation. The success factors and findings of the research on innovative projects are also valuable for the realization of an IC report. Commitment, promoters, participation, project management, and communication are substantial ingredients for successful realization. Through presenting and discussing the IC report within the divisions of ARCS, it was possible to communicate new values and evaluate the results.

The IC report also represents an essential cornerstone to better manage the corporate knowledge base since, for the first time, it provides a foundation for management intervention based on sound data. When reading the IC report, a variety of interpretations are possible. This is mainly due to the absence of standards and collective-reference frameworks. We believe the main challenge for the future will be the standardization of indicators as well as the establishment of guidelines for developing and applying IC reports.

To sum up the discussion of lessons learned from the development of an intellectual capital report, the most important factors for successful realization of valuing intellectual capital are summarized in Table 14-2.

Table 14-2
Check list of success factors for realizing IC reports in practice

☐ Define corporate goals as exactly as possible

☐ Define the objectives of the project and communicate that an IC report system is a management tool that requires discussion about corporate goals and strategies

☐ Do not use a complicated model and do not try to develop a perfect IC report

☐ Formulate the indicators exactly and transparently

☐ Try to reduce the amount of indicators to a few, but significant ones

☐ Initiate a collective learning process when interpreting indicators

☐ Define a project team with clear responsibilities and define the project in comparison to other management projects, including knowledge management projects

☐ Ensure the commitment of the top management

☐ (Internal) members of the project team should have experience in valuing intangibles, the research process, and performance measurement, and they should be aware of the limits of valuing knowledge

☐ Provide for the participation of the employees and the communication of the benefits of the IC report

☐ The IC report is a medium of communication: initiate a discussion process on all levels of the organization and with different external stakeholders

CONCLUSION

It is perhaps too soon to evaluate the project effects in detail, which is mainly due to the effect that an evaluation of the whole project would have to consider all aspects of communication and intangible effects. However, some results have already become visible. The image of ARCS as an innovative player in the transformation toward the knowledge-based economy has been strengthened. New corporate values have been communicated throughout the organization and its environment. The awareness for networking has been fostered and new argumentative strategies for the discussion with investors and owners have emerged.

However, there are several challenges to be targeted in the next issue of the IC report. To overcome the resistance of people with the traditional, solely financial-oriented mind-set, a financial measurement should be developed and integrated with the IC report. For the support of the new paradigm, it might likely serve our interests more to translate the logic of the IC report in traditional managerial terms—even at the cost of losing some of the important points—than to ignore this reality of the current financial measures to which our stakeholders are accustomed.

Additionally, we want to stress the crucial importance of interpreting intellectual capital indicators in the context of the specific situation, because, otherwise, we still do not have a commonly shared standard and face highly heterogeneous organizational situations. To support this, we focus the scale and scope of our framework model for divisions and maybe even smaller units.

Finally, we would like to further increase the internal and external communications aspect of the IC report. The more it is accepted as an instrument that credibly reflects soft elements of corporate developments and the more this influences the actual decision-making process, the better it will support the organizational development process. We believe the main challenge for the future will be the standardization of indicators as well as the establishment of guidelines for developing and applying IC reports.

REFERENCES

Anthony, R. and K. Reece. 1983. *Accounting*. Seventh edition. Irwin, Calif. Austrian Research Centers, Seibersdorf (ARCS). 2000. *Intellectual Capital Report 1999*. Seibersdorf, Austria: ARCS.

Becker, G. S. 1975. *Human Capital*. Chicago: Chicago University Press.

Bontis, Nick. 1998. Intellectual Capital: An Exploratory Study that Develops, Measures and Models, *Management Decision* 36, 2: 63–76.

Bontis, Nick. 1999. Managing Organizational Knowledge by Diagnosing Intellectual Capital: Framing and Advancing the State of the Field, *International Journal of Technology Management* 18, 5/6/7/8: 433–62.

Bontis, Nick. 2001. Assessing Knowledge Assets: A Review of the Models Used to Measure Intellectual Capital, *International Journal of Management Reviews* 3, 1: 41–60.

Bontis, Nick, N. Dragonetti, K. Jacobsen, and G. Roos. 1999. The Knowledge Toolbox: A Review of the Tools Available to Measure and Manage Intangible Resources, *European Management Journal* 17, 4: 391–402.

Brockington, R. 1995. *Accounting for Intangible Assets*. London: Addison-Wesley.

Canibano, L., M. Covarsi, and M. P. Sanchez. 1999. The Value Relevance and Managerial Implications of Intangibles: A Literature Review, *International Symposium: Measuring and Reporting Intellectual Capital: Experiences, Issues, and Prospects*. OECD, 9–10 June, Amsterdam.

Eccles, R. 1991. The Performance Measurement Manifesto. In *Harvard Business Review on Measuring Corporate Performance*. Boston: Harvard Business School Press.

Edvinsson, L. and M. S. Malone. 1997. *Intellectual Capital: Realizing Your Company's True Value by Finding Its Hidden Brainpower*. New York: Harper Business.

European Commission. 1997. *Second European Report on S&T Indicators 1997*. Brussels.

Foray, D. 2000. Characterising the knowledge base: available and missing indicators. In *Knowledge Management in the Learning Society*. Paris: OECD.

Gibbons, M. 1994. *The New Production of Knowledge*. London and New York: Pinter Publishers.

International Accounting Standards Committee. 1998. *International Accounting Standards: Intangible Assets*. London.

Leitner, K. H., K. Grasenick, H. Haubold et al. 2000. *Development of a System for Intellectual Capital Reporting for the Organization Research Austria*. Vienna: Research Austria.

Lev, B. and P. Zarowin. 1998. The Boundaries of Financial Reporting and How to Extend Them. Working paper, New York University.

Machlup, F. 1980. *Knowledge: Its Creation, Distribution, and Economic Significance,* vol. 1, *Knowledge and Knowledge Production*. Princeton: Princeton University Press.

Organization for Economic Cooperation and Development (OECD). 1999. The Knowledge-Based Economy: A Set of Facts and Figures. Paris: OECD.

————2000. *Intangible Investment and Firm Performance*. Paris: OECD.

Ohler, F. and K-H. Leitner. 1999. Die Wissensbilanz: Ein Instrument der Unternehmenskommunikation. Working paper, ARCS/Seibersdorf.

Reilly, R. and R. Schweihs. 1998. *Valuing Intangible Assets*. New York: McGraw-Hill.

Schneider, U. 1999. Bericht zur Erstellung einer Wissensbilanz. Working paper, University of Graz and ARCS/Seibersdorf.

Steward, T. 1997. *Intellectual Capital*. New York: Doubleday.

Sveiby, K. E. 1997. *The New Organizational Wealth: Managing and Measuring Knowledge-Based Assets*. San Francisco: Berrett-Koehler.

15

FOR BETTER OR WORSE?

ASSESSING THE COSTS AND BENEFITS OF CONTINGENT KNOWLEDGE-WORK AS AN INVESTMENT IN INTELLECTUAL CAPITAL

Shelley MacDougall
*Manning School of Business Administration, Acadia University,
Nova Scotia, Canada*
shelley.macdougall@acadiau.ca

and

Deborah Hurst
*Centre for Innovative Management, Athabasca University,
Alberta, Canada*
deborahh@athabascau.ca

ABSTRACT

Intellectual capital is an important source of competitive advantage in business today, and the brisk pace of change compels firms to continually invest in their intellectual assets. One means of investing in intellectual capital is the introduction of contingent knowledge-workers for the purpose of stimulating new ideas and importing public-domain knowledge to enhance core private knowledge. However, bringing knowledge workers to where they are exposed to the firm's core competency risks the dissemination of private knowledge, thereby jeopardizing the firm's strategic position. On the other hand, in knowledge-intensive and dynamic industries, the failure to develop new knowledge can likewise be very risky. In deciding whether to introduce a knowledge worker on a contingent basis, companies must weigh the benefits, costs, opportunities, and risks, many of which are intangible and thus believed to be immeasurable. This paper proposes a conceptual model for evaluating such an investment that first identifies the tangible outputs. It also discusses the research still to be done on assessing the net value of using contingent knowledge-workers, evaluation of investments in intellectual capital, and the implications for valuation of the firm's stock of intellectual capital in general.

INTRODUCTION

In today's economy, competitive advantage is becoming increasingly knowledge-dependent. To compete in an environment characterized by rapid technological development, shortened product life-cycles, production flexibility, and globalization, research and innovation are critical. Intellectual capital has become a primary source of wealth creation (Carayannis and Alexander 1999: 328).

Intellectual capital is made up of intellectual materials, knowledge, information, intellectual property, and experience used to create organizational wealth (Stewart 1997). Handy (1991) estimates the intellectual capital of modern organizations to be worth three or four times an organization's tangible book value. In his view, the intangibles are now brainpower assets, which reside in the minds of people. Still, despite the importance of intellectual capital and the success of companies in deploying it, we do not fully understand it or how to measure it.

The value of a company's intellectual capital is broadly measured by the difference between the book value and market value of the company. This credits the financial markets with the ability to recognize the value of the firm's intellectual capital and the potential profit it can generate, even though an objective measure has not yet been established within accounting standards.

Intellectual capital, by its very nature, is a unique asset. For instance, knowledge can be increased by sharing it with others (Inkpen 1998). Even failure can result in an increase in knowledge (McGrath 1999). Furthermore, acquiring a critical mass of knowledge can yield escalating returns-to-scale because it tends to attract increasingly more expert workers (Carayannis and Alexander 1999) and enables a company to "break away from the pack" competitively. On the downside, knowledge is a decaying asset. Simply maintaining the current stock of knowledge can result in lost competitive advantage as industry rivals make advances in their knowledge.

In order to maintain strategic advantage, firms must continuously manage their stock and flow of knowledge (Carayannis and Alexander 1999; Roslender 2000). In addition to the depreciation of the firm's knowledge assets from competitor advancements and developing public knowledge, some knowledge is lost as employees leave and private knowledge is disseminated to the public domain. Over time, the acquisition and development of new knowledge must be greater than the loss and decay of existing knowledge.

Firms undertake to develop their intellectual capital through a number of means. One is the employment of knowledge workers on a contingent basis. Organizations are increasingly relying on the use of contingent workers (defined in contrast to full-time, permanent workers) at all levels of the organization (Booth 1997). "Knowledge workers are people who use their heads more than their hands to produce value. They add value through their ideas, their analyses, their judgement, their syntheses, and their designs" (Horibe 1999: xi). Knowledge workers now contribute to the essential skills and competencies of producing goods and services. They are key drivers of wealth creation and are in scarce supply.

Matusik and Hill (1998) consider the importation of knowledge from the public domain essential to the stimulation and development of private knowledge, especially in the area of the firm's core competence. In highly dynamic industries, they recommend contingent knowledge-workers for this purpose. However, exposing core competency knowledge to contingent workers jeopardizes the company's competitive position. In contrast to Matusik and Hill, Quinn (1999) and others recommend core activities be protected from the view of outsiders. They recommend companies concentrate on developing and maintaining their own core competence at "best-in-the-world" levels and, partly as a defensive measure, contract specialist firms to perform only non-core activities.

As with any investment, companies seeking to develop intellectual capital by engaging contingent knowledge-workers should weigh the costs, benefits, and risks over time. However, the same impediment to valuing intellectual capital is inherent in evaluating investments in it: intangibility. This paper examines the use of contingent knowledge-workers in organizations as an investment in intellectual assets of the firm. We propose a capital budgeting approach to determining the net value. This is theoretically consistent with the measures of market value and has the potential to reconcile the difference between book value and market value that intellectual capital constitutes.

INTELLECTUAL CAPITAL AND KNOWLEDGE

Intellectual capital can be described in terms of human capital, referring to the knowledge and expertise of people, structural capital (systems, such as databases, that connect people to one another), and customer capital, such as brand awareness and customer loyalty, which ultimately determines the company's success.

Companies are becoming more knowledge-intensive in human, structural, and customer forms. Increasingly, we hear of organizations investing in research, development, and training as a form of capital spending to build intellectual capital. In fact, some organizations today are investing more in research and development than they are in capital equipment (Stewart 1997: 21). The rationale behind this is that the money spent on research and development will have greater returns, since the investment will not simply produce incremental improvement but innovations—whole new products, services, and processes that may be of a greater value than those they replace. However, organizations have difficulty managing and measuring knowledge as an intangible asset. "Brain gains," as a return on investment, cannot be seen directly or classified, nor can such capital be expressed or recognized because it is "soft" or tacit, rather than explicit.

The purpose of this section, then, is to organize and define the different forms of intellectual capital so as to move forward on how investment in such knowledge can be appropriately assessed and valued (Figure 15-1). Matusik and Hill (1998) provide definitions of the different forms of knowledge that are captured under the human, structural, and customer capital headings. The following

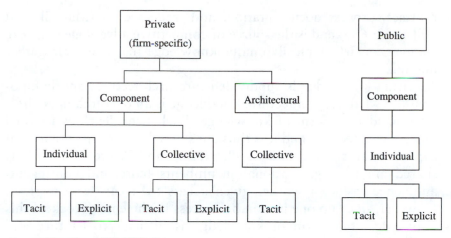

Source: Matusik and Hill, 1998, 684.

Figure 15-1 *Organizational knowledge components*

definitional summary will highlight the dimensions of individual versus collective knowledge, tacit versus explicit knowledge, private versus public knowledge, and component versus architectural knowledge.

Human knowledge, knowledge individually held, is defined as that which individuals bring into the organization. Some of this becomes collectively held. Within collective knowledge develops "organizing principles, routines, practices, top management schema, and relative organizational census on past experience, goals, missions, competitors, and relationships" (Matusik and Hill 1998: 683).

Knowledge can be tacit or explicit. Tacit knowledge, which is part of human knowledge, is acquired through experience and is difficult to describe and transfer to others (Matusik and Hill 1998; Nonaka and Takeuchi 1995; Polanyi 1962, 1966). Tacit knowledge can also reside within organizational collectives in the form of skills, habits, and abstract understanding, which make up architectural knowledge. Similarly, explicit knowledge is held both individually, as human knowledge, and organizationally. Explicit knowledge is somewhat more observable and can be easily examined. It is procedural, rule-bound, and transferable. Explicit knowledge is present in operating procedures, documentation, information systems, and rules (Brown and Duguid 1991; Lyles 1988; Matusik and Hill 1998; Starbuck 1992).

There exist both private and public knowledge. Private knowledge is specific to the individual firm. It is embedded in specialized routines, process documentation, and trade secrets (Matusik and Hill 1998: 683) and is the source of competitive advantage and core competency. It is typically unique knowledge that is not altogether imitable.

Private knowledge is subdivided into architectural and component knowledge. Architectural knowledge is an overarching, collectively held tacit form of knowledge. Each firm develops its own unique architecture, and it is thus considered part of its intellectual capital (Matusik and Hill 1998; Nelson and Winter 1982). It is shared among organizational incumbents (core and contingent) and, once inside, a worker given access to it can leave with it. However, since no one person has access to the entire stock of this knowledge, this form of knowledge is difficult to capture and expropriate.

By contrast, component knowledge consists of discrete aspects or subroutines of an organization's operation that underpin the organization's functions, development, and processes. Component knowledge can be held individually or collectively and is defined in terms of resources, knowledge, skills, and technical systems (Amit and Schoemaker 1993; Henderson and Cockburn 1994; Leonard-Barton 1992; Matusik and Hill 1998). It is at least partially derived from the public knowledge base.

Finally, public knowledge is shared by all firms and includes best practices. The latest technological information or system is relevant to the public domain where knowledge is advanced. Even though the knowledge is available in the broad domain and is not firm specific, a company may be disadvantaged if not aware of its developments and potential benefits (Matusik and Hill 1998).

Using each of these knowledge concepts, we can work toward an understanding of how to manage and integrate organizational knowledge to develop intellectual capital. All contribute to the firm's intellectual capital and competitive advantage. Tacit knowledge is difficult to transfer, whereas component knowledge is easier to appropriate and/or transfer. Architectural knowledge, on the other hand, is not possessed by any one individual. It can also be a source of competitive advantage, but it is difficult to transfer. If we consider these in the context of organizational flexibility and the use of contingent knowledge-workers to develop intellectual capital at all levels, we realize the importance of mechanisms to improve the generation, intrafirm diffusion, and interfirm protection of knowledge. Such is the new field of theory and practice called *knowledge management* (Carayannis and Alexander 1999: 331).

The task becomes even more complicated as we try to discern the type of human resource that constitutes intellectual capital and where the most sensitive, competitive, private knowledge must be managed. Stewart (1997) suggests it is important for an organization to collect and concentrate human capital for knowledge creation since such knowledge and intellectual capital are easily dissipated. The challenge is to find and enhance the talents that are truly assets for the organization and separate them from those human aspects that are more appropriately considered costs. Stewart classifies knowledge skills as follows: (1) commodity skills, gained through collecting knowledge and information to enhance individual abilities, (2) leveraged skills, which include knowledge valued by the company and are industry specific (e.g., programming), and (3) proprietary skills, which are company specific, related to the organization's core competency and upon which the business is built. In Stewart's view, the most important human capital knowledge assets exist among knowledge workers possessing the key talent and experiences that create wealth for the company as defined by customer behavior.

The focus of this paper is on those intellectual assets in the third category: the knowledge of individuals who are in many cases very difficult to recruit, difficult to replace, and who add high value to the organization's core competency. We extend what Stewart provides by considering the impact of the use of contingent knowledge workers in this highly competitive category. This is of concern specifically because the valuation of knowledge in this category is lacking, yet it is where the organization's private knowledge exists. When such knowledge is leveraged through contingent workers, it puts the company at competitive risk.

VALUING AN INVESTMENT IN INTELLECTUAL CAPITAL

If intellectual capital is considered an asset and expenditures to increase it an investment, one should estimate the value of this investment by estimating the net benefits (benefits less costs) and risk over time. Companies typically attempt to value such expenditures using the return-on-investment (ROI) measurement tool. However, this technique of valuation is severely limited when the investment and its benefits and costs are intangible and contingent.

Bontis (2001) and his colleagues (Bontis et al. 1999) among others (Booth 1998) describe a plethora of methods for valuing intellectual capital as developed by companies and researchers. Many of these methods propose measures of intellectual capital that are only proxies. Such ratios as personal computers to employees, and revenues from new products to total revenues, only loosely measure intellectual capital. They can be used for an internal trend analysis but do not translate directly into a market value comparable across firms. A measure that reconciles the dollar difference between book value and market value, reflecting the company's intellectual capital, remains elusive.

The market value of a company's equity is the present value of expected cash flows to the shareholders. The book value is the depreciated value of the recorded assets, which a company employs to generate profit (and hence cash flow to shareholders). How enterprising and intelligent the firm is will dictate the magnitude and duration of the cash flows to be generated from these assets. According to the tenets of fundamental analysis in investment theory, the present value of this potential profit is what makes up the difference between book value and market value.

Cash flows to be generated from the company's assets can be classified into two categories. The traditional capital budgeting valuation of an investment tabulates the present value of usual cash flows: the initial investment, incremental revenues, and costs and savings for the economic life of the asset. These medium-term cash flows are relatively foreseeable. However, such strategic investments as information technology, research and development, and brand development have an inherent ability to "pave the way" for future opportunities because of the flexibility or strategic position they afford the firm. This knowledge, capability, or flexibility creates options that can be exercised if and when market conditions are favorable. This strategic value, very much a feature of intellectual capital, is one that is not captured in techniques typically used for valuing it.

A considerable amount of research has been done in the field of capital budgeting for strategic investments in advanced manufacturing and information technology. The traditional net-present-value model for these complex investments has been expanded by adding their strategic value, calculated using the Nobel prize-winning option-pricing model (Black and Scholes 1973; Cox, Ross, and Rubenstein 1979; Merton 1977), which has been adapted for real assets. Although still in the early stages of development, the resulting real-option pricing model is designed to add to the traditional net present value model the value of the optional projects that can be undertaken in the future, made possible by flexible technology. This is revolutionizing investment decision-making by enabling the valuation of the strategic value that many intuitively knew existed.

Standard real options include the option to delay an investment, build in stages, expand, contract, shut down, restart, abandon, switch inputs or outputs, and grow (Trigeorgis 1993). Trigeorgis (1993) described real options as falling into two general categories: operating and strategic. Operating options arise from management flexibility to make positive changes to operations to respond to opportunities and threats, as external events unfold. These changes can alter the profitability of an investment, "skewing its cash flow distribution toward a higher rate of return" (Cheung 1993: 31). This adds to the value of the investment calculated by conventional discounted cash-flow techniques. Strategic options are the opportunities latent in an investment that, if exercised, enhance competitive advantage. As examples, the option to take advantage of changes in consumer demand, respond to or curtail competitors' actions or to make subsequent, contingent investments add potential and value to the investment.

Developing a company's knowledge generates immediate benefits, costs, and savings. However, there is more. The value of the real options, or perhaps, in the case of intellectual capital, *virtual* options, are in the cash flows of later projects made possible by today's investment in the company's stock of knowledge. These later projects are optional. If conditions do not warrant further action, then nothing more is lost; if conditions are favorable, benefits can be garnered with additional investment. Under these conditions, there is limited downside risk, although much can potentially be gained. The one-sided nature of the risk of these contingent investments is the value the option-pricing model is designed to capture.

The real-option terminology is borrowed from financial options as shown below (Trigeorgis 1988: 149). Call options in capital investment are options to invest further, such as a follow-on investment or a delayed new product launch. The options to abandon or switch use are real put options, the salvage value of the investment being the exercise price.

Table 15-1
Option Terminology

Real Call Option		Stock Call Option
(Gross) PV of expected cash flows of later project	P	Current value of the stock
Further investment required to undertake later project	Ex	Exercise price
Time until opportunity disappears	t	Time to expiration
Project value uncertainty	σ^2	Stock value uncertainty
Riskless interest rate	k_{rf}	Riskless interest rate
Expired profit opportunities, cash flows foregone	d	Dividends

Trigeorgis, 1988, 149.

As an example of a real call option, consider a pharmaceutical company that has developed a new drug for asthma (Micalizzi et al. 1999). Using this drug, they launch a product, not for asthma but for allergies, which has similar characteristics. If the product gains market acceptance and brand recognition, they will follow with the launch of the related asthma product under a similar, then-recognizable brand name. The investment in the allergy product launch includes an opportunity—an option—to market the asthma product as a subsequent, contingent investment. If the allergy drug does not gain market acceptance, the asthma product will not be introduced and no further expenditure will be incurred. By taking this wait-and-see approach, some of the uncertainty is resolved, making the new asthma product less risky. The downside risk is reduced while upside potential can be optimized. In fact, since the risk of the contingent investment is largely one-sided, the more risk the better. Real options have more value in a highly competitive or rapidly changing business environment than in one more staid, which is consistent with propositions put forward by Matusik and Hill (1998).

The financial markets recognize the potential of the new drug formulation, and the share-value reflects the perceived likelihood of future returns to shareholders. Furthermore, this market value will adjust with the changes in the competitive and economic environments that affect potential sales and profits.

The research and development and the resulting new drug is part of intellectual capital. The company's stock of knowledge generates not only immediate benefit but real options as well. The more intense the competitive environment, the greater the importance of this knowledge and the greater its erosion by external forces. To maintain competitive advantage, companies need to continually invest in their intellectual capital.

VALUE CREATED BY CONTRACTING KNOWLEDGE WORKERS

Using the strategic net-present-value framework, investment in intellectual capital can be valued in a manner that has the potential to reconcile the difference between a company's book- and market-values that is attributable to its intellectual capital. Lepak and Snell (1999) present a simple framework for the value generated by an expenditure in skills development: the ratio of strategic benefits to the customer derived from the new skills relative to the costs incurred to develop them. More explicitly, investments in intellectual capital adds value if they help a firm either offer lower cost or provide increased benefits to customers, enhancing strategic competitive advantage.

The use of technical and professional contingent knowledge-workers for work critical to the organization appears to be increasing (Booth 1997). Correspondingly, the loss of private knowledge, and the absorption of new knowledge and intellectual capital by the organization before these workers leave, is becoming more of a concern. This is particularly vexing if such contingent workers are performing work surrounding the core competency of the organization and in the creation of proprietary knowledge.

As noted by Matusik and Hill (1998: 680), "contingent work is an increasingly integral part of the world of work . . . to accumulate knowledge, create value, and establish competitive advantage." There are, however, considerable costs and risks associated with using contingent knowledge-workers in wealth creation, particularly if the knowledge and intellectual capital that develops is tacit, private, or competitive knowledge in the firm.

Benefits

Numerous benefits of contingent work have been identified over the years and are summarized by Matusik and Hill (1998). The main reasons firms use contingent workers are to acquire special expertise and gain labour flexibility in doing so (Booth 1997). This activity can produce lower employee benefit costs, provide companies with the ability to quickly change the size of the workforce in response to seasonal or cyclical changes in product demand and meet needs for higher-end skills.

These benefits are exceeded, perhaps by orders of magnitude, by the strategic benefits from contracting knowledge workers. Innovation occurs when two separate knowledge grids are brought together (Carayannis and Alexander 1999; Matusik and Hill 1998; Quinn 1999). The benefits to be gained from this include product innovation, process innovation, and optional investments. Each of these is described below.

Product innovation. Product innovation translates into new products and services or improvements in existing offerings that customers value and are willing to pay for, either more often (increasing unit sales), for a longer period of time (increasing the duration of unit sales), or at a premium (increasing profit margin). Product innovation can sustain or enhance power in the supply chain.

Process innovation. Process innovation can yield cost reductions due to more efficient operations, better quality output, and lower direct costs per unit and can possibly allow greater command over suppliers. Process innovation can also stem the erosion of knowledge assets as competitors move ahead, thereby maintaining strategic value that may have been lost had the company not enhanced its knowledge.

Optional or contingent investments. Subsequent optional product and process innovation can allow for more of the above benefits with additional investment. For instance, the development of new products or features can be commercialized at a later date, if and when conditions warrant.

Costs

In addition to many benefits typically associated with contingent knowledge-workers, there are costs. In addition to those commonly cited costs, summarized by Matusik and Hill (1998), organizations face concerns surrounding legal issues, loyalty, and commitment to the organization, and how benefits should be allocated to those considered contracted or contingent knowledge-workers (Booth 1997). The question of who the employer is, and how the organization should define rights and obligations of both parties, remains somewhat vague at this point. That contingent workers do not have the same degree of attachment to the organization in terms of loyalty and commitment is problematic. The psychological employment-contract terms cannot be applied. Further, there is no real job security, nor are benefits provided to contingent workers as they are to regular employees. Despite this, there is often a perception of internal inequities among regular employees, since contingent knowledge-workers are often paid a premium (Booth 1997). Other costs noted by Matusik and Hill (1998) include the potential losses associated with firm-specific private knowledge dissemination and leakage of private-component knowledge.

Potentially, the most significant of the costs of a contingent arrangement with a knowledge worker is the leakage of core competence knowledge to the public domain, allowing competitors to encroach on the market share. This would be measurable in the probable unit sales lost to competitors or producers of substitute products or reduced profit margin because of the smaller incremental advantage the consumer perceives in the product over the competitor's offering. As well, with lost proprietary knowledge, time-to-obsolescence can be shorter and power over the supply chain eroded, reducing cost-and-price advantages. Dispersed knowledge of process can allow competitors to gain efficiencies, nullifying cost advantages. As well, lost knowledge can close down options: namely, optional projects that would have had the potential for generating further unit sales and contribution margins.

Eroding-Base Case

It is important to stress that, particularly in knowledge-intensive industries, the status quo does not persist. A firm that is not continually advancing its knowledge risks loss of market-share or contribution margin due to advancement by competitors. Thus, in considering the incremental costs and benefits of an investment in intellectual capital, one must be mindful of the eroding-base case, or "do-nothing" alternative.

Varying Risks

When exposing core competency to contingent knowledge-workers, the firm's relative ability to absorb new knowledge will influence whether there is a net gain or loss of strategic value. Inkpen (1998: 76) writes of a learning-curve involved in the diffusion of learning, which includes the development of skills necessary for knowledge acquisition. These are refined with practice and enhanced by an organizational structure and culture that encourages the sharing of knowledge. The amount of benefit gained depends on the firm's own knowledge level, its absorptive capacity, and its ability to integrate it with its current stock of knowledge (Inkpen 1998). Thus, the amount of strategic value garnered by a company from hiring contingent workers is somewhat controllable.

Of course, the dissemination of valuable, private, core-competence knowledge to the public domain via the contingent knowledge-worker is a risk. This is the basis on which Quinn (1999) promotes the outsourcing of all but the core activities and possibly essential non-core activities. This protects the valuable private knowledge from being expropriated. Tacit knowledge, gained and shared, cannot be controlled, although this may be limited, anyway. Also, a company may be able to put some legal restrictions on dissemination of explicit knowledge.

The difference between tacit and explicit knowledge and the *appropriability* of these have led researchers to question whether the risk is all that high. In the example given by Carayannis and Alexander (1999), the reverse-engineering of a product reveals some explicit knowledge but does not reveal the tacit and architectural knowledge that contributed to it. Likewise, a contingent worker may not be able to capture and transport enough of the organization's or the workers' tacit knowledge to be a material threat. Thus, the risk of loss of valuable knowledge to the public domain may depend on the tacitness-explicitness of the knowledge being exposed.

As well, the rate of change in the environment can affect the risk of contingent work and exposure of private knowledge. Matusik and Hill (1998) suggest that, in very knowledge intensive and dynamic competitive environments, the turnover of knowledge is so great that no private knowledge-based competitive advantage lasts for long. In such an environment, there may be much greater risk of *not* importing public-domain knowledge into core-competency areas.

Matusik and Hill (1998) describe the circumstances under which they expect a net gain or net loss of knowledge from the employment of contingent knowledge-workers. They compare stable-versus-dynamic industries with mild-versus-intense cost-and-flexibility pressures and propose the most beneficial combinations for bringing in contingent knowledge-workers (Table 15-2) and how close to the core competency

Table 15-2
Considerations for when to use contingent work

Cost and flexibility pressures	Environment	
	Stable	Dynamic
Mild	• High value on knowledge preservation • Low value on knowledge creation • Low value on public knowledge accumulation • Low value on direct cost saving	• Low value on knowledge preservation • High value on knowledge creation • High value on public knowledge accumulation • Low value on direct cost saving
Intense	• High value on knowledge preservation • Low value on knowledge creation • Low value on public knowledge accumulation • High value on direct cost saving	• Low value on knowledge preservation • High value on knowledge creation • High value on public knowledge accumulation • High value on direct cost saving

Matusik and Hill, 1998: 690.

Table 15-3
Where to use contingent work

Importance, magnitude of cost saving and flexibility	Evaluation of knowledge importance	
	Dissemination risks outweigh creation gains	Creation gains outweigh dissemination risks
Low	• Do not use	• Use only in core value-creation areas
High	• Use, but not in core value-creation areas	• Use, especially in core-value creation areas

Matusik and Hill, 1998: 691.

they should be employed (Table 15-3). With this, they describe different competitive environments in which employing contingent knowledge-workers where they are exposed to core competencies may be essential to sustaining competitive advantage.

For Better or Worse?

As shown in Table 15-3, in a dynamic, intensely competitive environment, Matusik and Hill (1998: 690–91) believe the benefits of contingent knowledge-workers exceed the costs and potential for loss of competitive advantage. They therefore "challenge the one-size-fits-all adage that firms should insulate core areas" (680). Although evidence to support the propositions is not provided, they are credible. They are also consistent with the tenets of real-option valuation that likewise favors the investment in a more volatile environment.

To determine the validity of these propositions, a framework for evaluating investments in intellectual capital is needed. A capital-budgeting and/or real-option valuation approach, with identification of the potential net-cash-flows as described here, is appropriate for this task. This is not only because intellectual capital is considered an asset but also because such expenditures have the potential to generate incremental cash flows and options well into the future. These increases in projected cash flows and real options will eventually be reflected in the market value of the company's stock of knowledge and will correspondingly increase the gap between book value and market value. The strategic capital-budgeting and/or real-option valuation model has the ability to approximate this increase in market value.

With regard to the contingent knowledge-worker investment specifically, more needs to be known about the nature and magnitude of the various costs, benefits, options, and risks involved, and how they differ in the various competitive environments described by Matusik and Hill (1998). Research in this topic will also lend understanding to valuation of intellectual capital in general. In the meantime, at least adopting a capital-budgeting and real-option mind-set can assist with decisions regarding such investments in intellectual capital.

Conclusion

Booth (1998: 28) stresses the need for a model to measure intellectual capital, recognizing this is a difficult task. "The limits of what can be achieved do not depend on the mathematics or the modelling tools but only on the depth of understanding of what is being modelled. The real difficulty is not so much the classification, identification, and measurement of intellectual capital but instead, making the link between acceleration of intellectual capital and financial performance."

The underlying principles of the model for evaluating the introduction of contingent knowledge-workers presented here can be extended to the valuation of the company's stock of intellectual capital (Bontis 2002). According to investment theory, the market value of a firm is the present value of expected returns to shareholders. This fluctuates as opportunities gained and lost in the marketplace are revealed. The value of the company's intellectual capital arises from its ability to generate and sustain profits and develop new sources of competitive advantage and corresponding revenues. Although some of these benefits are latent and difficult to predict, they are tangible outputs and their value can be estimated using discounted cash-flow analysis and real-option valuation techniques.

REFERENCE

Amit, R. and P. Schoemaker. 1993. Strategic Assets and Organizational Rents, *Strategic Management Journal* 14: 33–47.

Bassi, L. and M. Van Buren. 1999. Valuing Investments in Intellectual Capital, *International Journal of Technology Management* 18, 5–8: 414–32.

Black, F. and M. Scholes. 1973. The Pricing of Options and Corporate Liabilities, *Journal of Political Economy* 81 (May-June): 637–59.

Bontis, N., M. Crossan, and J. Hulland. 2002. Managing an Organizational Learning System by Aligning Stocks and Flows, *Journal of Management Studies* 39, 4.

Bontis, N. 2001. Assessing Knowledge Assets: A Review of the Models Used to Measure Intellectual Capital, *International Journal of Management Reviews* 3, 1: 41–60.

Bontis, N., N. Dragonetti, K. Jacobsen, and G. Roos. 1999. The Knowledge Toolbox: A Review of the Tools Available to Measure and Manage Intangible Resources, *European Management Journal* 17, 4: 391–402.

Booth, P. 1997. *Contingent Work: Trends, Issues and Challenges for Employers*. Ottawa: The Conference Board of Canada.

Booth, R. 1998. The Measurement of Intellectual Capital, *Management Accounting* 76, 10: 26–28.

Carayannis, E. and J. Alexander. 1999. The Wealth of Knowledge: Converting Intellectual Property to Intellectual Capital in Co-operative Research and Technology Management Settings, *International Journal of Technology Management* 18, 3–4: 326–53.

Cheung, J. 1993. Managerial Flexibility in Capital Investment Decisions: Insights from the Real Options Literature, *Journal of Accounting Literature* 12, 29–66.

Cox, J., S. Ross, and M. Rubinstein. 1979. Option Pricing: a Simplified Approach, *Journal of Financial Economics* 7 (September): 229–63.

Handy, C. 1991. *The Age of Unreason.* Cambridge, Mass.: Harvard Business School Press.

Henderson, R. and I. Cockburn. 1994. Measuring Competence? Exploring Firm Effects in Pharmaceutical Research, *Strategic Management Journal* 15: 63–84.

Horibe, F. 1999. *Managing Knowledge Workers: New Skills and Attitudes to Unlock the Intellectual Capital in Your Organization.* Toronto: Wiley and Sons.

Inkpen, A. 1998. Learning and Knowledge Acquisition through Internal Strategic Alliances, *Academy of Management Executive* 12, 4: 69–80.

Leonard-Barton, D. 1992. Core Capabilities and Core Rigidities: A Paradox in Managing New Product Development, *Strategic Management Journal* 13: 111–25.

Lepak, D. and S. Snell. 1999. The Human Resource Architecture: Toward a Theory of Human Capital Allocation and Development, *Academy of Management Review* 24, 1: 31–48.

Matusik, S. and C. Hill. 1998. The Utilization of Contingent Work, Knowledge Creation and Competitive Advantage, *Academy of Management Review* 23, 4: 680–98.

McGrath, R. 1999. Falling Forward: Real Options Reasoning and Entrepreneurial Failure, *Academy of Management Review* 24, 1: 13–30.

Merton, R. 1977. On the Pricing of Contingent Claims and the Modigliani-Miller Theorem, *Journal of Financial Economics* 5 (November): 241–49.

Micalizzi, A., P. Pellissari, and A. Gamba. 1999. *Valuing the Launch of a New Pharmaceutical Product.* Northern Finance Association 1999 Annual Conference. Alberta.

Nelson, R. and S. Winter. 1982. *An Evolutionary Theory of Economic Change.* Cambridge, Mass.: Belknap Press of Harvard University Press.

Nonaka, I. and H. Takeuchi. 1995. *The Knowledge-Creating Company.* New York: Oxford University Press.

Pearce, J. 1993. Toward an Organizational Behavior of Contract Laborers: Their Psychological Involvement and Effects on Employee Co-workers, *Academy of Management Journal* 36: 1082–1096.

Polanyi, M. 1962. *Personal Knowledge: Towards a Postcritical Philosophy.* Chicago: University of Chicago Press.

Polanyi, M. 1966. *The Tacit Dimension.* Garden City, N.Y.: Doubleday.

Quinn, J. B. 1999. Strategic Outsourcing: Leveraging Knowledge Capabilities, *Sloan Management Review* 4, 4: 9–21.

Roslender, R. 2000. Accounting for Intellectual Capital: a Contemporary Management Accounting Perspective, *Management Accounting* (March): 34–37.

Stewart, T. 1997. *Intellectual Capital: The New Wealth of Organizations.* New York: Doubleday.

Trigeorgis, L. 1988. A Conceptual Options Framework for Capital Budgeting, *Advances in Futures and Options Research* 3: 145–67.

Trigeorgis, L. 1993. The Nature of Option Interactions and the Valuation of Investments with Multiple Real Options, *Journal of Financial and Quantitative Analysis* 28, 1 (March): 1–20.

16

MANAGING HUMAN CAPITAL WITH COMPETENCY-BASED HUMAN RESOURCES MANAGEMENT

Laurent M. Lapierre
Human Resource Systems Group Ltd., Ottawa, Canada
llapierre@hrmcanada.com

and

Lorraine McKay
Human Resource Systems Group Ltd., Ottawa, Canada
lmckay@hrmcanada.com

ABSTRACT

This chapter outlines for practitioners the conceptualization underlying the practice of competency-based Human Resource Management (HRM) as a method for effectively managing an organization's human capital. Management processes developed in accordance with such a framework are designed to hire applicants holding the most promise in terms of the human capital they bring to the firm and to then develop and reward employees in such a way as to ensure that they make the strongest possible contributions to the organization. The chapter ends with a list of best-practice features of current human resource information systems designed to facilitate the process of competency-based human resource management.

INTRODUCTION

Successful organizations in today's competitive global market place must be nimble and able to quickly capitalize on new innovations to gain and/or retain a competitive advantage. They must have systems, processes, and an embedded culture that allows them to quickly share and benefit from innovations, "best practices," and "lessons learned." Progressive organizations value and nurture the knowledge, skills, and experience that employees possess and that contribute to the achievement of the organization's strategic goals and long-term success. Indeed, it is these various employee attributes that define the organization's human capital. The key question therefore is: how can organizations measure and influence the specific employee skills, knowledge, and experience that will result in a competitive advantage?

COMPETENCIES AS A FUNDAMENTAL MEASURE OF HUMAN CAPITAL

In his recent book, Dr. Jac Fitz-Enz (2000) argued strongly for the necessity to measure the return on investment (ROI) of human capital. Indeed, costs related to the development or acquisition of human capital (e.g., compensation and benefits, training, recruitment, and selection) can exceed 40 percent of corporate expenses. It only makes sense to try to ensure that human capital investments are made wisely and that they have the desired impact on an organization's level of service and productivity as well as the quality of its products. A number of metrics exist to try to capture the bottom-line return on human capital investment. The human capital return-on-investment (HCROI) measure, taken as an example, looks at profitability per monies spent on employee pay and benefits. Thus, if the ratio is high, employees are worth their pay and benefits because they are presumably doing a very good job (i.e., they are highly productive, or they ensure quality of service or products). However, if the ratio is low, employee-related costs are not being adequately reflected in gains for the organization. Thus, there would be a need to get "better" employees in order to raise the ratio. Where the HCROI is an example of a measure that captures the return on human capital investment for the entire organization, other metrics can be used to form the basis of such measures at the business unit or team level (e.g., overall quality of service offered by the unit) and even the individual employee level (e.g., attainment of specified sales quota).

"Bottom-line" metrics, such as the HCROI, can be used to gauge over a finite time period the effect of human capital invest-ments on the success of the organization. Unfortunately, these measures do not capture why some employees are more successful in providing added value to their organization than others. In addition, these various measures fail to exclude other factors that would have an impact on the bottom line and that are outside the control of employees or managers (e.g., fluctuations in product or labor markets, defective machinery, changes in company policy or in business processes). Spencer and Spencer (1993) introduced the notion of employee competencies that captures the various knowledge, skills, abilities, experience, and other attributes that employees use to be successful on the job and bring added value to their organization. Competencies are defined in terms of pat-terns of employee behavior that lead to success on the job for either that immediate employee, his or her work group or unit, or for the organization as a whole. Because these are defined behav-iorally, they are observable and therefore measurable. In addition, competencies are strictly under the control of each individual employee.

Competencies define *how* employees achieve their business objec-tives (e.g., meeting a particular sales quota) or fulfill their areas of accountability (e.g., account management). They more clearly explain why some employees are more successful than others. For example, the *results-orientation* competency may be defined as "focusing one's efforts on achieving quality results consistent with the organization's vision." However, the specific meaning of "results orientation" is not clearly conveyed until defined in terms of a series of observable, and therefore measurable, actions or behaviors that successful employees display on the job. Thus, taking the definition one step further, employees who display the results-orientation competency could engage in the following types of activities:

- Set challenging yet realistic goals in line with team/unit goals
- Seek feedback from others on ways to improve
- Anticipate, identify, and effectively deal with problems or risks
- Plan for contingencies to deal with unexpected events or setbacks
- Identify and take advantage of opportunities as they arise

- Look for innovative ways to improve efficiency, stretch budget, and save resources
- Regularly evaluate their own work performance for ways to improve

These various activities or behaviors should be those that the organization feels would help the employee be successful in his or her job or role. Properly defined competencies translate the strategic goals, vision, and values of the organization into measurable behaviors that employees must display for the organization to be successful. They provide the framework and foundation for managing and focusing the organization's human capital on the organization's strategic goals.

Various categories of competencies exist and different organizations give them different names. Three very useful categories are presented as follows.

- Core competencies: these are competencies that organizations feel all of their employees should demonstrate to some extent on the job, because they underlie the vision, mission, and values of the organization. Examples could include "continuous learning" (the extent to which an employee takes active measures to enhance his or her level of work-related knowledge and expertise) or "teamwork" (the extent to which one works with others to support the overall objectives of the team).
- Functional competencies: these refer to competencies that are specific to particular business functions within the organization, such as "account management" (an employee's ability at ensuring the current and future needs of specific customers are dealt with in an expedient and appropriate manner), which could be specific to a firm's customer support function.
- Technical and/or professional competencies: these competencies would be specific to particular jobs or job families (i.e., jobs that are similar in their areas of accountability). Examples include, "knowledge of Windows NT operating system" or "knowledge of accounting and auditing." These types of competencies usually refer to areas of specific knowledge. It is important, however, for organizations wanting to use these competencies to agree upon a detailed definition that would describe them in behavioral terms (e.g., can reconfigure system-security parameters in accordance with departmental policy), so that it may be observable and easily measurable.

A *competency model or profile* refers to a set of unique and distinguishable competencies. Profiles may encompass various employee groups that require the same set of competencies. However, some employee groups (e.g., business functions) might require distinct profiles. Thus, the various competency profiles define which patterns of job-related behaviors set these jobs or groups of jobs apart. It is the variety of jobs within a particular organization that will dictate the number of profiles that are necessary.

Competency profiles may be defined in terms of graduated proficiency levels. For example, behaviors defining "results orientation" would probably be different for a director than for a front-line supervisor. Scaled competency profiles allow us to define the different behavioral expectations at different hierarchical levels within the organization for a given competency. Thus, though a group of jobs may all be assigned the same competency profile, not all jobs within that group will require the same competency proficiency levels. See Table 16-1 for an example of a scaled competency definition. This example includes a general definition of the competency, the notions underlying each proficiency level of that competency, and behavioral indicators under each level that more clearly describe expected behavior that would exemplify the competency. Please note that the different proficiency levels are cumulative, in that the demonstration of the competency at one level of proficiency assumes the employee demonstrates the competency at lower levels of proficiency as well.

Implementing Competency Profiles

Once competency profiles have been developed for specific jobs or groups of jobs within an organization or for the organization as a whole, specific HRM processes may be developed in accordance with these profiles, including recruitment and selection systems, employee performance management processes, learning and development, career planning, HR planning, and compensation. Since competencies are defined in terms of the various patterns of behavior that help employees achieve success at work, basing the various HRM practices listed above on competency profiles specifically created for a particular organization will help ensure that these various investments in human capital offer the highest return on investment. In effect, they establish the measurement standard used to make decisions in each of these various HRM processes.

Table 16-1
Example of a scaled competency

Teamwork: Through information sharing, works within and across organizational units to achieve common goals and positive results.

Level 1	Level 2	Level 3	Level 4	Level 5
Participates as a team member	Fosters teamwork	Demonstrates informal leadership in teams	Resolves interpersonal conflict	Creates and fosters a culture of teamwork
• Assumes personal responsibility and follows up on commitments to others • Deals honestly and fairly with others, showing consideration and respect for differences in opinion or in work methods	• Seeks others' input and involvement and listens to their viewpoints • Openly recognizes when a compromise is required for the greater good of the team	• Looks for opportunities to work with other groups or organizational areas • Initiates discussion of problems/issues with team members that could impact on results • Communicates expectations for teamwork and collaboration • Gives credit and acknowledges contributions and efforts of individuals to team effectiveness • Suggests or develops methods and means for maximizing the input and involvement of team members	• Coaches or advises team members on how to resolve differences or deal with conflicts to achieve mutually beneficial outcomes • Initiates collaboration on projects or methods of operating	• Promotes a culture and environment that fosters highly effective teams (e.g., breaks down historical barriers) • Establishes reward and recognition mechanisms and structures that promote effective teamwork

Recruitment and Selection

The purpose of any recruitment campaign should be to attract those candidates that will fit best with the job-to-be-staffed and the organization overall. The recruitment process allows prospective employees to gauge whether they would like to work within a particular organization. Put otherwise, they are given the opportunity to determine whether an employer will help them achieve their career ambitions and fulfill their ideals. It is therefore crucial for employers to give candidates the most realistic job preview so that their expectations are met, once hired. Research has suggested that realistic job previews can help ensure employee retention (Catano, Cronshaw, Wiesner, et al. 1997). Mentioning the required competencies in recruitment campaigns or job postings will undoubtedly help clarify what is expected of prospective employees, thereby increasing the realism of the job preview and helping ensure that those candidates who apply for the positions are those who truly want to work in accordance with those expectations.

A recruitment campaign usually results in identifying a number of employees who can potentially meet the requirements of particular jobs or roles. The organization must now select, among the candidates in this selection pool, those that would add the highest value to the firm. Competency profiles are instrumental in this regard, in that they tell hiring managers which knowledge, skills, abilities, and other attributes candidates must possess to be successful once hired. It is usually quite easy to determine whether a job candidate has the necessary technical or professional competencies to perform well on the job. Such information can be found via academic credentials, inquiring into previous experience, or job-knowledge tests (Gatewood and Feild 1998). What is more difficult to gauge, however, is whether a particular candidate has the necessary level of initiative, or required ability to work effectively with others as a member of a team or to provide regular coaching and mentoring. These "softer" competencies are more subjective in nature and are therefore more difficult to measure. They are, however, no less important to success on the job. Indeed, most terminated employees are fired because of poor soft skills than because of a lack of technical expertise.

Though more difficult to assess, it is quite possible to measure these softer competencies using various assessment techniques. The most commonly used approach is the structured behavioral interview, also referred to as the *patterned behavior description interview* (Janz

1982). This approach helps hiring managers determine whether employees have demonstrated the required competencies in previous roles or jobs by asking them to describe, behaviorally, how they dealt with particular types of work-related situations in the past. Such interview questions usually take the form of "tell me about a time when you. . . ." If candidates have not had enough previous experience to warrant asking questions about previous work behavior, then hiring managers can ask more hypothetical questions that assess the actions (behaviors) candidates would take to address a particular work-related situation. Questions posed using such an interview approach usually include the statement, "what would you do if . . ." This type of interview is commonly referred to as the *situational interview* (Latham, Saari, Pursell, and Campion 1980). Both of these interview types are successful in predicting future success on the job (Gatewood and Feild 1998), thanks to the use of a detailed competency profile that describes expected behavior on the job. Indeed, competency profiles can be used as an interview scoring-guide to determine whether the candidate has previously demonstrated, or would be likely to demonstrate, the required competencies. Using a scaled competency approach is quite advantageous in this situation, since it helps hiring managers distinguish between candidates who seem to demonstrate higher versus lower levels of proficiency on the same competency.

Performance Management and Employee Learning and Development

Performance management refers to the setting of work-related objectives for employees, monitoring their work toward the accomplishment of these objectives, giving useful and immediate feedback and positive reinforcement to ensure the continuation of effective behavior, formally evaluating the successful accomplishment of the set objectives, and determining steps that will allow the employee to improve his or her level of performance. One of the most difficult aspects of effectively managing the performance of employees is giving feedback that they can effectively use to improve their performance on the job. Many supervisors are less than clear when trying to describe better ways of performing one's duties. Competency profiles are quite useful in this regard by helping managers more clearly express the behaviors they expect and assess how employees are behaving on the job, against the standards set forth by the competency profile. The profile also guides the manager in giving behavioral feedback, such that employees can more easily grasp how they can alter their approach to work in such a way as to achieve their objectives or fulfill their areas of accountability. Thus, since competencies define how a job is done, well-developed competency profiles help managers coach employees on how to better do their jobs.

The performance management process usually incorporates decisions and actions taken to develop levels of employee competence. Indeed, when setting work-related goals with employees, managers can also set developmental objectives or learning assignments for the same review period that would be needed based on observed competency gaps. These learning objectives can be given to allow an employee to simply become better at his or her job, or to follow his or her preferred career path. Indeed, if the manager and employee know what the competency requirements are for the various positions along that employee's career path, then it is much easier to determine which competencies must be developed to help that employee fulfill his or her career ambitions. Providing employees with such career guidance and support has been shown to increase their levels of organizational and career commitment, thereby reducing their intentions to leave both their organization and their occupation (Hackett, Lapierre, and Hausdorf in press; Meyer and Allen 1997).

Competency profiles not only help both employees and managers clearly assess which competencies need to be developed to ensure success on the job or in future jobs but they also facilitate the development of specific training programs and learning activities targeted to the specific competency requirements of jobs or groups of jobs. There are various methods available to employees that would allow them to improve their levels of competence, such as on-the-job assignments or activities, books, videos, and offsite-, onsite-, or online-courses. Basing such learning activities on well-developed competency models helps to ensure that these activities yield the highest possible return on investment. In addition, if the organization has in place a method of rolling-up, or aggregating, the assessed competency levels of the members of a business unit or of the overall organization, such information can serve as a useful guide in determining and planning where the corporate training-and-development budget should be spent in order to fill the largest gaps in employee competence across the organization. One can see the strategic relevance of gathering such information. Finally, competency profiles can be used to measure the success of a particular training initiative. If the training was successful, it should be reflected in the observed competence of employees on the job. Such higher levels of competence should also yield stronger bottom-line results. Thus, changes in bottom-line metrics should also be tracked and compared to competency-based metrics. This comparison would help organizations determine whether the changes in bottom-line metrics are solely attributable to changes in employee levels of competence or to other uncontrolled factors as well.

Human Resource Planning

Human resource planning refers to the process of identifying the specific human capital needs of the firm in light of its business objectives and of determining whether such human capital exists within the organization or must be sought out externally. Competency models help organizations determine the specific employee requirements across the organization, and, thanks to the implementation of a competency-based performance management system, help HR planners determine whether the required competencies already exist somewhere inside the organization. If they do not, a well-designed recruitment and selection system targeting specific competencies would be of significant benefit. Alternatively, employee learning and development programs would help develop the competencies of current employees to take on new or modified roles. Again, one can clearly see the strategic relevance of building valid competency profiles for the various employee groups within an organization.

Compensation

There is some debate as to whether employees should be rewarded for the demonstration of competencies instead of, or in addition to, the successful achievement of their work objectives (e.g., increase sales target by 10 percent) or job accountabilities (e.g., conduct employee-performance appraisals). Indeed, if one rewards for behaviors and not work-results, employees might focus on behaviors at the expense of results. However, some types of behavior (competencies) affect other employees, departments, or the organization as a whole (e.g., sharing business-relevant information with other employees or departments, supporting the generation of ideas from other employees) that do not directly affect an employee's success in

17

A DIALECTICAL MODEL FOR BEST-PRACTICES DEVELOPMENT

Michael Charney
ServiceWare, Parsippany, New Jersey, U.S.A.
mcharney@serviceware.com

ABSTRACT

The practice of developing Knowledge Management (KM) systems for many different types of businesses relies necessarily on the expertise of KM practitioners. However, the practice of KM has itself rapidly become stultified through the overemphasis on static "best practices." In this chapter we discuss an alternate framework for the effective implementation and management of KM initiatives. The seven-stage framework is based on dialectical theory and recognizes that KM projects are themselves constantly involving creations, dependent on both the specific business and cultural factors being addressed, as well as the individual capabilities and talents of those performing the work. Rather than forcing individuals into a defined practice, the framework proposes, instead, that practitioners be given an overriding thematic and high-level methodology for performing their tasks, while leaving the definition and implementation of those specific tasks up to the individuals themselves, allowing them to account for individual differences across varied implementations. At the same time, the framework suggests a KM system for managing KM projects—thus encouraging the reusability of previously created techniques wherever possible and, as appropriate, for the subsequent projects being performed.

INTRODUCTION

As Knowledge Management (KM) grows as a business initiative, it becomes strikingly clear that nearly any business venture can benefit from the application of KM principles and practices, particularly those that are "knowledge-based": engineering organizations, research laboratories, consulting houses, marketing organizations, software organizations, and so on (Brooking 1999). Analysts report strong growth (Mullich 2000), and more corporations are embarking on KM, either departmentally or across the entire enterprise. How best to actually implement KM, however, is still the subject of discovery and debate, and the bulk of such advice concentrates largely on theory and critical factors: the importance of executive commitment, the need (or non-need) of developing a knowledge culture, and so on (Dixon 2000).

More recently, however, books and articles have begun to appear that attempt to bridge the gap between the theoretical and practical approaches to KM (Tiwana 2000; Bukowitz 1999; Rowland 2000). Though these approaches begin to clarify "step-by-step" approaches to the implementation of KM, there is still a dearth of targeted materials that translate into specific missions and objectives for particular business problems. Nowhere is this shortcoming more apparent than in the gap between the KM initiatives that need doing and the KM analysts who actually perform the work. In essence, there is a pressing need to develop a KM practice around how to implement KM, both for departments and for enterprises as a whole. Development of such a "meta-KM" has the potential for providing the fuel that will explode the growth of KM initiatives.

The common model for meta-KM definitions is to prescribe a set of "best practices," collected together as a methodology, and then use that methodology to provide a strict roadmap for the implementation of a KM project. However, this approach—inherited from both software development and process analysis (and used with varying degrees of success in each) stultifies the uniquely dynamic nature of knowledge and the combination of art and science that goes into knowledge-modeling. Simply put, KM initiatives are different from other business practice initiatives: they are more inclusive, more involved with people than with process or technology, and more subject to systemic flows that are chaotic, at best. The approach of developing a set of best practices for KM is doomed unless it treats this reality with respect and care, incorporating in any definition of competency models throughout the organization, strengths and weaknesses can be rated against expected competency levels or requirements for specific groups or across the organization.

- Interview question banks categorized by competencies. These questions can be designed to serve both reference checking and candidate interviewing purposes.

Though the HRIS provides potential for efficiency and access, such electronic support should not eliminate the dialogue that must exist among employees and between employees and their managers. Thus, the data collected via the HRIS should form the basis of useful discussions regarding the change and development of employees and the organization as a whole.

COMPETENCIES AND BOTTOM-LINE PERFORMANCE METRICS

As discussed earlier in this chapter, it is strongly recommended, where possible, to measure the impact of human capital on the level of service, quality, and productivity of a particular organization (Fitz-Enz 2000). Competencies do not tell organizations how successful they are, but they do offer them the necessary information for assessing why they are more successful, or why they are not as successful, as they would like to be. Thus, competency-based measures should be used in conjunction with bottom-line measures, so that organizations can implement HRM initiatives that will have the highest return on investment. Also, these two sources of information, as mentioned earlier in this chapter, can be used jointly to understand whether the level of success of an organization is largely attributable to issues of employee competence or to other situational or contextual factors outside of their control. Thus, tracking employee competence levels can be used as a diagnostic tool in understanding the factors underlying corporate success.

CONCLUSIONS

Competency profiles form the basis for the measurement of human capital within an organization. Determining the competency requirements for all jobs or roles within an organization guides the creation of value-added HRM processes, including recruitment and selection, performance management, employee learning-and-development, career-planning, and compensation. There is no single best method for developing competency profiles for an organization. It is important, however, that they be developed with the interests, goals, and objectives of the organization in mind and that they be defined in terms of observable patterns of behavior that are relevant to the work environment of employees.

REFERENCES

Catano, V. M., S. F. Cronshaw, W. H. Wiesner, et al. 1997. *Recruitment and Selection in Canada.* Toronto, Ontario: ITP Nelson.

Fitz-Enz, J. 2000. *The ROI of Human Capital: Measuring the Economic Value of Employee Performance.* New York: Amacom.

Gatewood, R. D. and H. S. Feild. 1998. *Human Resource Selection.* Fourth edition. Toronto: Harcourt Brace College Publishers.

Hackett, R. D., L. M. Lapierre, and P. A. Hausdorf. Forthcoming. Understanding the Links Between Work Commitment Constructs, *Journal of Vocational Behaviour.*

Janz, T. 1982. Initial Comparisons of Patterned Behavior Description Interviews Versus Unstructured Interviews, *Journal of Applied Psychology* 67: 577–80.

Latham, G. P., L. M. Saari, E. D. Pursell, and M. A. Campion. 1980. The Situational Interview, *Journal of Applied Psychology* 65: 422–27.

Meyer, J. P. and N. A. Allen. 1997. *Commitment in the Workplace: Theory, Research, and Application.* Thousand Oaks, Calif.: Sage Publications.

Milkovich, G. T. and J. M. Newman. 1996. *Compensation.* Fifth edition. Toronto: Irwin.

Spencer, L. M. and S. M. Spencer. 1993. *Competence at Work: Models for Superior Performance.* Toronto: John Wiley and Sons.

meeting his or her individual work objectives. It therefore makes sense that employees be held accountable for the demonstration (or lack thereof) of these particular competencies. Also, it might only make sense to measure some job accountabilities by focusing on employee behavior. For example, should we only measure whether a manager has filled out all of her employees' performance appraisals, or should we also be assessing how she went about coaching and giving useful feedback to them? If an organization is interested in the latter as well, then it is necessary to measure job behavior or competencies. Thus, basing merit increases or bonuses partially on the demonstration of these competencies could be an effective way of rewarding employees for behaviors that describe the extent to which one has been successful in his or her role. This process would certainly help ensure that variable pay systems are rewarding and helping to promote behavior that leads to organizational success.

It is also possible to use competencies when determining the relative value of different jobs within an organization. Their relative value is defined in terms of the base salary assigned to each type of position within the firm. The resulting pay scale is intended to ensure internal consistency and equity across jobs (Milkovich and Newman 1996). Compensable factors are used to determine the relative value of each type of job. These factors are those characteristics in the work that the organization values, that help it pursue its strategy and achieve its objectives (Milkovich and Newman 1996). Traditionally, compensable factors have been grouped into four generic categories: skills required, effort required, responsibility, and working conditions. It is the variance across these four types of factors that explain the relative value of different jobs within an organization. It is entirely possible for an organization to use a set of core competencies under the category of "skills" as potential compensable factors. For example, assuming one of the core competencies is that of "leadership," a scaled definition of this competency that clearly explains the various proficiency levels at which it can be demonstrated can be used as one factor (among others) in measuring the relative value of different jobs within the organization. This assumes that, all things being equal, the organization values, and is willing to pay more money (in the form of base salary) for, those positions that require higher levels of leadership more than those that do not. This approach would be warranted if the organization believes that its success is a function of the quality of leadership demonstrated by employees. Using competencies for the determination of job value is only recommended if these competencies are deemed critical to the success of the organization and can be objectively measured (i.e., they should be clearly defined in behavioral terms using a scaled approach).

ELECTRONIC SUPPORT TOOLS

Today, various human resource information system (HRIS) providers offer organizations automated tools designed to help facilitate the sometimes lengthy process of administering a competency-based HRM system. Below is a list of best-practice features that you should look for in an HRIS that will make your life as a manager or HR professional much easier.

- The ability to create a competency catalogue (i.e., list of competencies that can be applied to all or specific groups and/or functions within the organization).
- The ability to custom define competencies (e.g., define as many proficiency levels as you want for any given competency).
- An automated competency assessment function where employees and managers can log on and evaluate either themselves or others within the organization for the purposes of performance feedback. This function should also present the employee or the manager with a gap analysis between his or her assessed competency levels and those required for his or her immediate job or any other job they wish to move to in the organization (thereby facilitating career-planning development).
- An automated "developmental tips" function that would accompany the gap analysis presented after competency assessments, so that employees and managers can determine which training-and-development initiatives to follow in order to improve their competency levels and achieve their career objectives. These automated suggestions should be directly linked to specific competency gaps observed and should include options such as on-the-job development activities or assignments, books, videos, in-house-, offsite-, or online-courses, and so on.
- Report wizards that allow senior managers to assess the overall competency, strengths, and weaknesses within particular groups, departments, or across the organizations as a whole. This feature is obviously necessary for effective HR planning and strategic learning-and-development initiatives. Thanks to the proper

roadmap the need for individuals to regularly create new roads them-selves in response to the context of the environment in which they are designing. What is needed is a *framework* for KM initiatives, but one that maximizes the opportunity for knowledge creation *about* knowledge creation. This chapter proposes such a framework, using the form of the dialectic both as a design-conceit and as a process within the approach that drives growth and change.

WHY BEST PRACTICES?

The argument for the framework begins with the assumption that the term *best practices* and the notion that they can be universally applied is faulty, ignoring the context in which such practices occur. I would argue further that the notion of practice must necessarily be expanded and defined to include both passive and active modes: pas-sively, a practice can be viewed as the set of operations that are per-formed; actively, however, a practice can be viewed as the performance of these acts. The former takes into account a set of pro-cesses and procedures, whereas the latter acknowledges that the indi-vidual(s) performing these processes and procedures take an active role in their development. This leads to a contradiction in the way knowledge work should happen: on the one hand, a fixed set of pro-cesses ensures quality, consistency, and usability across a KM imple-mentation, but on the other hand, that same fixed set of processes limits the creative potential of knowledge workers and the overall growth of the intellectual capital being managed (Bontis 1999).

The reasons for developing best practices have to do largely with the need for consistency and quality across knowledge work and with the very real business need for speed and surety of that work to meet conventional goals such as revenue recognition, volume activi-ties, and so on. As companies grow in scale and as the staff of knowl-edge workers becomes both more diverse and more remote (hence less subject to organizational panoptics), the best-practices method-ology emerges to provide a standardized way of performing certain tasks. However, standardization is impersonal and removes from the knowledge worker the freedom for creating new structures that solve real context-sensitive business problems. That freedom to create is a human need, and the best-practices methodology lies in opposition to it. The seemingly counterproductive conflict requires the dialecti-cal analysis in order to seed synthesis: how do we standardize a set of best practices and yet preserve the creative component of knowledge work that leads to innovation, solution, and knowledge creation?

The solution I propose addresses these apparently contradictory needs not as an oppositional conflict but as a dialectic out of which a synthesis can be formed; it is such a dialectical analysis that has produced the accompanying framework.

THE DIALECTIC FOR A BEST-PRACTICES FRAMEWORK

Dialectics (from the Greek *dialektos*) is a dialogue-based analysis of competing ideas—the thesis and antithesis—that then produces a synthesis, which then leads to another thesis-antithesis pairing, and so on. The purpose of dialectics is to investigate competing logics in an effort to reach a new level of understanding—in effect, a new knowledge of a situation or theory (McTaggart 1896). An effective description and example is given by Daloz (1986: 17):

> To begin, a "thesis" is stated or an assertion made (A). This is countered by a contradictory statement, or "antithesis," (B). Out of the two positions emerges a "synthesis," which, in turn, becomes the thesis for a further dialogue, countered by a further antithesis, and so on. In theory, the process goes on forever; there is no resting point. Truth is where the disputants choose to take a break. But a synthesis is not formed simply by merging thesis with antithesis in a kind of intellectual detente. Synthesis is not a compromise. If I suggest that an object is black and you counter by calling it white, our synthesis is not that it is grey. Rather, to reach agreement, we must come up with a formulation that accounts for both positions, doing damage to neither. We do this by leaping to a higher abstraction, by distanceing [*sic*] ourselves from it sufficiently that we can see the whole process, not just our own side of it. The object, we might agree, is both black and white, depending on where one is standing.

With respect to KM, the dialectic that I propose sets up what it is people need to *do* against what those same people need to *be*. Simply put, both the goals of the KM practice (standardization and ease of implementation) and the goals of the individual (discovery and creativity) must be met.

THE FRAMEWORK: SEVEN LEVELS OF DESCRIPTION AND ANALYSIS

Introducing a theoretical framework always requires some care: by its very nature, a framework intended to guide actual activities is *methodics* in this framework, each itself composed of numerous parts.

The purpose for defining a set of methodics is to inject *practicality* into the KM design process. A methodic provides practitioners with two fundamental building blocks necessary for any business implementation. First, it provides the specific goals for any one phase that must be achieved to proceed into later phases. (Often these goals are in the form of deliverables that require approval— as in the case of statistical outputs, charts, spreadsheets, or reports.) Second, the use of methodics makes it easy to clump efforts into project-manageable pieces, making it easier to monitor and adjust the time, resource, and cost scales commonly associated with any project (Wysocki 1995).

Methodics themselves can contain sequential and/or iterative phases; that is, they can be nested when the scope of the initiative requires project management at low levels of granularity.

Procedures

Procedures are classes of activities that can be conducted during the execution of a methodic. Within the framework, the term *procedure* serves an organizational function; they are categories of things-one-can-do but do not specify the "how" of actually accomplishing a task. Examples of procedures include surveys, interviews, statistical methods, and so on.

Procedures develop as a synthesis of methodical need and situational analysis. As an example, consider a particular methodic that requires data to be collected from individuals but where geography makes direct interviewing impractical. An effective procedure would be to survey appropriate individuals. Note that the choice of survey is the choice of procedure. There is no specific intimation as to the form that the survey should take.

The procedure component is the first of the pyramid-bottom components; procedures are created and modified by KM analysts through the application of dialectic. In the example above, the implied thesis is that "there is a need to gather detailed information from people," and an implied antithesis that "people are not available." The reached synthesis is that "information can be gathered from people who are not available through alternate means," in this case through a survey. Note that the synthesis is *not* a compromise, which would have taken the form "information can be gathered from some, but not all people," but rather is a "formulation that accounts for both positions" (Daloz 1986).

Techniques

Techniques are the variations available within procedural classes. They represent types and imply the activities a KM analyst will perform. Techniques are always a combination of two major elements: *medium* and *method*.

Medium refers to the way in which a particular technique is implemented. To continue the survey example, twenty years ago a survey would likely have been conducted by telephone or by mail. Today the same survey can be delivered electronically to a larger group in less time. And even within the electronic medium, there are additional options: e-mail, e-mail with forms, web-form, web-form with auto tabulation, and more.

Method refers to the way in which the technique is executed, and a single technique may include more than one method. The web-form electronic survey, for example, could consist of both "open-ended" questions and scalar questions; each of these represents a collection of *rudiments* (the questions themselves). In this example, then, two *types* of techniques are used in a single *medium*: open-ended and scalar survey questions presented as a web-form.

Techniques are also created through the dialectic process, with the needs of the project synthesized against the realities of the implementation environment. The result is the choice and/or creation of usable techniques within that context.

Instruments

Instruments are the actual, physical items used for a particular task on a particular project and are the most critical components in the framework. In the case of the survey we have been using as an example, the *instrument* is the actual survey, numbered and cataloged as appropriate for storage in a knowledge base.

The instruments created and collected by KM analysts represent the media for actual work performed by KM analysts in the field. As such, instruments are the targets for KM initiatives associated with developing analytical and consulting best-practices approaches within this framework. It is the effective management (through creation, quality assurance, accessibility, and/or delivery and usability)

Table 17-1
Expanded framework example, with specifics

Stage	Description
Thematic	"Ask a Question, Get an Answer"
Methodology	Knowledge Reservoir Analysis (KRA)
Methodics	There are six methodics in the KRA: Business Requirements Gathering Knowledge Location Knowledge Reservoir Mapping Limiting Factors Analysis Knowledge Base Construction Knowledge Testing
Procedures	Examples of procedures used within Methodic 4, Limiting Factors Analysis: Interviews Surveys Review of Literature
Techniques	Examples of techniques used within Procedure 1, Interviews: One-on-one; in person One-on-one; telephone Group meeting; live Group meeting; teleconference Group meeting; Web collaboration
Instruments	Examples of instruments and elements used within Technique 3, Group meeting; live: Questionnaire; open-ended questions Tape recording and transcription; open-ended questions Workflow modeling revelation, Visio capture
Rudiments	Examples of Rudiments used within Instrument 1, Questionnaire; open-ended questions: What kinds of problems do you find most difficult to solve? Where do you normally go for assistance with a difficult question? How do you get training on new subjects you need to learn in order to do your job more effectively?

As an example, KM initiatives aimed at providing knowledge for Web-based self-service have adopted a belief system that people need to (and will) learn something quickly and immediately, but only at the point of need. The thematic that drives this model is, "ask a question, get an answer." Ask Jeeves follows this model: their consumer-facing website allows an individual to ask any kind of question, and the system will attempt to find the one "answer" (or location of an answer). Vendors also use this approach in developing products and service models for their customers. E-service products across the marketplace share common assumptions in the way knowledge should be presented and the learning model of end-users. The pedagogy, then, drives the type, quality, form, and so on, of the knowledge and of the analysis and construction processes that go into the development of the KM system.

Other pedagogies are certainly possible. One international consulting organization uses an internal KM system based on the pedagogical principles that the knowledge user is looking to do something and that learning is best accomplished by facilitating that "doing" through narratives (both textual and visual) of others' similar experiences. As a result, the company has built a system to provide that expert narrative, accessible through the use of a "similar qualities search." The pedagogical principle results in the thematic—in this case, one centered on storytelling.

Regardless of the pedagogical principle in use by a particular organization, KM efforts, when well focused, will rely on an overriding thematic that drives the KM development process.

Methodology

Perhaps one of the most overused terms in business, *methodology* is improperly used to refer to everything from simple process modeling to full-scale strategic mapping; the confusions associated with the term have led to muddled expectations on the part of analysts, consultants, and customers. The term *methodology* is properly used when it refers to an understanding of how methods are constructed, and how those methods (along with their constituent parts) compose an integrated whole, one that is the targeted at a specific problem domain (Arbnor 1997).

In its simplest form, a methodology is a table of contents or outline in which each step in the methodology summarizes the rules needed to complete that step and move on to the next. It is not a collection of elements, nor is it developed from analysis of a collection of elements, but instead has more in common with the epistemological frameworks used to create the developmental pedagogies referred to earlier. Methodologies act as a necessary bridge between theoretical approaches and practical applications. They serve to guide practitioners along a path without designating specific steps they must take.

Methodics

Methodics is the organization of methodical procedures into an overarching study or practice (Arbnor 1997). I have expanded the definition to interpret these methodical procedures as phases in a methodology; it is these phases that I represent as individual

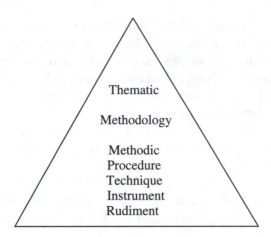

Figure 17-1 *The Pyramid Framework*

a semiotic system open to various interpretations, which, once decided upon, tend toward stasis. The risk is that the framework becomes a "recipe" rather than—as intended—a mental model. The framework presented below is intended only as a means for shaping ideas and not as a "roadmap" or "process."

Conceived visually as a pyramid, the framework contains seven components that emerge from the dialectic synthesis; the early (top) components are very general and become more specific as you move down through the framework (Figure 17-1). The components are the

- thematic: the overriding theme around which a KM effort will evolve
- methodology: a phased approach that describes the gross functions to be performed
- methodics: individual phases within the methodology
- procedures: the ways used to execute the tasks of a particular methodic
- techniques: variations of procedures that represent actual implementation
- instruments: the physical instantiations of a technique
- rudiments: the granular elements that make up an instrument

The framework is divided into "pyramid-top" and "pyramid-bottom" components. Pyramid-top elements (thematic, methodology, and methodics) are those that are generally defined by the organization, which means that, through discussion and facilitation, the KM implementation teams define the pyramid top in accordance with corporate goals and objectives, the assumptions of customer need based on target markets and penetration, analysis and consultative skills of the staff, and so on. Pyramid-bottom elements (procedures, techniques, instruments, and rudiments) are those created by KM analysts as a result of context-related implementations of KM within a specific organization. They are framed for the KM analyst based on work done previously by others, but they allow the individual to construct and create new elements and instruments as needed, based on individual analytical or consultative dialectics engaged in with a customer. Pyramid-bottom elements are collected, deconstructed, and entered into a knowledge delivery solution as part of the overall KM discipline. Others use such a knowledge delivery system on subsequent engagements to maximize reuse of elements and instruments wherever possible.

Table 17-1 shows a breakdown of the framework, with an example used for building KM systems for self-service and self-support. The component names were determined by the organization that performs the work; this analysis has placed those components within the overall framework.

Components of the Framework

The individual components are explained in the sections below. Each is defined with respect to its role in the KM initiative, the process by which it is understood, and its function within the dialectic.

Thematic

Any KM endeavor—whether large-scale or small—takes its direction from a corporate belief system. What is the organization attempting to accomplish? Is it inner-directed (toward employees) or outer-directed (toward customers)? What does it believe can be accomplished by maximizing the availability and movement of intellectual capital?

The answer to these questions, and the subsequent definition of a knowledge belief system, leads to the "theme" of the KM effort. Once articulated, the thematic designates the belief system surrounding KM within that organization. For teams that then implement KM for others, the thematic becomes a pedagogical principle, an assumption about how users will learn once knowledge is made available to them.

that moves the best-practices effort forward. The ultimate goal, of course, is to allow for a dynamic presentation of best practices for each individual engagement: a personalized best practice composed of appropriate instruments and based on the individual dialectic of each engagement.

Rudiments

Rudiments represent the individual (granular) pieces used to make up the instruments employed on a KM initiative. They are constituents used to construct those instruments. In a survey, for example, each individual question is a rudiment.

The combination of existing rudiments (wherever possible) provides an effective way of creating new instruments that meet the specifics of an engagement's dialectic. The rudiment is the atomic element of KM; it is both input and output to an evolving model.

It is possible to conceive, then, of a primary responsibility in KM as the management of rudiments as they enter the system. However, the management of rudiments is exponentially more difficult than the management of the instruments that serve as their containers. In an ideal KM system, rudiments would be individually managed and instruments dynamically constructed on an as-needed basis. In practical terms, however, such granular knowledge management may not be doable by many organizations. In either case, however, the KM system used to manage both instruments and/or rudiments should be capable of searching at the rudimentary level. (Table 17-2) I will return to, and expand on, the details of knowledge managing against this framework in the next section.

Table 17-2
An example of the framework, with examples of individual items

Framework Component	Component Detail
Thematic	People ask questions to get answers
Methodology	Knowledge Reservoir Analysis
Methodic	Knowledge Domain Analysis
Procedure	Survey
Technique	Web-based form with open-ended questions
Instrument	Survey # n
Rudiment	Individual questions

KNOWLEDGE-MANAGING PYRAMID-BOTTOM COMPONENTS

As should be clear from the discussion above, the organization looking to knowledge-manage its KM initiatives will succeed best by identifying and publishing the pyramid-top components and by systematizing, through the use of technology, the creation, collection, quality assurance, and delivery of pyramid-bottom components.

A model developed by the American Productivity and Quality Center (APQC), in association with Arthur Andersen, presents seven functions necessary to the KM process (O'Dell 2000): create, identify, collect, organize, share, adapt, and use. The model accurately captures the cycle of KM activity; mapping the APQC model against the framework presented in this chapter suggests that the concentration of KM for KM should be on the collection, organization, sharing, and use of components.

At first this may seem counterintuitive since knowledge creation is such a core function within the framework. However, *creating* is viewed as a result of dialectics in response to necessary tasks and/or goals to be accomplished and is not something to "manage" in a traditional, system-based sense. The assumption is that creation is *always* happening. Therefore *collection* becomes the first critical-path step in designing the system. Also, within this framework, *adapting* is considered axiomatic; the nature of the dialectic requires it, and so it is subsumed under the process of use.

Collection

Collection—or knowledge acquisition, the movement of knowledge into a technical environment or knowledge base—is always an issue in any KM effort. The process for collection is enabled most effectively through two methods: tasks that require collection for completion (Wolf 2000; Newman 2000) and incentives and/or external motivations (Bukowitz 1999; Angus 2000). However, there has been serious argument recently about whether incentives and/or external motivators are having the positive impact originally expected (Brooking 1999; Dixon 2000). In a KM practice designed to promote KM within other organizations, the expectation is that motivation is already high; the KM analysts building KM systems are de facto interested in the design and success of KM projects.

However, there are still very real practical limitations (time, geography, etc.) that can limit collection. The recommendation is to make it a standard part of the work process; that is, include the items to be collected as deliverables for the project. Rely on technical solutions and/or internal-knowledge managers to parse and store the knowledge in the KM system. Instruments (a survey, for example) are commonly required as deliverables; based on an encoding system, changes or additions at the rudimentary level can be flagged and both new rudiments and new instruments can then be added to the knowledge base.

Organizing

A knowledge base should be organized to increase the likelihood that a search will produce a targeted, useful results set. Since a knowledge base about and for KM aims to leverage previous similar experiences, the organization should revolve around three vectors. The first vector is *class,* and is made up of the instruments and rudiments that are the physical instantiations of the knowledge. These are modeled according to *type* (whether they are surveys, questionnaires, project plans, etc.) and *purpose* (whether they are used for planning, data gathering, data analysis, project management, etc.).

The second vector is *filters,* the dimensions in which particular instruments and rudiments have been used in the past. Examples would be geography (where a particular instrument is useful for remote data gathering, for example), time available, KM analyst experience level, business domain to which the KM initiative is being applied, and knowledge-gathering and/or domain requirements. The application of filters is a critical organizational element. To maximize the use of previous practices, it is important for individuals to know the "worlds" in which those practices have been used, as well as the outcomes of that use.

This last point leads to the third major vector: *results.* Knowing the objectives of a particular effort—and, therefore, the goals to which the instruments and rudiments have been applied in the past—is a critical path item for understanding whether particular instruments or rudiments are appropriate to any one circumstance or environment. Cataloging (or otherwise flagging) results-based, post-project analysis tells future users of the system what worked and what did not (Wolf 2000).

Sharing

Sharing the knowledge in the knowledge base is more than simply making it available to those who "need" it (Dixon 2000). Personal and task-motivated energy, work goals, and success and/ or failure feedback are all critical (Tampoe 1996). The need may not even be apparent; often people do not "know what they don't know" (Fisher 1998) and, in the particular case of building KM systems, what someone may need to "know" is very much context-sensitive, dependent on the emerging dialectic that takes place over the course of the project. A knowledge base must do more than simply contain data in the hopes that it may be useful knowledge for someone, at some time, and in some nonspecific context. And some knowledge will never reach a knowledge base. KM system design is part science and part art and so has a strong tacit knowledge component; sometimes people do not know why they have done something or why it worked, and the appropriate way of sharing that knowledge is not through a technology-based search and retrieval process but through both technology- and non-technology-supported knowledge-sharing sessions. Sharing must take place both inside and outside the knowledge-base technology itself and must be supported by other technical and nontechnical means.

Using

Using knowledge has been discussed in detail; it involves the entire dialectic between the KM analyst and the customer for whom he or she is designing the KM system. However, *using* can also be understood as being composed of two discreet parts: *accessing* the knowledge and *applying* the knowledge.

Accessing the knowledge is the function of obtaining from the knowledge base the necessary instruments and rudiments (and other background materials) appropriate to the effort, based on the filtering information that comes from the project itself and which has been entered by the KM analyst as search criteria. KM analysts must be able to access the knowledge through a simple interface, but one that allows for filtering.

The application of those instruments and rudiments (and the creation—through modification or anew—of instruments and rudiments) proceeds as part of the project. In this context, application becomes input to the dialectic and therefore merges cyclically with the knowledge creation process.

Advantages of the Framework

The framework is a coordinated design that simultaneously respects three competing needs: the needs of the organization performing the work for customers, the needs of the customer (either internal or external) receiving the work, and the needs of the individual consultants and analysts who drive the work forward.

Perhaps more important, however, is the importance of having a framework that encapsulates the critical KM functions of creation and application within that structure of needs. This framework respects the necessities of dialectic by allowing the appropriate concatenation of ideas into resulting syntheses, themselves resulting in additional dialectical possibilities. It is from the dialectical base and the emerging syntheses that new knowledge emerges through the development of new rudiments, instruments, techniques, and procedures. The framework also provides the data-points necessary for ongoing evaluation and reconstruction of higher-order constructs (the pyramid-top components) that drive the organization's KM model.

Appropriate Use of the Framework

Numerous works attempt to argue that a particular model or "recipe" is appropriate for a particular purpose, to the exclusion of other, similar models or ideas; these attempts may be skeptically received insofar as they present yet another "recipe" to be followed. It is necessary, therefore, in an attempt to avoid that same skepticism with this framework, that the discussion include how best to put the framework to use and, at the same time, avoid the very stultification that the framework proposes to eliminate.

A framework in the sense presented in this chapter is not a *process*; it does not provide step-by-step instruction for how to achieve a particular goal or set of goals. It is best construed instead as a high-level *schematic*, designed to provide guidance to the thinking that surrounds the eventual development of a process that, in this model, is dialectically driven, individualized when necessary, and completed through the creativity of those performing the work. Insofar as the framework seems directive, those directives would be that KM efforts proceed through the comparison of new efforts with old, determination of reusable KM components (techniques, procedures, etc.) previously stored in a library, modification of those components with respect to the inherent dialectic assumed in the engagement, synthesis of unique solutions for the engagement, and storage of the modified KM components for additional consideration in later engagements. Anything more structured than this "process" endangers the theory itself, risking the development of the very kind of fixed best practices that the framework hopes to avoid and surpass.

CONCLUSION: EMERGENCE OF THE DIALECTIC AND ITS USE IN BEST-PRACTICES DEVELOPMENT

The use of the dialectic in consulting and analysis is described as a way to ensure that the needs of stakeholders are represented in the final application of best practices against a specific business problem or problem set. It is used primarily as (1) a way to minimize the use of compromise as a solution, where compromise represents a lessening of expectation and solution for a particular stakeholder, (2) as a means for the emergence of new elements, instruments, techniques, and procedures within the context of actual work performed, and (3) as a way of preserving the needs of practitioners for creative and meaningful work. The resulting framework is decidedly not a best-practices model in the traditional sense but is instead a meta-model, one that encourages the ongoing creation and development of targeted practices based simultaneously on individual circumstance and expert experience.

There is a need to break free from conventional best-practices thinking. Too often best practices are developed in Aristotelian terms; that is, that there is a right way and a wrong way to implement a particular schema or solution within a categorized framework. Customers are assayed with respect to that predefined taxonomy and, based on where they lie within it, a set of best practices is deemed appropriate. I propose instead that KM initiatives are best served when they are conceived of as a continuing dialectic, where the partial resolution of a particular antinomy leads to a procedural or technical decision as to how best to allow the following dialectic to emerge; the goal is a final solution, necessarily impossible, but the movement along the dialectical trail leads to better and better solutions for the customer. When combined with technological and social constructions for knowledge sharing and knowledge delivery, the framework can provide a unique set of constructs for successful KM planning, design, and implementation.

REFERENCES

Angus, J. 2000. Reinforce Your Incentives, *Knowledge Management* 3, 9 (September).

Arbnor, I. and B. Bjerke. 1997. *Methodology for Creating Business Knowledge.* Second edition. Thousand Oaks, Calif.: Sage Publications.

Bontis, N. 1999. Managing Organizational Knowledge by Diagnosing Intellectual Capital: Framing and Advancing the State of the Field, *International Journal of Technology Management* 18, 5/6/7/8: 433–62.

Brooking, A. 1999. *Corporate Memory: Strategies for Knowledge Management.* London: International Thomson Business Press.

Bukowitz, W. and R. Williams. 1999. *The Knowledge Management Fieldbook.* London: Financial Times Prentice-Hall.

Daloz, L. 1986. *Effective Teaching and Mentoring.* San Francisco: Jossey-Bass.

Dixon, N. 2000. *Common Knowledge: How Companies Thrive by Sharing What They Know.* Boston: Harvard Business School Press.

Fisher, K. and M. D. Fisher. 1998. *The Distributed Mind: Achieving High Performance Through the Collective Intelligence of Knowledge Work Teams.* New York: Amacom.

McTaggart, J. M. E. 1896. *Studies in the Hegelian Dialectic.* Scanned and presented at *www.ets.uidaho.edu/mickelsen/*, January 17, 2001.

Mullich, J. 2000. Knowledge Management on Linux, *Knowledge Management* 3, 9 (September).

Newman, V. 2000. Viewpoint: Can You Embed Knowledge-Sharing into Everyday Work? *Knowledge Management Review* 3, 1 (March/April).

O'Dell, C., S. Elliott, and C. Hubert. 2000. *Knowledge Management: A Guide for your Journey to Best Practice Processes.* Houston: American Productivity and Quality Center.

Rowland, H. 2000. Managing Knowledge and Creativity at the BBC: Sharing Knowledge in the Ideas Warehouse, *Knowledge Management Review* 3, 2 (May/June).

Tampoe, M. 1996. Motivating Knowledge Workers—The Challenge for the 1990s, in *Knowledge Management and Organizational Design,* ed. Paul S. Myers. Newton, Mass.: Butterworth-Heinemann.

Tiwana, A. 2000. *The Knowledge Management Toolkit.* London: Prentice-Hall International.

Wolf, B. 2000. Embedding Knowledge-Sharing into Work at SBS: Making Collaboration a Natural Part of Daily Work, *Knowledge Management Review* 3, 1 (March/April).

Wysocki, R., R. Beck, and D. Crane. 1995. *Effective Project Management: How to Plan, Manage and Deliver Projects on Time and Within Budget.* New York: John Wiley and Sons.

18

DE-BIASING SCIENCE AND TECHNOLOGY INVESTMENT DECISIONS

Joseph J. Kranz
Requirements Engineering, KM and IC, Anteon Corporation, Rhode Island, U.S.A.
jkranz@anteon.com

and

Denis M. Coffey
Requirements Engineering, KM and IC, Anteon Corporation, Rhode Island, U.S.A.
dcoffey@anteon.com

ABSTRACT

The naturalistic decision-making (DM) literature documents that DM, whether individual or group, is biased. Biasing takes on many forms. Group biases arise from both naturalistic processes and from social influences. These biases cannot be eliminated at any intrinsic level. Practice, experience, education, and other techniques do not significantly change most DM biases in practice.

The science and technology (S&T) research investment domain is fraught with these natural biases. Competing internal alliances, and individuals and groups with notoriety, exercise more influence than is reflective of their value to the organization's objectives. Alignment of an organization's investments to its goals, objectives, and inherent value system is therefore problematic because the subject matter experts, and others, embed both explicit and implicit biases in their judgments.

This paper documents a metaprocess that enables the development of a methodology that mitigates organizational and naturalistic decision-making biases in science and technology investment decision-making. An example methodology resulting from the metaprocess is described that aligns advice from topic area experts with an organization's goals and value system. It creates a "value blind" process that diminishes overt and inadvertent bias effects. It has been validated in back-testing and can be applied to other domains.

Introduction

Decision-making (DM) in scientific and research investment is biased by social (egocentrism, alliance, notoriety influence), by naturalistic, decision-making biases and heuristics, by communications failure, and by a variety of other sources (Fischoff 1982; Senge 1990; Schein 1996; Piattelli-Palmarini 1994; Price and Kennie 1997; Summerfield 1997). This biasing causes institutions to fund research or to misallocate technology investment such that it does not optimally fulfill the values, goals, and objectives of the institution. In some cases the funding is applied to projects that have little or no chance to support the institution's value system, because the projects or their sponsor and proponents are "popular" or appear to be socially valuable, but are misaligned and directed away from the mission or focus of the organization. These factors cause valuable research and investment funds to be allocated to inappropriate projects and can exacerbate inadequate funding for well-aligned and -focused projects that lack notoriety.

De-biasing directly through education, training, or experience has been shown to be ineffectual (Fischhoff 1982). Biasing has great influence on the success or failure of research, as it relates to fulfilling the end goals of an organization. Values in organizations are usually not well defined in terms of criteria that will satisfy and fulfill the value system (Stewart 1996).

Objectives of Technology Investment

Technology investment is an action taken to satisfy the objective values of the (profit-research-nonprofit-learning) organization. Therefore it is a corollary that the values of the organization are (should be) embodied in the set of research and technology investments selected as a result of judgments by the managerial and scientific hierarchies of the organization.

Nature of the Organization

The structures, processes, and needs integral to a particular institution are unique to that organization, meaning, the National Cancer Society is not the same as the University of North Dakota, which is not the same as a U.S. Navy Laboratory. Even organizations of the same ilk (e.g., two universities) are different in their internal and external cultures, needs, specific interpretation of objectives, and, consequently, value systems.

Time Domain Issues

Decisions that must be responsive and/or reactive to immediate realities cannot consume more time than is available to react. Long-term consequences are not of significance in this case. However, when the outcome of a decision occurs far in the future, the decision must be as precise and aligned with the outcome intention as possible. Most organizational processes are dynamic in nature, and, accordingly, small differences in early activity and direction can have great consequences in the future (Senge 1990). These are only two examples of time domain issues in DM, the latter applying significantly to research investment outcomes.

Decision-Making Context

Organizational DM-complexity is compounded by multiple hierarchies and relationship lattices. There are multiple cultures and interests to accommodate as well as multiple conflicting objectives (Schein 1996; Diekmann et al. 1997; de Jong 1999).

The Actors

Organizational actors live in multiple, separate cultures and communicate with different languages (Schein 1996; Summerfield 1997). The actors are usually defined by their function and with whom they are tasked to interact. Marketing people tend to interact with sales,

SUBJECTIVE PROBABILITY UTILITY			
NATURALISTIC AND BEHAVIORAL			
CORPORATE VALUES (C.V.)	D-M'S PERCEPTION OF C.V.	D-M'S VALUES	NATURALISTIC D-M FACTORS
- ORGANIZATIONAL - MANAGEMENT		- PERSONAL - PSYCHO/SOCIAL	
EXPLICIT	EXPLICIT	EXPLICIT AND STATED	BIASES
IMPLICIT	IMPLICIT	UNSTATED	HEURISTICS
LATENT	LATENT	LATENT	CONDITION BASED BIAS

Figure 18-1 *Decision factor overlap*

advertising, and other marketing people; engineering tends to interact only with engineering; operational management interacts with finance and customers and tries to interact with engineering. The expertise, biases, communications, and values of these separate groups are defined by their roles and interactions in addition to implicit and explicit personal agendas.

In summary, the landscape of organizational factors and behavioral influences on project investment decision choices have overlapping characteristics that can be described in subjective probability theoretic terms and in naturalistic and behavioral terms. This overlap and some of the factors are illustrated in Figure 18.1.

Objectives

Rarely does an organization have well-defined, explicit, commonly understood value systems. Accordingly, they rarely have clearly stated objectives (Senge 1990).

Culture, Context, value system, environment

Our experience has shown that engineers and some scientists, by training and to some extent by personality dispositional affect (Myers and McCaulley 1985), tend to jump to technically based solutions and abstractions as soon as possible. Frequently, engineers and technically trained personnel tend to discount the "intellectual" content of solutions and focus on technology and quantifiable factors. Their own culture is based on abstract, impersonal solutions, developed with a notion that these solutions are, or should be, "free of human foibles and errors" (Schein 1996). This personality of the engineering and scientific community (not the individuals) has been observed to exist without being significantly modified by organizational cultures. Tragically, to a significant extent a similar effect is found in the managerial accounting community, even in the relatively enlightened activity-based costing discipline (Cokins 1996).

What results from this predisposition in a technology- and engineering-oriented organization, when applied to a business environment, are decision processes that emphasize directly quantifiable measures. The paradox is that the real attributes of the return-on-investment (ROI) problem are frequently not directly measurable. The entire nature of the ROI issue is a fuzzy one. Much work is continuing to be done to clarify and define ROI metrics that account for the value added by organizational intelligence and intellectual capital. The context, value system, and environment for one corporation, corporate unit, or research and development director are likely to be completely different than any other. These factors, or *attributes,* are usually based on latent and unstated corporate strategic goals. For example, retention of a world-class staff is an important success factor in a scientifically oriented enterprise. It is quite easy to draw the logical connection from a world-class scientific staff to corporate image and quality-product image, and from these latter factors in turn to success in the marketplace. The problem is that there is no satisfactory and generally accepted transfer function to provide computational consistency across these logical boundaries. The authors have used Figure 18-2 with several technical management groups to illustrate this conundrum and have received anecdotal confirmation that such value confusion in engineering and technology organizations is common.

WHAT IS "RETURN ON INVESTMENT"?

Improving the Bottom Line comes from:
- **Increased sales**
- **Decreased cost**
- **Market share**
- **Product image**
- **Corporate image**
  & *MANY* others

Latent strategic goals usually lead to the "real" returns and failures.

Figure 18-2 *ROI confusion*

Bias and Values

Human value systems tend to vary among cultures (Summerfield 1997). A *value system* is defined herein as a hierarchy of precedence or importance among alternative courses of action, states of being, and relationships to the physical and spiritual worlds. Cultural variations themselves have no value difference in any objective value system; they just exist. Cultural distinctions are not necessarily based on language, ethnic group, geographical region, and similar criteria; each human organization has its own identifiable culture (Senge 1990).

Values are logically equivalent to pure biases. They genuinely reflect a context and/or culture. The framing of an issue or concept becomes meaningful only with reference to some framework in which a pure bias can be placed. The decision-making-bias issue arises because of the noise or pollution of the pure bias caused by other factors. These factors arise from egocentrism, social expectations, illusory perception or cognition, and a variety of other sources (Bazerman 1998; Senge 1990; Schein 1996; Piattelli-Palmarini 1994; Kranz and Coffey 1997; Diekmann et al. 1997).

Problem Perception

The perception of ROI is key. Each participant has a different view. The corporate value system, though unerringly documented in the annual report, has substantial components that are implicit and latent. Corporate culture varies widely and has pivotal influence on research and development DM. The decision-maker's perception of the corporate value (CV) system is an order of magnitude away from direct measure of the CV, because, for each individual, it is modified by the explicit, implicit, and latent perceptions of the decision-maker. The decision-maker's personal values and psycho-social values no doubt have an explicit and stated component, but the unstated and latent ones may bear more weight. Finally, all of these are influenced by the biases, heuristics, and condition-based biases of naturalistic DM (Plous 1993).

Rationalistic DM is prescribed using Bayesian game theory or other subjective probability utility–based weighting and schema. They are applicable for the explicit components of the CV, decision-maker's perception of CV, and the decision-maker's values. However, they do not provide a vehicle to address the implicit and latent requirements nor take into account the inherent errors caused by naturalistic decision-making factors (Plous 1993; Tversky and Kahneman 1974). Classical methods assume that the problem is,

and can be, defined prima facie in technical and quantifiable
business terms. They assume that there is no change in the environment of the decision when there is an organizational or personnel change. Most of them are not documented as actually
used. They are sort of like a Boston traffic signal . . . a suggestion
of how to behave, not a discipline and dictate.

BIAS REDUCTION MODEL

The methodological approach to constructing a bias reduction, or
"de-biasing," model utilizes a synthesis of well-established process
techniques to identify, weigh, and align advice from topic-area
experts with an organization's goals. It needs to integrate a "value
blind" selection qualification process that diminishes or eliminates
overt and inadvertent effects of subject matter expert (SME) bias.
The procedure for valuing-and-decision-criteria development needs
to be a metaprocess that enables the technique to capture the unique
characteristics of each organization using the process and that further makes it extensible to other subject or topic-area domains.

It is known that addressing the problem at a personal, operational
level through education, experience, and tools, such as checklists and

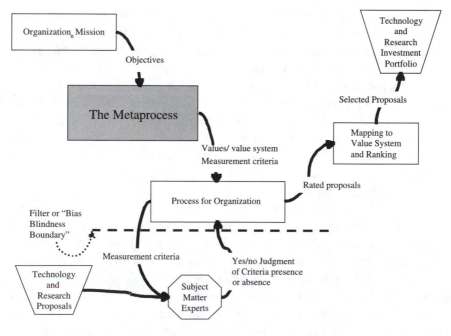

Figure 18-3 *Conceptual process diagram*

cognitive strategies, has, at best, a temporary effect and one only on very specific contemporary decision activities. This implies that the chosen methodology must not rely on such strategies and must be independent of them. From another perspective, the methodology needs to be based in a strategy that can accept "noisy," or biased, data and justifiably eliminate the bias. Figure 18-3 shows a concept of the needed process.

CASE STUDY

Project Goal: Investment Selection

The customer's question was, "How do I measure the ROI on my research and development dollars?" The constant effort by corporate management to reduce overhead expenses prompted this question. Curiously, management perceived research and development to be an expense and not an investment. The research and development director's call carried a plaintive and frustrated tone and clearly stated the need for some method to align the organization's values and DM process for research and development selection. The research and development director was also frustrated by obvious biases within his organization's technical and engineering staffs.

Whenever a new project or problem is undertaken, the authors routinely ask these basic questions: "Do we know what the problem is? Is it clearly defined? How do we know what the customer wants?" The authors have found that the *apparent* problem is frequently a description of the customer's *solution* to a given problem, and though pointing to the fundamental problem, does not characterize it (Kranz and Coffey 1997; Burchill 1995). A team consisting of a variety of engineers, scientists, and corporate managers, with no participation from the customer, met and discussed the problem. *This lack of stakeholder-customer participation is counter to recommended practice* (Kranz and Coffey 1997; Wilson et al. 1998; Burchill 1995). The outcome of this meeting was a revised requirements statement, or charter, as follows and the selection of Concept Engineering (CE™) as the structured manner in which to define the problem and reach a solution.

Task

"Develop a process to use in making investment decisions involving research and development projects. These decisions are to be

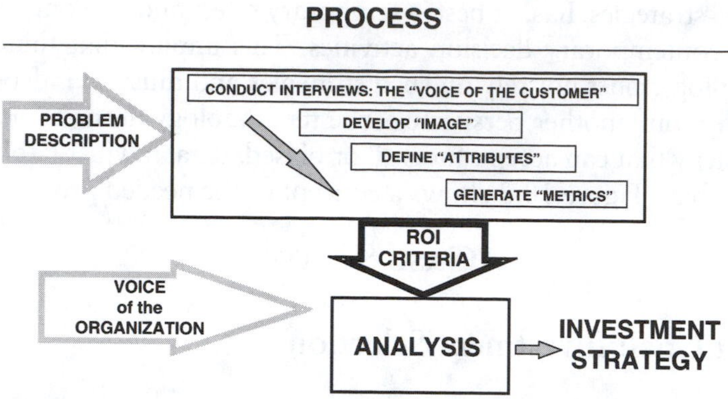

PROCESS

Figure 18-4

grounded in current values of the corporation and, at the same time, are to minimize the biases of the decision-maker and of the technical advisors, the topic area experts or SMEs in this case."

CE™, as developed by Gary Burchill and refined by the Center for Quality of Management (CQM), is a structured engineering process appropriate to the class of problems with a "fuzzy front end." Further, CE™ would produce:

- Latent needs of the customer
- Meaning to the users
- Requirements or attributes about the decision process
- Outcomes that would be measurable and validated

Though CE™ had been used extensively to define product solutions to customer requirements that are "fuzzy," the intended application of CE™ to this type of problem had never been tried (CQM User's Group Meeting, May 1997). The objective and result expected of CE™ in this case was *to generate a new process that applies to a service*, a new and unique application of CE™. Figure 18-4 presents an outline, or roadmap, of how the CE™ process was planned to be utilized in this case.

Concept Engineering™

CE™ is executed in five stages, with each stage requiring three steps. The stages are

- Understanding the customer's environment
- Converting the understanding into customer requirements

- Operationalizing what has been learned
- Generating concepts
- Selecting the concept

For this project, only the first three stages were used.

Stage 1: Understanding the Customer's Environment

A cross-functional team was formed and chartered. This team consisted of one corporate manager, one assistant program manager, two engineers, one computer scientist, and one staff-support person. Only the assistant program manager was from the customer's organization, and only two members of the team had previous experience using CE™.

Understanding needs. Strategy for developing a comprehensive understanding of the customer's needs and environment relies on collecting the customer's voices through a carefully planned interview process that emphasizes active listening. At this point the team prepared learning objectives ("what we wanted to know") and developed a customer selection matrix ("from whom to get that knowledge"). Customers or customers' organizations defined the rows, and the learning objectives defined the columns. Each customer was evaluated for the type and strength of information that could be provided with respect to the learning objectives. In addition, each customer was assessed and ranked as a weak, medium, or strong source of information for a given objective, and a corresponding symbol documented the appropriate intersection on the chart. Standard team methodology, notation, voting, and other processes were used throughout (Burchill 1995; Brassard and Ritter 1994; Kelly 1996; Scholtes 1992). The team added a final column to the matrix to identify specific individuals to interview from each customer organization. A customer organization receiving the strongest ranking for a given learning objective became the leading interview candidate for that objective.

In planning for the interviews, the team prepared a discussion guide that is a set of questions derived from the learning objectives. Pairs of team members were assigned as interview teams, and the necessary logistical arrangements were made to conduct the interviews. Team members practiced interview skills such as asking open-ended questions and active listening and probing, techniques that are crucial to the success of the interview (Graziano and Raulin 2000). It is critical that the team follow a strict discipline, using the discussion guide when conducting the interviews. Care must be taken so that the interviewees are not biased or led by the questioning. In this project a broad cross section of thirteen users or customers was identified.

Collecting the voice of the customer. The following steps are strongly dependent on the success of the interview process. In CE™, this step is described as "swimming in the customer's fishbowl." Instead of simply looking at the fish swimming around, the team experiences the customer's environment by swimming in the fishbowl. Hence the team can more effectively develop a 360-degree view of the customer's environment of use. Accordingly, the team conducted the interviews at the customer's facilities and work offices. The intention in this process is to engage the team member's "affect," so that they understand the problem at an intrinsic, emotional level.

Nine of the thirteen candidate interviews were conducted in teams of two members over a two-week period. After each interview, the interview team debriefed among themselves to share insights about that particular customer or user. All those interviewed, except one, consented to audio-recording. The tapes were transcribed and provided very valuable resource material throughout the remainder of the CE™ process. These transcripts were often referred to and reread whenever questions arose concerning what and how something had been described.

Developing a common image of the customer's environment. After all the transcripts had been prepared, they were distributed to the interview team members for image extraction. The team members went through the transcripts and extracted images of the customer's environment. This activity is akin to graphical coding in qualitative research (Maxwell 1996). More than one hundred images were recorded. Each image answered the question, "What scenes or images come to mind when you visualize the research and development program?" The Method for Priority Marking™ developed by Burchill in 1995 was used by the team during each selection round. The rounds continued until a manageable number of images was obtained. In this case that number was twenty-six.

These twenty-six images were classified, grouped, and organized into a Language Processing™ (LP™) chart (ibid.), the research and development image LP™. The image LP™ tells the story of the team's understanding of the customer's environment from the customer's perspective. An example of an LP™ is shown in Figure 18-5.

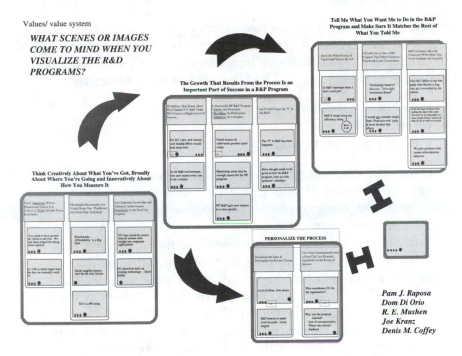

Figure 18-5 *Example language processing (LP™) diagram*

The team's summary story was:

"Think creatively about what you've got, broadly about where you're going and innovatively about how you measure it. The growth that results from the process is an important part of the success of an R&D program. That growth will also personalize the process. So, tell me what you want me to do in the R&D program and make sure that it matches the rest of what you told me. Then, the school principal, the corporate president, will have company at the Science Fair."

Stage 2: Converting the Understanding into Customer Requirements

The team had developed a shared understanding, and a common set of images, of the customer's environment. The next step was to identify the customer's requirements. The team members revisited the interviews and extracted over one hundred customer voices. A meaningful subset that connected to the image LP™ was selected for transformation. For each voice the team related the selected voice to at least one level of the image LP™ to ensure that the requirement statements would reflect the customer's experiences and that a trace could be maintained. A key thought or essential idea was extracted from the voice. The objective was to produce a set of well-written requirement statements that had the following characteristics:

- Simple sentence structure
- Free of solutions
- Clear and unambiguous

It must be emphasized that the statements must be free of solutions. The presence of solutions, to which engineers and scientists often gravitate, tends to restrict the process of creativity and exploration that is required at this stage.

Select the most significant attribute. Requirements were labeled "attributes" at this stage of the CE™ process. This change is appropriate for a process outcome versus a product outcome. The statements of attributes were processed in the same manner as the image LP™. This time the question, "What are the most significant attributes of the R&D program that can or do add value and/or provide ROI?" was asked. Twenty-three attributes resulted.

Develop insight into customer attributes. The team summarized their understanding and developed an LP™ for the attributes. The team's summary story for this LP™ was based on consolidating the twenty-three attributes into nine top-level attributes.

> "The users wanted a system that responds to key, externally defined business area needs so that strategic initiatives would be created for the business area establishment. Then, in conjunction with clear and open communications, the participation in the process would be attractive to the technical staff. Then the system would contribute to the organization's business base and reputation."

Stage 3: Operationalizing What Has Been Learned

The next stage of the CE™ process was "operationalizing." This stage ensures that the top-level attributes developed in Stage 2 are written clearly and concisely and unambiguously stated in measurable terms. Before the metrics were developed, an issue arose concerning the clarity and ambiguity of the nine top-level attributes. The team analyzed the clarity and ambiguity of each attribute on a scale from 1 to 5. A rating of "1" meant that everyone disagreed on the meaning of the attribute. A rating of "5" meant that everyone agreed that the attribute was clear and unambiguous. This step was taken to guide the team in deciding how many metrics to carry forward. (This process was conducted with intuitive guidelines for determining the number of metrics needed to adequately represent the ambiguity through to the next part of the process. The authors have subsequently developed a methodology based on sampling theory for determining the number of metrics needed for ambiguity representation.) The less clear or more ambiguous an attribute was, the more metrics would be needed to ensure that the attribute could be measured. This is one method of randomizing the biases. Traditional brainstorming techniques were used to generate a list of potential metrics, including a brief definition if necessary, for each top-level attribute.

Each metric was then evaluated on the basis of its validity and feasibility. Validity is the degree to which the metric truly measures the attribute. Feasibility is an assessment of how easy or difficult it is to use the metric. Validity and feasibility were assessed as "strong," "medium," or "weak." Only those metrics that had a strong assessment in either validity or feasibility were carried forward in the process. This screening produced the following seventy-seven metrics. Each of the metrics is a question and is answerable with a "yes" or a "no."

House of quality. Each of the metrics was then correlated with all the attributes. This correlation was captured in a quality chart (Cohen 1995). This quality chart, similar to a house of quality (HOQ), determines the cardinal and ordinal ranking of each project if the importance-column is completed. The importance-column reflects the value system of the organization. It is the "voice of the organization" (VOO) that must be considered by all personnel. In real practice, top-level management determines the relative value system of each attribute. In this project the value system was developed by the team. Each member voted on the nine top-level attributes and the summary weighting on a scale of 1 to 10 was used as the factor for importance. This simple additive weighting (SAW) technique has been shown to yield extremely close approximations to "true" value functions, even when independence among attributes does not exactly hold (Yoon and Hwang 1995).

It is this separation of importance from the assessment of each metric that minimizes biases from spoiling the ranking of each project being evaluated. This method is consistent with the CAT model that has been shown to be statistically de-biasing in this type of judgment context (Amabile 1996). Based only on a reading and content of the research and development proposal being evaluated, each reviewer can answer each metric independently of management's value system. Each reviewer may need to justify his review in cases where outliers exist. Only when the value system is exercised and computed by an independent management team will the ranking of all proposals be evident.

Results analysis

In order to reduce the likelihood of groupthink effects (Plous 1993), the team enlisted a senior analyst with research and development investment decision-making experience to utilize the process in a back-testing case. The analyst selected two projects that had both been "liked" by the organizational management and had been funded at approximately the same amount: $35,000. No previous, detailed analysis of ROI had been done on either project, so there was a form of "blind" test involved in this analysis. Each project was rated based on its initial proposal. They were found to correlate at 81 percent and 37 percent, respectively, to the corporate value system–based attribute metrics. The analyst then evaluated the actual ROI to the organization from each of these projects. The project with 81 percent correlation was found to have yielded approximately $3 million in revenues over five years with an ongoing revenue stream of approximately $600,000 per year. The 37-percent-correlation project had yielded total revenues of $375,000 with no likely continuing stream. It had, however, received high visibility and high notoriety that both served to support it being funded initially. These visibility- and notoriety-biasing effects obviously did not serve the organization's long-term financial goals. Further results-testing is desired, however; due to the long duration from project selection through completion and benefit accrual, it has been impractical to date to conduct a thorough long-term validation test.

CONCLUSIONS

This study constitutes the first known application of CE™ to research and development investment decision-making. Results of this study were validated by the application of the metrics developed to two selected past organizational efforts. Though the back-testing provided information that is far from statistically significant, it did provide some useful clues and inferences about this process.

First, it demonstrated that use of the process would have eliminated an obviously misaligned project from consideration, or at least provided management with information as to how closely aligned the candidate projects were with the organizational value system. The decision to fund a misaligned project may still have been made because of overriding community, notoriety, or other influences. Second, though the metrics for ROI that were used in the process were not, by and large, financial in nature, the process still indicated preference for the project that resulted in better financial performance. The authors feel that this implies that projects that are well aligned to the corporate value system will intrinsically produce improved fiscal results for that organization. Though the results derived in this project are not conclusive, due to a lack of controlled experimentation, there is a hint that metrics associated with other-than-financial measures can indeed predict better financial success. Does this mean that intellectual property, knowledge management, and organizational intelligence can be correlated to improved financial performance? Intuitively, this seems to be the case, but it still has not been proven. The transfer function from organizational intelligence to financial performance is still elusive.

POSTSCRIPT—NATURALISTIC DECISION-MAKING (NDM) EFFECTS

As noted early in this paper, much attention has been given to the biases, heuristics, and coincident decision errors that accrue as a result in investment decision-making. The operation of NDM effects on the team that developed this process were also monitored carefully.

The introduction of the analyst from "outside" the team was critical to thwarting the effects of groupthink. This team error occurs when teams are either "bullied" into thinking a given way, because it is "not acceptable" to think outside certain constraints, or when a team becomes so cohesive that none of the members are able to separate their views from the team's views.

Team decision risk biases were also carefully monitored. Teams tend to make more risky decisions and choose more risky alternatives, for a variety of reasons. The process advocate during this effort was tasked with consciously monitoring the relative risk of each team selection and with providing the team with self-assessment assistance to evaluate whether or not they, as individuals, would have selected the same approaches.

Social loafing is an effect that results in all teams. In short, it is the reason for effects such as the "mythical man-month." The team members were consciously aware of this effect and provided a self-policing function to see that everyone contributed equally.

Finally, attribution errors in teams can be insidious. In brief, it is an effect whereby group members make dispositional attributions for group successes and situational attributions for group failures. The team constantly reviewed its own performance and attempted to judge whether it was indeed the team's activities and approach that produced each success or whether luck and circumstances should be given the kudos.

REFERENCES

Amabile, T. M. 1996. *Creativity in Context.* Boulder, Col.: Westview Press.

Bazerman, M. 1998). *Judgment in Managerial Decision Making.* New York: Wiley and Sons.

Brassard, A. and D. Ritter. 1994. *The Memory Jogger™ II—A Pocket Guide of Tools for Continuous Improvement & Effective Planning.* Methuen, Mass.: GOAL/QPC.

Burchill, G. 1995. *Concept Engineering.* Cambridge, Mass.: Center for Quality of Management.

Center for Quality of Management (CQM). Concept Engineering User's Group Meeting of 8 May 1997.

Cohen, L. 1995. *Quality Function Deployment.* Reading, Mass.: Addison-Wesley.

Cokins, G. 1996. *Activity-Based Cost Management—Making it Work.* Chicago: Irwin.

DeJong, M. 1999. Survival of the Institutionally Fittest Concepts. *Journal of Memetics—Evolutionary Models of Information Transmission.* 3. On-line serial: http://www.cpm.mmu.ac.uk/jcm-emit/1999/vol3/de_jong_m.html. Accessed 5 September 2000.

Diekmann, K. A., S. M. Samuels, L. Ross, and M. H. Bazerman. 1997. *Self-interest and Fairness in Problems of Resource Allocation.* Unpublished working paper, J. L. Kellogg Graduate School of Management at Northwestern University.

Fischoff, B. 1982. Debiasing. In *Judgment under Uncertainty: Heuristics and biases,* eds. D. Kahneman, P. Slovic, and A. Tversky. Cambridge, Mass.: Cambridge University Press.

Graziano, A. M. and M. L. Raulin. 2000. *Research Methods: A Process of Inquiry.* Fourth edition. Boston: Allyn and Bacon.

Kelly, P. K. 1996. *Team Decision-Making Techniques*. Irvine, Calif.: Richard Chang and Associates.

Kranz, J. J. and D. M. Coffey. 1997. A Frame Normalization Method to Reduce Technically Dispositioned Solution Biasing on Integrated Product Team (IPT) Decision Making in the Requirements Definition Domain. Paper presented at the 16th bi-annual conference on Subjective Probability Utility and Decision Making, University of Leeds, Leeds, England, 18–21 August 1997.

Maxwell, J. A. 1996. *Qualitative Research Design: An Interactive Approach*. Thousand Oaks, Calif.: Sage Publications.

Mowen, J. C. 1993. *Judgment Calls*. New York: Simon and Shuster.

Myers, I. B. and M. M. McCaulley. 1985. *Manual: A Guide to the Development and Use of the Myers-Briggs Type Indicator*. Palo Alto, Calif.: Consulting Psychologists Press.

Piattelli-Palmarini, M. 1994. *Inevitable Illusions: How Mistakes of Reason Rule Our Minds*. New York: Wiley & Sons.

Plous, Scott. 1993. *The Psychology of Judgment and Decision Making*. New York: McGraw-Hill, Inc.

Price, I. and T. Kennie. 1997. Punctuated Strategic Equilibrium and Some Strategic Leadership Challenges for University 2000. *Second International Conference on the Dynamics of Strategy*. Surrey, England: Surrey European Management School.

Schein, E. H. 1996. *Three Cultures of Management: The Key to Organizational Learning in the Twenty-First Century*. Cambridge, Mass.: MIT Organizational Learning Center.

Scholtes, P. R. 1992. *The Team Handbook*. Madison, Wis.: Joiner Associates.

Senge, P. M. 1990. *The Fifth Discipline: The Art and Practice of the Learning Organization*. New York: Currency-Doubleday.

Stewart, T. A. 1996. Why Value Statements Don't Work, *Fortune* 133, 11(10 June): 137–38.

Summerfield, E. 1997. *Survival Kit for Multicultural Living*. Yarmouth, Maine: Intercultural Press.

Tversky, A. and D. Kahneman. 1974. Judgment under Uncertainty: Heuristics and Biases. *Science*, 185.

Wilson, D. G., D. M. Coffey, and J. J. Kranz. 1998. Product Development that Reflects the Voice of the Customer: A Team Case Study. Paper presented at the 8th Annual Interorganizational Symposium of the International Council on Systems Engineering (INCOSE). Vancouver, Canada, 26-30 July.

Yoon, K. P. and C. L. Hwang. 1995. *Multiple Attribute Decision Making: An Introduction*. Thousand Oaks, Calif.: Sage Publications.

19

AN EXAMINATION OF THE TRANSFER OF INTELLECTUAL CAPITAL ACROSS CULTURES

C. Anne Davies
School of Management and Economics, The Queen's University, Belfast, Northern Ireland
a.davies@qub.ac.uk

and

Joseph Magowan
School of Management and Economics, The Queen's University, Belfast, Northern Ireland
mcgowans@lineone.net

ABSTRACT

This interpretative study assesses the transferability of intellectual capital across geographic and cultural boundaries by presenting a case study of the experience of a western European bank in acquiring a Polish bank. Nahapiet and Ghoshal (1999) focus on the creation of intellectual capital as a "social artifact," and this paper builds on their work by examining their ideas in the context of diffusion of intellectual capital. The relationship between the banks has been successful, largely because of an attuned evolutionary approach that reflects the history and context of the company or country. The conclusion is drawn that intellectual capital is transferable even in a context where the extent of social capital is restricted if due regard is paid to cultural sensitivity and sufficient time and effort are expended.

INTRODUCTION

This case study examines the transfer of intellectual capital in the banking industry. A broad interpretation of intellectual capital, which includes the concept of social capital, is used. The shared narratives of executives involved in a World Bank twinning program between a western European bank (WestEuroBank) and an eastern European bank (EastEuroBank) form the evidence base for the study. These knowledge-intensive organizations have leveraged organizational advantage as a result of their relationship.

INTELLECTUAL CAPITAL

An important strand in the literature on intellectual capital has come from executives who have devised systems for managing and measuring intellectual capital (Petrash 1996; Saint-Onge 1996; Bontis 1996; Edvinsson 1997; Edvinsson and Malone 1997; Bontis 1998, 1999). This work has been extended by consultants who have developed what they regard as more widely applicable systems or approaches (Allee 1997; Roos et al. 1997; Sullivan 1998; Brooking 1999). Their approach can be encapsulated as one of converting knowledge into profit (Sullivan 1998). The seminal case study of Skandia provides "a new holistic and more balanced set of tools for growing" the company (Edvinsson and Malone 1997: 67) by means of the indicators generated from the core focus areas of the Skandia Navigator (Edvinsson 1997). They acknowledge the lack of relation between intellectual capital and the financial measurement of the business, although this is a strong research area in financial accounting.

For these authors, intellectual capital consists of three core components. First, human capital, which consists of employees' tacit knowledge, individual talents and knowledge acquired through education, experience, and training. This concentrates on value creation (Edvinsson 1997). Second, structural capital is comprised of the artifacts of human capital, including intellectual property, customer databases, organizational processes, and culture. The key task for organizations is to ensure that human capital is converted into structural capital in order to transform tacit knowledge into explicit knowledge. This implies a drive toward value extraction as opposed to the concentration on value creation in the building-up of human capital (Edvinsson 1997). Third, *customer capital* refers to the value of customer relationships to the enterprise. The relationship of a company to its customers is obviously of central importance to the company's worth (Saint-Onge 1996).

SOCIAL CAPITAL

An alternative perspective builds on the work of Kogut and Zander (1996), which views the firm as a social community. Nahapiet and Ghoshal (1998) focus on the creation of intellectual capital as a social artifact arising from the interaction of individuals. Their definition of intellectual capital stresses the socially and contextually embedded forms of knowledge and knowing as a source of value. The focus is on knowledge as created through combination and exchange among individuals. This requires that the opportunity must exist for such combination or exchange to happen, that those involved expect that this will create value, and that they will extract some benefit from the process. To achieve this, individuals must be motivated (Quinn et al. 1996a). A lack of motivation provides an inhibitor to the transfer of best practice, but the lack of capacity to assimilate and apply new knowledge is of greater significance (Szulanski 1996). In this perspective, social capital facilitates the development of intellectual capital by affecting the conditions necessary for the exchange and combination to occur. Knowledge and meaning cannot be considered outside the social context. Meaningful communication is essential for exchange and combination. This requires a shared context facilitated either through the existence of shared language and vocabulary or through the sharing of collective narratives. The extent to which their language and codes are different keeps people apart and restricts their access. Organizations are usually well endowed with social capital. It is the interaction between social and intellectual capital that underpins organizational advantage. Organizational advantage is constructed and retained through the dynamic and complex interrelationships between social and intellectual capital. Therefore, to the previous three components of intellectual capital, a fourth, that of social capital, should be added.

In the area of social interaction and its importance to the creation and exploitation of intellectual capital or knowledge, the sense-making view of organizations (Weick 1979, 1995; Choo 1996, 1998) assumes importance. Meaning is socially constructed and organizational members create their own subjective reality by making sense of what is happening in the organization by reference to previous experience (Choo 1998). It is only by developing a shared interpretation that organizations have a context for organizational action. Organizations are "loosely coupled" systems wherein individuals have scope to interpret and implement directions (Weick 1979). The powerful role of experience in this organizational model suggests that attempts to effect change must be grounded in a recognition that they must relate to, and resonate with, the existing culture and previous experience of the organization and its members.

Cultural distance raises barriers for understanding both partner organizations and the nature of their competitive advantage (Simonin 1999). His research highlights the difficulty of transferring tacit knowledge and the relative ease of transferring codifiable knowledge. Although this echoes the term *packaged useful knowledge* (Stewart 1998), it underlines the difficulty of transferring knowledge or skills gained through experience. In areas where knowledge cannot be unequivocally codified, learning from experience and learning by doing in the presence of knowledgeable partners become essential conditions for circumventing ambiguity and favoring knowledge transfer. This form of learning is resource intensive and often requires the costly expatriation of valued specialists (Simonin 1999).

The rotation of personnel is "a powerful way of transferring knowledge" (Garvin 1993), but such experiential learning requires a substantial investment in human resources (Simonin 1999). The importance of experiential learning echoes Nonaka (1994), who asserts that an individual can acquire tacit knowledge through apprenticeship or on-the-job training. Such experience can overcome the absence of a common language, which constitutes a major obstacle. What is needed is "shared experience" to give the transfer of knowledge or skills relevant "socialization" (Nonaka 1994). A shared language may be that of a particular professional field such as medicine (or banking, in the present case) (Davenport and Prusak 1998). This reflects the concept of tradition within particular trades or professions (Polanyi 1967) and the ethos of communities of practice (Brown and Duguid 1991).

CULTURE: ORGANIZATIONAL AND NATIONAL

Transfers of knowledge or practice between organizations are impacted by differences in organizational culture. The task is further complicated in cases wherein different national cultures are involved, as in the present case. There is a clear distinction between national and organizational cultures (Hofstede 1991). A national culture shapes an individual's values and is grounded in one's experience as a child, whereas organizational life or culture is characterized by common practices that are assimilated when one is an adult. Organizational culture is a shared perception of daily practices and does not involve the sharing of more deeply seated values. The individuals who are involved in the knowledge transfer process between cultures experience culture shock, because of the impact of alien traditions and values. Such people will then experience an "acculturation curve," as they gradually come to terms in their own way with strange new conditions in an environment of different values (Hofstede 1991). Language differences pose difficulties for foreigners assimilating themselves into a culture. Even where a basic knowledge of the language is present, the inability to assimilate the subtleties of a culture, particularly its humor, remains. This has obvious implications for the field of social interaction in obstructing the combination and exchange of knowledge.

The key to the development of an organization through knowledge transfer is the "effectiveness of the intercultural encounter" between those involved in the process (Hofstede 1991). Expatriates involved in this process can only be effective to the extent that they transfer their know-how in the local context and to the extent that the receiving country or culture feels a need for that knowledge. An identification of overseas effectiveness includes intercultural interaction, personal effectiveness, and personal and/or family adjustment (Hawes and Kealey 1979). For intercultural activity to be effective in the context of transferring knowledge, there must be a two-way learning process. Technical knowledge passes in one direction and cultural knowledge in the other. To facilitate this, expatriate personnel must first be aware of differences in outlook and then consciously learn about the foreign culture. A combination of these two processes must be put into practice by embracing the new culture that must also apply to the expatriate's family. Consciousness of differences in mental outlook can and must be developed if knowledge is to be transferred across cultures.

A further issue to be considered in relation to the transfer of knowledge and best practice is that of politics (Davenport et al. 1992; Quinn et al. 1996b). The political reality of organizational life, that knowledge is the source of power, requires a change in organizational culture if knowledge is to be shared and transferred. An awareness of the possible impact of information politics is vital to understanding and assessing the behavior of individuals.

This work, and its focus on the social interaction of individuals in organizations, can be regarded as developing a truer understanding of intellectual capital than the work of those whose focus is purely on the measurement of assets, however intangible.

Methodology

This paper examines whether, and how, intellectual capital can be transferred across countries, organizations, and cultures. In an attempt to provide rich and valid descriptions of knowledge transfer and practice, an ethnographic approach based on an in-depth examination of a case study has been used. The case study material was collected over the period of a year using narrative storytelling (Coffey and Atkinson 1996) to outline the history of the West-EuroBank–EastEuroBank relationship. Documentary evidence from the records of both WestEuroBank and the World Bank was used, and semi-structured interviews were held to gain a phenomenological understanding (Cresswell 1994) of participants' experience of knowledge transfer and to identify common themes. "Key informant" interviews (Miles and Huberman 1994) were conducted with seventeen people who were involved at various stages of the relationship. Eleven WestEuroBank personnel were interviewed, including eight executive or senior managers and three middle managers. The length of their involvement with EastEuroBank ranged from six months (in one case) to five years. Among the six EastEuroBank employees interviewed, three were senior managers and three middle managers. All had worked for EastEuroBank throughout its relationship with WestEuroBank. Each interview lasted from one to three hours. The semi-structured interview format was piloted with two individuals who were close to the project, and refinements were made in advance of the main field research. The validity of the data was checked during the interviews by re-presenting what respondents had said for their verification, by cross-checking the details provided on each side of the relationship with the perspectives and recollections of the other side to provide triangulation, and by allowing key respondents to read the final report of the study (Kvale 1996).

CASE STUDY

WestEuroBank Group—Background

WestEuroBank was formed in 1966 and operates principally in Britain, Ireland, the U.S.A., Poland, and Asia. It employs more than 30,000 people worldwide in more than 1000 offices and has 82,000 shareholders. WestEuroBank invested in the emerging economy of Poland by taking a minority shareholding in a bank in 1995. The expansion into Poland can be viewed as a strategy designed to diversify WestEuroBank's operations into another area of the global economy by gaining access to a large and growing market in central Europe.

EastEuroBank Group—Background

EastEuroBank was one of nine new commercial banks created in Poland in 1990, all emerging from the state-owned National Bank of Poland. These new banks were created on a mainly regional basis to facilitate management and control. EastEuroBank was given fifty-five branches, mainly in the most prosperous area of the country. The area has seen high levels of foreign direct investment during the 1990s by western European manufacturers, retailers, and financial institutions. EastEuroBank's relationship with WestEuroBank through the World Bank twinning program commenced in 1991. In 1993, EastEuroBank was privatized and listed on the Warsaw Stock Exchange. In 1994, WestEuroBank purchased 29.4 percent of EastEuroBank. WestEuroBank's stake was raised to a controlling interest of 60.2 percent in 1997. In 2000, EastEuroBank has 4500 employees and 190 branches, of which one hundred new branches have been opened in the last three years without any increase in staff numbers. The bank's strategy is to concentrate the expansion of its branch network on large cities and towns throughout Poland, by exploiting new technology and by leveraging the intellectual capital and best practice of the wider group.

THE WORLD BANK TWINNING PROGRAM

The need to transform the financial systems in central and eastern European countries after the change from centrally-managed, planned economies in these countries gave rise to the twinning concept. It was first designed in 1991 by the World Bank in cooperation with the government and Central Bank in Poland. Each of the nine newly created commercial banks was to be twinned with a foreign bank from a more advanced banking system in western Europe. In the event, seven of the Polish banks participated. Over a period of approximately three years, expertise was passed to Polish banks from their western twins in all key banking disciplines. WestEuroBank's relationship with EastEuroBank as part of the twinning program was routed through WestEuroBank International Consultants, an operation created to gain commercial advantage from WestEuroBank's expertise. The twinning program with EastEuroBank involved, in total, 653 consultant-weeks, covering thirteen separate modules over four years. A major issue in the twinning program was the ability of EastEuroBank to absorb, manage, and implement such a large program of change, while at the same time continuing to run its own operations. The level of disruption within EastEuroBank caused by the program was recognized at an early stage and modules were grouped together or rescheduled to ease the burden. Much of the work on modules overlapped because of criss-crossing responsibilities on the EastEuroBank side and also because of the lengthy decision times within EastEuroBank. In total, additional time spent on modules and the provision of additional assistance increased the original budget for the project by 20 percent. From a review of the documentation on the twinning program, it is apparent that both sides believed that the work undertaken was necessary for EastEuroBank at its particular stage of development.

The twinning program eventually extended over almost four years, having originally been intended to last two-and-a-half years. Analysis of the Polish twinning experiment by the World Bank presents this relationship as one of the more successful of the program. Through the program, EastEuroBank was regarded as having been equipped with a comprehensive set of modern banking procedures and guidelines for the continual upgrading of its operations. The risk level in its operations was substantially reduced. The bank was privatized. Much of the credit for this achievement has been given to the management board of EastEuroBank for its determination to follow through on implementation of changes initiated during the twinning program. In addition, joint reviews performed by WestEuroBank and EastEuroBank six months after the completion of each module helped to ensure that implementation took place.

The Polish twinning experience seems to have been very much a process of trial and error, as there were no case histories from which to learn. Of particular importance was the caliber of the people sent by

WestEuroBank to Poland as consultants. Those involved in this case had had little or no previous experience in such a role, though they brought enormous practical experience to their work. Little formal training was given to these people to prepare them for their role as consultants.

Cultural Empathy

WestEuroBank and EastEuroBank invested very heavily, both before and during the program, in building what they term *cultural empathy*. This was done by organizing frequent working visits of EastEuroBank executives and managers to WestEuroBank's head office, and vice versa. Despite this, however, implementation problems arose due to differences in business culture. At the commencement of the program, the management culture in the newly formed EastEuroBank was one where "the urgent drove out the important," as one WestEuroBank consultant stated. Prioritization was poor, and meetings were often cancelled at short notice or poorly attended. Senior EastEuroBank management had limited confidence in middle management, which meant that many minor decisions had to be referred to senior executives.

The language barrier between WestEuroBank and EastEuroBank employees presented problems during the twinning program. Interpreters and translators were essential throughout the program but varied in quality and availability. At times, it proved necessary to have documents retranslated back into the original language by a second translator to ensure that correct comprehension had been established. This communication problem was compounded by the fact that internal communications within EastEuroBank were poor, with little emphasis on team-building and open communication.

A further practical problem experienced by WestEuroBank personnel was the significant expectation on the part of EastEuroBank employees that WestEuroBank people had "a bag of magic solutions and would deliver them with little effort from EastEuroBank." The reality of the twinning program was different, in that it was intended as a partnership approach to solve EastEuroBank's problems. The nature of the project needed to be communicated more effectively to EastEuroBank in order to structure expectations more correctly.

Acquisition

By the end of the twinning arrangement in 1995/96, WestEuroBank had become a major shareholder in EastEuroBank. This provided the foundation for continued cooperation between the two organizations in the form of ongoing secondments of key WestEuroBank personnel to EastEuroBank. The level of involvement was significantly increased when WestEuroBank acquired a controlling interest in EastEuroBank in 1997. This enabled WestEuroBank to appoint long-term secondees to key senior positions in EastEuroBank. A new Polish president of EastEuroBank was appointed by WestEuroBank at this time. It would appear, in retrospect, that it was from this time that EastEuroBank began to fully embrace the changes sought by WestEuroBank. The commitment of WestEuroBank to EastEuroBank as parent company seems to have had a very significant and positive impact on the level of receptivity. It can, of course, be argued that the same factor may also have influenced the commitment of WestEuroBank and its personnel to the task. The relationship between the two was no longer fundamentally commercial and at arm's length. Despite this change, senior WestEuroBank management within EastEuroBank continued to adopt a "soft" approach to change, and senior Polish management remained in place, assisted where necessary by WestEuroBank deputies. This attempt to create a partnership with EastEuroBank appears to have been earnestly intended and critical to the development and acceptance of change by EastEuroBank personnel. A significant departure from the twinning approach during this period, and up to the present day, was the abandonment of a structured modular approach to the task. Since acquisition, WestEuroBank's approach to EastEuroBank has been collaborative and evolutionary, rather than based on the achievement of specifically planned outcomes.

Overall, it is noteworthy that it would appear that most lessons were learned by WestEuroBank personnel during the process of knowledge transfer. Although EastEuroBank assimilated and adapted new knowledge or intellectual capital, the force of the two-way learning process was apparently most keenly felt by WestEuroBank people in coping with the actual process of knowledge transfer across cultures.

DISCUSSION

The factors influencing the process of diffusing intellectual capital include the combination capability, social capital, impact of culture, acculturation, shared language, and collective narratives.

Organizational advantage emerged through a "third quality" that was seen to develop in EastEuroBank.

Combination Capability

The organizational heritage of EastEuroBank was clearly reflected in the bureaucratic and hierarchical nature of the organization at the beginning of the 1990s. The deep roots of such a structure were evident in the subsequent years, as Poles clung to established practices. The organization was rules-based, with individuals expressing a strong desire for certainty (Trompenaars and Hampden-Turner 1998). The cynicism within EastEuroBank regarding change is indicative of the power of national and organizational culture to shape attitudes and behavior. There was also significant evidence of information politics (Davenport et al. 1992) in the preexisting management culture of EastEuroBank. Communication was adversely affected by such political activity. There was no evidence of information politics in the behavior of WestEuroBank personnel throughout the process, and it is difficult to discern the motivation for any such behavior. The compliance culture of EastEuroBank, which remains strong, reflects the significance of power and/or distance within the organizational relationships (Hofstede 1991). The gradual acceptance of change over time highlights the power of collaboration (Simonin 1999) and the positive effect of the underpinning commitment evidenced by WestEuroBank's purchase of EastEuroBank.

Social Capital

The collaborative and evolutionary approach adopted by WestEuroBank to EastEuroBank can be regarded as culturally sensitive. This approach recognized that meaning is socially constructed (Choo 1996). WestEuroBank did not seek to impose change, rather, through collaboration, it attempted to facilitate EastEuroBank in creating its own organizational reality. This attuned stance acknowledges the scope of individuals within loosely coupled organizations to interpret and mediate direction (Weick 1979). It implicitly accepts the sense-making view that change must be grounded in the existing culture of the organization and must be in accord with the previous experience of the members of the organization. The process may have been further reinforced by embracing the idea of sending more

EastEuroBank personnel to WestEuroBank locations as a means of transferring knowledge (Garvin 1993; Davenport and Prusak 1998) and of accelerating the process of two-way learning. The approach adopted recognizes that information is given meaning by the receivers and not the senders (Sveiby 1997).

The Impact of Culture

The "soft" approach is not without its drawbacks. The absence of a structured approach to the process caused significant difficulty because an "end destination" was never in sight for EastEuroBank employees. In this environment, change appeared constant, without being linked to an agreed-upon achievable purpose. The level of uncertainty that resulted was plainly uncomfortable for many Poles who exhibited a strong inclination toward "uncertainty avoidance" (Hofstede 1991). The evolutionary approach was also perceived to be detrimental to the process of induction and acculturation. In the area of cultural difference and affinity, the research findings strongly support Hofstede's (1991) differentiation of national and organizational cultures. At a national cultural level, the most marked difference was the Polish suspicion of, and resistance to, change. This appeared to be greatly influenced by the Polish experience of the twentieth century, when change was almost universally regarded as unfavorable and undesirable.

At an organizational level, the public sector tradition of a former communist state remains evident within EastEuroBank. The emphasis on the need for regulation again reflects the strength of "uncertainty avoidance" (Hofstede 1991) within the organization. The culture of control in EastEuroBank stands in interesting contrast to the degree of what might be described as *anarchy within branches,* where individual branch directors exercized significant degrees of autonomy. This bears out the importance of power-distance relationships (Hofstede 1991) within the organization. The research's finding of a lack of personal responsibility within EastEuroBank reflects the collectivist nature of the organizational heritage, dating from the communist regime. It is, however, at odds with the specific findings of Trompenaars and Hampden-Turner (1998), who report that 80 percent of Poles saw employment as an opportunity to work individually and receive individual credit. Little support for such a conclusion was found in the present research, though there is the possibility that the impressions, particularly of WestEuroBank secondees, were originally formed up to ten years ago and may not have taken account of subsequent cultural shifts in the intervening period.

Acculturation

The process of acculturation was evident in the experience of WestEuroBank secondees, all of whom recognized the impact of the initial culture shock and the gradual acculturation process over a period of time. The experience of WestEuroBank secondees of this process was something for which they had not been properly prepared. The high level of training and preparation that is a necessary foundation for effective acculturation and assimilation was absent. The view was expressed that intercultural encounters must involve a two-way flow of knowledge concerning the practical realities faced by secondees.

Shared Language

The notion that the subtleties of a culture, particularly as expressed in its humor, are denied to someone who is not fluent in the language found support in the research particularly in the area of informal communication. WestEuroBank secondees have had little success in developing more than a rudimentary grasp of the Polish language. The issue of language was found to present problems in the area of the modes of knowledge-conversion. The combination and socialization of knowledge (Nonaka and Takeuchi 1995) are impeded by the language barrier. That an individual can acquire tacit knowledge without language through apprenticeship came across in this study. The paramount importance of "shared experience" (Nonaka 1994) is evident in this case. The shared technical language, in this case that of banking, can offset the intermediating effect of translation and help overcome communication barriers (Nahapiet and Ghoshal 1998; Davenport and Prusak 1998).

Collective Narratives

Throughout the research it was apparent that the degree of social capital that developed between WestEuroBank and EastEuroBank was constrained, particularly by the language barrier and the different organizational heritages. This restriction of social capital was mitigated, however, both by an emerging national cultural affinity and by the common organizational purposes of WestEuroBank and EastEuroBank, that is, collective narratives. The common goals compensated for the limitations to social interaction and served to endow the process of knowledge transfer with meaning through shared understandings and common experiences.

The knowledge transfer process overcame the obstacles posed by restricted social capital through EastEuroBank's gradual assimilation of new knowledge or intellectual capital. Collaboration over an extended period of time proved effective and might also be regarded as having contributed to an emergent form of social capital. A crucial foundation for this success was the level of trust that was evident in EastEuroBank's attitude toward WestEuroBank and the transfer process. This level of trust mitigated the inhibitors to social capital. Trust creates the conditions for the exchange of intellectual capital (Misztal 1996). Over time, the combination of cooperation and trust was found to be mutually reinforcing. The requirement for such conditions to develop over an extended period supports the approach adopted to the WestEuroBank–EastEuroBank experiment. There can be no effective alternative to "enduring relationships" in transferring intellectual capital or knowledge (Nahapiet and Ghoshal 1998).

Knowledge transfer in this relationship has focused on both tacit and explicit knowledge. Both tacit and explicit knowledge can only be transferred effectively over an extended period of time (Simonin 1998; Davenport and Prusak 1998). Knowledge transferred by means of a long apprenticeship is likely to have a high viscosity or durability, raising the hope that the WestEuroBank–EastEuroBank relationship can be judged successful. Knowledge transfer is indeed a slow and arduous process.

The Diffusion and Exploitation of Intellectual Capital

The important role played by those WestEuroBank consultants and secondees who worked in EastEuroBank highlights the significance of social capital, in that humans must interact. This is necessary to provide the opportunity for combination or exchange of knowledge. The enthusiasm expressed by EastEuroBank respondents to capturing new knowledge from WestEuroBank is evidence of their expectation that cooperation would create value and also of their motivation and commitment to the process of knowledge transfer. The difficulties and delays experienced during the ten-year period of knowledge transfer provide ample evidence of the importance of combination capability (Szulanski 1996; Nahapiet and Ghoshal 1998). Particularly in the early stages of the twinning program, EastEuroBank was overloaded with too much change at once. The organization simply did not have the "absorptive capacity" (Cohen and Levinthal 1990) in the form of its existing knowledge base and its internal network of communication to assimilate and apply the knowledge being transferred.

SOCIAL AND INTELLECTUAL CAPITAL AND ORGANIZATIONAL ADVANTAGE

The collaboration is seen, particularly by the Polish respondents, to have produced a "third quality." WestEuroBank personnel shared the view that what has been achieved in EastEuroBank is not simply a carbon copy of WestEuroBank. This agreement represents the strongest evidence in the research that the knowledge transfer process has been successful and that intellectual capital is capable of being transferred across countries, organizations, and cultures, but crucially so in an environment of two-way learning. In recording such a measure of success, the research bears out the importance of cultural factors, the learning process, and the need for an attuned, sensitive approach on the part of the exporter of knowledge. It is the interaction between social and intellectual capital that underpins organizational advantage. This evolution of a third quality in EastEuroBank through the processes of combination and exchange represents, to those involved, what can be described as *almost tangible evidence of actual organizational advantage.* Through the realization of this quality in EastEuroBank, we see the creation of an additional dimension for organizational advantage by combining social and intellectual capital across cultures.

CONCLUSION

This case illustrates the importance of access to experience as an effective means of knowledge transfer. The approach adopted, though far from perfect in the eyes of those involved, is best suited to the context of cross-cultural and cross-organizational knowledge transfer. There remains, however, a lingering doubt that, had

WestEuroBank known the full scale of the undertaking in advance, a less collaborative and evolutionary approach may have been adopted, thereby jeopardizing the success of the enterprise.

The collaboration of WestEuroBank and EastEuroBank suggests that intellectual capital can indeed be transferred successfully across countries, organizations, and cultures. The research provides strong support for the relationship between social capital and intellectual capital. The third quality in EastEuroBank, which has resulted from the process of two-way learning, adds to the understanding of the contribution that the interaction of social and intellectual capital makes to organizational advantage.

REFERENCES

Allee, V. 1997. *The Knowledge Evolution*. Boston: Butterworth-Heinemann.

Bontis, N. 1996. There's a Price on Your Head: Managing Intellectual Capital Strategically, *Business Quarterly* Summer: 40–47.

Bontis, N. 1998. Intellectual Capital: An Exploratory Study that Develops Measures and Models, *Management Decision* 36, 2: 63–76.

Bontis, N. 1999. Managing Organizational Knowledge by Diagnosing Intellectual Capital: Framing and Advancing the State of the Field, *International Journal of Technology Management* 18, 5/6/7/8: 433–62.

Brooking, A. 1999. *Corporate Memory*. London: Thomson.

Brown, J. S. and P. Duguid. 1991. Organisational Learning and Communities of Practice: Toward a Unified View of Working, Learning, and Innovation, *Organization Science* 2 , 1: 40–57.

Choo, C. W. 1996. The Knowing Organisation: How Organisations Use Information to Construct Meaning, Create Knowledge and Make Decisions, *International Journal of Information Management* 16, 5: 329–40.

Choo, C. W. 1998. *The Knowing Organisation*. New York: Oxford University Press.

Coffey, D. and P. Atkinson. 1996. *Making Sense of Qualitative Data*. London: Sage Publications.

Cohen, W. M. and D. A. Levinthal. 1990. Absorptive Capacity: A New Perspective on Learning and Innovation, *Administrative Science Quarterly* 35: 128–52.

Cresswell, J. W. 1994. *Research Design, Qualitative and Quantitative Approaches*, Thousand Oaks, Calif.: Sage Publications.

Davenport, T. H., R. G. Eccles, and L. Prusak. 1992. Information Politics, *Sloan Management Review* (Fall) 53–65.

Davenport, T. H. and L. Prusak. 1998. *Working Knowledge.* Boston: Harvard Business School Press.

Edvinsson, L. 1997. Developing Intellectual Capital at Skandia, *Long Range Planning* 30, 3: 366–73.

Edvinsson, L. and M. S. Malone. 1997. *Intellectual Capital.* London: Harper Collins.

Edvinsson, L. and P. Sullivan. 1996. Developing a Model for Managing Intellectual Capital, *European Management Journal* 14, 4: 356–64.

Garvin, D. A. 1993. Building a Learning Organisation, *Harvard Business Review* (July/August). Reprint 93402.

Hawes, F. and D. J. Kealey. 1979. *Canadians in Development: An Empirical Study of Adaptation and Effectiveness on Overseas Assignment.* Ottawa: Canadian International Development Agency.

Hofstede, G. 1991. *Cultures and Organisations.* London: McGraw-Hill.

Kogut, B. and U. Zander. 1996. "What do Firms Do? Co-ordination, Identity and Learning," *Organisation Science* 7: 502–18.

Kvale, S. 1996. *InterViews: An Introduction to Qualitative Research Interviewing.* London: Sage Publications.

Nahapiet, J. and S. Ghoshal. 1998. Social Capital, Intellectual Capital, and the Organisational Advantage, *Academy of Management Review* 23, 2: 242–66.

Nonaka, I. 1994. A Dynamic Theory of Organisational Knowledge Creation, *Organisation Science* 5, 1 (February): 14–37.

Nonaka, I. and H. Takeuchi. 1995. *The Knowledge-Creating Company: How Japanese Companies Create the Dynamics of Innovation.* New York: Oxford University Press.

Miles, M. B. and A. M. Huberman. 1994. *Qualitative Data Analysis.* Thousand Oaks, Calif.: Sage Publications.

Misztal, B. 1996. *Trust in Modern Societies.* Cambridge: Polity Press.

Petrash, G. 1996. Dow's Journey to a Knowledge Value Management Culture, *European Management Journal* 14, 4: 365–73.

Polanyi, M. 1967. *The Tacit Dimension.* London: Routledge.

Quinn, J. B., P. Anderson, and S. Finkelstein. 1996a. Leveraging Intellect, *Academy of Management Executive* 10: 7–24.

Quinn, J. B., P. Anderson, and S. Finkelstein. 1996b. Managing Professional Intellect, *Harvard Business Review* (March/April). Reprint 96209.

Roos, J., R. Roos, N. C. Dragonetti, and L. Edvinsson. 1997. *Intellectual Capital.* London: MacMillan.

Saint-Onge, H. 1996. Tacit Knowledge: The Key to the Strategic Alignment of Intellectual Capital, *Strategy and Leadership* (March/April): 10–14.

Simonin, B. L. 1999. Transfer of Marketing Know-How in International Strategic Alliances: An Empirical Investigation of the Role and Antecedents of Knowledge Ambiguity, *Journal of International Business Studies* 30, 3: 463–90.

Stewart, T. A. 1998. *Intellectual Capital—The New Wealth of Organisations*. London: Nicholas Brealey.

Sullivan, P. H. (ed.) 1998. *Profiting from Intellectual Capital*. New York: Wiley and Sons.

Sveiby, K. E. 1997. *The New Organisational Wealth*. San Francisco: Berrett-Koehler.

Szulanski, G. 1996. Exploring Internal Stickiness: Impediments to the Transfer of Best Practice within the Firm, *Strategic Management Journal* 17: 27–44.

Trompenaars, F. and C. Hampden-Turner. 1998. *Riding the Waves of Culture*. McGraw-Hill: New York.

Weick, K. F. 1979. *The Social Psychology of Organising*. New York: Random House.

Weick, K. F. 1995. *Sense-Making in Organisations*. Thousand Oaks, Calif.: Sage Publications.

20

KNOWLEDGE-SHARING IN NETWORKED ORGANIZATIONS

Eila Järvenpää
Department of Industrial Engineering and Management, Helsinki University of Technology, Finland
Eila.Jarvenpaa@hut.fi

and

Eerikki Mäki
Department of Industrial Engineering and Management, Helsinki University of Technology, Finland
Eerikki.Maki@hut.fi

ABSTRACT

This paper deals with knowledge-sharing in networked organizations. The organizational and individual conditions for knowledge-sharing are discussed in two kinds of organizational networks, in intraorganizational networks and in two kinds of interorganizational networks. Data were collected in industrial networks and in museum networks.

The results indicate that networked organizations did not fully utilize the benefits of the organizational networks. The prerequisites

374

for knowledge-sharing in museum networks were personal relationships, joint professional interests, and trust. In company networks, the understanding of the other partners' business, common goals and strategies of the network, and trust were important in promoting knowledge-sharing.

INTRODUCTION

The importance of knowledge as a critical success factor is recognized for the company, as well as for nations and for the global economy. Knowledge is seen as the basis of economic growth and productivity in the new knowledge economy. To survive and succeed in the new knowledge economy, companies need to successfully manage their knowledge assets, that is, their intellectual and social capital. This means both the creation of new knowledge and the sharing of existing tacit and explicit knowledge.

For companies today, networking and cooperation within, and between, organizations is a typical way to organize their operations and to conduct business (Hastings 1995; Ollus 1998). By building networks, companies look for benefits, such as time-to-market, cost-reduction, competitiveness, and, especially, an increase in, and broadening of, their competencies (Ranta 1998).

Networked organizations include a huge amount of knowledge. However, to utilize this knowledge, the entire network needs systematic knowledge-management. This study aims to identify critical factors and conditions for successful knowledge-sharing in networked organizations.

DEFINITION OF THE CONCEPTS: KNOWLEDGE AND NETWORKED ORGANIZATION

Knowledge and Knowledge Management

Knowledge includes both intellectual and social capital, as well as competencies of the employees and the knowledge and information a company needs to run its business. Knowledge consists of a tacit element and an explicit element (Polanyi 1966). Knowledge is a multidimensional concept related to most of the processes and operations of companies. For a company, knowledge may be a raw material and/or a product. Knowledge and information are needed, for instance, for production, logistics, product development, or new business strategies.

Knowledge-sharing means the sharing, diffusing, and transferring of knowledge between individuals, groups, and organizations. Knowledge can be shared using different media: face-to-face discussions, video-conferencing, phone calls, e-mail, letters, memos, and so forth. Knowledge can be shared between particular individuals, among a group of people, or between all the members of the organization.

In this paper, knowledge management includes the creation of new knowledge, the sharing and diffusion of knowledge, and the tools and methods to promote knowledge creation and knowledge-sharing.

Networked Organizations

The concept of a networked organization has several meanings (Nohria and Eccles 1996). First, *networked organization* may mean an internally networked organization. In this kind of organization, different units and functions work closely together. They are internally networked and form an intrafirm network. Operations and processes cross over organizational units, and, typically, cross-functional teams conduct operations. The borders of units or functions are crossed over in everyday business activities.

Second, *networked organization* may mean a network of several independent organizations. These organizations have built interfirm networks. Members of a network have a close and continuous cooperation; they have partnerships, common products and/or services, and even a common strategy.

Third, *network organization* may refer to an electronic network, usually inside the company. In this paper, *networked organization* refers to organizations that are internally or externally networked.

A networked organization may be characterized as "communication-rich" (Nohria and Eccles 1996). This means that there is a lot of informal communication inside the organization and with other organizations. The members of the organization have a lot of interaction within, and between, units, departments, and companies. Communication is informal, and employees on different levels and units are in contact directly, not through their supervisors. A networked organization is also flexible and responsive to customers' needs and to changes in the business environment.

In a company network, each company usually has its own role. The companies may have agreed about alliances or about a long-term partnership and cooperation. The companies in a company network need to have common goals. They usually have common products, and they may have common customers. Levels of cooperation in interorganizational networks are competition between subcontractors, cooperation with subcontractors, partnerships, and strategic cooperation within the network. The cooperation is very close if the companies have a common strategy (Järvenpää and Immonen 1998).

There are several reasons to build company networks (Ollus 1998). One of the most important reasons is the globalization of the world economy, that is, the needs of the global market. Competition between companies has become tight. Companies must develop and produce new products continuously and faster. In a network, companies can organize their product development, manufacturing, and demand-supply chains to operate faster and more smoothly to get the products to the customers as fast as possible.

New information and communication technologies (ICT) have been a very important factor for the development of, and work in, company networks. Moreover, by networking, companies can concentrate on their own core competencies and, at the same time, utilize the knowledge and competencies of other companies in the network. Optimally, the companies can increase their own knowledge and competencies by working closely together with their network partners.

There are several dimensions that characterize company networks (Paija 1998). Networks can be geographical, that is, companies in a specific geographical area have built networks. Examples of these include networks of Italian clothing companies and the Oulu area network of ICT companies in the northern part of Finland. Usually, a company network has a focal company, the most important or biggest company in the network, which is the central actor of the network. The central actor can also be a research center or a university. Company networks can be horizontal or vertical, or both. The vertical company network consists of companies in the value chain of the product. The members of the network build parts of the product according to the value chain, and the last company in the network supplies the product to the customer. Often, the customer is also a member in the network. An innovation network is a network of institutional actors participating in the development of new products or new processes. Usually, the innovation network is based on earlier cooperation between the partners. The innovation network looks for a synergy of competencies. The members of the innovation network have their own interests and approaches to the innovation to be developed. By networking, the members are looking for a synergy of competencies.

CASE STUDIES

Three kinds of case studies are the basis for this study. One of the case studies deals with museum networks. The other case studies are industrial networks. One of these latter cases is an internally networked company in the electronics industry; another case is an inter-company network in the electronics industry; the third industrial case is a company network in the furniture industry. The findings from the three industrial intercompany networks are discussed together.

All the organizations can be described as *knowledge intensive*. In knowledge-intensive organizations, knowledge is a very important asset. In museum networks, knowledge is composed of all the special knowledge about cultural heritage that the employees possess, create, and modify in their work. In industrial networks, knowledge is included in products, production, and market.

The amount and quality of cooperation within, and between, organizations were used as the indicators of knowledge-sharing. Moreover, conditions for knowledge-sharing, such as organizational culture and leadership practices, were studied.

Museum Network

Museums are one of the most important institutions in managing the cultural heritage of mankind. Museums create, maintain, share, and manage a huge amount of knowledge. Therefore, museums are typical knowledge-intensive organizations. Most of the jobs in museums involve knowledge work, such as research work, the maintaining of archives, or the designing and arranging of exhibitions. So far, museums have been rather independent organizations that have focused on their own special field of maintaining heritage, whether it is national heritage, technology and industry, or art. Only recently, museums have been looking for cooperation with other museums or even with public sector organizations or industry (for financial support).

Our case study aimed to find out what kind of networks museums have built and how the possible networks operated in cooperation and in sharing knowledge. Moreover, our interest was in investigating the cooperation of museums with other institutions. We selected twelve museums in the Helsinki area of Finland to participate in the study. Eight of the museums belonged to one museum organization, three of them to another museum organization, and one was an independent museum. Both art museums and museums that maintained national heritage were selected to participate in the study. The data were collected by open-ended thematic interviews of museum managers, and documents about the museums' activities were used as additional data.

The results showed both intraorganizational and interorganizational cooperation in museum networks. In the organization of three museums, all the museums had cooperation in their internal network. On the other hand, in the network of eight museums, six out of eight museums had intraorganizational cooperation. The cooperation was not systematic but more or less coincidental. The independent museum had only occasional cooperation with other museums, but after moving to the same premises with one museum belonging to the museum network, the collaboration with these two museums increased. The common artistic views and interests promoted cooperation and knowledge-sharing. The interviewed people emphasized the need for joint activities in supporting activities, such as storage management, marketing, and the search for extra funding.

Interorganizational networks consist of cooperation with both other museums and with organizations in other fields of expertise. Among different museums, the number of cooperative partners varied from a few to tens. The interorganizational cooperation was usually neither very intensive nor continuous. The basis for cooperation with other museums was good personal relationships, either based on friendship or shared professional interests. Lack of professional confidence was one of the obstacles for cooperation. Information about future activities was not actively shared with other museums, nor was the information actively searched. The lack of information had even caused, in some case, overlapping and unnecessary work. Museums seemed to have a quite internally oriented organizational culture, which may have prevented cooperation with other museums. Interorganizational cooperation included offering museums premises for concerts and other cultural activities.

Knowledge-sharing in museum networks was based mainly on both personal relationships and professional interests. The obstacles to knowledge-sharing seemed to be related to confidence, lack of trust, and poor personal relationships. Museums and their personnel in general seemed to be somewhat reluctant to share their expert knowledge with other colleagues and other museum organizations. The benefits of the networking were not very well identified or realized in museum networks, except in supporting functions, such as marketing, storage management, or funding. Core knowledge of museums and their employees was shared only occasionally. Personal relations, competencies, and trust seemed to be key issues in promoting knowledge-sharing.

Networked Companies in Industry

Case studies about company networks concern two company networks in the electronics industry and one in the furniture industry (Ranta et al. 1998; Järvenpää and Immonen 1998). The aims of the case studies were to find out what kind of networks companies build, what the reasons for building networks are, what the problems are, challenges in networking, and how to manage company networks.

Case companies had built both product networks and production networks. Moreover, one of the case companies had actively built its intraorganizational networking activities. It consisted of a network of five companies, or units. This case study was conducted to get an understanding about the characteristics and dynamics of intraorganizational networking. The main focus of the study was organizational culture and leadership practices (Immonen and Järvenpää 1998; Järvenpää and Immonen 1998).

Among the case companies, reasons for building networks were faster time-to-market, the ability to concentrate on their own core competencies, the increase in competencies due to networking, and the need to guarantee availability of resources and materials. Most of the company networks consisted of one focal company and several other companies. Some companies were members in several networks, sometimes even in competitive networks.

In the internally networked company, organizational culture and organizational climate were quite similar in all the member companies of the network. Only one of the companies differed in rules-culture. In that company, the rules were emphasized more than in other companies. In leadership, five managerial levels were identified. Upper-level management assessed the organizational culture in a more goal-oriented manner than the lower-level managers. All managerial groups (upper-level, middle-level, and lower-level managers) reported a difference in support between organizational culture and organizational climate. This means that they perceived an incongruity between support culture and the actual supportive actions in the organization.

For interorganizational networks, the problems and challenges in cooperation were related to the possibly conflicting goals of different companies. Trust was an important factor and a prerequisite for cooperation. To be able to operate properly, the members of company networks need to understand each other's business and production. The critical questions are: what kind of information and knowledge the other companies need, in which form the information should be presented, at what time the information is needed, and who needs it. Sharing of confidential information and knowledge between companies needed both trust and deep understanding of the other company's business. After creating trust and understanding the need for information and knowledge about other members of the network, the companies could really operate together for the common goal.

The findings about the internally networked organization provide understanding, which is related to knowledge-sharing both in intraorganizational and interorganizational networks. Organizational culture differed a little in different member organizations of the network. Five levels of management were identified, and the organizational culture and organizational climate differed across the entire network. Knowledge-sharing in this kind of organization may not happen as fluently as expected. A network itself does not necessarily promote knowledge-sharing. Knowledge-sharing needs to be actively promoted, both on the individual level and between companies.

The ways to develop knowledge-sharing in interorganizational networks included the following issues. First, official and informal agreements about common practices in sharing information and knowledge are needed. Second, the setting of common goals and a common strategy for the networks was found to be important. Third, the creation of communication practices between people in different organizations, and the promotion of informal communication among them, should be agreed upon. Fourth, communication media for information and knowledge-sharing between organizations should be agreed upon and implemented, and joint meetings and training among personnel from different organizations would promote knowledge-sharing. Fifth, information systems used in different companies of the network should be compatible to guarantee information flow between companies.

DISCUSSION

The results indicate that networked organizations did not fully utilize the benefits of the networks. This came out in all of the cases studied. In museum networks, the museums had mainly only occasional cooperation with each other. The prerequisites for knowledge-sharing were personal relationships, joint professional interests, and trust. One reason for the low amount of cooperation may be that the museum personnel did not seem to appreciate very much the expertise and competencies beyond their own expertises.

In company networks, the challenges for networking may be more on an organizational level. The understanding of the other partners' business seems to be one important issue in promoting knowledge-sharing. Moreover, common goals and strategies were important in creating positive conditions for knowledge-sharing. Trust was an important prerequisite for knowledge-sharing. It was also related to the willingness of sharing confidential information and knowledge.

When promoting knowledge-sharing in networked organizations, several issues should be taken into account. The network should have a culture wherein knowledge creation is emphasized, encouraged, and acknowledged. Management of the organizations should understand and promote the knowledge-sharing culture, both in their organizations and in organizational networks. The employees should have possibilities to communicate on a personal level with their colleagues in other units of the organization or of other organizations in the network. Personal contacts promote creation of trust and common understanding among employees. At the same time, the employees would learn to understand the knowledge-needs of their colleagues in other units or organizations. Employees from different organizations could have common meetings for knowledge-sharing. The meetings are needed especially for sharing tacit knowledge, which is hard or impossible to share without personal contacts. For company networks, common "language," as well as mutually agreed ways of knowledge-sharing, are especially important. Applications of information technology should be used effectively, both within and between organizations.

REFERENCES

Hastings, C. 1995. Building the culture of organizational networking, *International Journal of Project Management* 13, 4: 259–63.

Immonen, S. and E. Järvenpää. 1998. Building Network Organizations–Implications for Organizational Culture and Leadership. In *Human Factors in Organizational Design and Management—VI,* eds. P. Vink, E. A. P. Konigsveld, and S. Dhondt. Amsterdam: Elsevier. 27–32.

Järvenpää, E. and S. Immonen. 1998. Leadership and Managements of Company Networks (Verkostojen johtaminen ja hallinta). In *Company Networks—Competition Using Knowledge, Speed, and Flexibility. (Yritysverkostot—kilpailua tiedolla, nopeudella ja joustavuudella),* eds. M. Ollus, J. Ranta, and P. Ylä-Anttila. Helsinki: Sitra. 61–89. In Finnish.

Järvenpää, E. and E. Mäki. 1998. Networking in Non-Profit Organizations. A Case Study about Museum Networks. In *Corporate Networks: Emerging Strategies of Doing Business,* eds. E. Järvenpää and J. Ranta. Working paper no. 16., HUT Work and Organizational Psychology and Industrial Management, Espoo.

Nohria, N. and R. Eccles. 1996. Face-to-Face: Making Network Organizations Work. In *Networks and Organizations. Structure, Form and Action,* eds. N. Nohria and R. Eccles, 288–308. Boston: Harvard Business School Press.

Ollus, M. 1998. Approaches for Network Economy. In *Company Networks—Competition Using Knowledge, Speed, and Flexibility,* eds. M. Ollus, J. Ranta, and P. Ylä-Anttila. Helsinki: Sitra. 1–7. In Finnish.

Paija, L. 1998. Benefits, Forms and Risks of Networking. The Economical Point of View. In *Revolution of Networks—How to Manage a Networked Company,* eds. M. Ollus, J. Ranta, and P. Ylä-Anttila. Helsinki: Sitra. 9–54.

Polanyi, M. 1966. *The Tacit Dimension.* Garden City: Doubleday and Company.

Ranta, J. 1998. Networks and Network Companies—Competition with Time, Speed, and Flexibility. In *Company Networks—Competition Using Knowledge, Speed, and Flexibility,* eds. M. Ollus, J. Ranta, and P. Ylä-Anttila. Helsinki: Sitra. 8–27. In Finnish.

INDEX

385

KNOWLEDGE MANAGEMENT CONSORTIUM INTERNATIONAL

Managing Knowledge about Knowledge Management™

Knowledge Management Consortium International (kmci) - organizations and individuals coming together to develop a shared vision, common understanding, and aligned action about Knowledge and Knowledge Management.

KM as a Balanced System of People, Processes and Tools

kmci is a non-profit organization founded in 1997 devoted to developing a balanced view of knowledge management from the context of an organization. We seek to establish knowledge management as part of a complex adaptive system involving people, processes, and tools. People manage knowledge, not tools. Tools can help people manage knowledge more effectively. The end result of kmci's efforts is to provide a practical, measurable application of KM to businesses and other organizations.

The KMCI Network
Information and Resources for a Competitive Edge

KMCI is your leading resource for professional development, offering special training and certification programs, as well as access to the latest news, conferences, and educational events for today's knowledge workers.

Our online journal, *Knowledge and Innovation* offers a unique perspective which draws together the concepts and processes of Knowledge Management, Organization Theory, Systems Theory and Complexity.

We offer a variety of membership levels. Benefits include discounts on KMCI Institute's CKM cerfication course and other training and development courses, special offers with members of our network, access to discussion groups, today's news, white papers, featured websites, case studies, and a complimentary subscription to our Knowledge and Innovation online journal. Visit our website for these and other features including links to our affiliates, and corporate sponsors, job postings, and more!

Visit www.kmci.org for more details today!

General Inquiries (860) 280-3394 KMCI P.O. Box 191 Hartland Four Corners, VT 05049